At the Intersection of
Disability and Drama

At the Intersection of Disability and Drama

A Critical Anthology of New Plays

Edited by

JOHN MICHAEL SEFEL
AMANDA SLAMCIK LASSETTER
JILL SUMMERVILLE

Foreword by Calvin Arium

McFarland & Company, Inc., Publishers
Jefferson, North Carolina

LIBRARY OF CONGRESS CATALOGUING-IN-PUBLICATION DATA

Names: Sefel, John Michael, 1977– editor. | Lassetter, Amanda Slamcik, 1975– editor. | Summerville, Jill, editor.
Title: At the intersection of disability and drama : a critical anthology of new plays / edited by John Michael Sefel, Amanda Slamcik Lassetter, Jill Summerville ; foreword by Calvin Arium.
Description: Jefferson, North Carolina : McFarland & Company, Inc., Publishers, 2021 | Includes bibliographical references and index.
Identifiers: LCCN 2020050486 |
ISBN 9781476678474 (paperback : acid free paper) ∞
ISBN 9781476642208 (ebook)
Subjects: LCSH: People with disabilities—Drama. | People with disabilities, Writings of. | Drama—21st century.
Classification: LCC PN6120.P54 A8 2021 | DDC 808.82/93527—dc23
LC record available at https://lccn.loc.gov/2020050486

BRITISH LIBRARY CATALOGUING DATA ARE AVAILABLE

ISBN (print) 978-1-4766-7847-4
ISBN (ebook) 978-1-4766-4220-8

On the cover: Erin Ball, a circus artist and coach based in Ontario, Canada. She is the owner of Kingston Circus Arts and a partner with LEGacy Circus, specializing in adaptive and accessible performance (Grim Photography, with thanks to Arts Nova Scotia)

Printed in the United States of America

McFarland & Company, Inc., Publishers
Box 611, Jefferson, North Carolina 28640
www.mcfarlandpub.com

Table of Contents

Part Three—Alone, Together

Acknowledgments

The editors of this collection offer their admiration and sincerest thanks for the aid, wisdom, and labor generously given by our wonderful dramaturgs, readers, and consultants: Lindsay Adams (Saint Louis University), Lisa Aikman (University of Toronto), Brianna Berthiaume, Heather Elise Hamilton (Minnesota State University-Mankato), Andrea Kovich (LMDA), Maddie Parrotta (The Theatre Times), Sara Perry (Red Kite Project, Chicago Children's Theatre), Lily Shell (University of Wisconsin-Madison), and Lydia Valentine (empathos company).

Additional thanks for direct help, support, or encouragement in the creation of this book goes to: Erin Ball, Michelle Barry, Brian Be, Eric Brinkman, Suzanne Delle, Taylor Dodson, Avner Eisenberg, Brian Long, Edie Norlan, Adrianne Gibbons Oehlers, Nicolas Shannon Savard, Grace Riehl, Kira Rockwell, Jennifer Schlueter, Shirlana Stokes, Zoë Brigley Thompson, Katherine Williams, Vancouver's Playwrights Theatre Centre, our families, and, of course, Layla, Steve, Lori, David, and everyone at McFarland.

We would also like to acknowledge the guidance, instruction, and inspiration from the following lovely people—often before there was even a thought of a book and, for several, without even being aware of us or the impact they were having: Zach Anner, Anohni, John Belluso, April Biggs, Rachel Bloom, Josh Blue, Linda Bove, Naomi Brenner, Chris Burke, Cerrie Burnell, Stratos Constantinidis, Julie Goell, Kalyn Heffernan, Rosie Jones, Neil Marcus, Charlene Kennedy, Marlee Beth Matlin, Viktoria Modesta, Leroy F. Moore Jr., Susan Rogers, Rob Shimko, Ali Stroker, Susan Sanders, DeAnna Toten Beard, and Stella Young, as well as Deaf West, Graeae Theatre Company, Phamaly Theatre Company, Rocky Mountain Deaf Theatre, and all the troupes and artists out there creating amazing, accessible, disability-community-centric theatre.

Finally, as the introduction to this work explains, we have sought to create a work which balances rigor with accessibility; a collection useful and insightful for the scholar, but conversational and easily understood by the casual reader. One of the more unfortunate drawbacks of this approach is a hesitation to dive deeply into theory or to directly quote existing scholarship as much as we would normally prefer. With that in mind, and though some of their names do still occasionally appear in essays throughout this collection, we wish to acknowledge the overwhelming influence the following scholars had on this collection. It is in no way hyperbolic to suggest there is not one bit of editorial argument in this volume which cannot be traced back, in some way, to one or more of these pillars of the field. Our acknowledgments and sincerest respect to: Philip Auslander, Lennard J. Davis, Amy Fox, Bree Hadley, Petra Kuppers, Victoria Ann Lewis, Aly Patsavas, Margaret Price, Martha L. Rose, Ellen Samuels, Carrie Sandahl, Sami Schalk, Tom Shakespeare, Tobin Siebers, Rosemarie Garland Thomson, Tonya Titchkosky, Alice Wong, and uncountable others—far too many to name—who have brought their genius and academic rigor to transforming academic, social, and medical model presumptions about the disability community.

Foreword

"Welcome to This Book"

C<small>ALVIN</small> A<small>RIUM</small>

THIS IS DAKOTA. ZE IDENTIFIES AS DISABLED AND LOVES HOW IT CONNECTS TO THE HISTORY, ADVOCACY, AND PRIDE OF THE DISABILITY COMMUNITY.

HEY!

THIS IS MATILDA. SHE DOESN'T IDENTIFY AS DISABLED AND HATES IT WHEN SHE'S MISLABELLED WITH THE WORD

SALAM ALEYKUM!

BOTH OF THEM LIKE IT BEST WHEN YOU ASK FIRST.

THIS IS BOO-BOO. BOO'S THE LIFE OF THE PARTY AND MAKES JOKES ABOUT EVERYTHING INCLUDING DISABILITY.

YO!

THIS IS JACOB AND HIS SERVICE DOG MAXINE. JACOB IS ONE OF THE MOST CARING PEOPLE EVER, AND MAXINE HELPS HIM NAVIGATE SOCIAL AND HIGH-STIMULUS SITUATIONS.

HOLA!

(NEVER PET SERVICE DOGS)

DO NOT TOUCH

THIS IS COURTNEY. SHE LOVES POSTING GORGEOUS PICTURES OF HERSELF IN BIKINIS ON INSTAGRAM.

HI!

THIS IS KIM. SHE HAS A MEDICAL CONDITION WHICH SHE FEELS ISN'T ANYONE'S BUISNESS BUT HER'S AND HER DOCTOR'S.

SHALOM!

THIS BOOK IS FOR ALL OF THEM. AND ALL THE PEOPLE WHO AREN'T COVERED. FOR ANY WHO EXPERIENCE THIS WORLD THAT INVOLVES TOO MANY DOCTORS, TOO MANY TROPES, TOO MUCH INSPIRATION PORN. EVERYONE INVOLVED IN THIS BOOK BELONGS, IN SOME WAY, TO THIS COMMUNITY. MAYBE YOU DO, TOO. EITHER WAY, WELLCOME.

Disability is not a brave struggle or "courage in the face of adversity." Disability is an art. It's an ingenious way to live.

—Neil Marcus

Preface

How to Use This Book

This collection is designed to offer a wide range of perspectives and life experiences. No single play collected is expected to "speak" for any other play, for the disability/condition/experience in question, or for anything other than that one playwright's experience. There are times when included plays support each other's arguments beautifully—and times when they disagree vehemently. The collection includes voices from several countries and a range of gender, ethnic, religious, and political identities. Reading the plays in the order they are included will not make these tension lines any clearer. You are encouraged to pick up whichever play seems to call to you and boldly chart whatever course you like from there. Each play is accompanied by a short introductory essay by John Michael Sefel or Jill Summerville. These essays are designed to provide context as to possible interventions a play may make within larger conversations of disability scholarship, performance scholarship, disability culture, medical humanities, or any of a number of related subfields, but are certainly not meant to be a "definitive" way to understand a text.

Who Is This Book For?

Whether enjoyed at home or in the classroom, we believe the plays offer many valuable lessons. For the Critical Disability Studies student, this anthology presents viewpoints which both support and helpfully push back against assumptions and rhetoric in the field. For the Theatre Arts student, the varied approaches of these playwrights to direct-address, to autobiographical performance, and to performance-based activism are palpable. For the Medical Humanities student and health care provider it offers twenty-one examples of why understanding the individual patient is every bit as important as understanding the diagnosis. For the casual reader, whatever their connection to the disability community, it is a vital reminder that their perception is not the only perception. This anthology is for anyone who wants to learn more about the daily experience of belonging to the larger disability community. It is designed to help shed light on the many members of that community who do not, themselves, identify as "disabled," and yet are compelled to live with the medical, legal, or social term nonetheless, as well as those who do identify with the word, only to have others constantly question whether they belong. It is for anyone reading it, whether for professional, scholarly, or personal reasons. Most of all, it is for fellow members of the disability community, with our love and respect.

Notes on Language

There are a few matters of language in this collection that deserve a moment's consideration. First, although all the plays in this collection are in English, playwrights of several different nations are included. These diverse geographies often are accompanied with different grammar and spelling conventions, as well as a cornucopia of regionalisms. As McFarland is a U.S.–based publisher, we have chosen to standardize inconsistencies regarding grammar and spelling (e.g., commas will come inside quotation marks, "color" will be spelled without the "u," etc.). Word choices and regionalisms, however, remain untouched.

Then, there are disagreements and contradictions regarding genial address within the disability community. For many in the United States, and especially those primarily familiar with the medical system, "Person First" phrasing is considered the preferred, respectful way of addressing disability. "Person First" refers to ensuring that the person, not the disability, is named first, and is seen by many as a counter to the medical system's past tendency toward dehumanization. As such, one is not an "autistic child," but rather "a child with autism." Under this belief, "she's disabled" would be seen as incorrect, while "she has a disability" is viewed as a recognition that she is more than that singular aspect of herself.

This same view is not, however, held by everyone, and many in the U.S. disability advocacy community and a growing majority in Canada and Great Britain prefer "Identity First" phrasing. The "Identity First" argument is that disability can be far more than "just" a thing person has, as though it is an accessory. It seeks to include the culture, history, pride, and legal distinctions that come along with being a member of the group. As such, in "Identity First," "zie is Autistic" is preferable to "zie has Autism" and "Mr. Chu is an amputee" connects him positively with a community, rather than "Mr. Chu has had an amputation," which only denotes a loss.

Both sides of this debate have made excellent arguments as to the validity of their position while pointing to the potentially dehumanizing aspects of the other. In practice, many who work in disability scholarship, activism, or medical spaces have found that the careful application of both approaches, depending on the situation, can often result in an appropriate and genial method of discussing disabilities and members of the disability community, while always abiding by the golden rule of, whenever possible, asking the individual which identification they themselves prefer. At times, however, and especially in writing for a large audience, tough decisions must still be made.

Our guiding principle has been to utilize Identity First language—as is the commonly preferred approach in Critical Disability Studies—in scholarly passages, except if quoting or dealing with some other circumstance in which a switch to Person First makes more sense. Meanwhile, we will keep playwrights' words as they have written them and embrace that this is yet one more way in which the disability community proudly defies expectations of becoming a monolith.

Meanwhile, there are certain words that are deemed offensive to some and empowering to others. Seemingly simple words like "disabled" can carry various meanings depending on how they are used, and the capitalized "Disabled" versus the non-capitalized "disabled" can indicate the difference between political, cultural, and practical matters. Additionally, hot button words—like the reclamation by some of the Disability Community of "Cripple," "Crip," "Krip," and "Mad"—tend to encounter similar controversies as reclaimed words have in the Black, Latinx, and LGBTQ+ communities: some cheer the linguistic act as a bold power move striking against stigma and prejudice, while others decry the harmfulness of the words themselves and their painful history. There is no easy answer to this disagreement. Early drafts of the anthology frequently employed activist, "Crip"–loaded language and rhetoric, but through conversations with several of our playwrights it became increasingly clear that, in a setting intending to welcome and educate a diverse range of people, the benefits of such language were far outweighed by the potential to create confusion or—even worse—to alienate readers. As such, the editors have made extremely limited use of such words, utilizing them only when referring factually to specific ideas or authors working within "Crip-Culture." We will, however, let the importance of free-flowing ideas and diversity of voices win the day when any playwrights use the words and not intervene. Finally, while it is known by several names both in the United States and around the world, we have chosen to refer to the rhetorical and theoretical study of disability as a social, cultural, political, and legal identity by its most common name in the UK, Critical Disability Studies. We hope doing so will alleviate confusion by marking the distinction between the field and various disability-centric medical education, while also paying homage to its roots in Critical Race Theory.

Defining Disability

Some readers may very well quibble with our use of certain conditions, impairments, and circumstances as "disabilities." Several of our authors spend a great deal of time in their daily life trying to convince family, employers, and peers that, despite their assumptions about their condition, they are not "disabled," while several others end up spending the same amount of time in frustration trying to convince their own families, employers, and peers that they are. Some in Disability Activism prefer not to include some "invisible" chronic disease sufferers—especially those individuals in the geriatric community—with rationales described in this collection's essay for *Tales of My Uncle*. Others prefer to consider disability a natural part of several phases of the life cycle, and that healthy, unimpaired people are merely "temporarily able-bodied." The borders around this word have always been fuzzy at best, and all indications suggest the borders will blur more and more in our ever-changing relationship to this loaded political, legal, economic, public, and deeply personal subject.

In trying to set some boundaries for the purposes of the collection, we have chosen to look specifically at conditions, circumstances, alternative limbs, impairments, and/or illnesses which:

- directly and substantially affect a person's personal and/or professional life;
- necessitate regularly dealing with the complexities of the medical community (absolutely including mental health) and/or are labeled as illnesses, dysfunctions, or other forms of negative life occurrence by the medical community, regardless of whether the individual argues against this classification;
- whether "visible" or "invisible," produce barriers in communication, empathy, or social bonds between the person in question and "able"/ "normative" society, whether because of tangible qualities/conditions causing boundaries, social design standards which force exclusion, or internalized and/or institutionalized stigma and lack of understanding.

Adam Grant Warren's struggle with ableist design practices in a train station, Billy Bitter's ever-blurring line between medically prescribed and self-prescribed "treatments," Carly Jo Geer's tango with an anthropomorphized Taco Bell entree, and Ben Rosenblatt's "Antonio Banderas Exposure Therapy" may seem entirely detached from one another, and—save for Warren's—far from the "stock photography" idea of the word "disability." They are all, however, points of light in the constellation of the word, and—as has always been the goal of this collection—all offer diverse views regarding the realities of the disability community.

It may be useful to note that, of the four individuals mentioned, all four recognize that they have a place within the disability community, and yet only one of them regularly identifies themselves as disabled. You may be forgiven if you assume the one who does is Adam, the sole person above who is a wheelchair user; the wheelchair, after all, unfortunately being an internationally recognized *de facto* symbol for "disabled." You would, however, be wrong. If you are new to considering disability from a sociocultural perspective and are looking for a way in, that last point is a very good place to start.

Accessibility

Inaccessibility comes in many different guises. To encourage a greater number of early and/or interdisciplinary scholars, we have worked tirelessly to ensure information presented within the collection's scholarly essays were written as free of jargon as possible and suitable to the expectations of an advanced high school honors course or standard undergraduate reading comprehension. For visual/legibility concerns, a sans serif typeface, Optima, has been selected as informed by the most recent studies in legibility of fonts among people with dyslexia or low visual acuity. Most importantly, we have worked to ensure a reasonable price point for this book—far less than the many three-figure textbooks on the market, following our strong belief that if something is unaffordable, then it is inherently inaccessible.

The Plays

Twenty-one plays by twenty-one playwrights. You'll find everything from musicals to postmodern experiments to pieces that border on stand-up comedy. Some of these plays seem designed to live as rich dramatic literature, while others are a mere sketch of the experience intended once transferred and translated to the stage. The collection is lightly divided into three sections, grouped by their central character's relationship to the audience, the playwright, and other characters in their story.

Part One, "First Person Singular," is a collection of solo, first person perspective plays in which the writer speaks to the audience directly about their own experiences. These are all some form of autobiographical works, whether blatant in their exploration of the playwright's life or abstracted and fictionalized. The plays in this section follow the simple pattern of "one speaker, an audience, and a story to tell."

Part Two, "Past Is Present," collects four plays rooted in the past tense. Three of these plays are about people no longer here to tell their own stories. In each of these cases, the playwrights have worked with their direct memories and/or the subject's own words to call these voices back, as much as is possible. Beyond their inherent dramatic worth, these plays were chosen because they exemplify avoiding the pitfalls of so many plays about disabled individuals. In each, a character's disability is not reduced to a metaphor, and—even more importantly—each features the subject's own lived experiences and, whenever possible, their own words. Their journey is not there to be an "example" to a separate, lead character—their journey is their own and deserves to be honored. The fourth of these plays is an autobiographical text but, unlike other autobiographical plays in this collection, there is a clear distinction between "then" and "now"—the experiences of the narrator in the years before her diagnosis, versus her experiences now, making it feel very much at home with the other plays in Part Two.

Part Three, "Alone, Together," returns us, in many ways, to Part One, though with a notable shift in structure. Playwrights offering autobiographical works (semifictionalized or not) return, but now they have brought friends. Each of these plays include the "other" voices around the playwright—monologues become dialogues, and the role of able-bodied family and society makes itself loudly felt on the page. At times, as with *The Brechtones*, this includes other bodies on the stage; in plays like *Hiccups*, these other voices are expressed by a solo performer, mapping their external voices, influence, and pressure on the performer's body.

Rights and Restrictions

Each play remains the intellectual property of its author, and performance rights are not handled in any way by either the editors or McFarland. Their inclusion does not imply that a play is available for third-party licensing. These works are offered for individual and classroom enrichment—absolutely no public use, including educational festivals or audition pieces, is permitted without permission. Rights availability information is included throughout the collection, and questions regarding an individual play should be directed to its author.

Introduction

John Michael Sefel

In 2001, playwright John Belluso (1969–2006) offered what has since proved a seminal quotation within the interdisciplinary field of disability performance studies. In an interview with prominent scholar Carrie Sandahl, Belluso described his experiences with the public and social "performance" of disability in theatrical terms, saying,

> Any time I get on a public bus, I feel like it's a moment of theatre. I'm lifted, the stage is moving up, and I enter, and people are along the lines, and they're turning and looking, and I make my entrance. It's theatre, and I have to perform. And I feel like we as disabled people are constantly onstage, and we're constantly performing.[1]

Sandahl frames the moments that Belluso describes as the social "commotion" which often occurs with the introduction and presence of an unexpected, atypical body. Even in stillness, and simply by being introduced into an environment in which it is, for good or ill, an outlier, the ripples of this social commotion are palpable. Individuals stare, avert their eyes, try to engage, etc. Unlike a grouping of "typical" bodies, the appearance of one who is atypical seems to prompt a decision on the part of others; this new body's presence has shifted the social reality, and so many—logically or not—seem to compel themselves into a battle over whether to embrace, reject, or strenuously ignore that shift.

This sort of commotion is not limited to disability, of course. Any atypical body—whether marked with unusual clothing, celebrity, beauty, unusual height, etc., can elicit some degree of this phenomenon. What is particularly notable here is the assumed context which disability carries. Beyond "typical" and "atypical," it shifts to the similar—yet decidedly more pejorative—"normal" vs. "abnormal" adjudication. In this shift, the body "causing" the commotion is imbued with the power to unsettle, and yet is ultimately robbed of agency by being viewed as inherently "unsettling." Rather than the active difference performed by the wearing of an uncommon hairstyle, obtaining a certain status, or the action of singing a song, the bodily or cognitive difference is often registered by others as passive and unwanted, regardless of the individual's actual feelings and reality. The dichotomy lands this atypical body somewhere between Homi Bhabha's "Other" and Bakhtin's grotesques. John Belluso, however, unashamedly activates this power of commotion, bending the spectacle to his will in a manner which mirrors some contemporary considerations in Drag and Queer scholarship but is rarely spoken of in medical and other able-bodied considerations of disability. Belluso continues his thought: "There are times when it's fantastic to perform your disability, it's joyful, and it's powerful. Like when I enter on the bus, I love it. I really feel like it's an entrance, like, 'I'm ready for my close-up, Mr. DeMille.'"[2]

The statement is a potent expression of Disability Pride and an example of body positivity which far predates that promoted in the era of Lizzo and Viktoria Modesta. Of course, the words "there are times" implicitly means that it is not always the case, and if there are times when it is "fantastic," then there must logically be times when it is not. Furthermore, unlike some who intentionally model or cultivate difference, many disabilities—like race or gender in similarly lopsided settings—do not offer a choice of "invisibility" in these situations—rather, only the choice to engage or retreat. The privilege of homogeny, as seen in so many socially constructed gatherings, is seen in all its force when considering the commotion caused by the mere presence of a body publicly marked as "disabled."

The experience of disability—whether as a claimed identity or an applied label, and whether congenital or acquired—is as diverse as humanity itself. Still, as with the "bus commotion" described above, certain tensions and dichotomies appear as commonalities. These tensions—being both empowered and robbed of power; of loving and being frustrated by the uniqueness of one's body; of the medical community being both a source of hope and a source of distrust; of the ultimately infantilizing result of so many "inspirational" stories; of all the contradictions and balancing acts that represent disability—they are qualities that many living with or around the title of "disability" experience—and they are the very qualities at the heart of this collection.

What if we could take John Belluso's moment of theatre, however, and expand upon it? What if we could seek out individual voices within the disability community and see what they would do with it—how they would present their lives, experiences, and selves through their own moment of "joyful and powerful" expression? What if we could have the entire world—able-bodied and disabled alike—quiet down for a moment and listen to individual experiences of living within the vast, complicated world of the "disability community"? What might that look and sound like? How might one member express their pride, while another expresses their anger? How might one person naturally thrive before a theatre audience, while another would require adaptations to ensure their voice was heard? How glorious, insightful, funny, heartbreaking, cathartic, activism-inspiring, and *human* might our stories shine if afforded such a theatrical stage?

Many of the plays have already found this answer and have been performed before hundreds of audiences to great acclaim. Others are making their debut in these pages. They run the gamut of emotions, opinions, and styles. Individually, they deliver important messages; collectively, they offer powerful ones. We, the editors, are proud to offer this book stage to every single one.

Interventions

The classic first question demanded of any manuscript that dares take up a reader's time is the work's rationale for existing at all. What is this work attempting to do and what interventions does it make in the existing literature?

To answer that, we must first consider what we mean by "existing literature." As this project is interdisciplinary by nature, work in Critical Disability Studies, Theatre, Performance Studies, and in a myriad of disciplinary subgenres (illness and disability memoirs; bioethics and medical philosophy; solo, autobiographical, and memory-based performance work), all make up part of the theoretical landscape within which this collection operates. Importantly, the above are simply at the "macro" level—by digging down into each individual piece, we cannot help but become immediately aware of the power of intertextual forces that occupy space and influence within the disability community's experience.

Race. Gender. Sexual Agency. Religion. Class. Politics. Disasters. Pandemics. Fashion. Comedy. Fairy Tales. Standard lawful protections, from bodily autonomy to minimum wage. It's hard to think of any area of study, culture, or life that does not intersect in some way with the vast concept of disability—and very often in the negative. Furthermore, it is the single largest minority group; according to the U.S. Centers for Disease Control, one in four U.S. adults—61 million people—have a disability affecting mobility, cognition, hearing, vision, independent living, or self-care.[3] "Disabled" is a demographic signifier that is found within every single other identity. Whether identifying as a member of the Disability Community or not, anyone may become disabled at any stage of their life. For something so widespread, however, and for an identity that requires legal framework for a number of programs as well as one that binds a cultural and political community together, it continues to lack clear definition.

For much of the medical community, disability has long been treated as a binary concept—someone is "broken" and needs "fixing." At its worst, it is little different than one's car having a bad starter on Monday and then, thanks to a mechanic's expertise, running like new on Tuesday. Although the medical community undeniably includes a great number of caring, understanding people, this "medical model" nevertheless sets disability as an applied status, prioritizes the viewpoints of the doctor, and emphasizes the medically normative.

For the Critical Disability Studies community, being "capital-D" Disabled is to identify with a minority group disenfranchised by social and legal barriers—a wheelchair user, for example, only becomes "disabled" when faced with the barrier of a man-made staircase. A wheelchair user is not disabled by the fact that they are in a wheelchair, but the fact that most others are not and, therefore, have designed the world for an ambulatory population. You and I are not disabled because we cannot fly, and yet, Critical Disability Studies points out, if most of our neighbors could and, therefore, created buildings and resources only reachable through flight, then those conditions—not our inherent physical reality—would leave us "disabled."

For most Hollywood offerings and social media feeds, disability is an origin story—it is a challenge to be overcome. It is the source of inspirational moments that help the able-bodied community face their difficulties while simultaneously promoting, purposefully or not, the sort of dangerous and stigma-instilling "positivity" beliefs exemplified by figure skater Scott Hamilton's infamous—and frustratingly ubiquitous—"the only disability in life is a bad attitude." In the standard Hollywood framing, disability is inherently an aberration which must be "fixed" for the story to reach a satisfactory conclusion. It is a transitory state, which must end in either a cure or death as, once the able-bodied character's problem is solved (once Scrooge sees the error of his ways), the metaphorical usefulness of the disabled body becomes a liability to the future happiness of the able-bodied characters. Cure or death, Tiny Tim or Owen Meany, either offers the audience a cathartic, inspirational tear while getting the disabled body out of the way.

Not only could more be written on this topic and the various social, philosophical, and medical definitions of what "disability" means, more *has* been written. Bookshelves-full, in fact. If you are curious and at the beginning of your studies, I'd recommend picking up the latest edition of Lennard Davis' landmark *Disability Studies Reader*, turning to the bibliography section, and starting from there. Additionally, for those particularly interested in Hollywood's treatment of disability, there is no finer examination of the topic than Salome Chasnoff's vital documentary, *Code of the Freaks* (2019). For the moment, let us take it as acknowledged that the "definition" and "role" of disability in society is complicated and hydra-headed—and, as such, the literature on the topic could be described much the same way.

It is with that understanding that this anthology seeks to make a difference. If we step away from the "macro" understanding of disability and, instead, spend time with a range of individuals, we begin to see just how diverse an experience disability—whether as a claimed title, medical diagnosis, or a social assumption—can be. No demographic is a monolith, but is there anywhere that this statement is truer than among the Disability Community, if such a thing can even truly be said to exist?

In creating this collection, we purposefully sought performers with different experiences and perspectives who had taken to telling their story to audiences. Care was taken not to set up an "agenda" or an "approach"—this collection takes no sides in the Great Disability Wars. One playwright embraces the status of Disability with pride and defies the audience to think otherwise. The next looks at all the ways their impairment has stood in the way of their desires. The next views disability as the great mountain that they successfully climbed, while the next sees disability as something that others incorrectly label them as having. Playwright X sees disability has something they "have," while Playwright Z sees it as something they "are" …

…and they are all correct.

Rather than try to solve this disagreement, this collection seeks to amplify it, simultaneously speaking to the need for greater understanding, respect, and lawful protections toward the Disability Community while also forcefully demanding those steps don't come at the cost of homogenizing its members and their needs. This book, in short, seeks to spend intimate time with the micro, immersed in artists' own words, so as to better understand the macro.

What the reader gets out of it will undoubtedly be linked to what the reader brought into it. Physicians, caregivers, and teachers looking for a quick way to better understand their disabled patients, clients, and students will hopefully learn that no such "quick way" exists, any more so than with any other human. Scholars and activists within Critical Disability Studies will hopefully remember that, while the Social Model and its derivatives are absolutely essential to understanding disability, it is far from all-inclusive, and does little to alleviate chronic pain, a lack of oxygen, or the many other impairments which a person may choose not to feel pride over but rather eagerly wish away. It will, with luck, remind us all that there is nothing about race, gender, sexuality, class, or the law that can't be made all the more fraught—and all the more important—by the added factor of disability. From sexual abuse to housing, from employment to dating, from performing to public transportation, and for many, from standing to thinking to breathing, there is not an area of life nor a subject of study that is not touched in some way by disability.

We offer this collection with the sincere belief that it is unique—certainly, for all my research on the topic, I've never seen another like it. True, it is a collection of plays about disability by authors who either identify or are labeled by others as disabled, which is relatively rare in and of itself, and yet that alone is not enough to claim the distinction of truly unique. There have, after all, been several publications just in the past decade or so that match that structure, most notably the excellent work by Victoria Ann Lewis in her 2006 collection, *Beyond Victims and Villains*. Additionally, books examining individual disabled performers through a scholarly lens are most certainly not new. From Sandahl and Auslander's classic *Bodies in Commotion* to the majority of Petra Kuppers' oeuvre and more, academic works critiquing, investigating, and celebrating the evolving creation of a "Disabled Theatre" is—happily—a topic that has received excellent scholarly attention. Beyond that, there have been brilliant memoirs, and wonderful literary and essay collections, including recent notable works by Alice Wong, Rosemarie Garland-Thomson, and Peter

Catapano, not to mention the excellent *Disability Experiences: Memoirs, Autobiographies, and Other Personal Narratives* from editors Couser and Mintz, to which I am so proud and thankful to have been a contributor.

I still argue, however, that this collection stands apart and does so in four very specific ways:

First, the plays have been intentionally chosen to defy a singular idea, view, or definition of d/Disability. Previously, most collections have represented the works of those specifically associated with either Disability activism and Critical Disability Studies or, instead, frameworks designed to be "inspirational" or "therapeutic." The boundaries between these two approaches have long been firmly drawn and well-protected. This collection intentionally encourages the reader to recognize and grapple with that philosophical friction and its practical implications.

Second, the definition of "disability" has intentionally been left as wide open and muddled as it is in daily conversation. Cognitive, physical, and behavioral/emotional—visible and invisible—socially constructed and biologically undeniable—the door is open. It is fully possible that readers may find at least a play or two whose theme rests outside of their personal definition of "disability." This book isn't interested in proving that reader wrong—the definition has always been impossibly messy and uncontainable; our goal has been to embrace that fact.

Third, the plays collected here are entirely direct-address and fall within the realm of either autobiographical, biographical, or semi-autobiographical. While I have a deep and profound respect for each of the collections of "disability plays" on my bookshelf, both I and the entire editing team sincerely believe there is something important—something inherently different—that comes with a play in which a person on stage speaks directly to the person in the audience, with all conventions of a "fourth wall" stripped away. Some of these characters are the playwrights themselves, while others are fictionalized abstractions. Still others are the theatrical resurrection of now passed-on artists (though, in such cases, great care has been taken to recreate from their own words and messages). In all of these, however, there is a person onstage, staring down an audience and demanding that attention be paid. The safety of Fourth Wall voyeurism is nowhere to be found, making it that much harder to see the individual speaking as either a prop or metaphor. Through direct address, each of these voices is a force—the sort that demands to be heard.

Finally, and perhaps most difficult of all, the process of creating this collection involved the editorial team actively committing themselves to highly "accessible" scholarship. This meant holding ourselves to the standards of "serious" academic research and ensuring that we were providing content that would be useful to scholars of all of the subject's interdisciplinary areas while simultaneously avoiding language, frameworks, or costs that would alienate a typical first-year undergraduate student or a casual reader. More importantly, it meant creating a work that we honestly felt would be useful both to those in the medical and disability support fields as well as the Critical Disability Studies and activism fields—a means of telling stories honestly, with vulnerability, and with the diversity of thought, opinion, and experience that makes up the disability community.

All the while, of course, we were also trying to make sure that the collection felt at home among a theatre practitioner's library and would be useful in teaching and experiencing autobiographical single-person plays and disability theatre, both subjects currently in high demand in many university training programs.

The best thing about setting such impossible standards, of course, is that "success" is more about "getting it close" than "getting it perfect." I am thankful for this, since "perfect" this anthology is not. Still, I hope the finished product offers some suggestion of our well-intentioned goals and the lengths to which we went in our attempt to create a collection that welcomed all readers.

Perhaps nowhere is this better exemplified than through the comic Foreword by French artist Calvin Arium. We were faced with the creation of a lengthy essay explaining the difference between "Person First" vs. "Identity First" and other controversies of speech within the disability community, coupled with the need to ensure that all readers would have some sense of what the disability community "looked like" beyond any of their preconceived notions. It quickly became clear that such a multipurpose introductory essay may have been too overwhelming for the uninitiated and far too remedial for those who work and/or live in the field. After several tries, resulting in essays which either felt too academic or too remedial (both dreadful as introductions to the text), we instead approached Calvin Arium—a disabled artist popular in the United States and Europe with many in the disability community for their exploration of disability and ableism—to help sum up the wide diversity within the community. The result, I think, is as close to "perfect" as this anthology gets—offering a non-intimidating welcome to the casual reader and a reminder to the entrenched scholar or physician that, no matter what their background or preconceived notions may be, there are more perspectives in the world that are worthy of attention, understanding, and respect.

This collection has an eye on its scholarly business, but instead of thick essays that refer to and quote plays, we've placed the emphasis on the playwrights' words, allowing the reader to experience their stories and voices in full, only providing scholarly critique as supplementary framing. We have worked closely throughout the publishing process to ensure we were packing in as much wonderful material for as low a retail purchase price as we could negotiate, in the hopes that the book might be financially accessible to as many people as possible. Above all, we have fought to keep intersectional questions of disability front-and-center, listening to and learning from the critique that Critical Disability Studies has long been the province of the wealthy and white. I wish I could say we were more successful in this effort than we were, and the disability community is far more diverse than what we've captured here—but I hope, at the very least, we've been able to reach a "next step" toward that representation, and for now we'll simply commit ourselves to doing even better in the event of a second volume.

And so, what intervention does this collection seek to make? Perhaps that very word, "intervention," blocks us from properly answering the question. To "intervene" is to forcefully make a mark—to push one's way through and make a change. In some ways, that's the antithesis of this collection. The intention of this book is closer to a portfolio of Polaroids taken on a street corner than to a curated museum of masterworks. The world needs the latter, certainly—but the world can benefit greatly from a few good Polaroids as well.

Disability Aesthetics

If the above is all true, how is the reader to consider, analyze, and "enter" the book? One way is the same method that would likely be used with that metaphorical portfolio of snapshots: start thumbing through the pages and find what catches—and surprises—the eye. If the reader is coming from the medical humanities or theatre, there's a good chance something within will do just that.

"The idea of disability aesthetics," writes Tobin Siebers, "affirms that disability operates both as a critical framework for questioning aesthetic presuppositions," as well as "a value in its own right."[4] This second point being, he contends, "important to future conceptions of what art is."[5] The idea of collective identity-based aesthetics is, of course, nothing new. Even outside of academia, popular scholarship is increasingly becoming interested in such identity-based aesthetic choices in mass entertainment, from the Afrofuturistic costume designs of the film *Black Panther*[6] to empowering conversations detailing the differences between male gaze and feminist visual portrayals of feminine sexuality. Through cultural and group identity aesthetics, subjects may be understood through entirely different cultural lenses, gaining information not only through intellectual context and perspective, but through phenomenological feeling and emotional adjudication.

Like food, ritual, and other social practices, cultural/group identity aesthetic can both create and recall wordless narratives, forming and binding communities. Identity aesthetics may develop naturally over time through peer and generational repetition, or, as argued by Shailee Wilson, may be utilized to shore up weakening social bonds to create "alternative, self-defined identities in response to changes within their social and cultural environment."[7] In other words, collective identity aesthetics may be created formally or informally and within the collective subconscious or by individual artists intentionally seeking a community-specific visual language. The aesthetic appreciation of collective identity-fueled art involves the same basic principles and analytical skills as homogeneous works, but, at their best, help the receiver of the artistic experience appreciate the content through a cultural lens and empower the artist to work within their own artistic "language."

What, then, might we take as examples of disability aesthetic, especially considering this collection's repeated claims of the vast diversity of the disability community? What forms, functions, imitations, and conceptions of emotional beauty help create and bind a collective disability identity among so many diverse individuals? One of the most striking areas in which such an aesthetic has emerged has been in dance, in which "traditional" forms, designed for typical bodies, are adapted or, just as often, dismissed, in favor of new kinesthetic vocabularies. Defying years of "therapeutic" approaches in which disabled dancers were expected to adapt to traditional forms as best as they could in pursuit of ableist aesthetics, these new efforts subvert, if not totally abandon, those aesthetics for movement that follows the strength and shape of the artist's body and function. Similar artistic discoveries and experiments continue to occur throughout the fine and performing arts, with often stunning results. "Instead of working with well-made plays," writes Bree Hadley, Australian Disability scholar and author of this collection's *Ex/centric Fixations Project*, "performers with disabilities tend to be much more interested in working with contemporary comic, theatrical, performance, and choreographic practices."[8] A casual thumbing through this anthology will offer proof: of the twenty-one plays collected, very few retain the traditional model of the "well-made play." By each artist molding expectations to their own, highly individualized experience, the aesthetic expectation moves from technical imitation of an existing standard to experimentation of expression. To be sure, other, nondisabled artists have long done the same, but within critical analysis their work is primarily considered as a reaction to and subversion of a traditional default.

Critical analysis of disability theatre aesthetic, however, places the central default within itself, with no "typical" or "ideal" body or mind as archetype. It is in this that its seemingly paradoxical strength exists; the aesthetic of the collective is enhanced by individual differences. In *Scar of Visibility*, Petra Kuppers considers the work of Ted Meyer, an American artist who—bearing several scars himself—creates monoprints directly from the scars of his model-subjects, accentuated with gouache and color pencil. Scars, Meyer contends, "can mark entering into or out of a disability…. They freeze a moment in time, a car accident or gun shot,"[9] and so his artistic renderings seek to echo bodily narratives, the "portraits of those events that changed their lives."[10] Kuppers quotes Meyer's artist statement:

> A few years ago I met a woman with [a] large scar that runs down the length of her back…. The scar was not just a marker of a disability but rather part of what made her unique. It wasn't just a scar. It was her scar. Something that no one else had. No[t] only did it make her physically unique but emotionally [as well]…. My hope is to turn these lasting monuments, often thought of as unsightly, into things of beauty.[11]

Though there are countless examples which could be offered to illustrate this point, Meyer's work with scars highlights the intensity of the *individual* as subject. Scars are as individual as their owners, and yet by studying one with intense scrutiny and aesthetic appreciation, a collective aesthetic forms. This is a foundational aspect of disability aesthetic, and one found throughout this collection.

Away from the visual art of Meyer or experiencing live performance, what of disability aesthetic within dramatic literature and scripted theatre? As this book collects the work of over twenty artists writing on, around, and within disability, it seems a reasonable place to look for examples. Consider, first, the length of many of these plays. While able-bodied theatre has everything from one-minute play contests to Wagner's *Ring* cycle, there is nevertheless an assumed "normal" in which a "play" generally means two or three acts, lasting somewhere between two and three hours. Plays which don't follow this standard are usually given attached descriptives; they are "one act plays," "*fait divers*," "vignettes," or some other word that denotes they are apart from the assumed default form and structure. That default, however, is excessive—and even oppressive—for many in the disability community, for whom ten minutes may be possible when two hours are not. In this, we find a variation of the Romantic era's call for form to fit content; as disability theatre's content so often includes a focus on the disabled performer, form must fit performer as well. As such, and as is captured throughout this collection, approaches in aesthetic formalism of disability theatre consider the unique form of each work, without an assumed "default" as contrast.

Then, there is disability theatre's role as a minority theatre. While not absolute, most disability theatre will find their audience is made up primarily of able-bodied members. Even among disabled audience members, it is likely there will be few who share the same physical or cognitive experiences. Therefore, without becoming a lecture on ableism, many performers find ways to address and disprove ableist assumptions near the beginning of a performance, making clear that any infantilization or pity the audience may have arrived with should be immediately abandoned.

Note how both *A Performer's Monologue* and *Last Train In* feature author-performers taking immediate control over their surroundings: Connor Long controls the lights with a magical snap of his fingers, while Adam Grant Warren moves set pieces about the stage. Related, if not identical, are the beginnings of Kurt Sass's *Why This Monologue Isn't Memorized (A True Story)*, Anita Hollander's *Still Standing*, and Sherry Jo Ward's *STIFF*. Each takes a moment near the beginning of the work to directly address what an able-bodied audience member may perceive as their "weakness" or "the elephant in the room," immediately destigmatizing the subject. With equal parts formalism, imitationalism, and functionalism, an aesthetic analysis reveals how these artists play with form by introducing this structured moment of "proof of competence," rarely required from non-disabled theatre. These moments provide an imitative example (in Warren and Hollander's case, practical; in Long's case, mimetic and metaphorical), and function as a teaching moment for the audience. Removing infantilization and pity from the experience, then, serves an important part of exploring its aesthetic beauty.

At the heart of disability theatre, however, is the phenomenological—put simply, how the artist helps the audience actually *experience* phenomena, rather than observe them. Graham Bryant's repetitive use of circular media in *RPM*, the panic of Sherry Jo Ward's sudden attack, the entirety of the unrelenting rhizomatic dialogue captured in Bree Hadley's *Ex/centric Fixations Project*: these leave behind the ontological and "clinical" understanding, instead inviting the audience to exist within the world of the playwright, if only for a moment.

In the end, it is often not content which determines generic categorization, but approach. A play about disability or a play written by a disabled person (no matter the subject) is not necessarily well-described as disability theatre. While it would be counterproductive to suggest any hard borders could be established to denote what does and does not earn that particular title, disability aesthetics—which include more than those discussed here and are, as are all cultures, ever-changing and expanding—are a worthwhile place to start.

Before You Go

First, yes, we know, this collection is worse off for those perspectives, identities, and voices it does not include. Disability culture, for example, owes a great deal to over a century's worth of Deaf culture and activism, and yet there is not a single d/Deaf play collected here. The same could be said for a great many identities, cultures, disabilities, and circumstances. These missing entries are, in part, a matter of avoiding a checklist, "tokenism" approach, as well as a simple matter of binding widths. If you find that the absence of a given voice or perspective leaves this book lacking, I wholeheartedly encourage you to write McFarland and request a second volume. I promise, we'll do better next time.

Second, this book doesn't seek, in the end, to really "say" much at all. Instead, it seeks to listen to and learn from the voices we've collected, providing a resource for the reader to do the same. Knowing the potential for "curator bias," we have been intentional in challenging our own perceptions and viewpoints, and rather than bringing forward a collection of works that agree with our perspectives have, instead, collected plays which both buttress and challenge our personal views. Perhaps it is because we, the editorial team, are members of the disability community ourselves that we know we cannot possibly speak for it. Hopefully, however, we can act as a conduit to welcome more people into the conversation.

NOTES

1. John Belluso, interview by Carrie Sandahl, Los Angeles, July 2, 2001. Qtd. In *Bodies in Commotion: Disability & Performance*, edited by C. Sandahl and P. Auslander (University of Michigan Press, 2006), 2.

2. *Ibid.*

3. Catherine Okoro, et al., "Prevalence of Disabilities and Health Care Access by Disability Status and Type Among Adults—United States," 2016. *Morbidity and Mortality Weekly Report* 2018; 67:882–887. DOI: http://dx.doi.org/10.15585/mmwr.mm6732a3.

4. Tobin Siebers, "Disability Aesthetics," *Journal for Cultural and Religious Theory* 7 (2): 63–73, 2006, 71–72.

5. *Ibid.*

6. Buena Vista Home Entertainment, Ryan Coogler, Chadwick Boseman, Danai Gurira, Michael B. Jordan, and Lupita Nyong'o. *Black Panther*. [Burbank, California]: Buena Vista Home Entertainment, 2018.

7. Shailee Wilson, "Métissage Culturelle: Identity, Aesthetics, and the Social Roles of Portraiture in Saint Louis du Sénégal" (2014), *Independent Study Project (ISP) Collection*. No. 1863, https://digitalcollections.sit.edu/isp_collection/1863.

8. Bree Hadley, "Introduction," *Disability, Public Space Performance and Spectatorship: Unconscious Performers* (Basingstoke, Hampshire: Palgrave Macmillan, 2014), np.

9. Ted Meyer, artistic statement, published in VSA Arts exhibit catalog, Union Station, Washington D.C., 2004, accompanying the work *Trachea Reconstruction* (1998), as qtd. in Petra Kuppers, *The Scar of Disability: Medical Performances and Contemporary Art* (University of Minnesota Press, 2007), 5.

10. *Ibid.*

11. *Ibid.*

Part One

First Person Singular

STIFF

SHERRY JO WARD

Borrowing from Judith Butler and established theories of gender, Sherry Jo Ward's autobiographical play *STIFF* reveals multiple layers of performativity mapped onto Ward's presentation of her own body. She is female and disabled, as well as *female* and *disabled*. On an initial, surface level, the reader may recognize that the narrative of Ward's work explores her experiences with the assumptions, semiotics, and social mores wrapped up in the daily "performance" of disability as well as the many ways in which disability has interrupted the "rules" and standards set on her and her body as a woman. As wife, as daughter, as mother, as performer, as teacher, as intellectual, as actor, as comedian, as musician, and as sexual being, every aspect of her life is not only altered by Stiff Person Syndrome, but altered in an impossible-to-hide, immediately "public" manner. She grapples, in this way, with going from a performer-by-choice-and-vocation to the sort of performer described by John Belluso in the introduction to this collection, adding new layers of performativity onto those she already wore in her pre-diagnosis days as "just" an actor and a woman.

Beyond these ideas, however, there is another layer of performance at work in *STIFF*; one that—intentionally or otherwise—speaks directly to ethical hurdles surrounding the presentation of self that many disabled individuals face every day.

When Ward goes onstage to perform *STIFF*, she is, of course, *literally* performing her disability. Yes, this includes those Butler/Belluso-esque performative aspects that follow her into every public space, as well as the fact that this is a literal, tangible, tickets-sold-and-audience-attending performance in which she highlights her disability. More to the point of this essay, however, is a layer of "performance" that so many disabled individuals are familiar with, and one that is exemplified by a striking moment approximately two-thirds of the way through this script when Sherry "stages" having an attack.

I personally experienced this play as an audience member before I experienced it as a reader, and I am able to report that this staged and written attack was taken by myself and—as far as I could tell—the rest of the audience, as entirely real. It seemed in all ways to be happening *not* to the written and rehearsed "character" of Sherry Jo Ward, but in an extratheatrical sense to the "real" Sherry on stage, and no statement or indication was ever offered the audience before or after to suggest otherwise.

Sherry Jo Ward in *STIFF* (© Mark Oristano, all rights reserved).

Ward's "attack" is extremely effective. As a piece of theatre, it is undeniably powerful, and as an artistic choice that brings a tangible experience of the unpredictability of Ward's condition, it excels. It also, however, introduces complex questions regarding "true" theatre performances. Sadly, this limited space does not afford the opportunity to deeply consider the ethics of suggesting to an audience that the performer—rather than the character—is in physical pain, or to ponder how canonical master theorists of the craft might respond. What mustn't be allowed to go without comment, however, is how closely this act of "performing" an attack mirrors the daily (though often unspoken) reality of so many in the disability community.

Society at large has long applied expectations on the behavior, attitude, and consistency of symptoms shown by those with illnesses and disabilities—as Anita Hollander wryly offers in *Still Standing*, "Cripples ain't supposed to be happy." I imagine anyone who has a chronic condition (and most anyone who doesn't) is familiar with trying to "perform away" pain or illness. To smile widely, trying desperately to erase the pain from one's face, saying "No, I'm fine, really!" can readily be seen as an effort at performing good health. Perhaps less well-known, though anecdotally common, is the need many people with disabilities or other conditions feel to sometimes perform a "bad" day—whether to be taken seriously by a doctor or, quite often, to deal with a co-worker, boss, or other who doesn't understand that a disabled individual indeed has "good" and "bad" days just like everyone else, except, with certain disabilities, the impact on one's movement and productivity may be far greater.

With begged indulgence for a personal example, consider my three types of commute: I have bad mobility days, during which I use my accessible parking placard and my cane; good mobility days, during which I don't use either; and medium days, during which I need to use the placard as I cannot walk far, but don't necessarily need the cane. The performance comes as, on days that land in that third category, I have learned it is far socially easier to still use the otherwise unneeded cane, purely to avoid stigma. The dirty looks I receive when I use the placard and *not* the cane tend to be more than I can deal with while concentrating on my breathing and other various pain coping strategies. In these situations, I am having mobility issues, but perform my very-real-but-not-currently-happening need for a cane so that I might navigate social minefields. Similarly, ask any patient of chronic pain, shallow breath, etc., how inconvenient and annoying it is to have a "good" health day on the same day as a doctor's appointment; you are likely to hear that doctors are far more hesitant to prescribe much-needed pain relief or other treatments if the individual is not actively displaying symptoms while in the office. The result? Patients whose symptoms are usually at a 7 on the dreaded chart, but are currently at a 4, often hone their acting chops. Performing one's default experience (despite how one might feel at a given moment) means help and understanding, whether for prescriptions or for strangers feeling as though a parking space is "deserved." The same, of course, is also true in the reverse: it may be a bad breathing or standing day, but with a loved one visiting the choice is either force a happier face on things or be subjected to unsolicited attention, advice, and pressure. This struggle—"How 'disabled' do I need to appear to get through my day?"—is a performative balancing act that many in the disability community know quite well.

Sherry Jo Ward suffers from attacks—she warns the audience of this at the beginning of the show. When she has one, then, it is assumed to be an interruption in the performance—a "time out" in which Sherry's rehearsed performance-avatar disappears and we see the "real" Sherry, in pain, suffering on the stage. She shortly recovers and the show begins again. It works magnificently, and yet still seems to strain at theatrical conventions and the unspoken contract between theatre artists and audiences. How, then, are we to react?

I asked Sherry about all of this. She responded that, since she does get those attacks without warning, it's perfectly possible one night it won't be staged. Those attacks are her reality, whether they happen to be the reality of that particular moment or not. This led to the obvious follow-up: what will happen when that is no longer the daily reality—when either such progress is made in her treatment so they no longer happen, or things progress in the other direction, and they are no longer able to be faked. This question was asked in early 2018. I don't know how she would answer now—but at the time, her thoughts were simple: as long as they were real for her, she would use them as tool for helping the audience understand her reality. If they ever stopped being part of her experience, then the scene would change accordingly. I think back to the idea of the daily performance of pain or lack thereof for the benefit of those around us; to make them feel better, either that we're ok and they needn't worry, or that we're "impaired enough" that we're not getting some special treatment for no good reason. The pains and impairments and conditions and even the good feelings are all real; but at times they must be conjured up, even when they're not particularly in the mood.

Gender is a performance, age is a performance, authority and submission are performances, and, yes, disability is for damn sure a performance. The ethics of these performative identities are as complicated as they are ubiquitous, but rarely are they laid bare as starkly and imaginatively as Sherry Jo Ward has offered here.

—John Michael Sefel

STIFF

STIFF has received numerous awards, honors, and recognitions, including writing and acting awards from the Dallas Theatre Critics' Forum, the Kathleen Freeman Spirit Award, nominations for several Broadway World (Dallas) Awards, and special citations from Baylor Health and the National Organization of Rare Diseases. The version included in this collection is the originally toured iteration. Due to a progression of Sherry's symptoms, the play has since been modified to allow her to perform the entire piece from her motorized wheelchair.

Production note on projections: Throughout the play, a large screen will display words and/or images. It is placed so that the audience can always easily see it, and so that Sherry can easily turn and look at it, gesture, etc. The projections are controlled by a "helper" (either onstage or off, depending on the needs of the venue) with whom Sherry communicates directly.

STIFF © Sherry Jo Ward, all rights reserved. Performance rights for *STIFF* are available by application. Licensed rights come with an expectation of casting a performer who identifies as physically disabled, and priority is given to theatre companies with histories of actively promoting accessible theatre experiences. Those interested are welcome to contact the author at sherryjo2000@ yahoo.com.

*   *   *

Audience enters to find Sherry Jo Ward, a youthful-looking woman of middle age, sitting in a comfy orange chair with an ottoman. There is a walker next to the chair, a cup of water on the floor, and a large white projection screen at center. Far to one side of the playing space, Sherry has a "helper" who assists Sherry during the show should she need anything. For the most part, however, this assistant behaves as one more audience member.

In the lead-up before showtime, Sherry amiably chats with anyone who wishes to chat with her—in theatres whose stages easily allow this, she even allows individual audience members to come right up, sometimes encouraging them to sit on the ottoman so that she can be eye-to-eye with them. It's all extremely casual, and the comfy living room chair and ottoman, combined with her casual attire and attitude, give the play the feel of heading over to the playwright's house to so that she can update us on her situation rather than attending "a play."

At showtime, Sherry produces a harmonica from her pocket and plays a quick phrase.

[slide: blank]

SHERRY: I know what you're thinking

Another quick bit of harmonica

"She seems fine."

A bit more harmonica

So, I'm an actor. Before all this I was the go-to actor who knew how to make an entrance and command the stage and play those larger-than-life characters. The three actor tools are body, voice, and mind, and I'm down one of those. A pretty significant one.

I have a super rare neuromuscular disorder called Stiff Person Syndrome. That's the actual name, there's not a long scientific-sounding name, that's it, it's a thing.

[slide] text: Henceforth to be known as "SPS"

The good news is I finally, after forty years of just saying no, have discovered the joy of cannabis.

She enjoys a hit from her vaporizer, then suddenly remembers:

Oh, PAT!

Sherry gestures, and a photo appears on the screen.
[slide] a charming, "grandmotherly" looking woman with a wide smile. She is proudly holding a homemade sheet cake decorated as the American Flag, complete with strawberries lined up to form the red bars and a field of stars made of blueberries. Everything about the picture is, in a word, precious.

That's her. After I got sick we moved in with my mother-in-law, Pat. She's lovely. (*pointing at the photo of Pat with the cake*) That's not even a holiday, it's just a Tuesday.

And it's great, it's been … great. We've always gotten along great, really.

Pat didn't want me to do this. She thought it would be too strenuous. (*looking around*) I'm not sure what she was expecting me to do here—

I've actually had a few fans of my work tell me they would happily watch me sit and read the phone book on stage. Well, I'll tell you this is going to be just about two notches more physical exertion than that.

But I promised her that I would have a safe word. I said okay. But I wanted to choose a word that would catch my helpers' attention but still fit within the general theme of the show.

[slide] text: SUGARTITS

So, now you know.

[slide: blank]

I started teaching an Intro to Theatre class at a community college. I'm collecting disability but I can still work a little bit. It's been good to get out of the house for an hour a couple days a week. I can't drive so I applied for Fort Worth's Mobility Impaired Transportation Service. MITS!

[slide] text: Mobility Impaired Transportation Service

The MITS guy did his home visit, and said, "Yeah, we'll get you hooked up, door-to-door service." So, the first morning I was feeling an acceptable level of independence with this door to door service. I was expecting this:

[slide] photo: a sleek, expensive-looking sports car

But what pulled up was a bus:

[slide] photo: a standard city bus

Nope, not exactly. It was more of a condensed ... smaller ... two-rows-of seating...

[slide] photo: an eight-passenger MITS paratransit bus

Short bus. It was a short ... bus.

The bus driver said, "this your house? This a nice house!"

I said "thanks, yeah, we live here with my mother-in-law."

[slide] The photo of Pat again

She said, "Shiiiit, no thank you."

And the bus kept going.

[slide: blank]

When I sat down she leaned over her shoulder and said, "What you got wrong with you?"

I love that. It's always interesting to see how folks approach the delicate issue of why I'm like this. They see me, with my walker, or in my wheelchair, and they're curious. If they decide to ask, they have to figure out how. "What's wrong with you?" is kinda rude, so I see them going through words, "how did ... what's with the..." and then invariably it lands on "what happened?"

Honestly, I don't know what to tell them. There is no known cause, except that folks with SPS have a GAD Antibody—Glutamic Acid Decarboxylase

[slide] text: GAD = Glutamic Acid Decarboxylase

which shows up in a blood test, but no one knows where it comes from. It's just something that SPS patients have acquired that messes with an important neurotransmitter. Some researchers have said it often follows a period of stress, but when are we not following a period of stress?

She takes a long, luxurious hit from vaporizer
[slide] photo: a pot leaf, worthy of the Grateful Dead

It's medicinal.

[slide: blank]

My early symptoms were nothing extraordinary—pain, fatigue. Then some numbness, and muscles would start to seize up, like a rubber band tightening.

Then in the course of a week I started having tremors and falling. It was a very specific kind of fall. It was like stepping off a moving sidewalk, where the top half of your body starts moving at a different speed than the bottom half of your body. Then everything from here down just filled with cement and I would just crumple. I went to my doctor and he told me not to go back to work until I saw a neurologist.

Do you know that joke the little asshole kid would play when she'd say, "Do you know if your hand is bigger than your face it means you have cancer?" And then she smashes your hand into your face? That's what it felt like every time I went to a neurologist.

And I had to see three neurologists, which is actually not bad for an SPS diagnosis. This disease is literally one in a million, that's not hyperbole. There are about 330 people in this country that have it.

The first neurologist came in and we go through some tests. (*to audience*) Okay, are you with me? I'm going to give you three numbers to remember, okay?

3, 7, 4

Repeat them back to me.

> *audience does this*

Okay, remember them, I'm going to ask you to repeat them back later. Can you name these items?

> *[slide] three basic line-drawings arranged side-by-side (blank out-line on white background, coloring-book style): a camel, a sailboat with mast and sail, and an apple.*
> *The audience follows her instructions and names the pictures, though invariably some people call the middle picture a "sailboat" and others just a "boat."*

That's right. Good.

We're going to keep this simple and call this middle one a boat, okay? Do you know why it has the sail on it? Because if I showed it to you without the sail—

> *[slide] enlarged detail of the previous slide, showing only the sailboat. This time, however, it has no mast or sail—the result is a strange, roughly triangular shape*

At least half of you would've guessed parmesan cheese.

> *[slide] the camel, boat, apple slide comes back up.*

We're just going to say camel, boat, apple.

> *[slide: blank]*

He looked at the film of the MRI and said it was normal. Then he had me perform a few tasks, testing muscle strength, reflexes, double vision, etc.

> *Giving directions to the audience*

Look at my face, not my hands, how many fingers am I holding up? (*she changes the number*) Now? (*again*) Now?

Good job, and what were those numbers?

> *[slide] text: Sherry Jo Ward is an actor, not a neurologist.*

Great, now do this (*two fingers together, she keeps this up as she continues speaking*). I was worried about Parkinson's because my mom had Parkinson's.

She died at 72 with Parkinson's and diabetes and congestive heart failure. And I judged her. I thought, if only she did what the doctors said and ate like she was supposed to and exercised ... She became disabled in her fifties from diabetic neuropathy, but she was still able to work twelve years longer than I could.

> [slide] text: Sherry Jo Ward is a disabled, out of work actor.

Anyway, everything looked normal.

> [slide: blank]

He looked through my family history. He asked how my brother died at age nineteen and when I said "suicide," he looked up from the form for a brief moment, said "oh, I'm sorry to hear that," as he surreptitiously put a point on the side of mental illness.

Then neurologist number one told his assistant to show me how to google "psychiatrist" and sent me on my way.

By the time I got to neurologist number three it was different. Something bad was happening. He said, "It's not Parkinson's, it's not ALS. It might be stiff man syndrome." Stiff man syndrome? Is he making fun of me? Stiff man syndrome? That's not a thing. He said, "Don't drive and don't go back to work until we have test results," And that was it. Medical bills were piling up from doctors and tests that I was passing with flying colors, but no answers.

I got a call a couple days later telling me I tested positive for stiff person syndrome. They had changed the name from stiff man syndrome to stiff person syndrome. I'm telling you, feminists are on top of everything!

You know the other name for ALS?

> audience answers "Lou Gherig's disease"
> [slide] photo: American baseball player Lou Gherig, in his prime, Yankee ballcap on his head

Lou Gherig Syndrome. Baseball player Lou Gherig got ALS, so they named the disease after him.

You know who else had ALS?

> [slide] photo: famed theoretical physicist and cosmologist Stephen Hawking.

I have nothing against baseball, but I think it might be time to propose a name change. Stephen Hawking was a cosmologist who discovered black holes and was developing artificial intelligence with one muscle in his cheek.

I know it's good to put a face and a name with something like a disease. It makes it less scary and easy to remember, and cute baby-face Lou Gherig had a good face, but do you know what Lou Gherig would look like if he had lived with ALS for fifty years?

> [slide] photo: the same picture of Stephen Hawking, except now Lou Gherig's Yankees cap has been photoshopped onto his head.

So neuro number three got it right.

> [slide: blank]

And I got lots of "treat your symptoms" prescriptions, and he told me not drive. It's amazing what an immediate game-changer that is, not being able to drive. My first huge step toward total dependence.

But I thought, okay. It's not any of those scary things, we can take care of this! Then we looked it up.

As the following projection appears, Sherry reads it out loud
[slide] text of the following paragraph

SPS causes progressive rigidity to develop in trunk and axial muscles and a heightened sensitivity to stimuli such as noise, touch, and emotional distress, which sets off painful muscle spasms. Severe muscle stiffness develops in the spine and lower extremities. SPS can cause difficulty walking and significantly impact a person's ability to perform routine, daily tasks.

Well shit.

[slide: blank]

When I was thirteen I overheard my mom on the phone telling someone that my brother shot and killed himself, and among all the other feelings I was feeling, I had this idea that it didn't matter what I did anymore. Everything from that point on would be measured by my relationship to this event. The smallest success, like being in a school play, was a monumental triumph over tragedy. And if I was a total failure, it would be blamed on this tragedy. It didn't matter what I did.

And I'm ashamed … that I squandered that opportunity away and didn't take advantage of it. I was an exceptionally easy to manage kid.

I just couldn't misbehave, not after all my mom had been through. Guilt. And I'm not anti-guilt, I think on a certain level guilt gets things done. If there were no guilt, churches would be empty, non-profits would have to change all their fundraising videos, society would fall apart.

I also remember being immediately aware of the attention that would be unavoidable. I was super shy, and I really wanted to get that attention that was due me, but when someone would so much as put their hand around my shoulder, I would have to stifle a shudder.

So I thought losing my brother to suicide was going to be my event that would define me for the rest of my life. I remember a friend lost his sister to suicide and on the way to her funeral, he wrote on Facebook that he was about to begin the worst day of his life. I thought, "Oh, friend, no. this isn't going to be your worst day. This day this going to be part of every other bad day and this pain will be part of all of your future pain."

I have those feelings again now. I'm going to call attention to myself with this, and it also doesn't matter what I do anymore. Any accomplishment is a triumph, any failure is a symptom.

And, by the way, I DID google "psychiatrist" and I DID go to see one, because when you don't feel good you do whatever you can to feel better.

My mother-in-law Pat had been living with her ninety-year-old mother with dementia, but everyone decided that yes, Sherry needs your help more than great granny.

[slide] *the photo of Pat with the cake reappears*

That's right. Great-Granny wouldn't have made it past "camel, boat, apple," but still, my need was greater.

Also, Pat's a hugger, so I've been adjusting to that.

[slide] *the photo of the MITS bus*

The MITS driver went up to the next door and wheeled the next passenger onto the bus and she saw me for the first time and shouted, "Oh my God!" And she laughed, and I smiled. Her name, DeAndra, was on her backpack that was hanging on the back of her wheelchair. I just smiled.

DeAndra sang as we went along, and then we pulled up to the next house. She said, "George!," and a man walked onto the bus and took the seat in the last row. He didn't speak in words, just single syllable sounds.

They don't look like me. They have "special needs." I don't belong here.

George was obviously upset. He was moaning, but he never used words. DeAndra stopped singing and was listening to George. He paused and her voice was suddenly focused, and she said, "I know, George. I'm here. It's okay." And his voice immediately softened.

The bus kept going and she kept singing.

[slide: blank]

There's this thing called "the startle effect" with SPS. Sudden noises, stimuli, set off painful spasms, muscles seizing up. That makes going to the theatre a tricky venture. I saw a production of *All My Sons* which had a very loud, realistic sounding gunshot, and I knew the play, I knew it was coming, but still. When it happened, the whole left side of my body seized up. It hurt, but not cry out loud hurt. I just couldn't move for several minutes. Here's the thing. No one noticed. It was imperceptible. Kind of like doing your kegels.

How many of you just started doing your kegels? I'm not going to ask for a show of hands, but I want you to make eye contact with your neighbor and realize you have no idea what's going on inside their body.

If you don't know what kegels are, ask [*assistant's name*] after the show.

Speaking of "no idea what's going on," I haven't been auditioning. It's not that I'd be discriminated against or anything like that, just the opposite. I'm a white woman but now that I'm disabled I'm also a minority, so in terms of diversity casting, I'm suddenly an option. But it's the reality of the stamina required for the 6-day, 7–11 rehearsal schedule that's made me wary of auditioning.

Precious Little in 2015 was the last play for which I auditioned and got the role. I saw the post, and before auditions I read through the script very carefully. I decided to go for it and I got it.

It's a play about motherhood; it's a character in need of physical contact; in need of finding life-balance, and all the layers of communication.

A great role in a great play. And it was a lot of sitting.

[slide] A production photo from Precious Little. Sherry looks to be acting her heart out. She's seated.

Sitting.

[slide] Another production photo. Sherry is acting with a co-star. They're both sitting.

Sitting.

[slide] Another production photo. In this one, Sherry and a co-star are huddled close together—while sitting.

Sitting.

[slide] Another production photo. In this one, Sherry is lying on her back with a large smile on her face. She is looking straight up into the eyes of another actress who is straddled over her, close enough to kiss, looking equally happy with the arrangement.

…Recliiiining

Referencing actress in photo

That's Molly. I like her. That was fun. (*Sherry takes a moment to enjoy photo*) She was my first girl stage crush. I've come to terms with talking about my girl crushes. I think that's okay.

My husband Thomas … thinks it's fantastic.

It's more about that nurturing thing than it is about anything sexual. I'm learning to sink into an embrace without a shudder, partly because it feels nice to be loved, but also the literal compression is therapeutic to my condition.

And I don't mean to exclude men from this. I know there are dear, tender men with amazing bedside manners. I'm fortunate to have a man in my life who possesses that nurturing quality.

[slide] a promotional photo of Dr. Derek Shepherd, a.k.a. "McDreamy," the famously handsome doctor played by Patrick Dempsey on the U.S. television show Grey's Anatomy.

My other girl crush is my physical therapist, Jennifer.

[slide] a photo of "Jennifer," a professional-looking, attractive woman. She has kind eyes and a warm smile.

I see her once a week. The first time I saw her I walked in with my cane, like this (*demonstrating with two hands*). She said,

"Do you feel secure with that cane?"

I said, "Well, I really feel like I need two canes, you know, like for balance." Enter the walker.

Jen is so sympathetic and understanding, and not in a "bless your heart" kind of way, but just so pragmatic about my well-being.

No muscle is off-limits to SPS, and no muscle is off-limits to Jen. I mentioned once that my hip was bothering me and she hiked my leg over her shoulder and dug in with both abnormally-strong-yet-perfectly-manicured hands, twisting and rubbing my upper thigh. She said, "Oh wow, you're having lots of spasms in your groin."

Well yeah, NOW!

Do you know, not even one year before I started seeing Jennifer, I was riding my bike to work, about five miles one way.

I still have my bike. Still have hiking boots and high heels. I still have remnants of my able-bodied life. I'm not holding out hope for a miracle. That would be arrogant. I just can't let them go.

I cry at therapy a lot. I tried to do the leg press. Jen always removed all the resistance bands before I used any of the machines. This one day my legs couldn't push my body up at all. They began to shake and she smiled and said, "You can't do this today."

She went over to grab my cane. It was hanging on the balance bar about twenty feet away. She's about my age, in great shape, super strong, and I watched her just walk over to get it like it wasn't a big deal.

It wasn't. It wasn't a big deal for her.

She came back to me and it was obvious I had been crying. She whispered, "I'll grab a couple tissues." Then she brought them over and just sat for a minute. She said, "I don't know why this is happening to you. It doesn't make sense." She didn't try to tell me God had a plan for me even though she often told me she prayed for me. I just love her.

> [slide: blank]

My Ob-Gyn is hot too, like Dallas Cowboys cheerleader hot ...

> [slide] photo: Sherry's Ob-Gyn. Her description is accurate. Blonde hair, model-features, etc.

...but eh. Just nothing there. Takes more than a couple of fingers up my vagina to develop feelings, you know what I'm sayin?

> [slide: blank]

I have to do exercises for Jen, and they require body awareness. I studied Tadashi Suzuki during an acting apprenticeship. I have acute body awareness. I like to have control of my body in space.

> She demonstrates

But when I try to do the exercises Jen has instructed me to do ...

(to helper) Can you time me for 20 seconds? ...I have to stand up straight for 20 seconds three times a day, as soon as I adjust my posture and stand up straight. It's like the more aware I am, (shaking) the less control I have.

(to helper) How much time is left? Tell me when it's been 20 seconds.

After my five-mile bike ride to work, I would take the stairs up to the fourth floor. Now my body rejects 20 seconds of being upright.

I wish I had known this was going to happen so quickly, so I could've done a few more things one last time.

Ridden a roller coaster.

Walked on a beach.

Done one more brush hop step flap ball change.

Gone to a flea market by myself and take my time looking at Every. Single. Thing.

I don't go anywhere alone anymore.

>*The 20 seconds is up. Sherry slouches down in relief*
>*[slide] photo: The MITS bus.*

MITS! The MITS got me to the college early. As I left the bus that first day, I said, "Have a good day," to this new community I was now a part of, and DeAndra said,

"Bye Bye, I love you!"

I just smiled. And the bus kept bus going.

>*Sherry carefully bends her head over, rests on her cane*

A couple of times I've been asked "what's the hardest part." That's a hard question to answer. So, naturally, I practice my Diane Sawyer interview.

>*[slide] photo: American television journalist Diane Sawyer, mid-interview, looking inquisitive*

"What's the hardest part?"—that's a great question.

Truth is, it changes every day. I can't wear high heels. And I was good at walking in high heels. Swivel the hips, put one foot in front of the other. I'm 5'10" or so, in heels, I'm well over six feet, eye to eye with my 6'4" husband.

Well, I'm not 5'10" anymore. I've shrunk half-an-inch every year since my diagnosis. There's nothing wrong with being 5'9", but when you're 5'10" you can conceivably be an amazon. I can remember entering a room and being noticed. Now I enter a room, and I'm … noticed.

Honestly, a lot of what's hard has to do with vanity. And pain.

>*[slide] photo: Sherry's two young sons. They look happy, mid-laughter*

How're the kids?

They always adjust better than we do, you know? And whenever I'm having a bad day and am feeling particularly depressed, people remind me of how much the kids need me, "remember how much your boys need you," so that always helps. You know, because it's so easy for a mom to forget how much their kids need them.

>*[slide] photo: another shot of Diane Sawyer. This time, she wears a sympathetic look*

Our marriage? Of course it's hard on our marriage.

We had been married eighteen years when I was diagnosed, so he can't leave me now, he'd be an asshole. And this isn't going to kill me, so he won't be the handsome young widower. When he starts to worry about our future, I try to comfort him by telling him there's still a good chance he could die first.

We had a very similar upbringing. In seventh grade at our evangelical

Christian schools our sex Ed class was all about the dangers of heavy petting. I'm not sure what makes petting "heavy." I think it was an attempt to make second base sound less appealing. Granted, this was a less progressive time, when if a boy had his ear pierced, left was right and right was wrong, and LGBT stood for "Love God and be thankful" but still, the idea was if it felt good, it was dangerous.

> *[slide] photo: another photo of Diane Sawyer—a "consoling" look in her eyes.*

Now I've been partnered with a painful disease, so does that mean I'm perpetually safe now?

This is going to be with me for the rest of my life, and…

… …Sorry, Diane, that was where I thought I was going to cry. I know everyone says they're not going to cry, but that's bullshit, everyone does this so people can watch them cry, and that was the spot where I planned to do that. …Can we try it again?

There's no cure. There's no cure. There's not going to be a cure, they just treat symptoms while they can. Progressive rigidity until all mobility is gone and my body turns to stone… …Yeah, that's really where I thought I was going to cry, but I got nothin', sorry.

No cure, no prevention protocol, just try to avoid stress, and hope odds are in your favor.

Then there's the part of the interview they couldn't show on TV…

> *[slide] photo: Another Diane Sawyer shot—in this one Diane's eyebrows are raised in a faux-scandalized manner*

Yeah, our go-to sex position is my left leg over his right shoulder, but my leg won't quite straighten out anymore, so it takes some effort. It simultaneously takes precise maneuvering and tremendous strength. It's like in the middle of sex someone hands you a new key to put on a key ring.

And I'm taking so many downers that orgasms are hard to come by. Bless his heart. I had a fire hose installed in my shower head and still get nothing.

> *[slide: blank]*
> *Another pain hits, lower back. It hits quickly and intensely, Sherry shifts seemingly involuntarily in her seat*

Oh *shit*!

Sorry. Sorry—

I have some untouchable spots along my lower back and sometimes I lean back on something, or something shifts from moving too much, and it just…

… it takes me by surprise, and … …It's hard to talk about pain, right? It's embarrassing, and it's intimate, and oh yeah, it's also the only thing everyone in the world can relate to. I hate the pain scale, you know, rate your pain from one to ten. I took my son to a doctor with a stomachache when he was five and they had a pain scale for kids and they asked him to point to the face that looked like how he was feeling…

*[slide] photo: a typical "pain scale" chart, made up of several cartoon
faces which go from smiling to crying.*

… and he looked at the pictures and looked at me, like, "what the hell?" and I
said to the doctor,

"just look at his face!"

He's five. He is actually making one of those faces.

It's so hard to explain my pain and how hard it is to get comfortable. I went
to see a friend from high school, and after a few hours of just sitting up and
visiting I was hurting and exhausted.

I was on her couch with my feet on her coffee table, and the only thing that
brought me any relief was the half-second that their dog Smoky ran under my
legs and grazed my calves. It was just enough positive stimulus to take away
the pain for a moment.

[slide] photo: The MITS bus

So I taught my one community college class that first day, and then headed
back to the MITS stop. I got onto the bus for the ride home and I was
exhausted from class and hurting from the walking. The ride was bumpy
and I pulled my arms in to my side and started leaning forward for the least
amount of contact with the seat. I was rocking back and forth to keep the
cement inside my muscles from hardening, and I really, really saw myself
from the outside for the first time, and realized I do belong there. On the
actual short bus.

I'll admit something. I want pity! I don't know why pity got a bad rap! There's
nothing wrong with it, but everyone says, "I don't want your pity," but, fuck
that.

Also I want someone to come over every Tuesday and write down everything
I say and turn it into a book. Morrie was full of shit.

But I'm trying to learn the big lesson, whatever I'm supposed to learn about
turning pain into something positive, something bigger than myself, but I
haven't figured it out yet.

I'm glad my mother isn't here to see this. I think about her a lot and wonder
what lesson she learned. After I had kids I would call her a lot and she would
give me parenting advice. If I ever questioned it, she would come back with,
"well y'all all turned out all right!" And I'd say thanks and hang up.

Then I'd think, "Wait a minute! We didn't all turn out all right!" Four out of
five kids surviving to adulthood may have been a pretty good record during the
smallpox epidemic, but not in the 1980s. Her son killed himself! But I never
corrected her.

*[slide] photo: Diane Sawyer again. In this one, she's "leaning in" in a
manner that suggests practiced empathy.*

My greatest fear? Goddammit, Diane, I knew I should've pretend-interviewed
with Ellen.

Ellen would've been like:

[slide] photo: American television host and comedian Ellen DeGeneres from her "Ellen" daytime talk show. She's all smiles and the opposite of a "hard" interview.

"Hey, I hear you play the harmonica!"
   And I would say:
   "Why, yes, I do!"

She plays a little riff, then suddenly grabs her eye in great pain

Sugartits! SUGARTITS!

[slide: blank]
gesturing to helper

Sorry. Can you help me get to the ground? I just feel like I need to be closer to the ground.

Sherry tries to explain while getting her wind back ... it's messy

My hair got caught in my eyelashes and it pulled it out, and it—I wasn't ready for it. My muscles on this side, just kind of ... it hurts. It's not always imperceptible anymore. I don't do my kegels in public anymore either, it's kind of indecent.
   (*To helper*) Thank you.

There is a pause ... and then she begins the show again without getting up—talking while lying on the ground. As she continues, it's clear that the sudden physical pain is beginning to slowly subside, just as the emotional pain begins to rise. While the show's performance style was already "conversational" in nature, over the next few lines her voice and approach takes on an even more improvisational tone, as if she's left any sense of "script" long behind

You know when you go to the fair? And you see the big plush bear hanging above the games, and you play and play until you finally get that giant bear and you hug it and it crunches because it's not plush, it's filled with millions of little hard balls.
   I'm afraid that's what it's like to hug me.
   I'm finally admitting that it feels good to be touched and embraced, and I'm scared that my body is going to turn hard and untouchable. I already have spots on my body that are solid and so hypersensitive they can't be touched without hot, hot pain.
   I don't worry about dying, but I don't want to live so long that Thomas is relieved that I'm gone.
   I want him to be sad. For a while.

She takes a hit from vaporizer

I remember my thirteen-year-old self, and I know I can't follow her logic anymore—
   It does matter what I do.
   I believe heavy petting isn't a sin, it's a requirement…

… and I think I'm ready to shed some guilt and cash in some misbehaving points.

> *[slide] photo: The image of Molly straddling Sherry is back.*
> *Sherry takes a hit from her vaporizer, then notices the slide that assistant has put up.*

Hehehe

> *She gives a quick smile to the slide tech, thankful for the gift of this "pick-me-up." Sherry sits up, more in control, and back on track. She returns to the same curled up, rocking position as on bus ride*
> *[slide] photo: the MITS bus*

On that hard MITS ride home we picked up DeAndra and George. As we were stopped, I was enjoying the stillness. When they wheeled on DeAndra, she saw me and said, "Oh my God!" I couldn't help but smile. George was obviously in a better mood.

Then the bus started moving again and it was bad. The vibrations, my body just couldn't take it. My legs were straight out in front of me. My eyes were shut tight.

We stopped at a light and I opened my eyes and DeAndra was staring at me.

Her eyes were huge and they were penetrating me. She was obviously watching me and was visibly upset. She actually looked angry.

I tried to adjust my body and relax a little so she wouldn't be uncomfortable, but she kept looking at me. Her voice turned focused … She said, "Are you okay?"

"I will be."

She said, "I'm here."

"I know"

She said, "I love you."

"I love you too."

The bus kept going, and she kept singing.

> *[slide: blank]*
> *Sherry carefully stands, using the walker for support. As she does, she begins to quietly hum or sing a little tune. Perhaps something along the lines of Radiohead's "Creep."*
> *As she does this, Sherry uses her walker to move in front of the screen. Lights fade, until we are left in a darkened space with the silhouette of Sherry and her walker standing before the blank, bright white screen.*
> *Sherry finishes her tune by playing the last line on her harmonica.*
> *Projector screen and stage lights to black.*
>
> *End of play.*

The 2018 Invisible Man

Leroy F. Moore, Jr.

In 2017, Angel L. Miles, Akemi Nishida, and Anjali J. Forber-Pratt wrote an open letter to "White disability studies and ableist institutions of higher education,"[1] calling for greater intersectionality and recognition of the unique experiences of community members living with multiple marginalized identities. Their letter was the latest in a long line of voices calling for Disability Studies to acknowledge and dismantle the white, cis, het, middle-class assumptions in the work of many prominent scholars in the field. Echoing the decade-old critique in Chris Ball's groundbreaking article "Introducing White Disability Studies: A Modest Proposal"[2] and adding to it a call to dismantle an array of still-ubiquitous prejudicial, oppressive, and marginalizing practices in academia, these three scholars—who signed the letter under the collective "Radical Disabled Women of Color United"[3]— minced no words.

> Dear White disability studies and ableist institutions of higher education;
>   cc: racist, misogynist, cis-heteronormative and other interacting systems of oppression
>   We believe that in order for disability studies (DS) to be most relevant, it must accurately address the interests of the full range of people with disabilities. Likewise, for institutions of higher education to be relevant to disability communities, it needs fundamental transformation led by the expertise of disabled people of different backgrounds. Hence, we are advocating for a critical intersectional disability studies that centers the needs, perspectives, and interests of marginalized people with disabilities and enables the advancement of disability justice. Disability should not be an afterthought; rather carefully considered as an intersectional and integral part of all university operations, visioning and planning.[4]

The letter goes on to list a series of specific changes required to create an intersectional, fundamentally useful, and justice-minded field of disability studies. Among the series of demands were included the recognition of ableism as a "socially constructed complex system of disempowerment which intersects with, and is just as pervasive as, other systems of oppression," the need to financially support research and agendas which "center the interests and contributions of disabled people of color and other marginalized people with disabilities," and the guiding principle that Disability Studies should strive for "social change."[5]

Their call will only seem radical if the reader has not been paying attention. Mainstream Disability Studies' relative lack of engagement to the practical effects of intersectionality—especially regarding race/ethnicity—has been an ongoing conversation in the field for years. Although there has been some stellar work in this area, exemplified by scholars like Sami Schalk, the study of Black Disability retains a "niche" status. Meanwhile, too much of U.S.–based Disability Studies may still be summed up by Chris Bell's assertion that "far from excluding people of color, White Disability Studies treats people of color as if they were white people."[6] As seen by this open letter, change has been slow. While the medical industry in the U.S. has often been shown to be ill-equipped and negligent regarding race, especially toward Black and African Americans,[7] it is notable that Disability Studies, which has been built largely on appropriated methodologies of Critical Race Theory and is regularly housed within Rhetoric Studies, has also often fallen short of the mark in these very fields in which they specialize.

Considering the discipline's focus on performativity, social constructs, perpetuated prejudices, and rhetorical tropes, intersectionality must be a central conversation in any consideration or discussion of Disability Studies seeking to implement Critical Disability Theory / "DisCrit" methodologies. Overlapping identities—at times competing, at times complementary, and at times contradictory—reach into nearly every facet of society, from housing, employment, medical care, and lawful protection, to even seemingly mundane aspects of daily life.

Schalk, whose scholarship on Black, Queer, and Disabled bodies often includes popular culture critique and analysis, has deconstructed many of the everyday areas in which the presence of multiple marginalized identities creates tension and paradox. In an article examining Black Disabled characters in popular romance fiction, Schalk notes that, despite contemporary efforts to create inclusive works featuring Black and Disabled people, systematic barriers and long-held identity tropes remain culturally embedded. These can lead to friction of bifurcated identity markers in a marginalized character's perceived identity, as well as continue to privilege White and able-bodied characters and readers. In a character or story that centralizes intersectionality, in which "(dis) ability, race, gender, sexuality, and class all represent potential analytics,"[8] Schalk maps how disarming one trope may play directly into another: "(B)lack people are often represented in overly sexualized ways, while people with disabilities are often depicted as nonsexual. This creates a representational double-bind when attempting to depict the sexualities of disabled black people: do we want to emphasize sexuality to resist the desexualization of people with disabilities or downplay sexuality to reject the hypersexualization of black people?"[9]

These intersections can be found in nearly every aspect of social interaction—especially those which are the most negative. While research makes clear that Black men are 2.5 to 3 times more likely to be killed by police officers than their white counterparts,[10] it further reveals that nearly half of those men are disabled, including "a majority of those killed in use-of-force cases which attract widespread attention."[11] While women are more likely to be victims of sexual assault or rape than men—and Black, Latinx, and Trans women face even higher percentages[12]—those with intellectual disabilities are estimated to be *seven times* as likely to be victims as the general public.[13]

Whether grappling with bigoted stereotypes in a romance novel, understanding the epidemic of violence which is ongoing in care for intellectually disabled individuals, investigating matters of police-involved shooting, or studying any area of life and society that overlaps with identity, Disability Studies must center intersectionality to accomplish its own professed goals.

—John Michael Sefel

NOTES

1. Angel L. Miles, Akemi Nishida, and Anjali J. Forber-Pratt, "An Open Letter to White Disability Studies and Ableist Institutions of Higher Education," *Disability Studies Quarterly*, 37.3 (2017). https://dsq-sds.org/article/view/5997/4686.

2. Chris Bell, "Introduction to White Disability Studies: A Modest Proposal," in *The Disability Studies Reader*, Lennard J. Davis, ed. (New York, NY: Routledge, 2017), 275–82.

3. Miles, *et al.*

4. *Ibid.*

5. *Ibid.*

6. Bell, 282.

7. John M. Hoberman, *Black and Blue: The Origins and Consequences of Medical Racism* (Berkeley: University of California Press, 2012).

8. Sami Schalk, "Happily Ever After for Whom? Blackness and Disability in Romance Narratives," *Journal of Popular Culture* 49.6 (2016) 1249–1260, 1244.

9. *Ibid.*, 1245.

10. Frank Edwards, Michael H. Esposito, and Hedwig Lee, "Risk of Police-Involved Death by Race/Ethnicity and Place, United States, 2012–2018," *American Journal of Public Health*, 108, 1241–1248, 8 August 2018, https://doi.org/10.2105/AJPH.2018.304559.

11. David M. Perry and Lawrence Carter-Long, "The Ruderman White Paper on Media Coverage of Law Enforcement use of Force and Disability," *Ruderman Family Foundation*, March 2016, https://rudermanfoundation.org/white_papers/media-coverage-of-law-enforcement-use-of-force-and-disability/.

12. Asha DuMonthier, Chandra Childers, and Jessica Milli, "The Status of Black Women in the United States," *Institute for Women's Policy Research*, 7 June 2017. https://iwpr.org/publications/status-black-women-united-states-report/.

13. Joseph Shapiro, "The Sexual Assault Epidemic No One Talks About," *National Public Radio*, 8 January 2018. https://www.npr.org/2018/01/08/570224090/the-sexual-assault-epidemic-no-one-talks-about.

The 2018 Invisible Man

(a spoken word performance)

> I am an invisible man. I am a man of substance, of
> flesh and bone, fiber and liquids—and I might even
> be said to possess a mind. I am invisible, understand,
> simply because people refuse to see me.
> —Ralph Ellison, *The Invisible Man*, 1952

The editors are proud to include the work of Leroy F. Moore, Jr., a highly respected and influential leader in Black Disabled art and activism (please see his bio in the About the Contributors section of this book, and check out his groundbreaking work in Afro-Crip and with the platform he co-created, Krip-Hop Nation). Although Mr. Moore's spoken word performances may strain the boundaries of what many readers will consider a "theatrical" performance (and, even more so, a "play"), we offer the following three points:

- The work is a memesis-centric piece of performed art. It meets both Peter Brook's three structures of theatre and Horace's two purposes of theatre. To the idea of "dramatic literature," it is performance-based, yet has a text-based script. While "plays" have a great many conventions which we have become accustomed to seeing, extraordinarily few of them—arguably just those noted in the first two sentences of this paragraph—are "mandatory." Moore's piece is longer than plays presented by the Boston Playwrights' Theatre in their Boston One-Minute Play Festival, it follows rules of conflict and rising action with greater clarity than half of Beckett's catalogue, and its construction in "verse" is no more a detriment to it than it is to the Athenians, to Shakespeare, to Molière, or to Lin-Manuel Miranda. Any true genre-based boundaries between art termed "spoken word" versus art termed a "short, direct address solo play in verse" seem to be more about audience than art, and so, as this collection seeks to appeal to theatre-readers, the editors invited several artistic works that exist in the liminal "slippage" between genres and invited them and their creators to come hang out with the drama kids as long as they'd like.
- As seen in many of the plays collected in this anthology and as addressed at length in the Introduction, Disability Aesthetics centers the individual over collective standards and is built on an adjudication of what "works" and "doesn't work," rather than what is or is not the "right" or "traditional" way to construct art. For Mr. Moore and several

other included playwrights, a short, artistically worded, creatively delivered monologue is the perfect structure for their expression.

- If Points I and II are not enough to persuade, then we would suggest simply reading the works without worrying about media or genre boundaries and, once done, considering the massive hole in the conversation that would be left if we limited Disability Theatre to only those works which best mirrored non–Disabled standards.

The 2018 Invisible Man © Leroy F. Moore, Jr. All rights reserved.

* * *

Leroy F. Moore, Jr., a thin, handsome black man with cp, approaches the microphone. When he speaks, it is with a slow, measured baritone.

> **Leroy:** Who is the invisible man today
> He is still Black I'll say
> After all of these years he is still not paid
> In Hip-Hop generation he is still howling the Blues
> Like Ray Charles he is born to lose
>
> The 2018 Invisible Man
> Yeah Ralph Ellison, I understand
> Take my hand pull me in
> Two thousand and blah blah
> Still going through fingers like sand
>
> From Jim Crow to Porgy theft of his identity
> Hush hush by his own community
> He watches humanity
> Invisible to everybody except his family
> One book tells everything
>
> Father only saw his disability
> So he left leaving no role model
> Not seen by his own people
> Got caught up displaying toxic hyper-masculinity
> He tried but that role was not accessible
>
> The 2018 Invisible Man
> Yeah Ralph Ellison, I understand
> Take my hand pull me in
> two thousand and blah blah
> Still going through fingers like sand
>
> Now he is labeled as weakness
> In the same sentence as homelessness
> Not a provider
> He is always the other

Single man as an elder
The 2018 Invisible Man
Yeah Ralph Ellison, I understand
Take my hand pull me in
two thousand and blah blah
Still going through fingers like sand
In a rocking chair
He sees the cycle
Cute, overcome, pity then invisible
Black disabled new born boys
In one room next to where he is, the hospice
Yeah Ralph Ellison, I understand
Take my hand pull me in
two thousand and blah blah
Still going through fingers like sand
2000 Invisible Man
Yeah Ralph Ellison, I understand

An Open Letter to the Usher at the Theatre Who Asked Me if I Was "the Sick Girl"

Amy Oestreicher

Terms like "accessibility," and "inclusive" are finding their way into an increasing number of theatre mission statements. As a general principle, this is obviously an improvement—things have inarguably become better since the early half-efforts of decades ago, when many theatres interpreted accessibility laws (such as the Americans with Disabilities Act in the U.S.) to mean exclusively "wheelchair accessible," and, in turn, often felt "wheelchair accessible" meant "we can clear a seat to make some room for a wheelchair if someone like that shows up." By comparison, Open Captioning, adjusted stimuli / "Relaxed" performances, and audio descriptive services are increasingly common in professional theatre venues. Even among theatres making these efforts, however, there is still an unfortunate tendency to think of the task as a checklist made up of the most common barriers which, once addressed, can be crossed off and put in the "done" pile, as though creating an "inclusive theatre" is about a binary set of "accessible" or "not accessible" traits over which one can claim victory. Successful methods toward truly inclusive spaces for both audiences *and* theatre artists, however, require a paradigm shift in approach. As with considering the medical vs. social models of disability, it means not focusing on what adaptations must be made for an individual who "cannot," but rather "what unintentional barriers do our decisions, design, and structures create?" At its simplest, it means moving beyond accessibility and, rather, seeking inclusivity.

Terminology is a useful place to begin. Despite being often treated as synonymous, "accessibility," "Universal Design," and "Inclusive Design" have different applications. Within contemporary design philosophy, "accessibility" is an attribute—i.e., "is this accessible or not?"—whereas "inclusivity" and "universalism" are methodologies—i.e., "are we being inclusive/universal in our approach?" *Accessibility* is a judgment as to whether a space or experience is available to a given individual. A product on a particularly high shelf in a grocery aisle may be inaccessible to those under a

48

certain height, whereas a product on a particularly low shelf may be inaccessible to those with bad knees, wheelchair users, or anyone who has difficulty grasping near the ground. In terms of lawfully mandated accessibility for those with disabilities, it is often a matter of adaptation—ramps, flashing lights in fire alarms, accessible parking signs, etc. In short, they are often efforts to modify "normative" structures for those who "cannot."

Universal Design, meanwhile, is an architectural philosophy and methodology which has become widely applied in many areas of design. While traditional design tends toward an "average" user, Universal Design imagines a wide diversity of users with different needs and preferences. At risk of oversimplification, it is formed on the basic belief that making something accessible is not a matter of adaptive "add-ons," but holistic design which seeks to eliminate as many barriers as possible, coupled with the ethos that designing for accessibility inherently makes things better for all users.

Inclusive Design takes this further. Whereas Universal Design creates fixed spaces and experiences that are designed to be more universally accessible than traditional approaches, Inclusive Design creates flexible spaces and experiences, designed to be used according to the needs and preferences of each end user. Whereas Universal Design remains a "one size fits all" approach, Inclusive Design empowers the end user to mold it to their needs.

For an easy example of the above, consider seating for an outdoor performance. A set of bleachers are inaccessible for many. A set of bleachers with a ramp and attached landing suitable for wheelchairs has been made accessible for wheelchair users. Installed seating featuring no-step entrances, railings, wide walkways, etc., integrated as central aspects rather than add-ons, is an effort at Universal Design. An open seating area designed for multiple uses which empowers users to choose from—or even create—various methods of sitting (including not sitting at all) is an effort at Inclusive Design. As Susan Goltsman, an internationally recognized expert in creating inclusive environments, describes it, "Inclusive design doesn't mean you're designing one thing for all people. You're designing a diversity of ways to participate so that everyone has a sense of belonging."[1]

Multidisciplinary performing artist and Inclusive Design professional Jan Derbyshire addresses this necessary shift in approach with the title of her article for *Theatre Research in Canada*, "Infrequently Asked Questions, or: How to Kickstart Conversations Around Inclusion and Accessibility in Canadian Theatre and Why it Might be Good for Everybody."[2] The concept of "Infrequently Asked Questions" proves a particularly useful framework for approaching both accessible standards and inclusive methodologies. There is, first, the way Derbyshire uses the term—a methodology for theatre professionals which includes actively pursuing the "tough" questions and constantly evaluating one's own assumptions. She writes of working alongside a number of collaborators: dramaturgs, an artistic director, and playwrights (including Adam Grant Warren, whose play, *Last Train In*, appears in this collection).

> We all had an open, direct discussion about doing the best we can, and what that might actually mean. We talked more and more about where ableism intersects with privilege. We talked about how, for the large majority of professional theatre makers today, including those of us at this particular table, the systems work. We asked: if a system works for you, why would you question it? Why would you bother to look around and see who isn't there? We grappled with the thought that even though theatre people are said to be good at imagining things for our creations, we seem to be deficient in imagining what we do not know, inside our theatre spaces.[3]

Some of the systems that Derbyshire references are rehearsal periods, which tend to be long on the clock and short on the calendar; others are auditions, often unfamiliar territory to disabled actors faced with inaccessible training institutions; still others include the limited control over transportation scheduling that some audiences face, language and communication barriers, and the many socially assumed standards and conventions of theatre performance and attendance.

Imagine this relatively common scene in experimental and fringe theatre: a director, working in a black box theatre whose seating doesn't allow an audience member to leave without crossing through the performance space, decides to forego intermission for artistic reasons. "Tell 'em to pee beforehand, it's only two hours" is the solution offered, met with chuckles and nods around the table. What, though, of those for whom two hours is too long? Beyond the obvious accessibility questions regarding a performance space in which people cannot easily leave once the performance has begun, it is vital to consider the many people such a decision affects and excludes.

There are those with renal difficulties and related disabilities, of course—none of whom tend to be on that usual accessibility "checklist." But then, what about seniors, or those who are pregnant, both groups who regularly have more frequent bathroom needs than others? What of people who may be taking any of the many medications which have a diuretic effect? What of the many unknowable reasons why someone might not be able to wait two hours, while also not wanting the social stigma (and, in some spaces and performances, physical danger) of crossing through a performance space?

This question, "who is affected and excluded by this decision" is a vital step toward providing accessible theatre. Importantly, of those affected by the scenario described above, many likely would not consider themselves "disabled." Modern airlines have become routinely the target of humor and discontent over contemporary cabin design prioritizing passenger capacity over passenger comfort. They are guilty of assuming every passenger is an "average" size, and then designing to that standard. How is it that the theatre community, bastions of empathy and creativity, so often do the same thing?

This brings us to the second use of "Infrequently Asked Questions"—an expectation of not just offering accessibility to "known" challenges but fostering inclusive practices. Designer Kat Holmes uses the hypothetical of a children's playground.

Imagine a playground full of only one kind of swing. A swing that requires you to be a certain height with two arms and two legs. The only people who will come to play are people who match this design, because the design welcomes them and no one else.

And yet there are many different ways you can design an experience of swinging. You can adjust the shape and size of the seat. You can keep a person stationary and swing the environment around them. Participation doesn't require a particular design. But a particular design can prohibit participation.[4]

As Derbyshire points out, "one of the principles of Inclusive Design is that by designing for the eccentrics, everyone benefits."[5] Although only certain audience members might *require* more leg room, most will likely appreciate it. Although only certain audience members might *require* the ability to leave the theatre during a performance, I suspect every audience member would prefer the option be available. While no physical space can be wholly accessible to every human need, Inclusion means making the effort to extend hospitality to all by creating spaces and experiences which provide the flexibility to be utilized and adapted by the individual according to their needs, rather than by a management assuming an "average" need. A combined approach of Inclusive Design when possible, efforts at Universal Design when necessary, adaptive accessibility when nothing else is available, and trained house staff who are empowered to help patrons with needs that no one could have predicted, is the goal to which contemporary theatres must strive.

Amy Oestreicher's epistolary monologue demonstrates more than simply the need for front of house staff to speak with tact; it perfectly frames the problem with approaching "accessibility" as a dichotomy of "normal" versus "special needs" audience members. Every patron has needs; the compatibility of those needs with a theatre's ability to meet them will vary from person to person, theatre to theatre, and, at times, even performance to performance. No theatre can meet every need, but every theatre can do far more than make room for a couple of wheelchairs.

—John Michael Sefel

NOTES

1. Kat Holmes, "The No. 1 Thing You're Getting Wrong about Inclusive Design," *Fast Company*, October 16, 2018, https://www.fastcompany.com/90243282/the-no-1-thing-youre-getting-wrong-about-inclusive-design.

2. Jan Derbyshire, "Infrequently Asked Questions, or: How to Kickstart Conversations Around Inclusion and Accessibility in Canadian Theatre and Why It Might Be Good for Everybody," *Theatre Research in Canada / Recherches théâtrales au Canada*, n.d. https://journals.lib.unb.ca/index.php/TRIC/article/view/25327/29314.

3. *Ibid.*

4. Holmes.

5. Derbyshire.

An Open Letter to the Usher at the Theatre Who Asked Me if I Was "the Sick Girl"

(a monologue-play based on real events)

An Open Letter to the Usher at the Theatre Who Asked Me if I Was "the Sick Girl" © Amy Oestreicher, all rights reserved.

* * *

Dear Miss,

First of all, thank you for being an usher tonight.

I've always had an admiration for what you do, and for the whole world of the Great White Way. Tonight, I was really excited to see one of my favorite musicals being revived on Broadway. I used to live for this stuff, and after being estranged from the theatre scene for a while, I still do love it. However, it's been hard to get back to that world to after a few "medical detours." Physically and emotionally.

I came to the theatre with an equal mix of nerves and dread. In my old life, I would have just hustled right to my seat, 20 minutes before show time, devouring every last page of my *Playbill*, maybe running down to the orchestra to see if I could sneak a look at the musicians, and eagerly hurried back to my seat with elated anticipation as the first booming sounds of the orchestra flooded the building with astounding resonance.

But tonight, like every night I go to see theatre now, I felt like I was intruding on a world I didn't feel quite as at home in. I tentatively walked towards the ticket stand, with equal parts adrenaline and anxiety, as I anticipated explaining my unique medical situation to the house manager, taking in their stupefied look, and keeping my composure as I tried to answer their baffled questions as calmly as I could.

I get it, though—I would be confused too. It sounds weird that, because of all of my surgeries, I can't sit down. I have two bags on my body—an ostomy bag taped to my side, and a large bag in the middle of my stomach—where my bellybutton should be, over an open wound that hasn't healed for five years. It makes life a bit more effort, but it's worth it, because I love living. But the bags prevent me from sitting comfortably. I don't mind if I don't have a great view—I can just stay in the back, where I won't disturb anyone for the many times I'll be in and out of the bathroom throughout the show. No, I don't get tired standing, and yes, I'm used to it, and double-yes, I know it's weird. It's not a preference, it's a necessity. And I know it feels ridiculous that I can't wait until the end of a song to use a bathroom—I hate it too, and I certainly don't want to be a distraction.

And the food—I get it. Nine bottled drinks in my backpack may seem excessive for a two-hour show. As do the six blocks of cheese stuffed in the side-pockets. But no, I can't wait until the end of the show. I only absorb 20 percent of what I eat so it means I have to always be eating something. And because I malabsorb so much, it means for that 80 percent leftover, I'll need the bathroom—a lot. I don't have a stomach and it takes a lot of work and constant calories to keep up my weight—which I'm still trying to gain more of.

I get it, I do. it's a lot of weird accommodations I'm asking for. Not your usual "I need wheelchair access" or "I can't handle loud noises" or something like that. And I know I'm asking you for a lot of favors, and then you have to get a manager of the house to approve, or a supervisor, and I really feel bad that you have to do all that for me, in addition to the hundreds of people that are still waiting to be seated, staring at this skinny little girl trying to manage a backpack twice her size. I try to be as chameleon-like as possible—just tell me where to stand, and I'll fade into the background, really. Whatever I can get out of the show, I will, although I'll probably miss half of it in the bathroom. I know in some ways, it's easier to stay at home, but I really am looking for quality of life here, and I don't want to spend the rest of my life saying, "well, maybe I should just be thankful I'm alive." I'm living, but theatre is what makes me feel alive. And I really want to see this show—I'm actually an actress, although you may never guess that from all of my requests right now.

Tonight was a bit complicated, I know. This theatre was super-strict about any food or liquid in the building, and I'm sorry, but my body doesn't make exceptions, even if a theatre has completely legit reasons and great intentions. So there was a little back-and-forth between my needs and the "powers that be" of the theatre, and the staff member was very understanding and was really trying her best to work things out. Maybe it's difficult to understand how rigidly I have to stick to my constant eating, standing and bathroom access. So I went downstairs to the general ladies' bathroom and just hung out there while the show started. I didn't know what else to do, and I felt like I was causing more commotion that I wanted. So I just waited there, trying to hear what was going on in the show through the speakers.

I'm *not upset* about how hard it was for that usher to make these accommodations. I get that it's hard to appreciate exactly how extreme my crazy situation is. My stomach exploded, but that's another story—actually, I wrote a musical about it. See? I'm not just a sick girl with a disability, I do theatre too! I belong here!

There is only one thing that made me upset. It's how I met you.

You asked me a question when trying to work things out (*which I really do appreciate*). You came down, saw me in the bathroom, and before even introducing yourself, said "Are you the sick girl?"

I hate that word. I really do. I immediately snapped back (*and I'm sorry if that came across the wrong way, but it struck a nerve)* "No, I'm not 'the sick girl.' I have medical circumstances."

You didn't seem to be bothered by the difference in phrasing and went on with your well-intentioned attempt to make my necessary accommodations. Eventually, it worked out, and thank you for helping me find a nice place to stand in the back and eat my cheese while enjoying the show.

But I really hope you heard me when I said "I'm not *the sick girl.*" Believe it or not, I'm an actress. An actress that has a few extra … props and stage directions, I guess.

What I really wanted to tell you is, yes, I have crazy medical circumstances. *And I hate them.* I absolutely hate them and sometimes I want to scream like hell how unfair it is, that I can't even sit in a cozy velvet theatre seat, relax, and just enjoy the show. And more than that—I used to be just like those actors you're seeing up there now. I used to be SO in this world! Auditioning in New York, with an agent and everything. I knew all the latest composers, what the Broadway trends were, the most overdone audition songs to avoid at the time … that was me! I'm not just this skinny thing that should be in bed at a hospital, barricaded from the outside world. I have those moments sometimes, in and out of hospitals, but I'm strong, I'm vital, and I'm an actress, whether I also happen to be a patient or not.

I want to tell you that I still do what I love, but in a different form, and hopefully inspiring people. I may not be up there with my Equity card, but I'm sharing my story through the *magic of theatre*—my addiction since the time I could remember. And maybe one day, I *will* audition again.

I know right now I look thin as a rail, I'm hunched over, embarrassed, insecure and trying not to feel ashamed that I can't behave like everyone else and not make a scene wherever I go. But for five years, I've been "making scenes" touring theatres, even some just a few streets down, singing, dancing and laughing about all of this medical nonsense.

So you can call me whatever you want—weird, high-maintenance, difficult—although I really do appreciate all of the accommodations you are willing to make. But please, *do not call me sick.* I have *medical circumstances.* Circumstances that I cope with through the power of theatre. Circumstances that I *won't* let determine the course of my life.

After the show was over, I went back into my life with those same medical circumstances, and frantically searched for a bathroom on the way back to my place. Whatever it was, I was going back to my life. A life that is so much larger than sitting or standing.

So, the next time you meet someone that needs special accommodations, please, don't call them "the sick girl." Hundreds of people mill in and out of a theatre every day. What if we judged all of them with the first label that comes to our minds? What if we judged all the actors on stage with the costume they wore? Theatre's about opening up our preconceived notions. I hope I was able to do that for you. Even though all I said was "I'm not the sick girl." Maybe one day, you'll see my show, and meet the person behind the patient.

And I really did enjoy the show, by the way. So thank you. I had a great view.

Wishing you the best,
Amy Oestreicher

End of play.

RPM

GRAHAM BRYANT

In her 2014 article, "Passing and Disability: Why Coming Out as Disabled Can Be So Difficult," Rachel Cohen-Rottenberg writes,

> Last year, on National Coming Out Day, I officially came out as bisexual. It was a celebration. No angst. No fear. No second thoughts. Just a celebration. It was a such a contrast with coming out as disabled at the end of 2008, with all of the fear and dread that attended that decision. There have been many times since then that I've thought that coming out as disabled was the worst decision I'd ever made in my life. If I could have put the toothpaste back in the tube at those moments, I would have.[1]

To be clear, while there has been amazing progress in many countries regarding "coming out" in reference to sexuality, this should not be taken as a sign that there are no worries, concerns, or dangers to doing so; victims of hate crimes and family abandonment in the U.S., let alone state-sponsored violence in some nations, are ample evidence to the contrary. Analogies between different oppressed and marginalized identities and communities are both common and almost as commonly critiqued. Still, as Ellen Samuels notes in "My Body, My Closet: Invisible Disability and the Limits of Coming-out Disclosure,"

> A number of disability theorists suggest that disability has more in common with sexual orientation than with race, ethnicity, or gender—other categories often invoked analogically to support the social model of disability. One argument for this connection is that most people with disabilities, like most queers,[2] do not share their identity with immediate family members and often have difficulty accessing queer or crip-culture.[3]

The relationship between these two forms of "coming out," then, is complicated and should not be reductively treated as absolute or without problematic aspects; still, the increasingly mainstream understanding of one provides a useful "way in" when considering the difficult decisions around the other. As Ellen Samuels continues, "[l]ike racial, gender, and queer passing, the option of passing as nondisabled provides both a certain level of privilege and a profound sense of misrecognition and internal dissonance."[4] There are numerous reasons someone may fear disclosing

56

disability that echo similar decisions around sexual identity. For example, while Cohen-Rottenberg's experience was positive, many people who identify as bisexual are met with disbelief, both about their own status and regarding the identity itself.[5] These same demands of "proof" are familiar to many in the disability community. This is especially true when—especially in education—these demands are institutionalized in the name of "service," and may be similarly affected by intersectional identities, prejudices, and resource availability. In her article "Coming Out Disabled: The Politics of Understanding," Tanya Titchkosky writes,

> The proving of learning disabilities is an incredibly messy situation: the proving enterprise has grown exponentially over the last couple of decades and the tendrils of diagnostic desires and procedures reach out into classroom practices, psychological and intelligence testing, brain imaging, gene mapping. Students who have "proof" of learning disabilities may, indeed, share very few experiences in common with one another: what counts as a learning disability is becoming more and more diverse. Some people have spent a lifetime being treated as learning disabled and others only a week or two. Learning disabilities are tied into the inequalities surrounding race, class, gender, state, and nation.[6]

Then, consider Graham Bryant's statement in *RPM*: "I still don't regret hiding my label initially," he writes, describing his arrival at his university, "I was going into a new environment where people didn't really know me, and I thought that if I was open about my past it might put me in a box that I couldn't get out of. [...] after spending a few months listening to people's thoughts about 'the spectrum,' which were either negative views or very little knowledge on it, I knew I made the right call."[7]

Cohen-Rottenberg gives further context to these fears:

> It's very difficult to come out as disabled, I think, because we face the dual reality that most people (a) hate our bodies absolutely unapologetically and (b) consider that hatred entirely natural. It's for this reason that they can use disability slurs constantly and think nothing of it. It's for this reason that they can segregate and exclude us as though we're substandard merchandise to return to the manufacturer. It is still considered natural to react with revulsion against us in a way that other groups have fought against more successfully—not entirely successfully, obviously, but more successfully.[8]

Many Disability activists would prefer the solidarity of more people disclosing, just as Harvey Milk famously pushed—at times controversially—closeted gay men to come out for the cause. There is some validity to this approach; being personally acquainted with an individual from a marginalized group often lessens personal prejudice against that community.[9] Still, the ethics of encouraging others to "out" themselves are, to quote Titchkosky, "messy" at best. Cohen-Rottenberg muses on the reasons for lasting prejudice against those who are neurodivergent, cognitively disabled, and/or mentally ill:

> Partly, we face this hatred because the medical model has taken over as a metaphor for human life. People are no longer evil. People no longer make

bad choices. People are no longer victimized by oppression. People no longer act out of ignorance, or selfishness, or greed. No. Now they're *sick, crazy, brain-dead, retarded, mentally ill, have low IQs,* and on and on.

In the face of this hatred, it's very, very difficult to convince people that you love your disabled body because it's the one you live in. You say that you love your body, and people look at you as though you don't quite understand your own reality.[10]

RPM explores Graham Bryant's challenges—not in coming to terms with himself, but in the difficulty navigating the social gauntlets around him, with negative consequences whether he chooses to disclose or not. As with sexuality, to "come out" remains a daunting risk for many disabled individuals, and, as explored by Bryant and Cohen-Rottenberg, it isn't a decision that always results in universally positive experiences.

—**John Michael Sefel**

NOTES

1. Rachel Cohen-Rottenberg, "Passing and Disability: Why Coming Out as Disabled Can Be So Difficult," The Body Is Not An Apology, December 19, 2014, https://thebodyisnotanapology.com/magazine/passing-and-disability-why-coming-out-as-disabled-can-be-so-difficult/.

2. This loaded word, "queers," is quoted from an article which deals with contemporary queer culture and the reclaimed word and is not meant as the slur it may appear in this limited context.

3. Ellen Samuels, "My Body, My Closet: Invisible Disability and the Limits of Coming-out Disclosure," in *The Disability Studies Reader*, ed. Lennard J. Davis (New York: Routledge, Taylor & Francis Group, 2017), 344.

4. *Ibid.*, 348.

5. Chloe Sargeant, "Bisexual People Are Asked to Prove Their Bisexuality Daily, and It Needs to Stop," *SBS*, October 9, 2019, https://www.sbs.com.au/topics/pride/agenda/article/2019/04/08/bisexual-people-are-asked-prove-their-bisexuality-daily-and-it-needs-stop.

6. Tanya Titchkosky, "Coming Out Disabled: The Politics of Understanding," *Disability Studies Quarterly*, 2001, https://dsq-sds.org/article/view/325/398.

7. Graham Bryant, *RPM*.

8. Cohen-Rottenberg.

9. E.g., Daniel DellaPosta, "Gay Acquaintanceship and Attitudes toward Homosexuality: A Conservative Test," *Socius* (January 2018), doi:10.1177/2378023118798959.

10. Cohen-Rottenberg.

RPM

* * *

Preset: A record player, preferably with a horn, onstage [must play both 78 and 33 rpm]. Either a screen or a white sheet (able to be used as a screen) at midstage. A wheeled AV cart—the type that was popular in schools in the latter half of the 20th century, sits with a rotary/carousel slide projector on top. Underfoot is a circular rug which "ties the room together"—it's one of those knotted rugs that form a spiral of fabric, similar to a record's groove.

Every item has a small label with its name on it (i.e., "AV Cart," "Slide Projector," etc.). If the theatre is intimate enough, these are best done on one of those "label maker" guns that were popular in the early '90s. If not, Post-its or some other "low-tech" label is fine.

Lights up—it's a warm, amber glow—"cozy living room with dark wood" feel

Graham enters, holding a red plastic View-Master toy. As he crosses he changes out one round disk for another and then, in no particular hurry, enjoys it for a moment at center stage. He then crosses to the AV Cart, places the View-Master down next to the slide projector, and turns the machine on. A slide appears.

[slide] Text: RPM

Graham checks to make sure that it looks good on the screen, adjusts things if necessary, and then clicks forward to a blank slide [blacked-out or "neutral"]. He then crosses to the record player and pulls out an old 78 from underneath, and very closely inspects the label. It's extremely old, and so takes a moment of real attention to read it properly.

Graham: The label I was given never really helped define who I am.

He is satisfied that it's the right record, and places it on the machine. As he begins this next line, he goes about setting the needle to get the music to begin.

The label itself, "Asperger's," was named after a guy who was working for a Eugenics program during the Third Reich, so ...

[Richard Strauss—Serenade for wind ensemble Op. 7 begins to play from the horn. [If this can't be found or is otherwise unsuitable, other works by Wagner or Strauss may be substituted, but they should carry the same stigma of "favorite works of Hitler."]

... I can't really say I hold any affection for the term.

He crosses back to the AV cart, picks up the View-Master and clicks through a few pictures while listening to Strauss' Nazi-approved music. He allows this to go on for several beats—a tad longer than most theatre audiences expect. He begins to speak again (splitting his attention between the audience and the View-Master) starting at measure 10 in the music (around 40 seconds in—when the horn part starts). He speaks casually, listening to the music, looking at the slides, and including the audience in the way he might speak to a friend in the room while also distracted by a video game.

I feel like these days there's a lot of drive for social acceptance and understanding for marginalized groups because there are communities and languages being developed to give people a voice they didn't have before. But for people "like me," I'm not sure the same… "parameters" apply. I've met people "like me," and they don't tend to want to form a community with one another. They're more focused on and predisposed to pursuing their own interests, the things that drive them. I can certainly relate. I also feel like the purpose of the language surrounding these "disorders" has been to categorize and simplify individuals' behavior so that they can be better understood.

During these last lines, the music has grown louder and Graham realizes he's competing to be heard over it. He stops, crosses, lifts the needle. During the next two lines, he puts the record back in its sleeve.

But, that's not what happens. The label I was given instead functioned as a quick word that justified what made me … myself.

He bends, puts that record away, finds a different record, pulls it out, and begins setting it up to play

It encouraged acceptance, sure, but it discouraged people from wanting to understand me or better yet just know who I am by my own name rather than this broad, sweeping term.

The music from the new record begins. It's a very short, gleefully loud and chaotic punk / post-punk tune—think "We Hate You, Please Die" by Crash and the Boys. Graham cranks the music. As he begins speaking again, he is joyfully yelling to be heard over the music. It's like being at a rock concert, trying to talk to the person next to you.

By the way, I probably hate the word "spectrum" more than any other.
    Light and sound are spectrums and people just aren't the same thing. The nature of this word in the context of people reflects this incessant need to name something rather than understand it or figure it out. People are just now starting to figure out that we messed up our language the first time around and that these concepts like "gender" and "sexuality" are spectrums. So at the end of the day that all translates to "stop trying to box me into a word so that you feel secure, and I'll get back to you when/if it's any of your business."

The song ends abruptly.

[*still yelling*] THE REASON—

A moment of embarrassment as he stops the record player before it can go on to the next song. He then begins speaking again, now at a normal volume.

The reason why I was even diagnosed in the first place is because I can't write. I'd use the word "dysgraphia," but since I have weak wrists and I can't write by hand for extended periods of time, I'll just say that instead.

During the next few lines, he slowly, half-paying attention, begins to take the record off the player, and preps to put it away.

It didn't matter how much I practiced or how much physical therapy I had, it didn't go away. And in the twenty-first century, that shouldn't even be a big deal. But for some reason, I had to be tested to receive the accommodations that I needed to get through school. And what I needed was to use a keyboard, not be separated from everyone else. I did that plenty enough on my own, thanks. So now I have the word "Asperger's" and despite what you may have heard it apparently means that I can't write.

You know how I like to think about people?

He uses the record as a visual aid.

I picture a vinyl record. A record has grooves in it that go all the way to the center of a disc. When you're closer to the edge the needle has to go faster than it would near the center because it has to make a larger amount of distance in the same amount of time. And yet, no matter what the size of the groove is, the needle is still traveling at the same amount of revolutions per minute. It's okay to go at your own pace, you're making the same journey as everyone else.

And that would be a really great place to stop—but unfortunately, it's not what I'm going to talk about.

All business, he puts the record away, and then crosses over to the AV cart and picks up the remote control for the slide carousel.
[slide] Photo: Graham's high school "senior portrait"

I left high school thinking that I would pursue psychology in college. Instead, I fell in love with theatre.

[slide] Photo: A picture of Graham performing, now college-aged

When I was accepted into the department, I couldn't believe it. Really, I couldn't believe it. I thought that somewhere on an application it must have mentioned my diagnosis, and that was the basis of how I got in.

I was diagnosed in my first year of middle school—

[slide] Photo: Graham in middle school

—and attended two different schools in the following years.

[two slides] Photos (in rapid succession) of each of the schools

They were "therapeutic" schools with good intentions and trained staff but looking back I think I took away more bad than good from it.

> *[slide] Photo: Graham from those years. He looks a little … "lost"*

I was tired of being in structures that decided my path for me, so I resolved to attend an academic institution and try to leave it all behind. I was open about my past with other people, but obviously not much had changed. I hadn't changed. I still had trouble with relationships, but it was high school so who cares? What I got out of high school was that I loved being onstage and working with a team on productions. It's what gave me the courage to audition for the department at my college. And when I got in… …I just didn't accept it.

> *[slide] Processed Photo: Graham's profile silhouetted in jet black against stark white—something like Alfred Hitchcock's old logo, but much higher contrast.*

I got into my own head that it must have been done out of pity.
   So … I hid.
Looking back, after everything that I went through it was the only time in my life where I didn't really feel like myself. I still don't regret hiding my label initially. I was going into a new environment where people didn't really know me, and I thought that if I was open about my past it might put me in a box that I couldn't get out of.

> *During the following list of questions, he keeps advancing the slides at the same time—the slides are cumulative—the first one says "typecasting" in black on a white background; the second one still has "typecasting," but now adds "Othering." Then "Special Treatment." Then "Resentment." Then "Self-Censorship." Then "Isolation." By this time, the screen is packed tight with words. Then, blank.*

If he's "impaired," could he only play roles that are neurotic?

> *[slide]*

I can, by the way.
   Would he be able to connect with somebody else on stage?

> *[slide]*

Would it be fair to let anyone else have those kind of roles when he's here?

> *[slide]*

I didn't want anyone to either have those thoughts or make me consider them as valid.

> *[slide]*

I was scared.

> *[slide]*

I didn't know that it would happen for sure, but after spending a few months listening to people's thoughts about "the spectrum," which were either negative views or very little knowledge on it, [slide] I knew I made the right call.

> *[blank slide]*

The mistake I made was in waiting so long.

It took about two and a half years before I "came out," which I never thought I would have to do. Everything I said before about my label? I believed it, and I still do. I think it's dumb and unhelpful for the most part. But it still had power over me. I was worried that when other people met me I would either let some memory slip or that maybe they would take a look at me, make a judgment, and then it would surface again all the same.

So instead of reinventing myself I had this mask that was preventing me from getting close to people, again. Every time that I would miscommunicate, come off as rude, or decline to go hang out in large groups I could just tell myself "It's not your fault. It's because they don't get it, and they wouldn't even if you talked about it." So I had this neat little safety net that I could always fall back into so that I didn't actually ever have to grow. It took too long for me to realize that my silence wasn't about not having to acknowledge my own limits or about making a bad first impression. Somehow, after all that time, I was still afraid of what people would think about me. Viewing me through this lens that I thought wasn't necessary to know "me."

Because then what if every time that I had either messed up or failed could be explained now because of this word? Two and a half years went by at this point and everyone knew "me" except for me. There were breakdowns all the time and I kept isolating myself when I knew people were going to hang out.

By the time I did it, it wasn't because I wanted to. I just had bigger things to tackle and it was getting in my way. So one long evening before finals—

> *Graham reaches into his pocket, where he had pulled the View-Master slide disk from earlier—and now starts pulling disk after disk, stacking them up on the AV cart.*

—I wrote it all out. Not unlike how I'm putting it out here now.

> *Graham starts collecting the new pile of disks, holding them up in his hands, fanning them out like a deck of cards.*

It was a blog post that took about five hours to write before I was satisfied.

> *In the following lines, he begins to treat the disks as the blog, "sending them out," crossing and handing them out to different audience members.*

I sent it out in small waves: people I trusted…

> *He hands off a disk to one or two people*

…then people who deserved to know

> *He hands out three or four more disks*

… then my class

> *Several more, less careful about who they go to now*

… and then … everyone

Graham starts rapidly handing them out, putting them in people's hands without really checking to see how they're received—just disk-disk-disk-disk-disk until his pile is gone. Once they're all handed out, he stops and looks at the breadth of what he's done.

(*Tranquil*) It was a weight off my shoulders for sure. Did I feel comfortable about it?

(*matter-of-fact*) Absolutely not.

And I'm not sure how much it helped people "understand" me either.

He crosses to AV Cart.

In the end …

He grabs the slide projector's plug where it's plugged into the extension cord.

… it was about me getting rid of my mask.

He pulls them apart. The slide projector goes dark. As he speaks, he pushes the cart off to the side.

From that point forward, any unhappiness or difficulties that happened were on me instead of others. I think the only certain good that came out of it is that some people who read it reached out to me about their relatives or their best friends, and now they felt like they had someone to talk to about them.

The AV cart aside, Graham is able to look at the audience. Really, really look at them.

Some of them may have been hoping for someone to talk to for years…

And I guess that's as a good a reason as any to be open about it again.

Beat. Then he turns his attention to pulling up/off the screen, and, finally, unplugging and shutting down/putting away the record player.

What I would say about "coming out" about … anything I guess, is that you don't owe it to other people first. I still think I was right to not be open about my past at the beginning. There's a stigma around the "spectrum" that I feel like a lot of people either dismiss out of hand or they overestimate the generality of its application. I don't think we've reached the point where atypical neurology is something that most people will feel comfortable talking about over coffee, and that's okay.

Over the next line he reaches into his pocket, pulls out one last View-Master disk, and puts it into the viewer

Still, when I put it off for too long, I became paranoid and repressed about how I was viewed…

… and in the end, the only person that kind of thing matters to is yourself.

Standing at center stage, he puts the View-Master up to his eyes and looks through it, roughly over the heads of the audience. A beat, and then he pulls the View-Master down just enough to, maybe, make eye-contact with the audience one last time.

It's okay to go at your own pace.

He brings the View-Master back up to his eyes.

Nobody else can set it for you.

He enjoys the slide, beat, and then hits the lever to make it advance. Quick fade to black.

End of play.

Whack Job

KATE DEVORAK

In the social model of disability, it is a society's physical, attitudinal, and social barriers that actually "disable" an individual by preventing that individual from fully participating in their community.[1] According to this model, it is possible to "perform" one's disability in the real world. In other words, it is possible to conform to a stereotype about one's disability, intentionally or unintentionally, by choice or by necessity, during a particular social interaction. However, this kind of performance differs from deliberately performing one's disability while onstage in order to add complexity to such "performances" in the real world. Someone who is embodying his/her/their condition onstage is doing so deliberately. Most onstage words and actions are scripted, and all of them are deliberate. A performer can use the performer/audience dynamic, which privileges the performer, to reverse the able-bodied/disabled binary in the real world, which privileges the able-bodied body. Any performer can use the stage as a place to represent, re-present, or critique stereotypes associated with disability in the real world. A stand-up or sit-down comedian, who can embody a disability or condition without having to "become" a character who might not have that disability or condition, is especially well positioned to represent, re-present, or critique stereotypes about his/her/their own disability. In her solo play, *Whack Job*, Kate Devorak has adapted the structure of the irreverent nightclub comedian, providing the audience-entertainer conventions necessary to bluntly address her lived experience.

First, stand-up comedians usually write their own material, and most audiences attending a comedy show are aware of that convention. In most cases, a stand-up comedian has more control over how his/her/their body is represented onstage than an actor would. Second, a stand-up comedian is always working in what phenomenologist Bert O. States calls the self-expressive mode. States says the self-expressive mode reveals "an actor's particular way of *doing* his role."[2] Though a stand-up comedian may adopt a persona, he/she/they does not usually play a character. Therefore, a stand-up comedian who has a visible or apparent condition is revealing both his/her/their way of embodying that condition and the personal magnetism that allows an audience to enjoy the performance, even when the comedian deliberately "fails" to overcome certain negative stereotypes associated with the observed condition, in order to make that condition either the subject or the butt of a joke.

Unlike an actor forced into "performing" his/her/their condition in a reductive way because they did not write the script of a play, a stand-up comedian can use language choices, physical choices, and vocal choices that support their preferred representation or re-presentation to an audience. In addition, since the performer/audience dynamic is always openly acknowledged in a stand-up routine, a stand-up performer can create didactic moments in a performance that an actor in a play that does not include audience address could not. Comedy is the art of presenting alternative possibilities to accepted modes of thought for an audience, using humor to make the experience enjoyable. One standard comedic tool, the punchline, allows a comedian to create unexpected juxtapositions between familiar ideas and then use comic timing to make an audience potentially reevaluate those ideas based on the pleasure an unexpected juxtaposition affords. Even a relatively simple punchline, such as English and American stand-up comedian Henny Youngman's "Take my wife … please!"[3] destabilizes both the rules of syntax and the privileging of marriage in American culture.

—Jill Summerville

NOTES

1. "Models of Disability: Keys To Perspectives," Alaska Mental Health Consumer Web, 2019; October 7, 2019.

2. Bert O. States, *Great Reckonings in Little Rooms* (Berkeley: University of California, 1985), 165.

3. Henny Youngman, "Take My Wife, Please! Take My Album, Please, Or Take Two Sets For The Price Of One," YouTube, July 24, 2018, https://www.youtube.com/watch?v=Kzj cFTrieSo.

Whack Job

* * *

The place is here. The time is now, or, reasonably, around 7:30–8 p.m. The set is simple—a stool, a microphone and stand, all the fixin's for a decent open mic. String lights made from empty pill bottles help illuminate the stage for pre-show. Pre-show music should consist of songs that reference insanity—Prince's "Let's Go Crazy," Gnarls Barkley's "Crazy," Aerosmith's "Crazy," Madonna's "Crazy for You," take your pick, they're not hard to come by. There's a projected image on the back wall, reading "Whack Job. by kate devorak." Lights up on KATE. She looks nervous. No, concerned.

Kate: It's difficult to pinpoint the exact moment you realize your life has gone completely off the rails, but I think that being comically overdressed and crying your eyes out in the day old bread section of Ralphs while listening to a cover of "I Want to Know What Love Is" is a pretty good indicator. I'm Kate Devorak. I'm not altogether all together, if you know what I mean.

> *[Beat]*

I mean, I'm "crazy." A "wee bit touched in the head."

"Whacky. Nutty. Batty. Mental. Out to lunch. Off my rocker. Freaked out. Flipped out. Mad as a hatter. Mad as a hare. Unglued, unhinged, and unzipped."

Or, as I like to say, bipolar.

That's right, we're going to have some fun with mental illness tonight! I know that's pretty heavy, so if at any time you start feeling nervous, try breathing in on a count of four, holding for four, and exhaling for eight. Like this—

(*she demonstrates*) in, hold, out.

It's called four-square breathing, and, fun fact: *(the projected image switches the words "Fun Fact")* ... it will help keep you from going into shock. (*projector fades to black*)

All right, let's begin! (*projector reads "Part 1. Crazy"*) Everybody comfortable? Yeah? Great. I'm never comfortable. This right here (*gestures to the whole deal*), this is stasis for me. You know how some people just look pissed off all the time? I have "resting concerned face." Which often makes people concerned for me. Like, folks will constantly ask me if I'm ok. And I'm like, "Yeah. That's just my face."

"Don't freak out," they'll say. Oh, trust me, if I was freaking out, you'd know. Everyone would know. It'd be a whole to do. Don't worry, I'm stable. (*Winks*)

So, as I've mentioned, I have bipolar II, which is a moderate to severe mood disorder. It's actually the less extreme form of bipolar, which is kind of weird because it seems like it should be an escalation. Like:

Bipolar II: Son of Bipolar I!

or

Bipolar II: This Time It's Personal ... Problems.

Bipolar II: The Reckoning.

I experience more depressive episodes, and my elevated state is a less intense form of mania known as hypomania. In other words, I'm more likely to max out your credit card than burn down your house.

Not quite like *Bipolar the Musical* ... or, as you may have heard of it, "*Next to Normal.*"

I have so many issues with *Next to Normal.* If you've never heard of *Next to Normal*—which, let's be honest, you're in the audience of a one-woman show about mental illness, you've heard of *Next to Normal*—it's a Pulitzer Prize-winning musical from 2008 about a mother living with bipolar I with psychotic symptoms and its effect on her family. Now, I promised myself I wouldn't get into it tonight, but I also have terrible impulse control, so I'll just say this:

Should it get credit for handling a complex topic and raising awareness for bipolar disorder through a popular medium?

Yes.

Do I, as a woman living with bipolar disorder, find parts of it relatable?

Absolutely.

Do I cry whenever I listen to the end of Act II?

You bet your ass I do.

But it's also incredibly anti-treatment, it exaggerates and romanticizes mental illness, and the pacing is all over the place! And *what even is* Aaron Tveit's character supposed to be? Is he a hallucination? Is he an angel? Because the show leans pretty heavily towards angel at the end, despite the fact that there is an earlier song in which he tries to convince the mother to kill herself. Consistency, people! But it's cool. It's cool. I'm here. I'm cool. You can read all about it in my upcoming *Jezebel* article.

Basically, I fluctuate between two major states of being: depressive and manic. How are y'all feeling? You want the good news or the bad news first? Up or down?

> [*She polls the audience, gauging whether they'd like to cover depression or hypomania first. She proceeds accordingly, depending on audience reaction*]

Alrighty, let's start slow [*ALT—let's slow things down*].

I spend more time in the downswing, so it'll be easier for us to wade into that deep depression. I was diagnosed with capital-D Depression back when I was 13 or 14. I probably could have told you that around the time I was 9, but I'm sure I thought it was just an inevitable result of being raised Irish Catholic. Reluctance to process emotions, a lot of directionless guilt, obsession with death and the afterlife, thinking that wafers and wine make up an acceptable meal. But no, on top of that, my brain is a bit wonky, so into the mental health care machine I went. Since my bipolar disorder manifests with more depressive episodes, it took a sec for everybody to figure out I was a little crazier than first expected. A depressive episode is a period that can last from a couple weeks to a few months where I can experience extreme sadness or hopelessness, lethargy, lack of interest in pretty much everything, and persistent thoughts of death and suicide. So it's a ton of fun. Everything becomes pointless and exhausting. For me, it's not so much that I get sad as much as it I get so overwhelmed by dread and despair and self hatred that I just shut down and feel nothing but the ghost of sadness. Nothing has meaning, nothing has value. For some reason showering becomes the most difficult task in the history of time and space. In that headspace it is so easy to lose touch with reality. Your brain lies to you. It tells you that you're worthless and alone and that if you disappeared the world would keep spinning and it would have no consequence. Which is technically true, but it shouldn't say that.

Plus, I start thinking like a sad 15-year-old who's just getting into slam poetry, which nobody wants.

The lights dim as she gets close to the mic. She pulls a small notebook from her pocket. A low bass line starts to play.

Hello all you cool cats, and welcome to an evening with Kate Devorak.

I'll start with an old favorite—"Self Indulgent Thoughts I've Had While in Withdrawal #7"

I feel like a Pointillism painting
I seem complete, but if you look
Close enough, I come apart
Each cell shaking
And screaming
And if this sounds crazy, that's kind of the point Cheryl
Thank you.

       She snaps the notebook closed.

I thought I was a genius when I wrote this, can you even imagine?

       The lights come up abruptly.
       [During the next section, Kate's energy ramps up, starting around a 3 and escalating to an 8 or 9.]

Ooh! Hang on. Real quick, I wanted to try out some material on y'all. So: I've been more aware of just how casually we throw around terms for insanity colloquially. It's really … crazy. And here's the thing, I don't really mind it personally, like, on the whole, though I try to sub out other words when I can, like saying "yo that's wild" instead of "that shit's insane." Every once in a while, though, it does stand out. Like, this one time, I was driving and this song came on the radio, and the DJ announces that the artist's name is "Bipolar Sunshine." And I'm like, "Is that—that can't be right." But nah, it was totally Bipolar Sunshine. It was the specificity that was especially jarring. It's like if I asked someone what their astrological sign is and they said, "Leukemia." Yikes. And by the way, I looked him up, Bipolar Sunshine doesn't even have bipolar disorder. He's a poser. Anyway, sorry, I'm rambling, that happens sometimes. Point is—I figured since insanity's built into our vocabulary anyway, it was surprising that there weren't more dumb jokes about it. So I wrote some.

Ready?

What's a bipolar person's favorite hair dye?

Manic Panic.

What's a bipolar person's favorite day of the week?

Manic Monday.

I should have warned y'all these are pretty bad. Ok, one more.

Why is a bipolar person so popular at the club?

Because she's a maniac, maniac on the floor

> *At the second "maniac," the instrumental of Ty Parr's "National Aerobic Championship Theme" starts playing. It is the peak of manic energy. Kate launches into a frantic jazzercise routine. It is not very good. Her smile seems forced and her eyes are filled with a kind of panic. This continues for about 20 seconds before she begins to speak again, but she does not stop dancing.*

My mom loves to tell this story about how once, when she was chaperoning my fourth grade field trip, the kids in our group were all talking about their grandmothers. Like, "My grandma bakes the best cookies" or "my grandma made me this hat." And then I piped in, "My grandma smokes, drinks, and plays the slots." Which my mother thought was hilarious, and which I now recognize as textbook manic behavior. Mania can last for a couple days to a couple months, and boy is it a wild ride. It's easy to confuse this feeling with confidence, but confidence doesn't make you blow a married dude in a Stop & Shop parking lot on a Tuesday night. We're talking elevated mood, rapid thoughts, zero impulse control, self esteem through the roof, baby!

Sleep? Don't need it. Money? Just throw that shit away. Consequences? What are those? You think drunk texting your ex is bad, try manic texting them. Is this a booty call or a cry for help? Ball's in your court, Brendan. You decide.

Quick, quick, quick. Sex, drugs, rock and roll. You're a coked up '80s businessman on the brink of the next Big Deal. You are the second coming. YOU RUN THIS TOWN.

> *She stops dancing, and the music ends abruptly, but for the duration of the mania section, she never stops moving.*

Then you crash. It's always a crash. I don't think you can just gradually come down from that high, so watch out. Coming down from a manic episode is a lot because suddenly reality snaps back and you're stuck dealing with the aftermath, like somebody reluctantly checking their bank account after a bender in Las Vegas. Which, coincidentally, is probably the worst place on earth for a person with bipolar disorder. I've only been once, where I couldn't smoke, drink, or play the slots, and I still somehow almost managed to get myself arrested.

Now this might be a bit … controversial … I kinda like mania. It can be super fun if you can harness its power. You feel great. Like what I imagine a normal, confident, driven person feels like, but faster. I'll clean the entire house, sort through my wardrobe, start writing 3 scripts I'll never get back to, decide that I need a whiteboard to really get my life together, run out to Target, end up at Walmart because the Target was closed because it's 3 a.m. and they're cowards, wander around for half an hour listening to the music they're playing over the intercom because I'm pretty sure the Universe is trying to tell me something through every third song, but never mind about that, now I have to buy this notebook/clipboard combo as though it's my train ticket to the Land of Second Chances before I try to fight the only other person here because she wants to fight me I know it I can see it in her eyes.

It's a slippery slope.

I have enough self awareness at this point to recognize when I'm manic, I just have a hard time keeping it in check very long. Here's the thing—I know when I'm being crazy. I am uncomfortably aware when the things I'm thinking or doing are erratic or irrational. I also don't want to be doing what I'm doing. And yet here we are. It's like an out of body experience, like I'm floating somewhere above myself helpless to do much but scream like a heckler in a horror movie.

"No, bitch, don't go in there! Why are you going in there? Is anybody going to stop her from taking that shot? Don't take that shot, lady! Damn it, she's screwed."

On top of that, my thoughts are totally scattered. Have you ever seen one of those things … it's like a phone booth that you go into and they pump cash into it in a wind tunnel and you keep whatever you can catch? They were hella popular in B-grade game shows in the late '90s for some reason. It's like that, but the dollars are thoughts and the wind tunnel phone booth is my brain. Everything is swirling around so quickly, and I'm frantically trying to catch even one thought, and the timer is ticking down, and I end up with a fistful of odd ideas, which most likely are bad ones, and I don't have the impulse control to throw them out.

So you can imagine that fluctuating between these two extremes with little to no break can be exhausting. And it can lead to some pretty sticky situations, so I'll say this right now—

Mental illness is not an excuse for shitty behavior.

All together now:

Mental illness is not an excuse for shitty behavior.

My disorder can be an explanation for my actions, but regardless, there are always consequences to my behavior, and at the end of the day, I have to own up to that.

If you're lucky, though, you get to unlock the secret third mood—irritable.

And I'm not talking like mixed episodes, or as I like to call them, the quick and the dead. Those are neat because you get all the fun and excitement of a deep depression, but at 10x the speed. You're like a skeleton strapped to a rocket chair being hurtled into space. Irritable is like a grab bag of emotions. You don't know what you're gonna get. Am I going to start crying? Am I going to hurl this coffee mug against a wall? Irritable is a prelude to a mood swing. We could really go either way at this point, and if anyone comes near me I will scream.

When you tell people that you have a mental illness, everybody suddenly turns into an armchair psychiatrist. I had no idea that I was surrounded by so many mental health experts. It's amazing. All I have to do is mention that I have bipolar or anxiety, and it's like I've opened Pandora's suggestion box. I get this one a lot:

"Do you do yoga? You should try yoga." Ah yes. Since I have mastered Warrior I, I am no longer haunted by what Sarah Iske said to me in the 8th grade. Namaste.

"Just relax. Stop thinking so much." Thanks. I'd love to. I would love to turn my brain off, but this existential crisis isn't going to have itself, you know.

"Take a chill pill" is one of my favorites. First off, "take a chill pill"? What are you, my mother in 1998? Second … what kind? What have you got? Don't hold out on me!

Anyway …

(projection changes to read "Part 2. Chill Pills")

In the past year, I have taken 730 pills for psychiatric treatment. Give or take.

I'm currently going steady with Lamictal. Or rather, because that shit is EXPENSIVE, the generic brand of Lamictal the name of which I cannot pronounce and will not try here. Lamictal is an anticonvulsant medication that incidentally helps to prevent or delay depressive, manic, and rapid-cycling episodes. Side effects include—dizziness, tremors, drowsiness or insomnia, memory problems, headache, double vision, blurred vision, memory problems, nausea, vomiting, stomach pain, dry mouth, back pain, and coordination problems. Please see your doctor if you experience the following: rash, fever, swollen glands, numbness, pain, confusion, rapid weight gain, rapid heart rate, worsening depression or suicidal thoughts, flu like symptoms, as any of these could result in hospitalization, permanent paralysis, or death.

(Projector changes to "Fun Fact" sign, then fade to black)

But you know what they say, a gal can't live on Lamictal alone, so I've also recently been prescribed Lithium. Yeah, throwback. Now I feel even more like my grandmother. It's an oldie, but a goodie. I can't take ibuprofen anymore, I have to make sure I'm drinking enough water so the levels don't become toxic, and it'll most likely break down my kidneys over time, but it makes me want to die a lot less, so I'd call it even stevens.

It's always a fun dating game with meds. Some are super reliable, some are just terrible, some are good for, like, a night and then do nothing for ya. You never forget your first, though. My first was Zoloft, which I was on when I was 14. You might remember that commercial with the little bouncing ball under the rain cloud, then he takes Zoloft and the sun comes out and the ball is so happy. I remember seeing that and thinking, "Yeah, I feel you, buddy." And I couldn't wait for my clouds to clear so I could bounce off into my new life. And I'm trembling with anticipation. And I'm trembling. And I keep trembling. And it gets so bad I can't hold a pen or a glass, so that was the end of Zoloft.

Of course, I shouldn't even be on medication, because I'm an ARTIST. Artists have to be able to feel the whole range of their emotions, right? And boy, do I have a range. Why hide that under a bushel? I had an acting teacher tell me that once, "anyone who takes psych meds cannot possibly be an actor because they'll keep you from really *feeling*. How are you expected to act truthfully if you kill those emotions?"

Granted, she also believed that anyone who was born via C-section could not be an actor because they "missed that crucial first human contact." What does that even mean? Try reading *Macbeth*, Kay. Shakespeare wrote the book on what happens when you underestimate C-section babies. Let's not lose our heads over this.

Listen, my meds don't kill my emotions. Some can, and if that happens, you get yourself some different pills. Medication isn't perfect, and some can be downright scary, but it can really help. I've bounced all over the place, but I can tell you right here that if I were not medicated, I would be dead. And I'd say that would do a pretty good job of killing my emotions. What my current treatment path does is focus my energy. Trying to create without treatment is like trying to light a candle with a flamethrower. It'll do the job, I guess. The whole house is on fire now, but at least that candle got lit.

People love to point to Van Gogh as an example. "He turned his crazy into beauty, but no one appreciated it because he ate his paints and drank too much and cut his ear off. Then he killed himself and everyone finally realized he was a genius; thank god he was crazy. Isn't that inspiring to all those crazy suffering artists out there? You can make it too, as long as you suffer. You'll probably be dead, but you'll finally get the appreciation you deserve."

But here's the thing: Van Gogh knew he was crazy. So did his peers. He sought treatment. He was medicated. He spent time in a hospital. He did some of his best work there. *[slide: The Starry Night]* Then he had a relapse, and it killed him. He suffered, yes, but not *for* his art. His success only came once people could distance themselves from the man, which is a real shame. It's easy to romanticize mental illness when it's not right in your face. Let me say this right here: medication and treatment don't kill art. The fear and stigma of treatment kills artists.

But also the price of sanity is too dang high. Seriously. Sanity is a luxury item. Keeping myself together, medically speaking, is so expensive. I'm not even having a good time. Now, I have been so lucky so far in my life with finances and health insurance, but I can imagine how desperate the situation can get so quickly if I wasn't. Theoretically, what I need for a successful treatment plan is a psychiatrist to prescribe my medication, a pharmacy to reliably get me said medication, a therapist to talk to who will ideally give me the tools I need to adjust my behavior and keep me on an even keel, and health insurance and enough money to cover all that. At the moment, I've got two of those—a prescription and some money. My health insurance status is wibbly wobbly.

Hashtag Millennials, right?

I remember one time I went to get my Lamictal prescription refilled, and that's a pricey one. I'm talking nearly $200 for three months, and that's *with* insurance. So I go to the checkout counter, and the pharmacist there starts processing me out, and then he gets to whatever screen shows the med breakdown, looks me up and down, and then says, "You know, it's *very* expensive." Like, I'm in the beginning of gosh dang *Pretty Woman*! Yes, of course I know that. I've been on it for awhile. You can see that in your system, *Patrick*. They tell me that every time I pick it up. But it's usually a throwaway line like, "And you're aware of the price?" Yeah, I am painfully aware. But you know what, now that you've reminded me, I think I'll just pass for the next couple months. I don't need it *that* badly.

Plus, with some of these meds, you might need to get additional medical testing to track your progress. I had to get a couple blood tests done when I first started Lithium to check the med levels and to make sure my thyroid and kidneys were doing okie dokie so I wouldn't, like, die or whatever. Which is a big to-do for me already because I don't do super well with getting my blood drawn. I'm basically booking an appointment for myself to pass out. But even if you do have health insurance, it only covers so much, and it seems like they test for a lot. Do I really need to spend $200 to test my vitamin D levels? Because I can tell you right now for free, it's super low. I know, I bought that big thing of vitamin D supplements myself a year ago and I never remember to take them.

Then you need a couple of doctors. Generally, therapy costs anywhere from $65 to over $250 per session. I could buy at least six burritos for $65 and feel just as great and terrible as I would crying on a stranger's couch for an hour. Emotionally, I mean. But you may ask me, "Kate, what about the 2008 Mental Health Parity and Addiction Equity Act and its promise to make mental health care just as accessible as medical care?"

Great question! It's not helping much! Alrighty, buckle up for some fun facts, folks.

According to the Mental Health Parity and Addiction Equity Act, insurers have to treat mental health treatment the same as medical treatment. So they technically can't charge you more for a copay for mental health appointment than a regular doctor's appointment. (*projector image now reads "Fun Fact"*) But insurance companies are also notorious for not reimbursing mental health professionals at the same rate as medical doctors. (*Projector adds another "fun fact" without changing anything else [i.e., the screen now says "fun fact" in two different places].*) So more and more mental health professionals are reluctant to work with insurance companies, instead requiring patients to pay out of pocket. (*a third fun fact—things are getting somewhat crowded*).

Also, your doctor's office can do this at any time! So you can go from paying a $30 copay to see your therapist to paying $130 per session. Whoopie! (*"Fun Fact," ding*)

And with less doctors available in-network, it becomes more difficult for these offices to handle the patient demand. So if you do find an in-network provider, chances are you'll be spending at least three weeks on a waitlist for an appointment! (*"Fun Fact," ding*)

Need care right now? Well, you could try going to the hospital, but wait, if you aren't actively suicidal (which, let me tell ya, is pretty difficult to quantify for everybody involved), the hospital needs to call your insurance and wait for approval to admit you, unless you have that Kanye money, of course. You don't? You haven't been to work for over a week because you can barely leave your bed? Well then, you wait and hope you get that green light, because if you don't, the hospital can just turn you away. (*"Fun Fact," ding*)

Wait, you got approved? Great! Now you have to wait for a bed in the psych ward to open up, or for the hospital to figure out where to transfer you. That's right, you could be in for some travel. Exciting! Which means you could wait upwards of 20 hour to a couple days. (*"Fun Fact," ding*)

Can you imagine going to the ER with a broken leg or pneumonia, and being told that you would have to wait 20 hours for treatment? Or being turned away because your insurance outright denied coverage? It's discrimination, pure and simple. Right? Or am I just losing my mind?

> *She stops, realizing what she just said. She takes a moment to compose herself, does a few seconds of four-square breathing. She centers herself and smiles.*

So, yeah, why spend $70 a session to rant about my problems to a professional stranger when I can just spring for a venue and do the same thing in front of a crowd of paying strangers? It's just economical.

And besides that … I'm a little wary of therapists. My sincere apologies to any therapists in the audience, it's nothing personal. Come talk to me after the show. Just make sure to bill my agent. I'm kidding! I can't afford an agent. It's more that I haven't had the best luck with therapists in the past.

Partially, I'm afraid that I'll go in for a consultation and they won't let me go. I'm half expecting to walk into the office and they'll have a table with a prescription and a book of healthy coping mechanisms set out under a big stick box trap ready for me. Which is one part paranoia, one part experience. The last time I went in for a consultation, the doctor was asking me all the routine questions, which, as always, came to a grinding halt when we got to my unfortunate suicidal ideation, because of course she wanted to go into more detail. I don't know the therapeutic value of making me explain, at length, my various suicide plans, but then, that's above my pay grade. So we get to the end and she says, "Why should I let you leave?" And I'm like, "Because I would very much like to?" And she asks me to persuade her that I'm not a threat to myself or others and that she should be confident in, you know, letting me go home instead of holding me for observation. I'm feeling the box drop down over me. It *was* a trick! I knew it! So I looked her dead in the eye and said, "I have work tomorrow. If you want to call my supervisor, go ahead, but I'm not going to have that conversation." Which apparently was enough because I was sent on my merry way. I think my outfit helped too. Whenever I have any kind of psych appointment, I put together my "put together" outfit. You know, an ensemble that just screams "don't put me away!" Think business casual, nothing too flashy. I just want the doctor to look at me and say, "Why yes, that blouse/pant combo really highlights how little of a threat she is to herself or society. And with that sensible heel? Clean bill of health. You're free to go."

I've had a handful of therapists in the past, with varied success. I saw one from the time I had my first nervous breakdown at 13 until I was 17 or so. She was fine, but towards the end, I could sense that she was getting frustrated with my lack of progress, so I just started telling her what she wanted to hear. It was just easier that way. You know, like when you fake an orgasm so you can just go to sleep?

What can I say, I'm a people pleaser.

Honestly, the best therapist I ever had was at the student health center in college. He seemed immediately invested in my concerns, he introduced me to that good good Cognitive Behavioral Therapy (hell yeah, healthy coping mechanisms), he even used my Dungeons and Dragons characters to, like, unlock some shit about my personality. He's the one who taught me that nifty four-square breathing trick! Then he got weirdly fixated on the fact that I was a virgin and tried to get me to watch porn with him.

Look, I'm not saying therapy is bad or that it can't be incredibly helpful. I'm just saying they can't all be winners.

I am technically disabled. I say "technically" because I have been fortunate enough to be pretty high functioning, give or take a couple of speed bumps. I have never been hospitalized. For the most part, my mental illness has not affected my ability to work or live on my own. My experience is not universal, and there are many, many people out there whose bipolar disorder greatly affects their lives and livelihoods. It is a legitimate disability, even though you can't always see it. Admitting it can be difficult, though. I'm pretty open about my disorder with my friends, acquaintances, and strangers on the internet. I'm not ashamed of it. I'm ashamed of a lot of things constantly, but I figure since I am the way that I am I may as well get used to it. But it is difficult in other situations.

Example: I have never listed myself as having a disability with an employer.

You know, that "Disability Status" part of the diversity portion of job applications that's a trap really, we all know it's a trap? Ok, so according to the Americans with Disabilities Act of 1990, employers can't discriminate against you because of a disability, given that the applicant is qualified for the position and can perform the duties as such. Cool, awesome, thanks ADA. But also, who are we kidding? Heck, most job sites will tell you not to disclose any disability unless it will be apparent in an interview. It's an easy way for employers to wade through the sea of online applicants. Does that make me sound paranoid? Probably, but that tracks. Especially with mental illness, because that's a bit more difficult to explain. What are "reasonable accommodations" for mood swings? I don't know.

"Hey, so, just a head's up, I'm having a bunch of feelings today, so if I start crying randomly, can I just step off for a sec until I swing back around? Also, I don't know when or even if that'll happen. Great, thanks."

Yeah, that's not gonna fly. Especially not in service. I work as a barista now, and I cannot imagine calling up my boss and asking for a mental health day.

"Yeah, hey, Sarah, so I don't think I'm going to make it in for my shift tomorrow. You see, I'm in the middle of a pretty bad depressive episode, and I've got this persistent existential dread and an overwhelming desire to chug a Venti cup of bleach, so I'm a bit out of commission."

"Hmmm, I see. Are you throwing up at all?"

"Well, not yet."

"Ok then, see you tomorrow!"

Even in a doctor's office I feel weird about talking about my illness. When the bipolar diagnosis was still fresh, I told people that I had epilepsy because I was afraid of weird looks from the nurses.

Was it the most responsible thing?

No! *Duh*! I don't have epilepsy.

Did it make me feel better about myself?

Eh.

Look, if there's anywhere you can be open about your medical issues, it's in a medical setting … most of the time.

I had a dentist appointment awhile back, and I was going over my medical records with the dental hygienist. Now, I've been going to this office for awhile. We've developed a rapport. And she's going through the questions and gets to, "Are you currently taking or have you changed any medication?"

"Yeah, I actually recently switched from Lamictal to Vraylar."

"What's it for?"

And I can see on the screen where it says "Lamictal—Bipolar," so I say, "Same thing."

She looks at the screen, back to me, and says, "I don't want to write that. I'm going to put depression."

(*Beat*)

"You know … because of the implications."

> (*Beat*)

Yeah, I am aware of the implications, Andrea. I'm feeling them right now. "I don't want to write that." But, no, Andrea, you have to write that. You are a medical professional. And furthermore, you have no right to judge me. You once bought a human skeleton on the deep web!

> (*"Fun Fact" sign illuminates with a ding*)

Stay in your lane, Andrea.

Dating with a mental illness is fun. Perks to dating me: no matter how the relationship ends, you can say you have a crazy ex-girlfriend.

I was never great with any of the dating apps like Tinder, Hinge, Bumble, Happen, Match, Link, Coffee Meets Bagel, Kiss, now I'm just making them up. Or am I? I did do OKCupid for a sec in college. If you're not familiar—that's the one where you answer a bunch of questions, and then they match you with people based on your answers. And I mean a BUNCH of questions. They start off like:

"Do you want kids?"

"Are you a summer or a winter person?"

Then, they'd quickly escalate to—

"Do you think the death penalty is acceptable in some cases?"

"Do you think that in a certain light, a nuclear war would be exciting?"

"What's worse: starving children or abused animals?"

It was fun.

Anyway, one time I was scrolling through this dude's profile, and I see the question, "Would you date someone with a mental illness?" So I knew right away this was gonna be good.

And he answered, "Yes, but only if it's something light, like anxiety or depression."

Something light, like anxiety or depression. You know, depression, the Coke Zero of mental illnesses? Honestly, I was so offended that he was so dismissive about anxiety and depression, that I forgot to be upset that he was turned off by crazy folks.

Mental illness runs in my family, which is great because we can all not talk about it together.

I get the anxiety from my dad. He's not really uptight, you know, he's just tight. The bipolar comes from my mom. I always kind of knew, growing up, that she wasn't quite well. I did feel that it helped me relate better to my peers. Girls in the hall would be like, "Oh my god, my mom is soooo bipolar. Like, yesterday she said I could go out with Adam this weekend, and today she threw a fit because my room isn't clean. What the hell?" And I'd be like, "I know, right? Like, my mom will be all, 'Let's go out! Let's hit the park. Let's go shopping!,' and the next thing you know she hasn't showered in days and is lying on the floor in the dark because the world hurts too much. Sheesh … *Moms.*"

I am crazy like my mother and her mother before her. Thinking back, I think my grandmother fostered my love of comedy. I remember telling her my first joke:

How do you catch a squirrel? Go up in a tree and act like a nut!

She thought it was hilarious. Probably because she's a nut. Always has been. Mama Babe smoked, drank, and played the slots. She was delusional. Mama Babe was obsessed with death, specifically her death. She wrote up her own obituary once. Almost all of it was made up. She said she was a hospital nurse at one point. She was in a hospital all right, she just didn't work there. She never got to use it, seeing as she's still alive and well. To make a long story short, there were a few mishaps, she ended up in a coma, and when she woke up, stopped drinking, and got medicated, she became a totally different person. I had a healthy fear of my grandmother for a good portion of my life, and now she's just a sweet old woman propped up on a couch.

Which is weird.

On the one hand, she's my Mumsy Babe and I love her. On the other hand, she did try to strangle my sister at Christmas. So it's weird. One summer, when I was 13 or so, the two of us were sitting out on the back porch of my aunt's place, watching the sun set over the lake, and suddenly she started to tell me about her time in the hospital. She didn't give too many details, none that I remember anyway, but I remember she said, "It's all about treading water out here. You can't be too deep or too shallow. If you're too deep and kooky, they'll pull you under and put you away. If you're too shallow, eventually you'll get tired, and they'll see you've been faking all along, and they'll put you away. You have to be very careful, tread somewhere in between, and see how long you can last. But either way, we all drown in the end." And I asked her, "Why are you telling me this?" Then she looked me dead in the eyes and said, "Because you're just like me."

    (Beat)

Yikes.

    (Beat)

Sorry, I couldn't come up with a good joke to end that one. "We all drown in the end."

That shit's just *grim*.

Oh! Speaking of grim, suicide's been back in the news recently. There's really no good way to get into that, so I figured I'd jump right in. Coincidentally, I've always seen myself as a jumper, *ba dum tish*. Remember to breathe folks, we're entering choppy waters here. The undiscovered country, as it were. But here's how I see it, in my experience, it's kind of funny if you think about it. Go on this journey with me.

If we break human beings down to their prime directive, it's to stay alive. That goes for all living beings. Stay alive for as long as possible. That's it. But there is a chemical imbalance in my brain that sometimes makes me want to die. Not just die, but to actively kill myself. That is absolutely absurd. That goes completely against the prime directive. It's like a self-destruct button in a Bond villain's lair.

Why is that button even there? Who thought that was a good idea?

Suicide's been on the rise over the past decade or so. And whenever there's a high-profile case, I hear the same things—

"It was so unexpected."

"We were blindsided."

"What could have prevented this?"

And then you see that 1-800 number. The suicide hotline. People like to post that on social media in the wake of high-profile suicides as a show of solidarity. Now, I know that everyone is likely doing that in good faith. But it's also the Livestrong bracelet of mental health awareness. It looks nice on your blog, but I doubt anyone you know is actually going to get much use from it. Whenever I see that, I think, "Oh, that's nice. You're informed, you care, but you also have probably never used that service." Because that is exactly what I want when I'm at the end of my rope, and I'm about to do the "unthinkable," and I believe that I have nowhere to turn and no one to help me—to make a phone call to a total stranger. I get anxious calling my parents on the phone. Can't we just do this over text like a normal person? I'll settle for a rambling e-mail at that point.

Plus, and I swear, this is absolutely true: I got hung up on by the suicide hotline.

I'd been going through a bit of a rough patch, and I was desperate, and I just needed someone to talk with. From what I understand, that's mostly what people use the hotline for. If a person is dead set on killing themselves, no pun intended, they're not going to reach out for help. They're just going to go for it. But if they're on the fence, or just lost and afraid, talking to someone, anyone, can be beneficial. So I thought I'd give it a go. I actually called twice. The first guy I talked to asked me if I had ever tried yoga.

> (*Beat*)

Yep.

> (*Beat*)

I said that I had, and it wasn't really doing it for me, so he came back with, "Well, at least you aren't one of the nearly 32,000 homeless in Los Angeles."

Ok. That's very true and very terrible, but not very helpful or relevant in this specific situation. I saw his homelessness statistics and raised him chronic illness. To which he responded, "You know there are plenty of successful people out there who are bipolar. Like Jean Claude Van Damme." He couldn't name anyone else other than JCVD. "There are also people out there who give TED talks about this, or write about their experiences. Maybe take a look at those?"

> (*Beat*)

But doctor ... I am Pagliacci.

> (*Beat*)

So I ended up hanging up on him and calling again, which you can do if you want another operator. But by this point, I was a bit upset, as I'm sure you can imagine. Then I was on hold. For 7 minutes. So by the time I got connected with someone, I was in a bit of a state. And I'm crying and crying and this woman keeps asking me the same question over and over again—"Where are you?" Which I do *not* want to answer because the last thing I need is to have the cops called on me with a one way ticket to the loony bin. I've never been on the Ward before. Ask any of my exes, I have a terrible fear of commitment.

And I told her to shut up. I snapped, I'm not proud of it. I immediately started apologizing and crying harder, and she said, "You obviously don't want my help right now. Call back when you feel like cooperating," and she hung up on me. The whole thing was so absurd I didn't know what to do. So I went home, got drunk, and went to sleep.

You have to have a good laugh about it. When you find the humor of the situation, you rob it of some of its power. It becomes less scary. That's the whole point of this here. This whole play, performance, thing that I'm doing. It's to make this illness, this way of being, a little less frightening.

Because I'm going to be honest, I am scared. Kind of a lot. I am scared of the shitty devils in my brain. I'm scared of losing control. I'm scared of what other people think. When I first workshopped this show, I almost couldn't bring myself to get into the suicide stuff. I stood at that ledge, and I nearly chickened out. Because I didn't want anyone to be afraid of me. Then I finally made that leap, and I looked out into the audience and I didn't see fear. I saw understanding. I saw sympathy, but not pity. Though I did get a note afterwards from this one guy who told me that it was hard to watch. He said, "I didn't really like the stuff about suicide. It was a bit much. We've gone on this journey with this character, we've had some laughs, and we've grown attached. I don't like seeing her get to such a dark place. I'd prefer you keep it light."

Well, random guy, I'm sorry, but that's me. That's my real life. I can try to sugarcoat it, but that's my reality, for better or for worse. I can't hide that, and won't. Not anymore. It took me a long time to learn to laugh with my demons. And it's hard. It is a struggle every day, but just because I'm depressed doesn't mean my story has to be depressing.

I'm Kate Devorak.

And I'm still here.

> *Blackout*

End of play.

I Come from Hoarders

CARLY JO GEER

Characters with physical, emotional, or psychological conditions have often served symbolic functions in the works of able-bodied playwrights. In Rudolf Besier's 1830 play, *The Barretts of Wimpole Street,* the poet, Elizabeth Barrett Browning's, physical weakness is a symbol for her initial lack of courage to pursue her romantic love for the poet, Robert Browning.[1] In Maria Irene Fornes' 1977 play, *Fefu and Her Friends*, Julia's physical disability symbolizes how completely she has been immobilized by the judges' abuse.[2] In Tennessee Williams' 1947 play, *A Streetcar Named Desire,* Blanche Dubois' mental instability serves as a reminder of her past sexual promiscuity; her mental strain is caused by the loss of her teaching job, the result of her affair with an underage student.[3]

Regardless of the skill of the playwrights who created them, all of these characters embody conditions that are symbols, as opposed to natural parts of the characters' daily lives. Even if they do not identify as people with disabilities—deciding whether particular terminology applies to one's life is, after all, a personal choice—playwrights who depict their own conditions in their work are providing an audience the opportunity to see a given condition as part of a complex life, instead of seeing it as a symbol for the lack of one. In this play, for example, the protagonist's childhood home could be a symbol for the hoarding that is a part of her family history. Her memories of the home her mother filled with objects are not unlike the home itself; they create a familial bond with her parents and her siblings that is both comforting and confining. However, not all of the scenes she describes take place in the house, because her mother's diagnosis defines neither her childhood nor the woman she becomes. In this case, the family home is not merely a symbol for the hoarding disorder that affects the people living inside of it.

This symbol, the family home, possesses semantic mobility. In other words, what the play symbolizes, both to characters in the play and to the audience, changes over time. Within the play itself, the house represents the protagonist's childhood memories, as it is where some of her most significant childhood memories take place. When she shares those memories with the audience, her retelling is a physicalization of her internal struggle to escape those memories. When her childhood home is embodied onstage, the reality of living in a house with hoarders becomes as inescapable for the live audience as it probably once felt to the protagonist. One place, a family home, symbolizes a familial bond, hoarding, the psychological condition that complicates and strains that bond, the protagonist's shifting psychological and emotional relationship to the home and all of the people who live in it, and a physicalization of the experience of coming from hoarders—and returning to hoarding, even if against one's will, for the live audience. In short, in this play, the family home symbolizes, not just one woman's relationship to hoarding, but one woman's whole life. Because the family home sometimes symbolizes the protagonist's relationship to hoarding without solely symbolizing it, the complexity of the use of the family home as a symbol is itself a symbol of the protagonist's emotional and psychological complexity. A complex symbol resists an audience member's attempt to make it representative of a definitive truth. When a playwright depicts a condition he/she/they embodies in the real world as both a multifaced symbol and a reality, he/she/they is inherently resisting any attempt to inaccurately conflate that condition only with negative qualities that may be associated with it in the real world. When the playwright is also embodying his/her/their condition during a performance, that complexity extends to the most recognizable symbol of the playwright's condition, his/her/their body itself.

Every time the playwright confirms a negative real-world association with his/her/their condition during a performance, the audience must admit that the choice was deliberate. Every time the playwright critiques a negative real-world association with his/her/their condition during a performance, the performer can complicate that real world association for the audience by simply performing the scene effectively. Of course, many playwrights are especially gifted at creating characters who are unlike themselves. Likewise, not every playwright who embodies his/her/their own condition onstage will consistently write or perform skillfully.

—Jill Summerville

NOTES

1. Rudolf Besier, *The Barretts of Wimpole Street: A Comedy In Five Acts* (Toronto: Proofreading Canada Team, 2011).

2. Maria Irene Fornes, *Fefu and Her Friends* (New York: PAJ Publications, 1990).

3. Tennessee Williams, *A Streetcar Named Desire* (New York: New Directions Publishing, 2004).

I Come from Hoarders

Scene: A mix of present day and past events

The set is minimal. Designated rooms are acknowledged by the actor as well as set props mentioned in each room. Lighting helps to denote scene changes as well as show which room is being focused on. "Parent's bedroom" area is used for the "hospice room" as well as "the attic." For the most part, the piece should be performed directly to the audience. Making eye contact with them is important when performing this style of theatre. It is also important to note that this play should be performed as a comedy with tragic elements.

I Come from Hoarders © Carly Jo Geer, all rights reserved. Those interested in licensing *I Come from Hoarders* for production may contact the playwright at Carlyjogeer@aol.com.

* * *

House lights off, stage lights to dim state

Music starts playing: "Conga" by Gloria Estefan

Carly enters holding a large plastic tote that holds certain props needed in future scenes.

She stands and looks at the house, then enters it. She goes to her room. When she mimes flicking the light switch and Lights go up: full— Upstage area if isolation possible, if not, a general wash. Music stops.

I enter my childhood bedroom for the last time. Decorated the same way since I moved out at 22 and left untouched as if it belonged to a dead child.

A home, that was once inhabited by five Geers, dwindled to four, to three, to two, and then one. But the memories are the only living things here now.

It only makes sense to sell the house. Why should dad pay a mortgage on a home he doesn't live in? But the memories need to be evicted.

I try to take in as much of it as possible. The stained fuchsia carpet has been there since my mom picked the color in 1988, the pale-yellow walls with the mural of the sun fading into the glow in the dark stars on my ceiling have been painted that way since the 6th grade.

I don't make the trip to New Hampshire for my nephew's first birthday. I don't make the trip to New Hampshire when my friend Courtney dies. But when my sister tells me at 10 a.m. on a Thursday that my dad's house is being cleared out and prepped for selling, I leave Chicago at 4 p.m. on Friday and I drive for 16 hours over night to get my stuff. My stuff. I need my stuff.

I tell myself that I am allowed to bring home two plastic totes of things with me to Chicago. Two totes out of a collection almost three decades old.

In December of 1987, mom brings home a onesie that says, "Baby's First Christmas" and tells my dad that she wants a third child by the following Christmas.

And suddenly, their two-bedroom lake home will no longer hold their family.

Our home, my only home, is purchased on May 31, 1988, and I am born six months later on November 20.

22 Seaverns Bridge Road

A fixer upper, the upstairs is yet to be finished. I imagine my mom and dad wandering the bedrooms as my mom spouts off numerous renovation ideas, only half of which are actually practical.

Starting as a three-bedroom, two-bathroom home with an in-ground pool, my father builds over the years an additional master bedroom, a family room, a mud room, a two-car garage, two gabled dormer windows and three porches.

This is my home.

Painted barn red with black shutters and cream-colored garage doors, it sits on 1.3 acres of land with a short dirt driveway.

22 Seaverns Bridge Road is the fourth child in the Geer family and she too screams for my parents' attention.

The thing about having a home and children is that sometimes you need to outsource their problems. Sometimes, mom and dad can't fix everything that needs fixing.

But mom double-majored elementary ed and psychology and dad was a carpenter. So, they're pretty sure they got this.

My mother thrives on being a caretaker both in her work as a teacher and as a mother. She wants so badly to be able to take care of her family without anyone's help. She is a housekeeping martyr. Never allowing any of the children to do laundry or dishes because those are mommy's jobs. I don't put a dish directly in a dishwasher until I move out at 22.

Mom stays at work late. Everyone knows that teachers get off around three but mommy isn't usually home until around eight. Masked by the love of her job and there being just "so much to do" I realize as an adult that mommy avoided coming home on purpose. Kindergarten teachers don't have THAT much grading to do.

> *Music cue: Secret Garden music*
> *a green light downstage left to indicate the "secret garden."*

Mom and dad's room is the home of lost toys. Although this room is built when I am in first grade, it remains a junk room for many years before it ever sees an actual bed. Leaving my dad on the couch and my mom on a futon in the living room next to me. Bags and boxes squished from being sat on and gone through fill this newly added master bedroom. Toys kept for the future grandchildren my mother will meet. Mom will need them for when she babysits in this house that was never safe to have children in in the first place. This is my secret garden of toys. I imagine pushing vines off of this hidden door and discovering this oasis of childhood bliss. No floors, just wall to wall toys of every kind, you could literally swim in them.

I sit on a child-sized dinosaur stuffed animal that my sister won for selling the most magazine subscriptions in elementary school, because sitting on a bunch of plastic toys is uncomfortable. I love rummaging through the boxes and bags discovering things I haven't played with in years. Old homework assignments, books I loved as a toddler and action figures that belonged to my siblings.

Music fades, lights return to general wash

On an occasion that I actually try to clean, I bring mommy a bag of trash from my bedroom.

The bags of trash go in the garage until it's time to go to the dump but you can't get a bag of trash to the garage without passing the mommy inspection. She takes out a cabbage patch doll that's been colored on that I, as the youngest child, haven't played with in years.

"This isn't trash"

"But mom, I don't want it anymore."

"But it isn't trash."

Half of the stuff in the trash bag is returned to me and the other half has been deemed actual trash.

What should I do with a bunch of stuff I don't want?

Eh, I'll just leave it on the kitchen table. I'll figure out what to do with it later.

A recording of "Have Yourself a Merry Little Christmas" begins to play. Carly sings along.

The red sparkly booth at Joey's Diner clicks as I wipe it down at the end of my waitressing shift. "Have Yourself a Merry Little Christmas" sung by Judy Garland is playing on the jukebox and I pause for a moment and really listen to the lyrics.

Music changes to the theme song from the television show Roseanne.

It's December 23 and I have finished my holiday shopping and baking. The only thing I have left to do is wrap my presents and put the Chex Mix puppy chow into their special holiday tins.

I sit in the family room at the sewing table my Grammy Geer gave me, carefully counting how many Twix, Kit Kats and mini peanut butter cups there are so I can put the same amount into each tin.

My *Roseanne* DVD is on "play all" and before I know it, it's about 7 a.m. and my father opens the door letting the cold air in from outside.

Music ends.

I am the first one he tells.

"The doctors don't think she's going to make it much longer."

"Like how much longer?"

"Today."

We are the only two awake and I can hear my dad making a moaning sound in the bathroom that I have never heard him make before and for a moment,

I'm confused about what it is he could be doing in the shower until I realize that he's crying. An angry, exhausted, soon to be widower's cry. And then we cry together on opposite sides of the same wall.

Carly sings a bit more of "Have Yourself a Merry Little Christmas"

As my immediate family gathers around my mother's hospice bed, we each take our moment to hold her hand tell her we love her along with our own individual message.

Dad says

"Please don't leave me and thank you for marrying me."

My brother Timmy says

"I'm sorry I was such a fucking asshole teenager."

My sister Bethany says

"you were a great mom."

And I say

"Thank you for always letting me be me and for letting me dye my hair weird colors."

I take the time to think about what it feels like to hold her hand because I never want to forget what her skin felt like.

After a long day of waiting a nurse enters the room. She places a hand on my mother's shoulder and speaks in a soothing voice.

"It's midnight, Penny, which means it's Christmas Eve and you can let go now Penny. Your goal was to make it to Christmas Eve and you did it! And you can let go now."

I am at the foot of my mother's bed and I want to touch her so badly but her closest body part is her foot and it seems weird to just reach out and grab her foot. Like, should I just grab her foot?!

And I wonder if she can hear what this nurse is saying. And I wonder if she's in pain. I still wonder if maybe she'll just open her eyes and make some kind of miraculous recovery.

After about an hour of waiting and watching my mother's lips move ever so slightly as she takes her final breaths I begin to think:

Just die already mom! Can't you see we're suffering here! I'm tired and I wanna go home mommy. I don't wanna sit here and stare at you anymore. Let go so we can begin to heal! I don't wanna hurt anymore and I don't want you to hurt anymore.

And not long after 1 a.m., her lips stop moving. And it is quiet and unnoticeable if you aren't really staring at her.

When what's left of my immediate family returns to our home, we all go to our separate rooms. And I wonder what all of us must look like, quietly crying to ourselves and I wonder how long it will take for the chapped skin under my eyes to heal if I continue to cry every day.

Carly sings more lyrics from "Have Yourself a Merry Little Christmas"

It's been almost 10 years since my mom passed away.

Leaving behind a house filled with 28 years' worth of toys and knick-knacks and a family that needs to move on.

You may have been the first to go mom, but your stuff is still here.

lights to general wash

My mother, Penny Geer, the Queen of Avoidance in her passing bequeaths to her family the different factions of her coping mechanisms.

Her husband, Phil, receives avoidance by watching television.

Her eldest child, Timmy, receives avoidance by drug use.

Her middle child, Bethany, receives avoidance by ignoring the problems.

And her youngest child, Carly Jo, receives avoidance by overworking.

Along with our coping mechanism, our bedrooms are all messy in their own individual ways.

Just like Timmy's emotions, no one is allowed to see his bedroom from the time he is in high school up until he moves out at age 35. The frame surrounding Timmy's door is no longer fully attached to the wall from it being slammed so many times.

And although I haven't specifically tried to open his door, I know Timmy keeps a baseball bat lodged between a dresser and the wall, sticking out in front of this door making it impossible for anyone but him to open when he's not home. He is guarded, even when he's not around.

My friends are always surprised to hear I have an older brother and want to meet him when they come over. I knock excitedly on his door giggling with my friends but he refuses to answer. He later tells me that he doesn't want to be paraded around in front of people like a zoo animal.

Timmy's room is his untreated borderline personality disorder. Once he moves out and the damages are assessed, we discover a room with moldy green carpet that smacks you with the smell of cigarette smoke when you enter. Butts and beer cans lay strewn about the floor as the sports illustrated swimsuit model poster decorates one of the only walls that has not had its sheet rock punched in and torn apart.

The upper portion of my brother's closet door has also been punched in leaving only half of the door intact. VHS tapes of old episodes of *Lost*, wrestling and *Dragon Ball Z*, sit on the steps that lead to loft in my brother's room where we would once line the floor with pillows and blankets and jump down from the steps laughing hysterically until someone ultimately got hurt.

A room were we once played *Sonic the Hedge Hog* into the late hours of the summer nights had now been reduced to a literal shit hole.

My cousin Patrick is the one who we pay to clean out my dad's house when we begin the selling process. I almost feel bad for my brother as Patrick tells us multiple times that he's lost all respect for Timmy.

I think about drinking beers with my dad at Uno's when he tells me he feels like he failed as a parent because Timmy isn't a functioning member of society. I try to reassure him that 2 out of 3 functioning kids is still pretty good.

Without letting the tears actually fall from his eyes, my dad tells me he can't help but worry he's gonna find Timmy hanging in his room one day.

But it's really hard to help someone who doesn't want to be helped.

Besides the expected nastiness of my brother's bedroom, Patrick finds multiple pairs of binoculars, Gatorade bottles filled with urine and lists of items in the house with prices next to them, to which we can only assume was Timmy planning to sell my mother's things.

Timmy's room is trauma and guilt displayed through toxic masculinity.

The theme song to Pepper Ann *begins to play*

I am 8 years old, sitting on the forest green, dog fur covered rug in the living room watching Saturday morning cartoons.

In between episodes of *Pepper Ann* and *Recess*, I see a PSA of a ballerina talking about how she is going to wait to have sex so she doesn't become a pregnant teen. She has goals and aspirations she wants to accomplish before having kids.

Jingle for the PSA "The More You Know" plays

And suddenly, it clicks. Babies come from sex. Sex is when the penis and the vagina kiss. I had sex with Grant in Timmy's room when I was 4.

I'm crying so hard that my breath is erratic and only pieces of words come out of my mouth. I have to calm down or the words will never come out. I think if I just start the sentence, then the rest will follow.

"Mommy, I'm pregnant."

We don't hug. We never hug.

What's at the bottom of that pile on the kitchen table?

What's in that box in the back corner of my closet?

What's in those plastic tubs behind the Christmas tree in the attic?

Do I wanna ask my sister about my childhood?

I mean, she's older, so she'll remember. But like, do I really want to clean out that attic?

I mean, I gotta, right? I gotta! Cuz shits gotta get worse before it can get better. Ain't that the fucking lesson of the century.

Bethany doesn't mind sorting some of this dirty laundry for me.

"If 4-year-old Carly had been in my pre-school class, I would have called Child Protective Services. Knowing what I know now about early childhood development, you exhibited many signs of abuse."

Damn. How did I not know that? It was my childhood; I should know what the hell I did right?

But when shit's buried that deep, it's really easy not to see.

Bethany continues.

"Remember how you used to say 'sex is when the penis and the vagina kiss' where do you think a 4-year-old got that from? You clearly didn't make it up. You had a much clearer understanding of what sex was before I did. And we just chalked it up to the fact that you didn't have any restrictions on what you watched on TV and you hung out with your older teenage brother a lot."

I never thought about it that way. "Sex is when the penis and the vagina kiss." Where did I get that phrase from? A phrase that my family has joked about for years.

"Oh Carly, you said the craziest things when you were little! Remember how you used to say 'Sex is when the penis and the vagina kiss.'"?

How. The Fuck. Was no one in my family concerned about where 4-year-old Carly got that phrase from?

And even when I straight up told you, mom, you did nothing. Why didn't you do anything about it mom?! Why did you just take it in as knowledge, assure me that I wasn't pregnant and move on? Why didn't you put me in therapy? Why didn't you call the police? You should have done something, mom. Seriously, anything. You could have done fucking anything and it would have been better than just sweeping it under the god-damn rug. Leaving me sitting here 23 years later wondering why the fuck I have these memories of the way Grant smelled like Tommy Hilfiger cologne and how soft yet balmy his skin was and wondering why sometimes nipple play triggers me into a panic because I remember the way Grant's mouth felt on my undeveloped toddler chest.

And the thing is mom, you were a teacher. You should have known this shit before I even told you. You should have known the signs mom. Your daughter Bethany knows the signs because she's a teacher just like you.

But I get it now. You put it in the attic. And you hoped if it was way in the back, you wouldn't have to think about it anymore. And maybe, if you keep buying me toys, I'll be so happy, I won't remember what's in the back of the attic. I don't need to go back there, right? There are plenty of toys in front of me to play with.

Well, fuck mom, now I'm 28 and you can't sell a house without cleaning all that shit out.

"It's a fire hazard."

Mom tells Bethany this for the millionth time.

It's hard to tell exactly how thick the layer of trash on the floor is but your toes will never feel the tan colored carpet. With each step you take, magazines, old tissues and paper plates spill on top of your foot as you sink an inch into the mess.

Bethany doesn't care about the mess. She's not ashamed of it the way my mother thinks she should be. And she's not attached to her mess, she's simply too lazy to bother cleaning it up.

Dishes pile around her bed, an assortment of plastic cups, bowls, and silverware. Bethany has never had a trash can in her room because her room is a trash can.

Posters of Hanson and The Moffatts line her bedroom walls because Bethany likes her boy bands like she likes her mental health: forgotten about.

A square, black, desktop computer sits on a broken, backless kitchen chair next to my sister's bed while a square, black TV, sits on a dresser at the front of the room, giving her no reason to ever leave her bed.

Bethany's sheets are always softer than mine. And despite the fact that she never washes them, they smell clean, like her. She showers everyday and refuses to wear the same pair of jeans two days in a row without washing them.

Laying in her bed when she's not home gives me comfort. Her twin mattress is about a decade older than mine and it has a warm, loving divot. I stare at the posters on the slanted walls in this alcove-like room and I remember how I used to sleep next to my mom in this room when it was my parents' room, before the addition.

I co-sleep until the age of 11. It started when I was a baby, suffering from asthma attacks that could only be prevented if my mother was holding my infant body. Mom would wait patiently for me to fall asleep and sing my "The Carly Jo Song" in a soothing tone.

(Singing to the tune of "Let It Snow")

When Carly's awake, she's frightful,
But when she's asleep she's delightful,
But since we all love her so…
Carly Jo, Carly Jo, Carly Jo
She doesn't show signs of sleeping
So I brought some brooms for sweeping
Her night light's turned way down low
Carly Jo, Carly Jo, Carly Jo
When she finally says goodnight
Then mommy gets to go to bed
But when she wakes up in the middle of the night,
Mommy wants to punch her in the head
When Carly is finally sleeping
Then mommy can stop her weeping
But as long as we love her so…
Carly Jo, Carly Jo, Carly Jo

I am asleep now and my mother gently places me in my crib.

But shit, this whole asthma thing is making it so I can't breathe lying on my back, and I start to cry before my mother even makes it out of the room.

Sorry for the carpal tunnel mommy, but you're gonna have to hold me all night if I'm going to sleep…

Bethany thinks the co-sleeping began so that mom would know I was alive if I was next to her and later probably continued knowing that I wasn't being abused by anyone if I was next to her.

As I grew up, my asthma went away but my desire to have my mommy rub my back until I fell asleep did not. And mom can't say no to her baby.

Not until the summer before middle school, do I decide on my own that

I want to sleep in my own room. I am obsessed with clouds and I want to decorate my room accordingly. I spend the entire summer organizing the room that had been mine my entire life. I place all the childhood toys in trash bags and boxes, knowing I'm not allowed to throw any of it away and I move it all into the attic.

My parents buy me bunk beds per my request and I cannot wait to have my first sleepover.

Because I am no longer a child.

> "What's Your Fantasy" by Ludacris begins to play.
> Lights shift to suggest a '90s roller skating rink feel. Pink would be great! The following story is performed while eating the largest, juiciest, messiest piece of watermelon possible.

I am a baby fawn in a pack of wolves.

The year is 2001.

I am in 7th grade and Good Times Roller Skating Rink is where all the kids go to have a bit of unsupervised and frisky fun.

The kids who go to Good Times come from the lower middle-class homes of Merrimack, New Hampshire. The ones who live in condos or apartment complexes with single parents.

The kids whose parents either don't know or don't care that Good Times is the go-to make out spot for all the 7th and 8th graders. Even a select few 9th graders who try to use the coolness factor of being in high school to try to score some 12-year-old pussy.

I'm not one of these kids. Sure, my parents are hoarders but they're still married and we live in a house and we're certainly not on the struggle bus when it comes to finances.

Sitting on one of the built-in benches at the back of Good Times, I wonder when will it be my turn? I've been practicing kissing on my hand, and I think I'll be good at it. At least I hope I'll be good at it. Envisioning what it would feel like to kiss any one of my numerous crushes, I am approached by Billy Steeves.

I don't know him, but I know of him. He isn't in my cluster, as we call it at Mastricola Middle School. He has a whole different set of teachers in a completely different section of the school.

All I know about him is that he sang some rat pack song in the 6th grade talent show in a suit and everyone thought it was hilarious. He is known as the funniest person in our grade.

Billy waves around some condoms that he and his comrades have purchased from a quarter machine in the bathroom. Another hilarious show. Everyone laughs, not knowing what he is going to do with them until he spots me. The fawn.

Without even introducing himself to me, he grabs the collar of my dark blue shirt with the sparkly star on the front and drops the condom down upon what small breasts I have begun to grow.

"Whoops. I better get that." He says as he shoves his pudgy fingers down the neck of my shirt grazing my favorite and only Limited Too sports bra. My favorite bra, because it is the only bra I own that isn't white. This bra was meant to be shown off.

Everyone is laughing. This is funny. I mean, I guess this is funny. I'm laughing because everyone else is. I'm not the butt of this joke, I am in on this joke. It's ok. I'm fine. I'm a cool girl. I'm not gonna freak out. I'm not a prude. I'm wearing a cute bra from Limited Too for Christ's sake. I am one of the cool kids, duh, why else would I be here at Good Times.

As I am about to leave, Billy approaches me before I make it out the carpeted door.

"So, are you my girlfriend?"

"Sure." I say. I mean, I might as well be right? Everyone is already talking about us as if we are dating so, might as well just give the people what they want.

But oh shit. I'm his girlfriend. That means—

Before I can finish my thought, Billy's face is pressed against mine. I can feel the sweat of his face on mine. He is a chubby kid, the funny ones usually are.

Backed up against the carpeted wall of the DJ booth, his lips are soft and moist. And not moist in the way you want lips to be when you kiss but moist like how the word moist makes most people uncomfortable.

His tongue is dancing around in my mouth which is open a lot wider than it probably should be but I have no other choice with Billy's face, inching deeper and deeper into my mouth as if he wants me to unhinge my jaw and swallow him whole like a snake.

He tastes like onions.

Everything about the kiss is wet and rank and I begin to wonder why people even like kissing in the first place. If that is what kissing is like, it is gross, gross, gross.

When I make it into the lobby, away from where Billy can see me, I wipe my mouth on the back of my hand. I really hope I don't have to do that again.

But I am now part of the elite crowd. I have unlocked the coolest area of Good Times. I can now sit in the wooden booths by the laser tag.

Only couples sit over here.

Billy and I sit at a booth with his arm around me. He lowers his hand just enough to grab my boob. Just on the outside of the shirt at first and we all laugh but eventually, as the night goes on, his hand slips down the collar of my shirt and inside my sports bra, where his soft, fat fingers hold my left breast.

He is still sweating. His hands are sweaty. But as long as we don't have to kiss, he can cup my boob for as long as he wants.

This is what it's like to have a boyfriend.

Music ends, lights return to general wash

And now that I have my own room, I have a place to hang out with my boyfriend, away from the rest of the family.

Dad tells me he doesn't think it's appropriate for me to have boys in my room.

"Seriously dad? I can't believe you don't trust me. Are you kidding me? What's the big deal? Nothing is gonna happen! We're just friends! I can't believe you don't trust your own daughter!"

Having bunk beds makes my room a convenient spot for double dates.

My bedroom is always cluttered but never "gross." Mommy doesn't have to come in my room on the weekends to collect dirty dishes, like she does with Bethany and Timmy because for the most part, I bring them down myself.

My walls are lined with trophies, medals and sportsmanship awards where my name is spelled wrong, but since I'm a good sport, I don't say anything.

It's not that I don't want a clean room, it's just that I don't have time. Between soccer practice every day after school, homework, and seeing friends, who has the time to keep a tidy room?

If I just had more time, my room would look better. And in the summertime, I usually get my shit together enough to at least get it into decent shape.

I ask Bethany why mom used to clean her room from time to time but never cleaned mine.

"Because she knew you'd eventually do it yourself."

Oh. Right.

But unlike Bethany, the stuff in my room isn't trash. It's my stuff.

I keep every playbill in an old shoe box.

Every ticket stub in an old altoid tin

Every fortune cookie fortune in a sky blue, plastic Chinese food take out container

My clothes from middle school hang in my closet, regardless of the fact that they will never fit again after I've grown boobs.

My beanie babies are displayed in whimsical poses on doll chairs and little red toy wagons, all organized by their different factions in the animal kingdom

My VHS tapes live on a rack next to the empty cd cases that I might need one day even though I keep the actual cds in a binder.

Every school assignment from 1st grade through my associate's degree live in thick plastic bags durable enough to hold large stacks of paper.

Notebooks that still have blank pages sit on my bookshelf because I could still potentially write in them.

Teen magazines from the '90s stand up right under the alcove in my room in case I want to take a stroll down memory lane.

I keep. And I keep. And I keep.

I might need it, I might want it, it was a gift, it was important, if gave me joy, it used to fit, I used to play with it, I loved it, I needed it, I had to have it. Stuff. My stuff is so important.

Except, there's dried cat poop on top of the magazines…

Ok, that's fine, I'll just throw that away and I won't touch that top part of the magazines. Why are they all stuck together? Why are the pages stiff? Why does it smell like cat piss over here? Oh fuck fuck fuck, I just touched a bunch of magazine that have been pissed on. Fuck, gross.

Ok. Ok … these need to get thrown away. That's fine. I can let go of them. But, I just don't feel like dealing with it now. I'll do it later.

After I leave for college, I tell Timmy not to let the cats go in my bedroom while I'm away because every time I come home, I am treated to surprise cat poop and bed sheets that are matted with fur.

Timmy obliges and when I return home again for break I am greeted by small mouse droppings all over my bed. Guess the cats where keeping the mice at bay. Great. Fuck. You know what Timmy, let the cats in my room sometimes, that's fine. But just make sure my sheets are washed before I come home ok? Thanks.

> *Carly starts to walk out of house to retrieve Febreze bottle. Boyfriend by Justin Bieber begins to play*

At 26, I bring home a boyfriend, to meet my family.

Despite growing up in homeless shelters, he is disgusted by my childhood home and insists on showering at Planet Fitness instead of at my dad's house. He isn't convinced when I explain that the reason the tub has green soap scum is because our tap water comes from a well in the back yard as opposed to town water. Mom always said the well water had extra minerals in it and that's why it turns the tub and sink green. No big deal … But there are also too many spiders in the shower for his taste. I guess I never noticed the fact that there were cobwebs in literally every corner of the house as if it were haunted.

We sit up the first night he sleeps over and argue while he tries to clean my childhood bedroom. He continually sprays Febreze until the air is thick with it, insisting that it still smells like cat piss. Even though of all the rooms, I think mine smells the best. I feel powerless, being made to feel like my room is a problem when I am the only proactive one in my family "stop cleaning my room! You don't have to do that. I can do it myself! I have other rooms in the house that I need to worry about. My room doesn't need the attention right now!"

"I just don't want you to end up like your family, Carly."

I never thought I would end up like them … but maybe the clutter in my room in Chicago is more of a sign than a coincidence to him…

This is the first time I ever feel ashamed of my childhood home.

The next trip I take home to visit, my dad tells me that there's something wrong with the cold water and that only extremely hot water is coming out of the shower head.

"But don't worry Cahly, I figured out if you just use a wash cloth while you're in there and get that wet, it's not too hot to use on your entire body!"

I will never take a shower in this home again.

I guess showering at Planet Fitness is probably the better option after all.

I enter the dining room, which is attached to the kitchen. I accidentally kick a cat food can across the floor. Both the cat food and dog food cans are left out for our Golden Retriever Lucy to lick clean. Because she'd surely complain if we just threw them away…

The brown juice stained paper plates that the dog and cats eat off of also remain on the floor. New plates are used for almost every meal, leaving the old ones to just live on the once impressive real hardwood floor. A floor, I can only recall being mopped once in my lifetime.

Cases of empty beer bottles sit on the kitchen table, looking as if there had been a rager the night before when, in actuality, it has just been a few months since anyone had taken the empties to the dump.

Mom never kept a tidy home, obviously, but since she died, the garbage can is filled to an all-time high.

The lid to the trash can adds about an extra foot of space for the trash to pile above the bag line. Rather than take the lid off to remove the bag, I keep the lid on to help contain the overload, even then, an assortment of trash still spills on to the floor as I try to bring the draw strings together as quickly as possible.

Trash bags lean against the fireplace, filled to the brim with recycling and garbage to be taken to the dump. Bethany and I have tried to convince dad to pay for trash pick-up, but he insists that neither he or Timmy will bring it out front to be picked up. Well, it's not like you're taking it to the dump in a timely fashion either dad…

The Chili's restaurant jingle ("Baby Back Ribs") plays

Deciding what we will eat for dinner has always been our biggest family argument.

I dig through the drawer of take out menus, we have at least 3 of every menu, so that multiple family members can decide what they want at a time. We're too hungry to take turns. Many of the menus that remain in our home still have items circled with our names written next to them. Mom writes "Penny" next to her choice as opposed to "me" and often orders over the phone "and my husband will have…" like the waitress gives a shit about who's eating what.

"I'll buy, you fly"

My dad tells my mom this, or me, once I've gotten my license. He doesn't want to get up off the couch and he knows that mom most likely already spent her paycheck on Walmart and Target runs for herself and us kids.

When mom comes home with the food, it's placed on the stove top. The only cleared surface in the house for obvious reasons.

"SUPPER!!"

We exchanged greetings about how hungry we are while asking "what did you get?" After collecting our takeout containers, we all retire to our separate rooms to eat. Mom and dad sit on the living room couch, while the kids all eat in our individual bedrooms. Often times, we are all watching the same TV show from different rooms.

I learn as an adult that sugar is addictive. And sugar, is in pretty much allllll takeout food. So, without meaning to, my parents hooked me on a substance.

It's 3 a.m. and I flop my drunk ass into bed.

Don't call…

Don't do it…

You know it's not a good idea…

You only want it 'cause you're drunk.

45 minutes later I'm having a 4-way with Papa John, Ben and Jerry.

I wake up the next morning, my head is foggy and I have pizza sauce lingering under my fingernails.

I see my empty cardboard box one night stand, lying next to be in bed, look at me as if it's my fault because I called him. I wanted him inside me so badly and I got it.

I have got to stop waking up like this.

I spend every weekend of high school in Tim Scadova's bed, eating Domino's because he gets a discount.

This is what love feels like.

I'm at Wal-Mart picking up a few things.

I casually stroll down the ice cream aisle, not looking for anything in particular.

Blueberry cheesecake ice cream!

My dad would love that!

I think I gave my dad diabetes.

Because he didn't have it before I started buying him sugary treats but I don't know how else to show him that I love him.

As a child I eat bacon, mayonnaise and cheese sandwiches.

I don't like the taste of water so my mom gives me Surge in my water bottle at soccer games.

Spaghetti sauce is gross, so when we have spaghetti for dinner, I just melt Velveeta cheese and pour it on the noodles.

Speaking of neon orange cheese…

I have to find a way to cut my drug dealer out of my life. My drug that comforts me when I am sad, my drug that celebrates with me when I am happy, my drug that doesn't even make me get out of the car to get it!

> "Whenever Wherever" by Shakira plays
> A man dressed as personified Taco Bell enters from audience with a bag of Taco Bell. (Specifically a crunch wrap supreme, cheesy Gordita crunch and a chicken chalupa supreme.) Man and Carly do a choreographed dance, after which the food is handed to audience members, the TacoBellMan exits, and the music ends.

God, it's probably been like two months since I've had you, Taco Bell. And I can't even remember which trip to get you was the last one. And that, like, weirdly makes me sad. Like, I wish I could have savored you. I wish I could have taken the time to really enjoy every last sour creamy bite. But I didn't know that I was gonna give you up. I thought I was fine having you whenever I wanted to. I thought that if I exercised regularly, I could eat whatever I wanted cuz I wasn't trying to lose weight so who gives a fuck. I wanna be active but I don't need to be skinny. I look at you T-Baby and I feel great about the way I look so why bother changing my diet when I love you, T-Bell. So that's the game plan, work out regularly and eat Taco Bell so that I can be happy.

But T-Baby … I went and saw an orthopedic doctor and he had some bad news…

"Carly, you have so much arthritis in your knees that if you were older I would recommend knee replacement surgery, but since you're only 27 I would highly recommend weight loss surgery"

And I'm like "whaaaat?!? Is he for real?!"

It's not like I'm so big I can't move around. Like, what is he talking about? Sure, 230 pounds is a lot for someone who is only 5 feet tall, but I live a perfectly normal life. Right TB? You think I look good.

So I asked him, "Can't I just diet and exercise?"

"Well Carly, I would assume you've already tried diet and exercise and that they haven't worked. Lots of people have trouble losing. 50% of the population is overweight."

Here's what I am hearing the doctor say to me:

"Well Carly, you're fat as fuck and I would assume that if it was possible for you not to be that way, you wouldn't be. So clearly, since you can't control yourself around the chalupas and the cheesy gordita crunches, surgery is the best option."

And maybe I should have seen the arthritis coming, Taco Bell. Like, I know it takes me a longer time to get up off the floor than most people but I just figured it was cuz I was bigger and whatever. Like, I can get up so it's not a huge deal. And sure my knees feel stiff when I've been sitting on a bar stool for a long period of time but I think that happens to a lot of people. And maybe it's not super comfortable for me to sit crisscross apple sauce but I'm not a fucking child, so I'm not really supposed to be sitting that way anyways.

It is so hard not to eat you, Taco Bell. When I eat you, I am full for several hours. Because I'm like half sick. But when I eat healthy, I want to eat again like 2 hours later and I'm like damn, why do I need to eat?! I just ate! But T-Bell, you make me feel so full. So full, I can't eat another bite full. So full I wanna take a nap, full. Because I like napping too!

I feel like I have body dysmorphia except when I look in the mirror, I see a beautiful, curvaceous, sexy woman, it's not until I see pictures of myself that I know I'm fat. When Melissa McCarthy lost weight, I cried. I felt betrayed. How could she drop 50lbs and then come out with a plus size clothing line?

I'm not going to lose weight for my career. I will be the fat actress that all the little fat girls look up to. Fuck the Hollywood standard of beauty. I am beautiful and I am a great actress and I don't need to be thin to act. But maybe Melissa lost weight because she has kids and she just wants to be able to run around with them. And I wanna run around with my kids one day too but I can't do that if I'm laying around with you Taco Bell.

Damn. I guess maybe I just like everything in excess...

Once I graduate from college and bills need to be paid, it's easy for me not to buy physical objects. I can't afford them, so how can I?

But food, well, I need food.

I would much rather spend my money on the experience of dining out with friends than buying a new outfit.

And if there is one thing us actors like to do, it's drink!

I don't drink alone, I never found a reason to, but when I drink with friends, I find it hard to not drink just to be drunk.

Being drunk makes for good stories, being drunk helps you forget why you're sad, being drunk is an experience that I am willing to spend my money on.

> *lights isolate her downstage right. Two chairs get set up next to each other: one for Carly to sit in and one to hold the cue cards that represent dad. Two PBR tall boys, one for Carly to drink and one sitting on the floor next to dad chair.*

"Cahly, would ya like to have some cocktails on the veranda?"

This is dad lingo, for "wanna drink beers on the porch?"

Get a couple of beers in my dad, and he'll tell you a great story.

We sit in the white wicker rocking chairs on the farmers porch and watch the cars fly down our busy street.

The grass is rarely mowed, but we don't seem to notice as dad tells me about how he once drove across the country to California in his friend's van.

Lou Dog, or Lucy, lays at my dad's feet as we enjoy the warm weather and talk about the flowers that hang from the roof of the porch.

"Your mothah, woulda liked them purple ones"

"Ya, she woulda dad."

"There is no one like ya mothah"

"I know dad"

I try to hold it together. I don't want my dad to think he can't talk about my mom because it makes me cry. I want him to talk about her. I want him to feel like it's ok to talk about her.

Mom always wanted this farmers porch. But dad enjoys it in her honor.

> *A collection of voicemails from Carly's father begins to play, moving from one voicemail to the next. Throughout, Carly holds up cue cards which read as follows:*

Dad wants me to check if his math is correct when he adds the tip at a restaurant
Dad tries to pick me up at the airport, a night earlier than he is supposed to.
Dad hits the mailbox pulling out of the driveway
Dad knocks over his beer at Longhorn Steakhouse
Dad needs my sister to do his taxes for him

Dad needs me to do the math for him when he adds the tip at restaurants

Dad isn't going to pick me up from the airport if I come home after dark anymore

Dad needs to push the grocery cart so he has something to hold on to

Dad tells the waitress he'd like more coffee when there's no waitress at the table

Dad goes to the police station and tells them there are undercover cops disguised as trash bags living in his recycling

Dad's not allowed to live alone anymore

Dad tells my sister there are men trying to burn the house down

Dad shits his pants on the way to apple picking

Dad puts his cat in his truck at 1 a.m. because he thinks the house is on fire

Dad pees on my bedroom door

Dad comes in my room naked and says "you again!"

Dad thinks ISIS lives upstairs and that my brother-in-law let them in

Dad has both of his legs in the same hole of his depends.

Dad can't drink beer anymore because it makes him confused and off balance.

>   *Lights back to general wash*

When you lose one parent, it's very easy to see the mortality in your other parent

You start to think about things you don't want to think about.

If dad dies before we sell this house, what would we do?

None of us are going to live in it. None of us can really afford to fix it up. And none of us want to deal with it.

As the manual labor child, I know it is my responsibility to clean up this house. My value in this family is the manual labor I provide. Dad provides us money, and Beth takes care of dad, and I moved halfway across the country and if I don't clean this house, I won't be contributing anything to my family. It's the only thing I can do, that no one else can. It's not mommy's job anymore, it's my job.

But coming home and cleaning a mess that I didn't make is becoming tiresome. I can only clean the common areas in a house I don't live in so many times before I feel unappreciated.

I decide to focus on cleaning out the house instead of cleaning up the house. Dad and Timmy might continue to make a mess but they're certainly not going to fill it with more stuff once I clean it out.

I make arrangements to rent a 17-foot dumpster.

17 feet should be enough room for all the stuff in the attic and the garage.

>   *Sound of truck backing up as Carly retrieves plastic tote from off stage.*

But when it shows up, it looks tiny.

I open the door to the attic and pull forward the piece of plywood leaning against the wall that covers the light switch. I do so carefully, as to not touch the pink insulation that was never enclosed. A lesson I've kept with me since childhood, "Don't touch the pink insulation, Cahly, it's made of fiberglass and it will make you itch." Apparently, dad never planned on covering any of the insulation in the house because that lesson was always stressed.

The door to the attic doesn't open all the way. It stops short when it hits several boxes stacked on top of each other. And there is only about a foot's worth of space to stand when you enter. The only way to go deeper in is to climb on top of that person sized dinosaur stuffed animal again, that lays on top an assortment of cardboard boxes filled with other miscellaneous toys. Regardless of the fact that this room is set up exactly like my childhood "secret garden of toys" room, I no longer see it that way. The room I see now has rusty nails sticking out of the ceiling, holes in the corners where squirrels chewed their way in and lived comfortably for the winter, and hanging pink insulation where those same squirrels most likely fell through.

This is not an oasis of toys, even though there are toys everywhere.

It's hard to know where to start. But I start.

Sorting through bins of barbies with matted hair, missing limbs, and miscellaneous make overs, I quickly realize that my entire childhood is in this attic. This refugee camp for toys, game pieces never to be reunited, stuffed animals stained with unknown substances, and sports equipment from the late '80s saved for those grandchildren my mother would never meet.

And even if she had, what would she have given them? The Stacy Dash Barbie or the Beanie Baby collector's guidebook?

I struggle with the idea that the things in front of me could be donated. I mean, they're not trash right? Mom told me this stuff wasn't trash, I have to be able to do something with it.

After the first load of stuffed animals is washed and prep for donation, my friend Michelle stops me, "Carly, it's not worth it. This stuff isn't worth anything. It will take you more time to sort through it than it would if you just threw it out. You need to get rid of it or you'll never finish cleaning out the attic this week."

Fuck. This is it, ya know, I have a week to get this room cleaned out. I don't want to go back to Chicago feeling like I didn't do enough. Granted, I always go back to Chicago feeling like I didn't do enough, but if I don't let go of this stuff right now, in this moment, this house will sit here and fester like an open wound. Rip the band aid off, Carly. Deal with it. Deal with it now. This stuff has to go. You have to let go.

Why.

Why is this house like this?

Why is my family like this?

Why am I like this?

Dad stops me as I carry a box towards the dumpster and points out the sock monkey sitting on top.

"Your grandmother made that, ya know."

"But we didn't take care of it, dad."

We didn't take care of any of it. And nothing is worth having if you don't take care of it.

We didn't take care of 22 Seaverns Bridge Road, dad, and now, maybe it's time to sell her to someone who can.

Hoarding has been an issue for my mother, my father, my brother, my sister, my grandmother, my great aunts, my great grandparents and me.

Hoarding has been an issue for me.

Up until this point, my life has been this attic filled floor to ceiling with stuff from the past. I keep the door closed so that no one has to see my stuff. I don't need help taking care of it because it's my stuff and my responsibility. But if no one has noticed my stuff then it can probably wait until later to take care of.

Except, my stuff was starting to spill into the other rooms in my home and it hurts when I see it.

So, I guess now it's later and I can't put it off any longer.

> *"Wild World" by Cat Stevens begins to play. Carly gathers everything on stage into the blue tote, dumps it in the "dumpster," then walks off stage to go fill the tote with more.*

> *End of play.*

A Performer's Monologue

Connor Long

The term "inspiration porn" is generally attributed to the Australian journalist, comedian, and Social Rights activist Stella Young (1982–2014), who used it in her July 2012 piece for the Australian Broadcasting Corporation titled "We're Not Here for Your Inspiration,"[1] and then introduced it to a far wider audience when her April 2014 TED Talk, "I'm Not Your Inspiration, Thank You Very Much," went viral.[2] "I use the term 'porn' deliberately," she said, "because they objectify one group of people for the benefit of another group."[3] In her 2012 article, she wrote,

> Let me be clear about the intent of this inspiration porn; it's there so that non-disabled people can put their worries into perspective. So they can go, "Oh well if that kid who doesn't have any legs can smile while he's having an awesome time, I should never, EVER feel bad about my life." It's there so that non-disabled people can look at us and think, "well, it could be worse…. I could be that person." [… U]sing these images as feel-good tools, as "inspiration," is based on an assumption that the people in them have terrible lives, and that it takes some extra kind of pluck or courage to live them.[4]

This idea of "inspiration porn" has become a foundational idea in contemporary Critical Disability Studies, and once one begins to look for it, it can be found in abundance. By understanding and defining inspiration porn strictly by the ideas explained above, it would seem any media, image, or performance designed for a non-disabled audience to gain inspiration from a disabled person should be condemned under this label. Instead of accepting such a limited view, however, we should remember what else the great Stella Young wrote and said about the construct:

> Inspiration porn is an image of a person with a disability, often a kid, doing something completely ordinary—like playing, or talking, or running, or drawing a picture, or hitting a tennis ball—carrying a caption like "your excuse is invalid" or "before you quit, try." Increasingly, they feature the Hamilton quote.[5]

Young's allusion to "the Hamilton quote" refers to Scott Hamilton, a figure skater and cancer survivor whose ableist statement "the only disability in life is a bad attitude" has become a common platitude on self-help memes and other internet posts. Young continues, specifically noting that the images and videos she is arguing against are ones that show disabled people "doing something completely ordinary."

> When I was 15, a member of my local community approached my parents and told them she wanted to nominate me for some kind of community achievement award. My parents said, "Thanks, but there's one glaring problem with that … she hasn't actually achieved anything out of the ordinary." They were right. I went to school, I got good marks, I had a very low key after-school job, and I spent a lot of time watching *Buffy the Vampire Slayer* and *Dawson's Creek*. I wasn't feeding Chlamydia-infected baby koalas before school or setting up a soup kitchen in the main street or reading newspapers to the elderly at the local hospital. I was doing exactly the same things as my non-disabled friends. When my parents explained all this to the well-meaning nominator, they said, "yes, but she's just such an inspiration."[6]

That, according to Young, is the problem; the sense that the mere act of a disabled person getting out of bed and going about their day—and even, yes, smiling about it—should be cause for inspiration to the great able-bodied majority. As Anita Hollander sings in *Still Standing,* one doesn't expect disabled people to happy,[7] and so, when they are, it must represent a Herculean feat of angelic grace and indomitable determination.

"Many Deaf people do inspirational things," writes Jolanta Lapiak, creator of Handspeak, "and some have done amazing things. Many of them lead a normal life. Others struggle. Just like everybody else. Those Deaf people are not inspiring simply because they are deaf but because some of them are genius, talented, hard-working, successful, or whatever."[8] Young offers a typical example,

> I was on a train with my earphones shoved in my ears completely ignoring my fellow commuters […] a woman patted me on the arm and said "I see you on the train every morning and I just wanted to say it's great. You're an inspiration to me." Should I have said "you too?" Because we were doing exactly the same thing; catching public transport to our respective places of employment.[9]

That distinction—the insultingly infantilizing applause and approbation for doing the mundane—*that* is the heart of inspiration porn. One of our chief reasons for including Connor's work is because it is the opposite of what the young actor wants.

These statements, from Young's work in Australia and Lapiak's article "Inspiration Porn: A Look at the Objectification of the Deaf," are the perfect summation for what Inspiration Porn is and isn't. The problem, however, is that no matter what the experience, mastery, or accomplishment of a disabled person, there will always be some well-meaning ableist who continues to hold to these tropes. Could it be that some will read these playwrights' words and be impressed not by the content but rather by the simple act of writing—of these artists "doing something" with themselves?

Though it is a sad possibility, we certainly hope—if this book does fall into the hands of someone with that mindset—this collection will help "cure" them of such ridiculousness.

—**John Michael Sefel**

NOTES

1. Stella Young, "We're Not Here for Your Inspiration." ABC News, July 3, 2012, https://www.abc.net.au/news/2012–07–03/young-inspiration-porn/4107006.
2. Stella Young, "Stella Young: I'm not your inspiration, thank you very much | TED Talk," TED.com.
3. *Ibid.*
4. Young, "We're Not Here for Your Inspiration."
5. *Ibid.*
6. *Ibid.*
7. See *Still Standing*, later in this book.
8. Jolanta Lapiak, "Inspiration Porn: A Look at the Objectification of the Deaf," Handspeak, n.d., https://www.handspeak.com/culture/index.php?id=155.
9. Young, "We're Not Here for Your Inspiration."

A Performer's Monologue

* * *

Connor enters, lights at a general stage wash.

Connor: While *it's not actually true* that "all the world is a stage," *it is true* that Life is a lot more amusing if you treat it that way.

> *Connor snaps his fingers, cueing: lights to black except sharply focused follow-spot on him*

I am *blessed* to be an actor, athlete, and advocate, because I came to understand that the *potential and pursuit of my abilities* matters far more than the challenges I may face as a person with Down syndrome.

I am here because Someone believed in me. Someone *believed* in my humanity, my potential, my abilities and my right to *not only exist*, but to *flourish*—uniquely and fully—as *ME*.

And I am here on stage—or on a set, at the podium, starting block, or out on the trail—not just because *someone else* believed in me, but because I, too, *came to believe in me*.

I came to understand and act upon the fact that my set of abilities is *not fixed* by genes or outdated stereotypes and expectations. That my abilities grow with supports and opportunities.

My search for *the uniqueness of me* and *a true belief in myself* brings me to the stage, just as surely as *a search for something to believe in* brings an audience to the theatre or screen.

My talent, skills and strengths lie in my performances and the stories told or examples offered by them. When I am on stage, I can be Me *by being someone else*. For those moments it's *okay* for people to watch my every move, to react and respond openly, to laugh, sigh, maybe even cry.

When I am on stage or screen, they have *my permission* to stare at me in a way that in other, everyday settings might be uncomfortable for us both. They have the right—and maybe even the responsibility—to wonder:

"Who is this guy and why is he up there?"

"What does he offer and have to say to me, to us?"

When I perform I don't have to compete with anyone. We can engage in shared experiences and emotions that I help to steer.

From Seuss to Shakespeare to Stevens and beyond, I am guided and encouraged, but not constrained, on the stage or the script, by words. I have an element of control over them if I perform well, while adding my unique perspective and flavors.

I can be a Superhero version of me! I can use words and emotions and expression to paint pictures to be seen in your mind and felt in your heart.

What "super-power" could be more *awesome* than to be able to grab and reshape hearts, minds, actions, and maybe, just maybe, a sliver of the future of the world?

Performing is a place when we, for a few moments or hours, share what is not just mine or yours, alone, but ours, together.

A place where I can share laughter, insights, and even the heartaches that we should not shoulder, or suffer, alone. Where I can reach beyond the stage or camera to cajole or console. To shine or reflect light, if only fleeting, into those darker places.

In my acting I've learned to exchange being nervous for being prepared, excited, and brave. I've learned that when I stumble, freeze or am distracted, I need just a moment, a cue, a centering breath to get back in flow.

I've learned that despite those awkward or even painful moments, the world still turns, my heart still beats, I still breathe, that I am still loved and valued, that the show can, and must, still go on, imperfect as it may be.

I ACT because *there are other people I can be*, with other stories that should be told.

In those moments and hours, I get to share the better parts of me with the hope that I will touch and maybe, just maybe, motivate the better parts of you.

I SING because there are songs in my head and music in my heart that seek to join with the rhythms of others and of the world.

Wouldn't it be great if the *imperfect* songs from my lips reminded you that there are *perfect-enough* songs in your heart?

Wouldn't it be great if a smile on *my* face led to a smile *on your face*? A smile that you could share with others? Wouldn't it be great?

If I can dare stand on this stage and share stories and the contents of my own tender heart, can you, will you?

Together, as performers and audience, let's go with bravery and truth, and change the world, one smile, one tear, one heart, and one mind at a time.

…Annnd "scene."

Connor snaps his fingers again, cueing black out.

End of play.

Why This Monologue Isn't Memorized (A True Story)

Kurt Sass

In her 2005 essay "The Tyranny of Neutral: Disability and Actor Training," Carrie Sandahl explains why an acting technique that privileges what she calls "the neutral body" is humiliating for an actor with a visible or apparent condition. When such an actor is held to the unrealistic standard of achieving the neutral body in the classroom or onstage, he/she/they is re-experiencing the degradation faced in the real world, where being able-bodied is regarded as more desirable.[1] The evaluative standard wherein the neutral body is privileged influences audiences as well as artists. Especially within the tenets of psychological realism, a "good" actor is one who "becomes" a character, ensuring his/her/their identifying physical and vocal mannerisms are not visible to an audience. An actor with a visible or apparent condition will never fully "become" a character, because the presence of the condition will always make the actor visible as himself/herself/theirself. If a "good" actor is one who "becomes" a character, an actor with a visible or apparent condition will never meet that evaluative standard.

Of course, this evaluative standard is subjective. Psychological realism is not the only genre, and "becoming" a character is not the only method of acting. Still, both determine the dominant evaluative standard for what is considered admirable acting. In that case, will an actor with a visible or apparent condition always fail to meet the evaluative standard for "good" actors?

In his 1985 book, *Great Reckonings in Little Rooms,* phenomenologist Bert O. States discusses another mode of performance, one that gives pleasure to an audience precisely because a performer does not become his/her/their character. According to States, an actor who is working in the self-expressive mode, "awakens our awareness of the artist in the actor [and...] reacting to the actor's particular way of *doing* his role."[2] A self-expressive actor does not "become" a character. Instead, the actor adopts the character as a "mask" underneath which his/her/their personal magnetism is always visible. An audience is doubly pleased by a skillful actor who is working in the self-expressive mode, because the audience enjoys both the quality of the actor's performance and the moments when the actor lets the "mask" of a character slip, revealing his/her/their own magnetism.

The self-expressive mode could be useful for an actor who has a visible or apparent condition. Such an actor's condition is revealed beneath the "mask" of a character in addition to personal magnetism. Therefore, a performance may be evaluated based on how successfully the actor makes the audience take pleasure in a role, insofar as it embodies both charisma and a particular visible or apparent condition. Even if the actor is not playing a character, the visible or apparent condition is evoking two performances, his/her/their own and the absence of an able-bodied actor, who embodies the ideal, neutral body. In this case, working in the self-expressive mode allows the actor to reveal his/her/their personal charisma. Ideally, the audience will take such pleasure in the actor's presence that it will cease to imagine an able-bodied actor in his/her/their place.

Someone with a visible or apparent condition who is working in the self-expressive mode could complicate the current evaluative standard for performance, which privileges the neutral body onstage, just as the able-bodied/disabled binary privileges ablebodiedness in the real world. Judging the effectiveness of an actor with a visible or apparent condition by comparing him/her/them to an able-bodied performer in the same role is not just potentially humiliating for the actor, whose work is being held to an unrealistic standard. In his 2001 essay, "What We Talk About When We Talk About Good," Todd London, the artistic director for New Dramatists, argues that an evaluative standard based on a narrow vision of what a theatre piece *should* be is reductive, not just for individual artists, but for the art form. London says, "We respond to art with an intense and intricate subjectivity, comprised of mind, body, spirit and heart. Our critical responses, meanwhile, are usually centered [...] on what we like, or don't like."[3] In other words, sometimes audiences are so focused on what *would* please them that they forget to enjoy the play they are actually watching. An actor with a visible or apparent condition who is working in the self-expressive mode can challenge this evaluative standard by reminding the audience, through performance, that the able-bodied performer they are conditioned to expect is not the only expressive performance worth watching.

—**Jill Summerville**

Notes

1. Carrie Sandahl and Philip Auslander, eds., *Bodies in Commotion: Disability and Performance* (Ann Arbor: University of Michigan Press, 2005), 17–28.

2. Bert O. States, *Great Reckonings in Little Rooms* (Berkeley: University of California, 1985), 165.

3. Todd London, "What We Talk About When We Talk About Good" (New York: Theatre Communications Group, 2001), October 7, 2019.

Why This Monologue Isn't Memorized (A True Story)

* * *

Note: Kurt looks at script constantly throughout the entire performance.

Kurt: Okay, let's get right to the point. As you can see, I am holding the script to this monologue in my hand. I did not memorize it. Made no attempt whatsoever. It's not that I'm lazy. If I were lazy, I wouldn't have written this script in the first place. And it's not that I don't care about you as an audience. In fact, I happen to think there are a lot of fine, intelligent people out there.

The fact is, the reason I didn't memorize this monologue is because I **can't** memorize this monologue. **Im**-possible.

I believe some explanation is required at this point. Between the years of 1998 and 2000 I had 22 ECT Treatments. ECT stands for Electric Convulsive Therapy or what many people call Shock Treatments.

ECT Treatments are actually performed by sending electrical currents throughout your brain, *(nods head up and down)* yes on purpose, with the hopes of stimulating the release of endorphins and other chemicals inside your brain. They are not done at all like you may have seen in the movie *One Flew Over the Cuckoo's Nest*, where Jack Nicholson was completely awake and he felt the current and was thrashing about like a fish just out of water. I was completely asleep and given muscle relaxants.

Now, there was one really **good** part of ECT for me and one really **bad** part of ECT for me. The really **good** part of ECT for me was that it cured me of a year long deep and dark depression at the time, which included total bed confinement, daily suicidal thoughts, and numerous psychiatrist hospitalizations, as well as me cutting myself up to 70 times a day. The treatments truly saved my life. The really **bad** part of ECT for me, however, was that those very same treatments that saved my life also f'ed up my memory something fierce. For example, unless I have contact with someone on a regular basis, chances are they will become totally lost to me. I can't tell you how many times someone has come up to me:

(Pantomimes a big hug)

"Hey Kurt, how's it going? How's Community Access doing?" *(to audience)* Community Access is the organization I work for. I have absolutely no idea who this person is who is right now hugging the S-H-I-T out of me. We may have met possibly upwards of 5–10 times or so in the past, but I still have no clue. I don't even remember their face. And I hate to tell you, dear audience, but to be honest, I doubt that I will be able to remember any of your faces after today, either, although there are quite a few cute and adorable faces out there I wouldn't mind remembering after today.

And that brings me to dating. Hell, dating is hard enough, but try dating while dealing with severe memory loss! Ring! Ring! Ring! Ring! Ring! Ring! *(to audience)* Wow! Excuse me! I guess I never got around to updating my make believe ring tone Ring! Ring!

> *(Picks up a phone)*

Hello? Who? Robin? Robin who?

> *(Looks completely puzzled throughout entire conversation)*

Oh, of course I remember you, Robin, how could I forget. What? Of course I remember where we met!

> *(Shrugs shoulders to audience)*

You said it was Saturday, right? Could you hold one second, the doorbell just rang.

> *(Puts down imaginary phone near right foot. Takes calendar book out of pocket, thumbs through it)*

Um, um, Saturday, Saturday. Er … Er … Finish term Paper, no, Dentist, no, Exterminator, no! Dog park, um, Museum, um.

> *(Shakes head left and right) (raises both hands, palms up, looks at them)*

Dog park, museum, dog park, museum, dog park, museum.

> *(Picks up phone from floor near right foot)*

Sorry about that. So yes, Saturday, at the, er, museum, right?

> *(Pause) (Pumps left fist in air and blows out air)*

What? Of course I didn't forget? How could I forget you, Robin?

> *(To audience)*

Fortunately, I lucked out that time. Over the years, I have learned many coping skills, the most important of which is to write down as much information as possible as soon as possible. If this same scenario had happened today, I would have already had written up an index card, with all important information, such as name and location we met. Now if only I could remember where I put that damn index card!

Work can be another issue of great concern when it comes to memory loss. Now, I know my limitations. I know a person with severe memory loss like myself should not be working in certain capacities. I don't think for example you would feel very comfortable or confident with me as your pilot. *(Finger on cheek, looks up—pretending to fly a plane)* Are we headed to Dubuque or Dubai? Fortunately, I work for a great agency, one that knows all about my history of depression and what comes with it, so I don' t have to worry about hiding anything from them, which is a great relief, believe me! Even with their understanding, it can still be very difficult with all the many e-mails, phones, meetings and conversations that take place each day. I've learned to cope by writing down E-VE-RY-THING! Here's an example.

(Shows date book to audience)—(Walks throughout audience)

As you can see, almost every single line is filled in. I mean, my follow-up lists have follow-up lists. I've been praised by many people for my diligence on keeping track of so many things, but what they don't realize is that for me it is as much a necessity as it is diligence.

Another problem with work is that sometimes I literally don't know if I'm coming or going. Let me explain. My memory is always at its worst when I first awake in the morning or from a nap. I try my best not to doze on the subway, but sometimes I just can't fight it. When I do nod off, once I awake I have no clue whether I am on my way to work or headed home. Fortunately, the train has a better memory than I and will let me know within a stop or two which way I am going. This can be very disconcerting when I think I am on my way home, only to realize it is 7:30 a.m. and I will have a full day of work ahead of me.

But I hope no one feels sad or sorry for me. I've been able to cope with this and actually have held the same job for over 10 years, have a 32-year-old son that actually still visits his dad twice a week (and not out of obligation) and am in a long term relationship.

Well, that's it for me. As I said earlier, unfortunately, as much as I might like to, I may not be able to remember many of your faces after today, but I hope some of you will remember mine.

Thank you.

End of play.

Tinted

AMY BETHAN EVANS

In their 2005 essay, "Men in Motion: Disability and Masculinity," Lenore Manderson and Susan Peake write that, "being feminine and disabled are consistent and synergistic; the traditional notions of woman and disability converge, reflected in the ascription of characteristics such as innocence, vulnerability, sexual passivity or asexuality, dependency and objectification."[1] The convergence of the characteristics associated with disability and those associated with traditional feminine gender roles ensures a person with a disability who identifies as feminine is doubly invisible, experiencing both the social invisibility associated with disability and the social invisibility associated with embodying the feminine gender. This double invisibility complicates any discussion of the sexual assault of people with disabilities who identify (or are identified by social institutions involved in sexual assault cases) as conforming to a feminine gender role.

According to the website Disability Justice, 83 percent of women with disabilities will be sexually assaulted at some time in their lives. Disability Justice also reports that women with disabilities are sexually assaulted at three times the rate of able-bodied women.[2] According to the 2015 U.S. Transgender Survey, 61 percent of respondents who openly identified as both transgendered or non-binary and as having a disability or disabilities have experienced sexual assault.[3]

Even though people with disabilities are three times more likely to experience sexual assault than able-bodied people, the stories of survivors with disabilities have not yet been integrated into the #MeToo movement. Only two disability narratives related to #MeToo have received widespread media coverage. As an octogenarian who is legally blind, Bill Cosby needed a cane and a guide when he entered the courtroom where he was convicted of drugging and sexually assaulting Andrea Constand. Cosby embodied the weakness and helplessness that are (however inaccurately) associated with disability. At the trial, Cosby's attorney, Joseph Greene, said, "Eighty-one-year-old blind men who are not self-sufficient are not dangerous, except, perhaps, to themselves."[4] Greene's words signaled to the jury that it was Cosby, not Constand, who was vulnerable. Like Bill Cosby, Harvey Weinstein, who arguably became the first powerful, predatory figure of the #MeToo movement after Ronan Farrow published survivors' accounts of Weinstein's sexual harassment and sexual assault in *The New Yorker* in October of 2017,[5] used a mobility device when he appeared in court. Weinstein's defense lawyers claimed he needed the walker due to injuries suffered after an incorrectly performed back surgery.[6] However, after Weinstein was found guilty of a criminal sex act in the first degree for forcing oral sex on the former Project Runway production assistant Miriam Haley and rape in the third degree for sexually assaulting Jessica Mann, he was taken into custody without his walker.[7] Both Cosby and Weinstein were embodying the stereotype that people with physical disabilities are incapable of performing physical acts independently. Of course, that stereotype is reductive. In these particular cases, however, it also implicitly invites a presumption of innocence, as someone who could not act independently could not easily commit sexual assault. Bill Cosby's and Harvey Weinstein's narratives certainly are part of the #MeToo movement, but these men are convicted sexual assailants, not survivors.

The stories of the #MeToo movement are stories where females (primarily) have been denied autonomy over the own bodies by males (primarily) who are taking advantage of their dominant position in the male/female power dynamic. The presence of the body of a female with a disability complicates this #MeToo narrative, for three reasons. First, a person with a disability may have difficulty physically or verbally indicating lack of consent. Further, that person may be dependent on caretakers for assistance with daily activities. This dependency might make a person with a disability especially vulnerable to a sexual assailant, and it might complicate any attempt to report a sexual assault to the authorities. Second, while an able-bodied female's lack of personal autonomy in a particular moment may be regarded as a social aberration, a lack of personal autonomy is a social norm for many people with disabilities. Because of this, authorities often deemphasize the importance of consent in the sex lives of people with disabilities. In 2012, Richard Fourtin was convicted of the sexual assault of a woman with cerebral palsy. The woman, who was 25 at the time of her alleged assault, had advanced hydrocephalus, and she could not walk or talk. A Connecticut court later overturned Fourtin's conviction, because his alleged victim did not "indicate her displeasure by means […] including biting, kicking, and scratching."[8] Sometimes empowering females with disabilities requires reexamining what constitutes consenting to sex, taking into account factors such as cognitive delays, lack of physical autonomy, and lack of access to disability-related sex education.

—Jill Summerville

NOTES

1. Lenore Manderson and Susan Peake, "Men in Motion: Disability and Masculinity," in *Bodies in Commotion: Disability and Performance*, ed. Carrie Sandahl and Philip Auslander (Ann Arbor: University of Michigan, 2005), 230–244.

2. "Sexual Abuse," Minneapolis: Disability Justice, 2019.

3. "Violence Against Trans and Non-Binary People," Harrisburg: National Resource Center on Domestic Violence, 2019.

4. Jessica M. Goldstein. "At Bill Cosby's Sentencing, Two Men Emerge: An Elderly Blind Man and a Sexually Violent Predator," ThinkProgress, September 24, 2018.

5. "Harvey Weinstein Timeline: How The Scandal Unfolded," BBC News, February 24, 2020.

6. Ed Pilkington, "Harvey Weinstein Convicted of Rape at New York Trial," *The Guardian*, February 24, 2020.

7. "Weinstein Taken into Custody Without Walker After Guilty Verdict," NBC News Now, YouTube.

8. Cindy Luo, "He's Not Guilty Because Disabled Woman Didn't Fight Back?" *The Hartford Courant*, October 9, 2012.

Tinted

Tinted was commissioned by Extant Theatre Company (UK) for their slot in the Bloomsbury Festival as an extension of a 10-minute play called *To Be My Eyes*, originally performed as part of *The Words Are Coming Now,* a rapid response project to #metoo at Theatre 503.

* * *

Laura: Ugh. Late show. Full of twats.

People who hang out in boxes and refuse to go home like "We just need a photo. We paid a million pounds for these tickets." Gary's like "Laura, go in with your cane" and I proper exaggerate like "No, I can't take a photo" and they just sort of shuffle out like… "sorry … so sorry." Good to help any way I can. I'm in my tinted glasses (square frames) because it was a late finish (take the hint you twats) and I can't wear my contacts for too long. I've got a Rapunzel gig tomorrow up the mall and I need my eyes to look their best. When I went in to audition they were like,

"the thing is, we want to be accessible to you … but with kids…"

—I didn't let 'em finish. I just started singing. And they were like "Yeah, your singing will convince them." When in doubt, just sing at people.

Finally, I've got back, and my tights and pants are in the wash and I'm doing that millennial thing of watching my laptop before bed. It's late and there aren't any buses at night, so Dad has to pick me up even though his gout's getting bad and it knackers him. I've been action planned for cashing up too slowly and it's been agreed that someone's gonna help me do it, but otherwise they're good. There's also the customers that see me count pound coins out holding them right up to my face and say, "Isn't it good they employ you?" Thankfully Gary's got his head screwed on there and tells the guy to fuck off. Well he doesn't say *fuck off*. He says "jog on" though, or he did once.

I'm in the changing room about to leave and this girl, Alice—who's like cash-up *supergirl* doing till stuff the managers are doing and knows how do her hair in a fishtail plait and sells knitting on Etsy—talks about her psychology dissertation. She's like, "our generation"—meaning hers and mine even though I'm like 8 years older than her—"our generation, we have helicopter parents and it really has an effect on our mental health … it's like we have a prolonged childhood because of what our parents have done to the economy. By the way Laura, we still need a housemate for next year and we all watch *Bake Off* together—we'll put the AD on for you," and she leaves.

I imagine telling Mum and Dad that I've been thinking of moving out and

I think it hits me because it's late and I've been dealing with twats all day, but I burst into tears. I didn't know that it was okay to feel like … to feel like … see, I even feel guilty saying it now … to feel like too much is being done for you. But every time I try and bring it up, I get told "That's them. This is you. It's not a race." They can't see me cry under my glasses, so I just leave and get in Dad's car and practice for my Rapunzel gig on the CD. Dad's like "you know Rapunzel actually means lettuce, because of the rampion. There are patriarchal connotations in the witch and the prince isn't supposed to get his sight back … it's the idea that they're both damaged now …" A grown-up conversation that only Dad can start.

This morning before work I had, "Laura, we care about you and memories you share on Facebook. We thought you'd like to look back at this post from 5 years ago."

Did you, Mark Zuckerberg? Is that what you thought?

Hey, Mum, what's in this photo?

"It's you and … him … and you're wearing those star glasses … funny, you never wear 'em now, do you?"

No, Mum. I don't wear any of the bloody glasses you bought me either. Especially not the first sodding pair. Hello, Deidre Barlow, may she rest in peace.

Those glasses. Those bloody glasses.

But that isn't what Mark Zuckerberg's showing me now. Now … it's you. #metoo. "Glad to see things are finally coming out of the woodwork and women are finally speaking up. #nogreyarea." What is that? Is it a dare? You? Posting that? "Laura, we care about you and the memories you put on facebook." The memories you post on facebook. They're not memories when you post them. They're brags. Memories are … memories are…

I'm four years old and Mum whacks my first glasses on my face and they're the size of hub caps cos it's the '80s and everyone wears them but I'm 4 and my face is tiny. I'm peering over the top of them because they're too heavy like the world's cutest mad scientist. Pink frames. *My Little Pony*. With them, I look at this photo of me on the wall and for the first time I see that my eyes are rolling inwards like this … And I look in the mirror with them and I see through the dark lenses that they're all like changing again … They're gonna keep changing. And those glasses need to be there while they do it. I get my My Little Ponies out and I'm always Sweet Stuff. "Come on Galaxy, we need to save the rainbow from the trolls. They've already got pink and they're coming for the other colors." "Well actually, Sweet Stuff, pink isn't in the rainbow." "What? Am I seeing it wrong?" "No, it is in My Little Pony's Rainbow but in a real rainbow—'All right Dad can we just use the rainbow we've got please?'" "Sorry love. Just thought I'd give you a taste of the real world."

When that hashtag came out … I felt … I felt bit sick. This stuff being like mainstream seemed to make it all so … simple. I knew. I knew it wasn't as easy as … and I thought of things I'd said. Stuff I'd done. And I didn't see it that way at the time.

I'm 11 (Glasses are smaller but not much, mosaic frames. I look more like an owl than a mad scientist) and I'm about to have my second eye op. They know better than to give me a Bravery Award when I wake up because I can't open my eyes and I'm grumpy. I just sit eating chicken nuggets with my eyes closed. Mum's like "well when your eyes open, you can draw them a picture. Draw the *Rugrats*. You like drawing the Rugrats." Mum's good at stuff like that. I draw a very average picture of the Rugrats. Sometimes Mum does know better than me what I want.

When I first played a Mario game at your house … I wanted to do the stuff you were doing with your mates. But I was like "I can't play Mario. I'll meet you after." But you were like "Come anyway" And you'd gone on the internet and downloaded an audio reader for bloody Mario! I did not know that was a thing. I'm playing Mario for the first time! I love the little ghosts—they're too cute to kill. I love the games. How much of a geek would I be if I'd known about this?!

So then it's my turn—show you all the My Little Ponies! And you're googling them and telling me how much my pony castle is worth now it's vintage and how I should look for ones on e-bay but something you do on e-bay is look for typos because people don't bid on listings with typos … It's … sweet. You're taking an interest … in me … and like there's nothing to stop me doing that with Mario or whatever … It's just … you want all of me…

Galaxy was the purple unicorn. I think she was purple. They've got a new My Little Pony out now haven't they, and there's another purple unicorn? Is She-ra coming back as well? I was in H&M the other day and I couldn't tell by feeling whether something was a top or a sports bra or what, and the assistant's like "it's a crop top" and I'm like "from the '90s?!" and she's like "Yeah. People bring stuff back but like … ironically." I'm just there feeling, well, old.

Like, I know all the guys are doing it since #metoo. "I solemnly swear that I have never mistreated a woman, not even to steal her last Rolo." And there's something about guys who post that … like, why do you need to? But there's something … something in particular about yours … your #nogreyarea. I mean, when I look at stuff, there are a lot of grey areas to me. That's about half a joke. If there's no grey area, where does that leave you? Where does that leave us?

They talk about our generation being dreamers, about never being satisfied. I dream about … about living in a flat … doesn't have to be alone … could be with randoms … and just … going to the chippy at 10 p.m. cos I want to and knowing that it's a poor life decision and tweeting about my poor life decision. Mine. I don't know what I'll want if I ever have that, but that's where I am right now. I want to tell Mum and Dad that I have this dream. I couldn't even tell Dad I could find my own way to school because we always listened to the same music in the car every morning and I knew he liked it. It was part of his routine. Driving me. Knowing I was safe. It made him feel better. People said I was lazy and it was actually a longer journey from the carpark to the school than it was from my house to the carpark, but I thought if I could show Dad I still needed him for some stuff, he might be okay with me not needin' him for other stuff ... people like to feel needed. They like to do things for each other.

There was that time you saw me on Fisher Road when I was going to my singing lesson. (Twenties, so contacts). I knew where I was going but ... I like using the cane for that bit of road cos it's a bit dodgy in the ice. And then you're there and you kiss me and it's not the "yes it is me and I'm letting you know I want you" kiss, it's the "guess who, it's me, I'm here to help you!" kiss. And you whacked my arm through yours and it was like ... and I know couples do that but I guess ... it is different. I'm not gonna say it shouldn't be because I don't think we should talk about shouldn't.

The first time you and I did stuff ... I didn't know we'd do stuff. I just thought I was staying over. Dad's like "be careful" and I'm like "I'm not gonna do anything." I don't even know what to do. Like when Mrs. Dickins in Sex Ed who was like 55 and wore pleated skirts and a netball whistle would talk about this stuff, I'd zone out. She wasn't talking to me. I'd never do that. She got this model cock out of the drawer at the front of the class, but it was blue, and I was like "what's that?" and everyone laughed, and she went "it's a penis, Laura" and I was like "don't laugh at me—it's fucking blue!" So, Mrs. Dickins passes it to me to feel and I'm like "oh yeah, it is a penis" and everyone laughs again. I'm not saying you should have ... passed me yours to feel ... I mean, I suppose that's one way to do it. I think my glasses were silver ovals then.

The thing with #nogreyarea is, well ... it's just not true, is it? Like, you can't say it's a culture *and* say that everyone who does it is a monster. This isn't My Little Pony. With the ponies and the trolls fighting over a magic rainbow. Everyone wants to save the magic rainbow, but they've all got different ideas how to do it. If people with sighted girlfriends are confused, what hope did you bloody have? There's no access guide to sex: how to consensually shag your blind girlfriend.

Like, I can put my boots on on my own. I have trouble with trainers. Mum forgets that sometimes and helps me with the boots—and like all kids—like adult kids get it don't they, even ones my age are like "Mum!" when she's wiping their face whatever. I mean I don't actually mind her wiping my face as long as she tells me she's doing it. Just like "Laura, you've got pasta on your cheek so I'm gonna wipe it off for you." I mean, I think I'd like "shall I wipe it off for you?" a bit better. Sometimes when we cross the road, she just grabs my arm and I scream because I don't know it's her but then she just goes "hold Mummy's hand" and like...

That's what we were all like. Ironic. Like, you could all make jokes about women in kitchens and the chain being too long ... about how being different races made people different and like ... how gays were ... gay. It was obvious we didn't mean it, so we could say it and anyone who thought we meant it was stupid! But then after that you'd read stuff on, like, facebook. You read it to me because facebook didn't do screenreaders then. And like ... there were people who meant it. And I should have known then ... where this was all going ... I should have seen … I should have seen where thinking like that and laughing at stuff like that would bring you … would bring us.

That first night we're lying together and you just start … touching me. You're all like, "It's all about you. We can do whatever you want." I stop listening to my brain as my brain has always told me that this isn't for me. But now it is. It so is and "No!" I stop you at going the whole way. When you stop listening to your brain and listen to your body, that's called seduction. I don't know what's happening, what my body's doing but in the movies the women have all got their eyes closed anyway so I thought maybe it was just like that. If my body says … if my body says it's enjoying it, maybe I should listen. But my body isn't reliable is it? It tells me a lot of things that aren't true.

I go downstairs the next morning in one of your hoodies and your housemate's like "hi" in that way you do when you know your housemate's had sex. She doesn't know that actually we haven't had sex. I keep that bit. Because even my body still says no to that.

I mean, I used to talk like I'd had sex. We were all gobshites a long time ago. But now people are talking about stuff from a long time ago and … I can't help wondering if you're a bit scared. Like, when you say you've never mistreated a woman … that you've never … Like, who are you actually telling that to? I have to put on special glasses to read a computer screen and that's the only time I speak to you now. If I'm not in those glasses, I'm not talking to you. What glasses are you using?

Because I can. I can hear how many crisps are left and when you eat them you make the most annoying noises ever. I literally feel like you are building a picture of half masticated potatoes swirling around the endless abyss that is your mouth. It makes you smell like onions even if the lighting's a bit off and I can't see you. Like, when we watched the football (Radio Five Live on so I know everything that happens even though it's mildly annoying for you because it's a couple of seconds ahead of the picture), I don't want any crisps. If I wanted them, I would … I would reach out and take them because I can hear where you put the bowl and if I can't I can ask you. I don't … need them waved under my nose every five seconds … or even worse, like … shoved into my mouth.

I used to like cheese and onion. Maybe I ate too many of them as a kid. It takes me a while to work out if I like something to eat. I'm seven. (Glasses are still round, rainbow frames with a cross bar). The TA's like "Laura, you're not still eating your lunch, are you?" I'm really slow that day because my apple is covered in bruises and I'm not sure when I get to one, so it just goes all soft and weird but still really sweet, so I can't work out if I like it or not. It's a school trip to a power station. We all have to wear hard hats and ear plugs (yeah, well-done school, take away my main sense, I'm gonna learn loads today, aren't I?) and the most fascinating thing is the chocolate lollies in the gift shop. At seven, we have no idea why we're there. Twenty-five years later I still don't. The thing I remember most is looking for my class and seeing them through the tinted glass door, lining up outside the coach with their coats and their Mr. Men lunchboxes. Except it isn't a door. It's a glass wall. Like a really big fuck-off window and I just walk straight into it—BAM! And a chip falls off my rainbow-framed glasses. There's a weird pattern in the corner of the glass. I'm screaming cos I bumped my head and that night I hear Mum on the phone to the school like "my daughter is visually impaired, and you left her to get out of the building on her own?!" "Mum, what's visually impaired?"

That photo from this morning. I'm in my sunglasses and my head's on your shoulder and I'm making lemon face cos I was like "is this ginger beer?" and you weren't looking and were like "yeah" but it was bitter lemon and ugh! It's got lots of likes cos my face is funny. Someone's saying I should make it my profile picture. I used to have a printout of it but when we broke up you said to move it out the way. "Break-ups are hard. This will make things easier for you. Trust me." Funnily enough, pictures don't have the same effect on me, but then that's just another thing you don't know, isn't it?

I'm 18. I've lost loads of weight because apparently that can happen when you're 18. I keep getting told I look great, but I should wear contacts. I can't wear contacts because you can't tint contacts though I'm really into *Harry Potter* at this time and love the idea of my eyes changing color like they do when Lupin turns into a werewolf. I get so angry at the end of *Prisoner of Azkaban*. I don't know why and then when I'm older I realize that Dumbledore is being an apologist for werewolf discrimination. I mean, yeah, the job was cursed but still…

Okay, yeah, I've always been a geek.

I know that everyone in Sixth form is copping off with each other except me. I say this to my learning mentor Marie who's a strawberry blonde which isn't a concept I quite get but okay and she says, "well who do you want to cop off with?" And I'm like … "no-one" and she seems confused and looks at me with her big blue eyes which apparently aren't strawberry blue because that isn't a thing. Like, that's not the point. I just wanna know that I could cop off with someone if I wanted and I convince myself that the reason why I'm not is the tinted glasses. I mean, I also have Dad dropping me off everywhere, but I could do something about the tinted glasses. I know … I know … copping off would eventually lead to … and who knows … no-one can really know … I'm working this out … So, I work it out with Mr. Markham that I can wear contacts if I wear sunglasses when I'm outside. It takes the guy in Vision Express (I think his name's Sid, really mild-mannered Australian bloke) over an hour to get them in as no-one's ever touched my eyes while I'm awake. He's like "not to worry. I'll give you a little break" But I keep going with it. I'm determined. And soon I can get them in in 5 minutes. I'm still not copping off but, in my head, I look like I might.

The thing that really draws me to you was that you get it. Or you act like you get it. And I think you want to get it and you want other people to get it. That boozy guest lecturer with the sick on his front, he used to think I couldn't hear him. I mean, I know people only want to do the right thing, but he speaks really slowly to me and I'm like "mate, I'm not deaf and even if I was that's not how you speak to anyone." Then he doesn't talk to me at all. He'll say "tell Laura" whatever he wants to say. He's not in his job long with Mum like "Has he been given any training at all?" And you really help with that shit. You sing, "Tell Laura I love her" every time he says it. Then you sing it to me yourself. And of course, you're joking. But you're not. And it's great. Because me and my blind eyes are something to banter with. That's where I want to go.

The first time we cop off is outside the club. I'm 23. Contact lenses. I know I fancy you. You wear a trilby, so I can tell who you are except it's an arts college and everyone wears something a bit like that. I've got pink streaks in my hair and my lipstick matches cos my color perception's bang on and everyone's like "for someone who can't see you can really paint your face" and that isn't without help from Mum but they don't need to know that and even if they did they wouldn't judge cos it's not like that here. "For someone who can't see." They all take shit like that so literally. "For someone who can't see, you sure know how to put an outfit together." "For someone who can't see, your boyfriend's really fit." I know you're fit. Just because I can't see it as well as others doesn't mean I don't know. I get it by your voice and you knowing it and I get to touch you and smell you and the bits I can see are very clearly fit. You've got a girlfriend when we first kiss. She's fit too. But we're in the club and "Poison" by Alice Cooper is playing and I can hear you singing it in my ear and I'm not sure if you're singing it to me. But you're getting closer and closer and our lips touch but if I'm gonna kiss you I want to know that that's what's happening so I ask if we can go out and I take your hand and I ask if you want to kiss me because I'm not gonna be that bitch that comes onto someone else's boyfriend and you respond by kissing me. Your tongue's in my mouth and I'm not sure I'm doing it right and there's no fireworks or anything but it's a kiss. And I don't like being that bitch. But I've got to take what I can get. I'm 23.

It's my 12th birthday. Glasses are dark orange framed. All my mates are coming round and we're going to the AD showing of *Antz* and they're all really excited cos they've never been to an AD showing before. I'm worried cos I've still got Teletubby figurines on my bookshelf. At primary school we used to watch Teletubbies ironically but at seniors that's still watching it. It just never occurs to me to take stuff down. Should I hide them? Mum says "Just tell them you collect cartoon characters because you do." And it's true. But I'm in the wanting to be cool stage and I hate myself for it. But then they like them. They think they're sweet. They think I'm sweet. So, it's ok. I'm still cool. I'm just cool and sweet.

You know, I was ready to get over it if stuff went wrong. Because that's what I've always done. I like him, but I know he'll never like me, so I'll get over it. Not because he won't want me ... I mean ... from what I've *heard* I'm quite attractive ... that was a joke ... but because he's gonna get pissed off meeting me places and reading menus and going to AD cinema showings. I thought maybe I didn't like boys. But then one would come along, and I'd know I did. I get pissed off with it, so he definitely will. Or he's got a girlfriend or he's really, really into sex and I don't want to get into that because he won't get it … but you … you don't seem to care.

It was Polly Pockets as well as ponies. Not the new ones where they have to make them all bend and shit these were the really little ones that bent over with a hinge. And they didn't have big fuck off houses.

It was those really simple smooth cases. I could see better then but even when I closed my eyes, I could feel them well enough to make a good story. They had English accents even though I watched all American TV. And some of them married my Mighty Maxes (which was weird—he was a kid) and some of them married each other which was well progressive back then. I made all my toys get married but I never really thought about doing it myself. I just put them together and worked out who looked together. I was never in my games. I was the director, controlling everyone else. I put couples together if the colors went together, like Galaxy with the yellow pony.

When I started the seniors, they didn't know what to do with me. I had my statements and that, but I didn't throw chairs and run out of lessons like the other statement kids. Though I did like going to photocopying building. With Angie and Sue and Nat's mum saying which teachers were dickheads and smoking and drinking coffee, so sometimes I'd say a sheet wasn't big enough, just so I could go and hang out with them. There was a story on the wall about a sparrow singing in a pile of shit that I used to get them to read to me until they enlarged it. That place got closed. And I couldn't stick being in lessons with no way of getting out. So, I started being one of those kids who threw chairs cos I knew they got to leave.

Those glasses. Those other glasses. There was Pete, do you remember? He was in our Performance Art group. I've got my instructions for the workshop blown right up but we've got a guest lecturer, so I had to wait for them and he's like "Instead of getting everything blown up, why don't you just get new glasses?" For one moment, I wish I'd gone to science college instead and never mind that I'd have blown myself up as soon as I got in. You're straight in like "Yeah Laura, your optician must be really stupid." Like you've said stuff like that before but this is when I think maybe … you get it. And we find these giant star-shaped shades in the SU shop and I start wearing them and telling Pete that I can see if I've got them on, but they're the only ones they make so I have to wear them. And everyone's in on it. And Pete is the joke and maybe it is a bit mean … but seriously what a twat. And people always thought I was bit funny but when we did that, they thought I… we … were really funny. We got together at some point during that. And I wore those glasses, even when Pete wasn't around. I did an audition with them.

The other day I tweeted about how I get sexually harassed more when I've got the cane because it isn't about sex. It's about power. Autocorrect changes sexually harassed to sexually harnessed and next thing I know you've tweeted me a pictured of a pony harness and a winky face which you then transcribe. Tom from work who I tell everything to pops up in my facebook chat like "why is he making that joke? OMG I hate him!" I wonder if I should tell my feminist friend who gave you a like. But it isn't really worth it. Tom's enough for me right now.

Sometimes I still freak out if someone goes near there. When I had my last smear they asked about it and it was really hard to explain as I didn't really get it myself … the nurse, Linda, who's got the most massive fuck-off fob I'ever seen like even I can read it and she's proper Bristol with "l"s on the ends of all her words … she's like "I'm not a blind specialist." Then she asks me what kind of music I sing, and could I demonstrate … as she shoves her hand up my twat. Now I'm scared to shag anyone in case I burst into song. I know she wanted to distract me because it had to be done. I guess that was your thinking too. I was just there like "Yeah … maybe not now … come to one of my gigs though …"

I remember the first time I went to look at a uni—I was only about 15 but Dad took me anyway because he knew it had a recording studio and he was fed up of me moping around. I liked it mainly cos other people were there with their dads. At school nobody had dads and their relationships with whoever they had instead weren't great. I know that makes me the lucky one but when they're all sodding off to town and you're waiting around to be guided everywhere you feel a bit like … and thinkin' your parents don't understand you is part of being a teenager, but I don't think they'll ever understand that … or you…

I know it's hard for them too. Dad's always dropped me off at school and I just didn't have the heart to tell him I knew the way because I knew he'd worry. It might not have helped, but the people I love have always been more important to me than … than street cred. And that goes for you too.

Mum said … never change for a man. We never had the sex chat. I never listened when they tried to have it in schools. It wasn't for me. It was for people who were actually gonna do it. I would make a life for myself not doing it. I would work alone, and I would love all my friends and they'd be all I'd need. It would be easy. Then you came along, and it was … amazing.

I'm 15. Oval glasses. All me mates are going to town. Mum says "You're not going. If you want to go to town we'll go together another time." "Aw Mum, I don't wanna go to town. I just wanna go out with me mates!" "Well why can't you go out with your mates … round here?" "You don't get it!" I'm ready to go home after school but Nat takes my arm like "where you goin?" and I'm like "home. I need to practice this stuff." She says, "I'll look after you" and it's before everyone has phones so I just go. It's fun. I'm having an adventure. On the bus with them saying the stops when they remember … but then I'm chatting away … and there's no-one there for me to talk to. They've left me on the bus. And I start to panic, and the driver comes upstairs and he doesn't want to touch me cos I'm a young girl alone on a bus but when I say "I don't know where I am" he's proper worried and he phones his boss "I've got a young lady here, she's a bit anxious and disorientated. Says she's got sight problems" and then a police officer comes in and discovers that I'm blind not senile and phones Mum. Then Nat comes back like "Come on! I thought you were behind me!" but I never want to speak to her again. And Mum says "I didn't want to send you to a school for the blind because I wanted you to integrate and know you could do all the things everyone else could do but if that's what you're gonna do, maybe it's the best option!" It's okay because I'm never gonna do it again. Until the next time I do.

Sometimes my body freaks out all on its own. I have to take control of it. Remind myself that I can … I can move away if I want to. That I can feel if anything comes near it, even if I can't see. That's part of anxiety apparently, your body always preparing you for stuff that isn't happening but might, and when you can't see what's happening … well the possibilities are endless. You don't need boring numbers about sensory impairment and mental health. Unless you're out there looking for someone else to "educate" … someone who literally doesn't have perception or someone who hasn't met one of you before … someone who … who wants to be saved and educated like their brain and their fanny is just on the receiving end. But I think you're right—it does always hurt the first time. Fanny and head. It hurts that you … it hurts that you didn't think I could make that decision. It hurts that you took it away.

Do I want those glasses? The purple ones with the stars? I don't think I do. They don't … they're not … they are the bit of us that belongs here.

Those glasses were on the windowsill. The purple ones. They weren't that bad at blocking the sun, actually. But they were purple. They turned you purple. Everything purple.

It was quite early on when we first tried. Apparently, it's an anxiety thing that women can close up down there. And of course, it's gonna happen when you can't bloody see what's coming. You were genuinely alarmed when I said I didn't want to do it. You said we'd try again and then you put *Ren and Stimpy* on. You said it probably would hurt the first time and we'd try again another day. I said nothing. I don't know if you noticed. We didn't try again that first night. Maybe I just really wanted to watch *Ren and Stimpy*.

Once I had a dream that Galaxy was trotting 'round the pony castle. She spoke to me. But not in the voice that Dad used for her. But that wasn't Dad's fault. He didn't know what was in my head.

What's in my head now is that … is that … that jobs aren't for me unless I'm really convincing … that I'm too young for my age … is that I can only have sex when I'm not expecting it.

The glasses. The purple glasses. They're on the windowsill in their big camp star shape with the light making shadows of purple stars on the white ledge. It's mid-afternoon, Orange Wednesday so cinema later. *Rango*. We're kissing. Your bed isn't the comfiest. People joke and say we broke the mattress. You're inside my bra and I let you take stuff off because you do it pretty much the same way every time now, so I know what's going on. And it's hands but then … then there's something else…

I said … I said … what's that?… and you said, "it's my penis, Laura" and I was like… "but you didn't say" and I felt the push and the slight prising apart and I was like "oh yeah … it is your penis." And I said, "can you take it out" and you were like "yeah … sorry. All right. But we've got to find some way round this." But you did. Something felt like it was burning … I didn't know … I didn't know if I'd done more of my body saying yes… "Am I bleeding?" "A little bit. I'll get a tissue." "Well … we may as well do it again now." It hurts when we do it again. And again. Not just down there. And not just me.

A month later, you're ringing me asking if you can pick me up from work. You want to do this face to face. I know what you're going to say. Face to face doesn't serve me. You're not enough for me. You need a girlfriend you can have sex with.

Your words chime out like a really shit xylophone where they only let you have one key. I don't feel anything. Your words and your body have just made me numb. Maybe the next time I let someone inside me, it'll be better. And I'll know I'm doing it.

You took it out when I asked you. You took it out when I asked you. I kept saying that over and over in my head. You took it out when I asked you.

You took it out when I asked you. And with it, you took us. You took the glasses and the crisps and the My Little Ponies and everything we did together, every laugh we had. Because those laughs weren't with me or at me. You were laughing for me. "You never liked condoms, Laura. It hurt less without. I was just gonna withdraw." Nice to know you had a plan. Maybe you could have let me in on it? But that's just it, isn't it? I don't get let in on things. That didn't start with you. None of us disableds get let in on things. My whole life … maybe not my whole life but most of my life … has just been a series of other people's plans. Maybe everyone else really did know best. Like all the times I've gone against it, it hasn't gone well. But it would have been nice to like … fuck something up by myself.

Maybe I fucked this up. Maybe I just really wanted to watch *Ren and Stimpy* that night.

I wear my contacts cos I've gone through too much bloody pain not to. And I still date men. I like my glasses too. It's taken a while, but I do. They're comfy in the sunlight. And if I want to take them off, I'll take them off. Because sometimes, that makes things clearer.

And I message Alice like "hey what are the details of that room again?" and I forward them to Dad. He's seen it. He replies through my screen reader "It probably doesn't have tinted glass." He's typing. "Let's go and look it together. Can't do this week but next." And I put my Rapunzel wig on its nightstand. And I smell it to make sure it's clean. And then I type the thumbs up sign, shut my computer and go to bed. I've still got my glasses on. I take them off and put them on the windowsill.

I don't need them tomorrow, but it's good to know they're there.

End of play.

Invisidisability

a multiple sclerosis play

ANONYMOUS

As discussed in the essay leading into Graham Bryant's *RPM*, disclosure of disability is a complex series of decisions, social negotiations, and often—even in cases of "best intentions" on the part of all parties—negative consequences. Additionally, unlike the standard rhetorical narrative in which disclosure (or "coming out") is framed as a singular and immediately transformative/emancipative act, the decision to disclose is ongoing, re-adjudicated with every new meeting, environment, and situation. As noted by Margaret Price, et al., in their consideration of disclosure within the academy, "Instead of being a single occurrence that leads to subsequent understanding, disability disclosure is better understood as an ongoing rhetorical process in which faculty members repeatedly need to address their disability for various audiences, across many different contexts."[1]

Anonymous describes several instances in which those around her have known about her disability, and yet she remains largely in a state of non-disclosure. Is she "out of the closet"? If not, at what point does an individual reach that threshold? Is there a percentage of social disclosure that must be met? What expectations are placed on her if she chooses to disclose? Price, et al., query the rhetoric of disclosure, policy decisions which demand disclosure for access to accommodations, and even question the helpfulness of terms like "invisible disability."

> The "visibility" metaphor implies accountability: it assumes that the disabled person who is "invisible" is responsible for making himself visible, or discernible. When we make this assumption, responsibility for alleviating injustice is placed upon the person suffering the injustice in the first place. Oppressed persons should not bear the burden of educating and reforming their oppressors, and yet, that is what the visible/invisible metaphor asks of disabled people.[2]

If she does not disclose, is it "her own fault" if she faces inaccessibility at work or in public spaces? If she does disclose, what level of information and "performative" disability does she owe to others? Utilizing an accessibility parking placard or plate, many of which are still emblazoned with the inappropriately specific wheelchair icon, is a forced act of public disclosure to any stranger who may pass her car. As seen in her monologue, many take that discloser as an invitation to look with a diagnostic gaze to determine whether the driver is "disabled enough" to justify the accommodation. If she passes the test and is believed, she then faces "well-meaning" suggestions of diet changes, pseudoscience, and more. If she stays silent, she is at fault for inaccessibility; if she discloses, she is judged as a potential fake; if she passes judgment and is deemed authentic, she is at fault for not doing more to cure herself.

In her influential piece "Disability and Representation," Rosemarie Garland-Thomson takes up this idea of the disabled individual—whether ill or not—being received as guilty of their disability:

> Modernity pressures us relentlessly toward standardizing bodies, a goal that is now largely accomplishable in the developed world through technological and medical interventions that materially rationalize our bodies under the banner of progress and improvement. We are told that if we buy the right products, cultivate the right habits, pay careful attention, and use the most sophisticated medical technology, we can banish disability from our lives. Strong disincentives such as social stigma and a sense of somehow having failed to "overcome" or "beat" life's inevitable limitations pressure us not to identify ourselves as persons with disabilities.[3]

Despite her "outing" herself, Anonymous still ends the play with her secret. Disclosure of any marginalized identity still invites a cornucopia of anxiety and practical concerns, and disclosing a chronic illness like M.S.—especially in as exhausting a field as technical theatre—risks, paradoxically, losing the trust and faith of colleagues and employers. Once again, she's at fault if she does, and at fault if she doesn't.

—John Michael Sefel

Notes

1. Margaret Price, Mark S. Salzer, Amber O'Shea, and Stephanie Kershbaum, "Disclosure of Mental Disability by College and University Faculty: The Negotiation of Accommodations, Supports, and Barriers," *Disability Studies Quarterly* 37, no. 2 (2017).

2. *Ibid.*

3. Rosemarie Garland-Thomson, "Disability and Representation," *PMLA* 120, no. 2 (2005): 522–27, www.jstor.org/stable/25486178.

Invisidisability

* * *

On the stage, there is a stool with a mic on a stand immediately down-stage of it, the cable trailing offstage. A small table is next to the stool. It looks like a standard, fairly boring, lecture-type setup. House lighting is at full, with a general stage wash creating a typical preshow look.

A female stagehand enters, wearing a wired headset, its cable running offstage from the direction she entered, and one of "those" tech theatre t-shirts—black, with text that says "Stage Crew: If you can see me something has gone terribly wrong!" or something quite similar. She brings a bottle of water for the performer and sets it on the table next to the stool, double checks the placement of both pieces, ensures they are on spike. A cursory glance at the mic to ensure everything is in order. Nods to herself and begins to exit in the direction from which she entered. She hears something on her headset. Presses the talk button briefly.

Stagehand (*into headset, still walking offstage*): Yeah, what's up?

Full stop, listening. Turns, looks up at the booth with an expression reminiscent of the "blinking man" meme. Speaks into the headset while making eye contact with the booth:

Excuse me? (*pause*) What? Why? (*longer pause, becoming incredulous*) Like what? (*another pause*) Are you serious?... I mean, no, are you actually serious right now?

She turns away from the booth, as though to try to leave the stage again, seeking some modicum of privacy for the following. It might begin at a volume that the audience can't hear clearly but by the end they can understand each of the last five words:

What...?! How come I... But what about ... I don't see why that's something ... no ... I get it ... I'm not saying that, I just ... I KNOW what the professional model is, but what if ... no ... no ... but ... because ... I'M NOT AN ACTOR, DAMMIT!

Still facing offstage (she almost made it to the safety of the wing), we see her stop, tense up with the sudden realization that she's not getting out of this. A brief moment while she composes herself—a big breath, then she turns and takes a few steps back onto the stage.

To Audience:

Hi there!

Umm...

so...

Welcome to the show!

I mean, you're probably astute enough to realize this isn't IT… So … yeah… I'm the ASM… "assistant stage manager."

It appears that the … performer … um, the playwright, or … whatever … um, the person who does the show got into some sort of mishap on the way here… (*interrupts herself to reassure the audience*) I mean, it sounds like she's FINE. Like, everything is FINE. She's just … not … here right now. But (*uncomfortable chuckle*) I mean, HERE WE ARE! And you know what they say … on with the show! Or … the show must go on! Or … whatever.

Which… (*getting a little amused*) I mean, really … It's a one-person show. Like what are we ACTUALLY supposed to do if she's not here?

So… (*slowing down, to explain*) there's this precedent, like this thing that happens sometimes, where the ASM goes on for the performer, right?

I mean, it goes back to before there were always understudies, and actually still sometimes they'll even add it to contracts on Equity shows … it just goes back to the ASM's duties being basically whatever needs to be done … Like, preset all of the props, sweep the stage, maybe get the coffee or whatever…

… but USUALLY you, the audience, are NEVER supposed to see me or have any idea I'm there. I mean, that's why we dress all in black (*gestures to herself, realizes the text on her shirt is exhibit A*) I mean, it's such a thing they sell us t-shirts about it, right?

Like, usually, if you see the crew on stage during the show, something has gone really wrong. We're like ninjas backstage. And even if we do a scene change or something onstage, it should be in blackout or you should be focused on the action and we should just be, like, invisible. And I'm SO OKAY with that, I mean that's actually WHY this is my thing.

Now, I know a guy … a stage manager in New York, and when he was working on this Nathan Lane play … *Front Page* I think it was? I mean, this is BROADWAY, folks … and he's the stage manager backstage, which means he's running the deck, kind of like what I'm doing here … except, you know … on BROADWAY. And he's ALSO the Understudy for the Sailor. Like, on his Equity contract. So, after a few weeks of running this show, I see him post this photo from his ASM station backstage? And he is in this SAILOR COSTUME and was actually going on stage as the Sailor that night. Which was just hilarious to me, because, you know, it's so antithetical to so much of what you think of as a backstage tech type of person, like there he is next to his prompt desk in this BRIGHT WHITE sailor costume, which was just adorable, by the way, and he's about to go OUT ONTO THE STAGE of this, like, BROADWAY SHOW and ACT behind NATHAN FREAKING LANE!!! I mean… (!!!) So anyway … Like, it's a thing that happens, that ASMs sometimes go on for actors who can't make it or if something happens.

But, like … that's not really me. You might have noticed that I am NOT a "performer" type of person…

… or someone who's comfortable in front of a…

> *She chuckles, a little self-consciously. She crosses over to the stool and drags it downstage of the mic, closer to the audience. Perching a bit, becoming slightly more comfortable. At this point, if the technology in the venue permits, there should begin a super-slow fade of the house lights down to a dim glow. The shift should be imperceptible as it's happening.*

But then ... viola ... the performer doesn't show and the stage manager up there in the booth says talk to the audience and tell them what's going on and "buy some time"... (*maybe another glance shot at the booth here*) and here we go ... the unexpected ... which, you know ... is FINE... because that's basically the job. I mean, prepare and anticipate as much as possible, but when things go wrong ... Adapt. Creatively problem-solve. Wing it.

So.

Here I am.

And here you are...

> *awkward pause*

And HERE'S the funny thing about this situation, is that it's like this one-woman show, right? So, like, I don't even have a SCRIPT I can read from! Like, this was supposed to be an easy gig, you know? Sweep the stage, set some water, hang out backstage in case anything goes awry, and make a few extra dollars, easy ... And then "awry" happens. ...But yeah, this is fine, and apparently she's on the way, so...

> *another awkward pause*

What is this thing actually ABOUT, anyway? (*Genuinely asking the audience*) I mean, do you know? Like, what IS the show, actually? (*Seeking an audience member who has their program readily available, making eye contact...*) I mean ... Do you mind? Can I just see your program? I mean, it's not like the ushers hand them out to us backstage ... Could I maybe just ... yeah?

> *She crosses to the patron, takes the program, with appropriate thanks. She scans it as she returns to the stool. Remember that big ongoing lighting shift? It shouldn't even be halfway done yet.*

(*perching again*): Huh...

(*a dry chuckle*) MS, huh? A "disability play"? (*maybe a little bit of judgment there*) ...That's cool... (*To the patron who gave her the program, or perhaps another who seems particularly engaged ... or disengaged*) Do you know anything about MS? (*Improvises in response to the audience member/s and then picks up, conversationally, when appropriate*):

Yeah, I, uh ... I have this really good friend with MS, so I know a lot about it... 'cause, um...

We actually lived together, you know ... yeah, we were roommates in college. Yeah, she's awesome. (*chuckles*) It's funny ... because now there are commercials for some of the MS drugs on the TV, and I asked her about one of them last time we talked, which, you know ... I'm sure she hated.

(*confidentially*) Like, I remember whenever anyone ... like, if they actually found out that she had MS...

> *Interrupts herself with the realization that maybe she should explain that*

I mean... (*to any audience member that expressed familiarity with the topic earlier*) you know, right? Sometimes it can be really obvious, sure, but sometimes people can have it and you'd never even realize.

And she's one of those people. And boy, does she prefer to keep it that way...
For people to not know about it. At all.

So, she would just go through an entire day, and then she'd get home and would just be, like, useless. Just completely worn out. And, I mean, I also reached a new understanding of the word exhaustion during college, don't get me wrong, but this was ... different.

So, the way I understand it is, like, if you take an extension cord ... or... (*looking at her headset cable*) really any kind of cable, it's transporting signal from one end to the other ... and there's this insulation and shielding around it (*she uses her cable as a prop*). So ... the actual conductive part, the part that the signal runs along from one end to the other, is way deep in the middle of this wire, and so the nervous system in the body works the same way ... the nerve cells conduct the signal and they have this shielding and insulation and THAT'S the part that gets messed up with MS...

Like the body ATTACKS it, basically it's like friendly fire, like...
If I cut through this headset cable and expose that inner part—

> *Quick stop, hears something over headset and looks at the booth like "seriously?"*

Which I am NOT GOING TO DO RIGHT NOW, OBVIOUSLY!!!

> *Slight shake of the head, perhaps a "can you believe that?" look*

Anyway, so if I were to cut this cord, like not entirely sever it but just kind of maul it...

Obviously the signal either isn't going to get through or it's going to have a lot harder time getting from point A to point B. And (*looking over at the mic cable*) like, the shielding part of it is that it keeps the signals from getting crossed or from interfering with each other, kind of in the same way as how we have to be really careful to keep sound and lighting cables from interfering with each other's signal, because otherwise things get really fuzzy and there's feedback, or they overheat...

> *By now that cue has completed and the house lights are at a dim glow — just bright enough to where the Stagehand can see and interact with the audience easily.*
>
> *Remembering where she was going with this:*

Yeah, so basically it just could cause this crazy exhaustion or, like, muscle weakness where things would just ... give out.

So she had this cane.

And she went through this whole thing of picking it out and it was really pretty—like this purple marble swirly kind of pattern—and then she just … hid it in the trunk of her car.

Did you see the thing Selma Blair did where she kind of like, came out with MS by showing up to the *Vanity Fair* red-carpet thing with her cane? And she has just been rocking the whole cane look ever since…

> *Perhaps connecting with any audience members who know what she's talking about*

Right? It's awesome. But yeah, this was very much NOT that. It was like that's what she wanted to do … the whole picking out something really beautiful … and then she just left it in her car, for "in case she needed it." But it was like her own idea of what would make her need it was so extreme … like, she would never use it … until this one day when things got so bad that she ACTUALLY used the cane. And I was talking to her in the hallway, and everyone … I mean EVERYONE who passed by kept stopping and asking her what had happened and was she okay. And I could tell she was so embarrassed and trying to explain to them that it wasn't an injury but it was this thing that happened sometimes but not other times and … just watching the way their faces would go from concern to puzzlement to this weird kind of disbelief or accusation of her … exaggerating? or faking, I guess? So, yeah, then the cane went back into the trunk and stayed there.

> *There's a sudden putting-together-of-pieces, one of those things that really suddenly strikes you as hilarious. She's laughing to herself.*

The cane was like a techie… (*gesturing once again to the shirt*) Like, if you saw the cane something had gone terribly wrong!

> *She's really amused by this, although probably nobody else is. Making the realization that she's alone in her humor … A pause … Looks around, obviously uncomfortable at having spoken so much…*

Wow. I'm thirsty. I am NOT used to talking that much…

> *A self-conscious chuckle, still looking around. She spots the water, crosses over to grab it.*

(*into headset*): I WILL set another one … when she gets here. If she gets here … Unless you'd like to trade places? … No? (*another glance at the booth*) … Yeah, that's what I thought. Thanks.

> *Shaking her head bemusedly, she heads back to the stool with the water, picks up the program.*

So who is it we're waiting on, anyway? (*reading. stops. looks at audience…*) Anonymous? You came here to see someone ANONYMOUS? How would someone even do one of these one-person show things anonymously? I mean … Why would…? … (*putting things together*)

I mean, I guess…

It's great the thing that Selma Blair is doing, but did you know Annette

Funicello had MS, too? Do you know who Annette Funicello WAS? (*depending on the audience response — nodding in agreement or shaking head*) Yeah, she was one of the original Mouseketeers on the *Mickey Mouse* show, and then she did all those Beach Party movies in the '60s? So she got diagnosed with MS in the '80s, I guess it was, but she hid it for YEARS. And not just from the public, but from some of her family and friends, too. Apparently, the only reason she came out about it at all is because she was losing her balance and everything, and someone started a rumor that she had become an alcoholic? And that was just so upsetting to her that it prompted her to finally go public.

So, yeah I guess she would have understood wanting to be anonymous.

(*pause*)

Which is like my friend, I suppose. It's like she really didn't ever want anyone to see or know about any of it because she was always really worried that people would look at her differently, like they did when she used the cane.

And then there were times when people DID find out about the MS, and they would mention how they had some friend or cousin or something, like SOME PERSON that they knew with MS, and then they would tell her all about how they changed their diet and started running marathons or whatever and how these … lifestyle changes … just helped them, you know, BEAT the disease or how this one diet was a CURE and it would just piss her off so much … I mean, she's one of those people-pleaser types, so she wouldn't ever actually say anything to them at the time, but wow would I hear about it afterward… (*laughs*) She'd be like "What the hell? That sounds great! Why didn't I think of just ADOPTING A HEALTHY LIFESTYLE to just GET OVER IT?" (*laughing at the memory*)

So, I asked her about the drug advertisements on the TV. And, you know, it was like she sort of had two responses to it.

Like, on the one hand it was like her … condition … actually had "made it" you know? Like into the ranks of ED and RA and whatever else … like all of these so-called "invisible diseases" … the ones that get primetime airplay for their pharmaceuticals. Which, really, apparently, is just because these things are like… "designer drugs." Did you know that? I mean, when we started living together, she was doing these daily self-injections … which apparently had been a huge thing for her, because she was super needle-phobic before all of this and then suddenly she's got to inject herself every day??? But I guess she did get over it because by the time we moved in together it was just a thing. I mean, at that point it was WAY weirder for me … because she would get these prefilled syringes from the pharmacy, and they had to be stored in the refrigerator, so like open up the fridge to grab the Riesling and … boom … syringes. Like HELLO! But the price tag … I mean it all worked out to where she could afford it and get her medicine, but with all of the hoops she had to jump through, and the actual cost … was $4000 A MONTH!!! I mean, yeah, there was this way that they moved the money around between the pharmacy and the drug company, but the whole thing just felt kind of weird and skeevy, you know? Like, worse than student loans. And then, I guess suddenly the shots weren't working any more…

So with all of the symptoms of those "crossed wires" and everything, apparently, these "treatments"—those aren't actually meant to do anything to help with the symptoms. Really. All of these drugs, therapies, or whatever are just to try to stop more damage from happening. Like, that's it. That's the goal … just for it to NOT GET WORSE. Did you know that? Like, there's no cure, which is bad enough, but, like, there's not even a way to fix what's gotten messed up. When, after all of these years, and, I'm sorry … after $4000 per MONTH the big goal is "let's not let this get worse than it is" and then it can't even do THAT? I mean… (*mimes "mind blown"*) That's crazy, man…

> *Settling into storyteller mode*

And do you know how they even tell if it's getting worse or not? Because whatever it looks like from the outside has NOTHING to do with what's going on inside. That's WHY they call it an invisible illness. Like … you just can't tell. So, I mean, obviously they CAN tell, but only by taking an MRI of your BRAIN. Can you imagine having this thing that's wrong with you and you have no idea what it's doing, and you have to do this crazy brain scan magnet picture thing to find out? And then what happens if it's nothing? Like … that's the "good news" version of events is you go through all of this crazy expensive testing just to find out that there's nothing new. So, like, whatever prompted them to check and see if it was getting worse is actually just the same old damage maybe manifesting in a different way. Which it can totally do. Because there are these things … check out this word… "pseudoexacerbations" (*eyebrows raised, let's that settle for a moment, delighting in the sound of it*) Right?

"Pseudoexacerbations." What a word. And it sounds like it's talking about something made up, right? But it's not. Not really … It just means that it's the existing damage suddenly getting stirred up and causing symptoms that it wasn't before, but without new damage. So like, if we take that frayed cable and we add heat … the heat will actually slow down the signal. I mean, that's why computers have fans in them and stuff, right? And so with the whole MS thing, it's actually really similar … It's like those coffee cups where you add hot liquid and then all of a sudden you see the picture that was invisible before, you know? So when she got overheated, it was like … BOOM. And not just the exhaustion, but it would be like, there's the limp or like there she goes dropping things, or even, like, the cognitive stuff … because you know there's cognitive stuff too, right? So it was almost like this on/off switch, but she wasn't the one in control of it.

Fortunately she had the parking thing … the handicap tag that goes up on the rearview mirror in the window? But that was just another thing that she was really weird about using. I mean, I think there was still that whole thing of being "disabled" but not in the usual way that you think about, and with the fact that her disease was so unpredictable and so it was almost like … like she was part-time disabled, if that makes sense? Ohmygosh, I mean I know that sounds so insensitive, but … you know? And so people just didn't get it. So if she parked far away in the morning she was fine getting into the building for classes, but then when she tried to leave … there was this one time that she literally called me, crying, to come help her because she couldn't get back to her car. So … again, at first I didn't get why she didn't just use the thing that the doctors and the DMV gave her to keep this from happening … But the problem was when people saw her getting out of her car and walking fine … they'd get really nasty, and they would leave these horrible notes and stuff on her car about how she was a fake and a fraud and using it to get good parking. Just crazy … and, I mean, it would really mess with her. Like, emotionally. So she would sometimes, sort of … I can't believe … but like, she would sort of act it out a little more sometimes … Like, if she knew someone was watching. (stops, thinks) …I mean, how messed up IS that? Like, you have this disability … this invisible thing that's attacking you that nobody can see, I mean the doctors can't even see unless they put you in an MRI machine, and you have to PRETEND to be … what … more disabled? differently disabled? more VISIBLY disabled? or else risk public shaming for using a tool that these medical and regulatory authorities gave you? I mean, there are lots of people with MS who DO need wheelchairs fulltime. But my roommate was … what … less disabled? (she's working through this, logically, as she's speaking) … I mean, but then I think of her calling me from the parking lot. She was literally physically unable to put one foot in front of the other. But … because that was a temporary condition … does that mean it … means less? I don't know… (a bit of a reverie…)

So when I saw the drug commercials! I mean, on one hand, it was like MS has kind of "made it" or whatever. I mean, because more people are talking about it and that means new research and new "treatments" and all of these things… (off onto another tangent) I mean, which is great, right? Because after those injections, after those stopped working, by then there was a PILL she could take, and she was so stoked. And she tried it, and it was actually keeping the invisible stuff from getting worse, and no more shots, and that's awesome, and then … she has to STOP taking it… (a pause) because of SIDE EFFECTS.

Isn't that just crap? … (A shift in tone, with a corresponding fade out of the house lights and increasing isolation on the stagehand. At some point she rises from the stool and paces a bit.)

I mean, here's something that's actually working and then I guess it was working TOO WELL… because, like, it did the job by making the white blood cells … the T-cells … go dormant and not attack the nerves, except only like MOST of them were supposed to go dormant but instead ALL of them were going dormant but the doctors got all freaked out because, like, her immune system was just GONE, but YOU COULDN'T TELL! I mean, she wasn't sick, she felt fine, actually … SHE FELT GREAT! And sort of almost … normal??? And they made her STOP… It was so … UNFAIR! (a pause)

So now it's infusions. Which need to happen at the cancer center because … it's NOT chemotherapy but it's LIKE a chemotherapy drug? And they actually use it to TREAT CANCER, so I don't know what makes it different, really. But the worst part about it is… (*her agitation is shifting to something else*)

… there's this bell on the wall. Like, with a string hanging down from it. And they ring the bell whenever someone has done their last dose of chemo. So it's like this big triumphant thing, and the person gets unhooked from their last round, and they walk or wheel over to this bell, and they ring it … and everyone is cheering for them and it's awesome and it represents hope for everyone else who's sitting there hooked up to their own private IV cocktail for however many more hours and however many more "treatments," but… (*she's very vulnerable, very alone on the stage*)

I'll never get to ring the bell.

Like, there's no "done" with this thing. I mean, I know there's no cure for cancer, either, but there's an END to the treatments. There's HOPE… for an end to each stage or type of intervention, to maybe reverse the damage, to make it shrink or go away, even. And then, if they're lucky, they get to go on with their lives … as a "Survivor."

But with this? "No progression" …and that's as good as it gets. It just goes on … and *I* just go on…

> *She looks around, realizing she has "outed" herself.*

Oh.

> *She removes her headset and places it on the stool.*

So … yeah…

> *Pause*

You know the thing about the TV commercials? The thing that really got me?

It's the paradox … This invisible enemy, taunting me from prime time. But it's not some foreign agent, you know? The thing is … the enemy IS my own body. The enemy is ME. I mean … that's really messed up, you know?

> *A wry laugh*

How is someone supposed to talk about this stuff "anonymously"? Why even try? I don't know … maybe that's why it helps to have a "friend." It just seems easier to stay behind the curtain.

Because usually you, the audience … you're never supposed to see me or have any idea I'm there.

I mean, that's why we dress all in black.

> *A smile, then she turns, leaving the headset behind on the stool, and exits to the wing she entered from. Blackout. There is no curtain call.*
>
> *End of play.*

Crooked

SEELEY QUEST

Perhaps the greatest challenge of intersectionality is finding one's position on the crossroads. Acknowledging intersectionality complicates two fundamental questions about the human experience: Who am i, and how does how i speak to the world reveal (or conceal) who i am? Intersectionality, simultaneous identification with multiple minority identities, is inseparable from visibility, insofar as it is an admission that certain aspects of one's identity (race, gender, sexuality, disability) may not be granted equal visibility in every circumstance, whether due to the sociocultural standards of a particular place and time or due to one's personal inclination. What then, are the benefits and the costs of revealing more than one aspect of one's identity in a particular place, the stage, especially if one is not playing a character? Does watching a performer with a disability struggle to button a blouse, for example, change how an audience evaluates that performer's embodiment of femininity?

The stage offers a performer an important advantage over the real world. Onstage, any revelation about one's identity must be viewed as a deliberate choice on the part of the performer. The audience members, all of whom have voluntarily paid for admission to the show, have tacitly agreed to accept the performer's self-presentation, insofar as no audience member is permitted to remove a performer from a public performance space. In the real world, someone who identifies as a member of more than one minority group must decide which identity will be most advantageous in a particular space. Someone who is queer and has a disability, for example, may more strongly identify as queer while attending a queer pride parade, because the queer identity is the one that is specifically being celebrated in that space. Onstage, on the other hand, it is possible to present all of one's minority identities as fluid and simultaneous, revealing the artificiality of both the hierarchies presented within certain types of identities (race, sex, gender, and disability) and the falsity of the belief that one's identification with a particular identity cannot be fluid.

When seeley quest dresses and undresses onstage, sie is complicating the audience's assumptions about both gender identity and disability. quest wears clothing associated with masculine and feminine gender identities. Because sie is dressed in layers, the pressure of conforming to a particular gender identity in a particular moment adds figurative weight (significance) to quest's stage presence. However, the weight and heat of the layers of costumes also potentially creates a physical strain on quest's body. This costuming choice is a visual embodiment of the significance of both gender identity and disability identity in quest's life. Apart from choosing to publicly represent, or decline to represent, a certain gender identity through their clothing choices, sie must also choose whether sie want hir clothing to conceal or accentuate hir back brace. Moving quest's costume changes onstage also invites the audience to confront that, if quest is wearing hir brace, sie can only wear clothing that accommodates hir brace. Separating intersectional identities may be useful for academic analysis, but someone who embodies those identities in daily life does not have the luxury of entirely separating from certain identities in certain spaces.

An audience member who is watching a performer embody more than one real world identity is confronting the possibility that the question "Who am i?" may have a fluid answer. It may be different, not only for each individual, but for any individual on a given day. In that case, perhaps the question of how one's voice reveals (or conceals) who one is is not as important as whether the voice one is using is authentic. Of course, what constitutes authenticity when one is performing the self is different from what constitutes authenticity when one is playing a character. In the latter case, a performer is adopting certain characteristics, presumably to give pleasure to an audience. That self, then, only exists for the length of a play. Its authenticity may be determined by how successfully the performer elicits a response from the audience, or, in more familiar terms, how believably a performer becomes a particular character. In the former case, a performer is revealing an identity the performer embodies regardless of whether or not anyone is watching. Then, the performer's authenticity cannot justly be determined entirely by how the performance of a particular identity affects an audience. (An openly gay drag queen, for example, might make a closeted audience member uncomfortable precisely because of the authenticity of his performance revealing the fluidity of gender identity.)

For performers who are performing their real world, minority identities, their authenticity is preexisting. They were who they were before they entered the stage space, and they will be who they are after the lights go down. The advantage of the onstage world is that it allows the performer to put the interplay amongst various real-world identities under a spotlight. A spotlight, after all, makes visible what was once in darkness. By making their various real-world identities visible in front of an audience, performers challenge the invisibility of those identities in the real world. Their presence in front of an audience is a demand to restore vulnerability and complexity to human communication. What does it mean to be someone with an intersectional identity? The answer is simple (and complicated): It depends on when and where you ask.

—Jill Summerville

Crooked

Author's Note: The great majority of this play was written in 2000 and 2001; the first version was performed as a thesis show in 2001, to complete my BA in Performance Studies and Gender Studies at New College of California in San Francisco. During the course of senior year studies, i finally came out to myself as disabled and trans at the same time, December 2000. *Crooked* has physical, mental, sexual, and gendered layers, and is a piece which now cannot be performed, as my body has changed, and i let go of a key prop in 2011. After taking sixteen years to return to full time school, while working toward completing my graduate diploma in Communication Studies at Concordia University in 2018, in December 2017 i learned i am also autistic. With increasing physical and cognitive impairments now, this historical text presents some work of my mid-twenties.

Crooked © seeley quest, all rights reserved.

*   *   *

> sq comes on stage, wedge spot on
> set is a small chair downstage, full spine x-ray hung midstage with fishing line, framed by dowels and with lightweight clamp lamps hooked on from behind, a tall box crate standing behind it and a sack of costumes on that. sq takes a firm stance facing the audience near chair, wearing boxer briefs, black drawstring pants, black corduroy pants over them, femme maroon shirt, blue workman shirt over it, yellow check vest, and black porkpie hat (which conceals a rolled scroll of paper inside)

sq: The Crooked Song!
Crooked is the deepest thing i know
i know it in the cells of my Crooked marrow.
Thrusting jut shifts to dimpled dip
one torso side's lippy curve before rut
the other's absence of a hip.
There's no straight tunnel through which to see
just what this Crooked means to me.
Nests and nooks of knots and twists
the angles in my plots, what's finer than this?
Correcting molds it's pushed on through
now Crooked is my only true.
The framework's interruption, the span of gap
chasms to cross before sense's resumption
a queer undertaking to read my map.
And, at end, you'll find only Crooked tales
in my wild, cunning, Crooked entrails.

blackout. beat. warm lights up to find sq with hat off

The first time i'm *publicly* marked as deviant i'm eleven. i'm generally well-behaved, quiet, marginal; why should my classmate start to tease me? But there she sits, going at it just under the radar of our teacher, and i'm paralyzed in my seat.

"2, 4, 6, 8, let's go meditate!" *[repeat and laugh]*

And here i am: *[staring at her, at a loss]*. i try to have my own joke by imagining her as a giant, kid-sized frog, croaking it at me. *[sq demonstrates]* But i don't know what else to do.

And still without knowing, one day suddenly i'm waiting by the door for her to come out to the playground after lunch, to trail some yards behind her walking to gossip with a friend. What's gonna happen? i'm just gonna keep staring at her silently and not move closer or step back.

"What are you doing?" she says, perturbed. i stare hard, silent, hold my ground, each time she stops and asks. She's taunted me relentlessly because she's *sure* i'm a meditating deviant. Now *i* initiate. i hold *her* attention. *She* doesn't know what to do, forced to face Sinister power—and she starts to cry. Then she tells a teacher, and soon the assistant dean is subscribing my dad to a flurry of curative measures for me. That starts my first year encounter with the mental health system.

Luckily, i don't tell any of them that i've known since earlier in grade school i couldn't possibly marry! Little matter if i might desire to be with someone—i don't much know. i just deeply know i want freedom to follow my own path. Don't want to compromise my dreaming, and who could fit with me in my particularity? i fall far when i'm dreaming; sometimes wake up on the other side of the looking glass. Mom leaves Dad when i'm six, and my younger sister and me to be raised by him, so often without babysitters i have to spend time entertaining myself with my imagination.

My folks both stay busy teaching smalltown-college theatre; i take in all this scene of books and performing, and early dwell in the world of storytelling. People don't always notice me, but when they do, they see i'm a southpaw who knows how to inhabit a different space. When i learn the word "sinister," i'm not scared. Its power is just something left to me, and feels familiar.

So i'm younger now, maybe seven, eight, nine or so. i do this a lot.

twists limbs in a manner that most people cannot

i hold it and sit this way while eating at the table, or while standing on one leg near my father as he cooks. The control feels good, a shape to contain myself with; all the parts of me are bound tightly as possible to my core. i guess i'm nervous; being with my dad is stressful, along with other adults and uncontrollable situations. This braiding up comforts. It's just one more quirky thing i do; no one ever tells me to stop.

then untwist while sitting in chair, and take off vest, roll sleeves

When i'm thirteen, folks notice my vertebrae slouching into curves.

Doctor says, a brace. My dad has some scoliosis too, but mine is worse. He's educated, but doesn't trust he might know better than the doctor in considering other alternatives. My body's starting on a long, strange trip: what is he supposed to do? Even though a cousin is also recommended this and my dad's brother decides they'll try negotiating that curve without a brace, dad says yes, and i raise no objection. i almost *never* do; complaints have to be dragged out of me—it doesn't occur to me to make them. So doctor says get long cotton tank tops, something to wear under its mold, or else the body suffers. My skin rubs away daily in the compromising tank-tops, where the armhole gap weds it and the plastic-encased rib-strap it adheres to. Brace forever stains with my body's productions—plastic, sweat, glue, salt, hair, steel mix together.

My classmates wonder about the new look. In 1990 the first *Robocop* film is big; after a day a boy coins "Roboneck"—it sweeps the school. Because i help pass on the name. Who i am through junior high and high school, you challenge me to expose my own ridiculousness to the world before anyone else can have the power to pin it on me, i'll take it on and also toss you Iron Maiden sometimes too. But you'll just wince and laugh weakly, and Roboneck will stick as my name for two years. Strangers think i'm "retarded." Dismiss me like folks in wheelchairs and the rest of my excellent "lame," "dumb," and otherwise "crippled" clan—i get to learn about what it's like being in this clan.

To this day, when anyone tosses off something or somebody as *lame* or *retarded* and i let it slip by, part of me dies, because those folks have been the only family i've had sometimes. Crooked will convert your children.

> *raps knuckles against side of head*

Knock knock. *[pause]* Who's there? Knock *knock.* Ah—

> *sq walks behind x-ray, carrying vest to put into satchel. Starts humming and singing "Brass in Pocket" by the Pretenders, while stripping off blue shirt (into black tank top bag) and cord pants (into satchel), then putting on from the bag heel boots and a scarf, then carrying out Brace crate to sit it on chair in front*
>
> *sq presents camp persona: precious. straightens up before audience, carefully removes neck-to-pelvis Milwaukee brace from where it's been hidden in the box and hold hir at arm's length, turning this way and that, admiring. Treat's come knocking at Brace's doorstep, seeking to make a connection again*

Hey! Mmm Brace! It's good to see you! i've been sentimental ... been visiting all the old places lately, and it's just not the same without *you* in the picture! *[pause]* Oh, you remember me—Trixxy! Trixxy Treat! *[aside to audience]* (Brace actually does remember me, and just likes playing this game.) Yeah, we were companions! Linked! *[show fingers tight]* You really held me up for a couple years there. i remember people even saying you were like my face to the world. Now i'm the one people notice, and they don't care so much to get to know *you*. But i still want to tell stories with you—come on, i want an m brace one more time! *[wink]* Sit down with me; i'll tell you a story.

> *sq takes crate from seat, sits and crosses legs, putting Brace on lap like a child, then pulls out "storybook" from the box to read from; addresses it directly, with great enthusiasm, to Brace*

This is called, A Crooked Tale.

Once upon a time there was a fair child named Crooked, who one day went into the deepest thrusting forest. The marrow there was dimpled and shifting. But torso was brave and lippy and would never absent hir in a rut. Sie went through no straight tunnels to see a nest of mean twists awaiting. They asked: what was finer than knotting nooks to moldy plots? Correctly, sie pushed on through until sie was interrupted by hir only true. This queer undertaker gave a map. Hir sense of chasm gapped hir frame until sie worked to cross. And at the end found a wild crook where sie cunningly ate entrails, and lived happily ever after!

> *Blackout, then warm lights up. Brace and book have been returned to crate*
> *sq quickly shucks maroon shirt and shoes, then scarf. Presses tit, pinches skin with surprise*

Is this me?

> *drops face to floor, turns head on side to audience, twists around to look at back*

Fuck, is that my back?

i've been pushing myself to do queer porn shoots nowadays, where i get images of how my back actually looks.

[runs hands down it] Every time i feel it it freaks me out.

> *rolls over, ass high, froglegged in air*

Is this me? Legs so wide open?

> *rolls into kneeling, grabs crotch, and mack-eyes the audience*

Is *this* me? How am i supposed to perform? And how am i supposed to really take care of myself—if i fail to embrace my body, in my confusion? On my way to finding out how far my body can go, sometimes i fall into the place where i remember i can take nothing for granted, not even it, and i'm *back* in the fire, nerves seized in spasm for a day or more, bowing me to the most humbling and holy pain i know!

> *turns to face audience on knees, explodes in pain*
> *blackout, then wedge spot on*

Thank you pain!
The spirit is upon me
Came down to walk along me today
Every time you touch my eyes roll in my head
Hallelujah

Blanch me in your grip until i dissolve
Set me aflame and remind me what freedom is again
Until i fall to ash in your teeth, all my ways are childish
You put that all away for me; thank you

> *Blackout. moves flashlight or lamp slowly down length of x-ray to illuminate while talking*

These are things i hold in this body: lucky to be raised among theatre queens and to have learned i can protect myself with saying, "it's okay, 'cause i'm *just* a performer; i'm not *really* threatening you"

lucky that my education, usually, helps me *talk* my way out of getting hauled off by an authority after disturbing the peace with agitation, *and* my whiteness helps get me hauled off *first* instead of shot

lucky i wasn't a gentile crip in Poland in the Holocaust: i've seen the exhibit room of braces and crutches at Auschwitz;

though i could mask my queerness or craziness a while, they'd soon enough see my back twist out, and i'd be gone

lucky to not be electroshocked for a therapeutic experiment like *some* friends with scoliosis, 'cause i already dissociate from and hate my body enough

lucky i haven't walked into the wrong men's room yet.

i'm *lucky* for so many other reasons—and to have things that inspire me and people to fight for.

> *Full blackout, including the x-ray light. A beat, the half-light up to find sq, now donning hat (roll of paper still inside) and holding a satchel. The satchel contains a vest, cord pants, makeup tin, and mirror that sq uses in the following scene.*
>
> *sq sets down satchel and surveys the territory; changes pants and hooks thumbs into belt loops, bemused. Considers:*

"i've traveled all my life to get here."

> *Shuffles elsewhere to stop, put on vest:*

"i've worn all these masks to get here."

> *Shuffles elsewhere, stops, puts on eyebrow and chin colors:*

"i've packed up all my sorrows to get here."

> *Shuffles elsewhere, stops, puts on nose and cheek colors:*

"i've had to face my Fate to get here."

> *Warm lights up*

Yeah, i can't help being a clown sometimes. Because it's a gee-willikers of a job to get naked, but *somebody's* gotta do it!

> *sq makes a gesture of "zipping lips," then begins a silent routine: offers hat to front row of audience, with great excitement regards scrolls inside which get unrolled one by one. sq silently get folks to take each one—each has a word on it that, when read together, says: CROOKED*

IS CONVERTING YOUR FATE. sq reacts with pleasure at first when they
read each one aloud, but, hat back on, freezes with surprise at the last
word, "fate."
   Blackout, then wedge spot
   With smeared face, sq focuses on washing all off with rag while look-
ing into the hand mirror

Crooked Reverse
Entrails are eaten and ends are cunning,
Crooked is wild and the only thing found.
A queer map undertakes crossing chasms;
frameworks are read and interrupted.
Crooked only now is true,
correcting molds are all pushed through.
Plots knot into fine angles,
and nests are twisted out of nooks.
Tunnel me there mean and just;
see this Crooked through and through.
No absence of sides before other ones;
torso curves to hips to lips to rut.
Juts dimple and shifts thrust;
i know my cells dip.
i know Crooked's deepest marrow.

   blackout
   take off hat and cords, leave on vest, walk to chair
   warm lights on

Being shirtless doesn't *quite* reveal how i am vulnerable. i do it and refuse
being female. And then of course there's the hair.
   When i'm thirteen, i have no blood, no breasts, no pubes yet. i visit mom
and see her do this.

   puts foot upon seat and mimes leg shaving with razor

So then i shut myself in the bathroom. *[turn, shut door, shuck vest]* i shave here
… and here … and here…

   gestures shaving arms, navel, toes and fingers, reachable hair on back,
   upper lip, between eyebrows, around nipples and against sternum—
   dons vest, opens door, walks toward front-row

i finally emerge and show my work to her husband: "i shaved my arms." He
tries not to laugh; "what?" You mean people don't usually do that? Just maybe
legs and armpits? All i've known is females aren't supposed to have hair, so
logically i must eliminate any single one i see on my body. Neither dad nor
mom nor anyone else raising me has talked about such things: what women
actually do. i don't tell anyone about my misconception, but regret to find
the formerly fine down grows back much darker and coarser. As i'm entering
puberty, hormones bring you back in sturdy, long, witchy rings of pubic hair

around my nipples. You're like the circles hairy-chested men have. How can i fit the category of female then? [*crosses by edge of x-ray*]

i'm twenty-two now, and staying in the shower during a visit from my second lover. He peeks in: "hey, what are you doing in there?"

> *sq pulls back side of film, then clutches it like a shower curtain with a jump to hide razor*

Nothing! Go away! [*pause, then hastily resume shaving nipple*]

i've been doing this for years, paranoid anytime someone might see my breasts, after i've stopped all my other shaving habits. Not till after being with him for a while do i risk saying i prefer not to hide it anymore. My sister says my fierce body hair is powerful; i should have respect for such Crooked strength. This throws light on the shame i've lived in for years, and i'll try opening to new possibilities. i'll fail as a woman in mainstream culture, but hold ground as a saucy freak.

> *blackout, then warm lights up—sq brings bag and dresses in 3-button domme top, skirt, boots, gloves, and wig/snood with mirror, finishes and poses sweetly*
> *hums and start singing:*
> well i hear some people talking 'bout their monkey yens,
> they want those no-love jokers and their trifling friends
> peaceful people sit around all day and moan,
> they're wondering why the wandering hotties don't come home
> but wild seeley don't worry, wild seeley never gets the blues.
> well, if you've got some seeley better get your share,
> 'cause i know i wanna get something everywhere
> i never have been known to treat no one kind right
> i keep 'em working hard both day and night
> and wild seeley don't worry, wild seeley never gets the blues!

Do i get to show this? Does it forfeit any masculinity i could have?

> *pulls off wig, starts peeling off gloves*

It's a thrill to play with these diva pleasures sometimes. Still i get stuck on how this skirt hangs on my hips askew—which you might not see now, but i'm sure you will. i'm terrified navigating here, that you'll see me as too disabled, my gender too disjointed, to be desired. Prefer to believe i'm camouflaged in costumes—anything *truly* body-revealing remains a hard choice. Wearing the clinging tank tops i have now is revolutionary. i do *want* to, sometimes, welcome my body and identity as a girl. i just don't know how to feel like one.

> *Blackout, then warm lights on. sq changes clothes, pulls tank top, blue shirt and black dress package from same bag, puts back on cord pants, tank, all the while regarding and caressing Brace before and after putting it on*

i wear you when i'm thirteen through fifteen, fitting almost as awkwardly as you do now. Only my family and locker room classmates see how we look under my regular clothes, see that i have small breasts divided by your center bar. Only with my family and locker room classmates can i steal stares at what other breasts look like, females' bodies. i tell myself i'm fascinated because i don't have any breasts, that's why i'm so taken with looking at others—and i still believe this has truth.

i eat lunch mostly with a couple boys during ninth grade, drifting together as rejects. At this time other girls seek popularity by going properly feminine, but i won't look like them no matter what. The boys banter, joke constantly; talk of girls occasionally, but mainly don't because it's easier not to dwell on what one can't have, all our hormones at the cusp of rage. They test boundaries, and one day Leon, gentle-hearted, full of bluff and a face of acne, says, "Will you go out with me?" With the other boy waiting for what i'll say, i think it's a game and say i won't play in with an answer. It never occurs to me till years later it's sincere, and not till four years later does anyone ask me out again, when i have long hair, and am somewhere no one's ever seen me with you.

> *sq just sits in fully fastened-up Brace for a bit, till putting back on shirt at end*

i've lived in East Bay ghettos years now, traveling alone each gritty neighborhood, carrying myself much as when i wore you 23/7. i'm startled to realize i'm so divorced from safety concerns had by women around me. It's not like butches and transguys don't get raped. It's not like i recognize the possibility of an attack enough to feel prepared should one come. It's just that in my commonest clothes and walk, i never worry. i don't threaten, i don't provoke. i'm a bit slight, but that just makes me the boy next door. Like when a Chicano guy from Salinas stuck overnight in Oakland from a Greyhound hold up approaches me for help, a place to crash because the black guys down the street scare him, it's not because i'm a girl, not with how he talks of the rumored homos in San Francisco. i fade to invisible; i barely make a target for anything. i know the world won't confront me with the demands for females. i'm untouchable. i say, yeah, Brace, sometimes disability is invisibility. And disability is sometimes a friend.

> *Blackout. Lights back up—wearing just boxer briefs again, stands to stretch*

Someday i *could* stand three inches taller, unkinked on the rack: everything in alignment even though it would tear to pieces what i am now.

> *sq poses taut as though strung up—then brings Brace in slow walk into audience as house lights rise. sq puts hir on while talking, encouraging audience members to touch Brace while sie's being worn. sq then takes Brace off again, but continues through crowd during next monologue, inviting folks to touch bare bones and feel the difference*

But it's still easier to remain in what's familiar, not have to re-work how to carry myself in the world.

When exposed in my awkward body, my identity can just be: gender traitor.

When in a brace, when psychiatrically diagnosed, my identity can just be: disabled.

i've relaxed inside bars and plastic against the shell of a defining framework, and know nothing else so awfully delicious. How can anyone else know what's inside that space, what's there for me? i find out years later that the assistant dean i talked to told my dad i believed i could *actually* turn that girl into a frog. But i've always survived in states of contradiction. Know the difference between truth and story: sometimes is a gulf. Sometimes is a hair. To this day i armor myself with how i'm askew. i valorize and defile my experience; this is my self-mythologizing. i've inherited my fortune, and i'm determined to share it with you.

You. Be my family. i need you to know i can be, and *am,* a young one who needs to sit on public transit sometimes because my back and arms don't always feel spry. A faggot. A girl. A force channeling something from your dreams. i want us to make that ok for each other. i kept Brace in my closet for years, and when i first looked at hir again, there was a spider living in the shell. i didn't disturb it because i decided that spider found a better home there than i ever had. The other day i looked at Brace again and saw another spider, but this time moved it because i want to reclaim all the homes i can get. Be my challengers.

Show me how to be open to a touch, an accounting, a pressure i haven't felt yet. Yeah, reach both hands in and press hard.

sq leaves the audience, walks back to front of stage

The fortune to find is the marvel of our minds, bodies, embodiment—willful, ungovernable. We Crooked survivors are *ourselves* articulations of anarchy. We don't have to run away from how we're queer, and we don't have to run to it, either. We can allow ourselves to be Crooked when it's the deepest thing *we* know; we know it in the cells of our Crooked marrow.

blackout.

End of play.

Last Train In

A Solo Play in One Act

ADAM GRANT WARREN

Dancer and choreographer, Bill "The Crutchmaster" Shannon uses the term Condition Arriving to describe social situations in which someone with a visible or apparent condition is rendered invisible due to observers' fascination with the condition.[1] To put this in theatrical terms, the person is upstaged by his/her/their visible or apparent condition. In social situations, Condition Arriving might be inevitable. After all, a person has limited control over how he/she/they is perceived upon entering a room. A performer onstage, on the other hand, has much more control over how an audience perceives his/her/their physical and vocal presence. Could the stage presence of a performer's visible or apparent condition be upstaged by the stage presence of the performer? The answer to that question is partially dependent upon how skillful the performer is during a given performance. However, it varies based on the reputation of the performer, namely, the magnitude of the performer's stage presence. The more well-known the performer is, the more likely an audience is to collectively acknowledge the impressiveness of that person's stage presence.

According to phenomenologist Bert O. States, an audience always tacitly compares an unknown actor who is playing an iconic role to the most famous actor who has played that role. An unknown actor playing Hamlet, for example, must persuade an audience to accept both himself-as-Hamlet and the absence of, say, Laurence-Olivier-as-Hamlet, in order to be regarded as having played his role successfully.[2] Regardless of whether or not he/she/they is well-known, an actor with a visible or apparent condition is similar to States' unknown actor playing Hamlet. Instead of being compared to the most famous actor who has played his/her/their role, an actor with a visible or apparent condition is compared to an able-bodied actor. If the actor uses a mobility device, that device itself evokes the able-bodied actor he/she/they *could* be if not for the disability that makes a visible mobility device necessary. In order to be considered a "good actor," an actor with a visible or apparent condition has to overcome the audience's expectation that an able-bodied actor will appear onstage when the curtain

150

rises. An actor with a visible or apparent condition must make an audience prefer watching him/her/them to watching either an able-bodied actor or a mobility device with a stage presence that might rival his/her/their own.

In *Last Train In*, performer and playwright Adam Grant Warren, who has a visible and apparent condition and uses a manual wheelchair, claims public space both onstage and offstage, though the offstage spaces are only evoked through the narrative. When he is taking the subway, Warren's physical condition subsumes any other aspect of his individual identity. If he wants to ride the subway successfully, he has to emphasize his condition, since he will need everyone whom he encounters to accommodate it. In his classroom, Warren overcomes Condition Arriving, insofar as his adolescent students are as indifferent to his instructions as they would be to any other teacher's. Warren addresses inaccessibility in public spaces in the real world, but his offstage spaces are evoked. The only space an audience actually sees Warren navigate is the stage space. Warren confronts Condition Arriving, which could happen onstage or in the real world. Because he is onstage, he confronts the audience's expectation of seeing an able-bodied actor at the same time. Instead of asking the audience to reevaluate his condition based on a positive re-presentation, Warren reminds his audience that anyone could experience a personal failure. Neither the challenges he faces in the classroom nor the emotional strain of his long-distance romantic relationship are directly related to his disability. When he does experience disability-related personal failures, they are failures for which the inaccessibility of the city of London is arguably to blame. In this play, the scenes when Warren's condition may upstage him are the same scenes where he has an advantage over an able-bodied actor. No audience member would argue that watching an able-bodied actor try to take the subway would be equally compelling. It is impossible for someone with a visible or apparent condition to entirely control how others perceive him/her/them, onstage or in the real world, but he/she/they can ensure those perceptions are as complex as possible.

—Jill Summerville

Notes

1. Bill Shannon, "Definitions of Phenomena: Conditions Arriving," *Bill Shannon: What Is What*, www.whatiswhat.com, accessed 14 March, 2019.

2. Bert O. States, *Great Reckonings in Little Rooms* (Berkeley: University of California, 1985), 120–121.

Last Train In

Following development as part of the National Writers' Colony at Vancouver's Playwrights Theatre Centre, *Last Train In* premiered at Victoria's UNOFest, and went on to critical acclaim at Vancouver's 2017 rEvolver Theatre Festival.
Last Train In © Adam Grant Warren, all rights reserved.

* * *

The stage is divided into a 5 × 7 grid—either literally or conceptually. Designer's choice. There are three set elements positioned on that grid. For convenience, let's call them "bridge boxes"—identical cubes that are roughly shoulder-height to a seated actor.

Each box has a set of metal handrails across the top and is on wheels. All handrails are flat to the audience.

Measuring from SR:
Box 1 is 3 spaces SL and 3 spaces DS
Box 2 is 4 spaces SL and 2 spaces DS
Box 3 is 5 spaces SL and 2 spaces DS

The lights are set in anticipation of some kind of pre-show speech. When it ends, there is an audible CLICK from OSR and the lights go to black. Another CLICK in the dark and there's the sound of a train pulling into a station. One last CLICK and the lights come up to begin the show.

ADAM enters from SR. He's in his mid-30s, wearing a light hoodie, and using a low-profile manual wheelchair.

He's also pushing a fourth set element ahead of him. It's like the cubes in all respects—handrails, casters, etc.—except that it's a staircase. He parks the staircase in the USR corner of the grid and addresses the audience directly.

Unit One—"So I Tell People ..."

I live in Vancouver. But I'm originally from Mount Pearl. Which is in Newfoundland.

Adam crosses to USL, retrieves a second matching staircase, and pushes it all the way to DSL.

But the only place most people in Vancouver know in Newfoundland is St. John's. Which is pretty much right next door to Mount Pearl. So I tell people in Vancouver that I'm from St. John's.

I've been in Vancouver for about eight years now. I'm a teacher. Well, I teach in Richmond, really. But that's, like, a twenty-five minute train ride south of Vancouver, and no one outside BC really knows where Richmond and Vancouver are in relation to each other. So, I just tell people in Newfoundland that I'm a teacher in Vancouver.

I teach SAT-level English and Composition. Essay writing. I'm also a private consultant on U.S. university applications: UCLA, NYU, Columbia, Princeton, Harvard, Yale … All the big ones. Been at it for about a year now. I mean, I've always been teaching one thing or another, but this is my first time working with high school kids in more than a little while.

Last week, I was in the middle of a lesson on semicolons when one of my consultation students sort of stumbled into my classroom…

"Adam! Adamadamadamadamadam! I got in! I got in! I got in! I got in! I got in!" And she comes over, and she's my student, and I'm her teacher. And she's kind of tall, and I'm not so much. So, there's this really awkward series of, like, near-hugs … Until finally she just sort of plunks down onto her knees so she's just a little lower than I am, and she reaches up and she hugs me. And she hugs and hugs and hugs. And then, she gets up and she smiles down at me and she says, "Okay. Thank you. Bye." So she's off kicking ass at Columbia now. I haven't seen her since.

My last high school gig ended just before I moved to Vancouver. In 2007. In 2007, I spent a year teaching English and Theatre Arts in London. England. Not Ontario. Well, I wasn't in London exactly. I was in Essex. But there aren't many people outside the UK who know where Essex and London are in relation to each other, so I tell people I taught in London.

> *Adam unclips something from his belt. A black box with a white button in the centre. Slightly smaller than a deck of cards. He points the box at the lighting grid and clicks the button It's the sound we heard from off-stage at the top of the show. The lights shift, and Adam observes the effect.*

No. *(He moves somewhere else and clicks again.)* Ew. No… *(Again)* …
   Okay. Yeah. Let's go with that.

Unit Two—When, Where, and Why

> *Adam pushes a third staircase in from **SL**. Parks it **3 spaces in and 3 spaces DS on the grid.***

2007. It's December. No snow, but there's the kind of wind that whips around corners and finds all the cracks, you know?

> *Adam clicks his button again, and the sound of WIND comes up.*

These fat, stupid raindrops that blow right into the side of your fucking head and I swear to God they stick to your skin.

> *Another click and the sound of LIGHT RAIN joins the WIND.*

The town in Essex where I was teaching, Hadley Cross. Over there…

> *Adam gestures off. He clicks the button again, the lights shift and there's the sound of a nearby bar.*

…that's the pub. The Crown and Bell, I think it's called. I've only been there once because I'm a high school teacher and every decent high school teacher knows that you do your serious drinking at least—*at least*—two towns away from your students. Across from the pub…

> *He clicks again. Another shift and the sound of a supermarket from somewhere else close by.*

That's the Tesco's Express Grocery. And just up the road from the Tesco's…

> *A click, a shift, the appropriate sounds…*

…I think you can see the edge of the roof from here—yeah that's my school, Hadley College. And … that's about it, really. I think there's a hardware store somewhere, but I'm not sure. Could be a flower shop.

> *Adam clicks again to end the final sound and pushes the fourth and final staircase in from* **SR**. *Parks it* **2 spaces in and 3 spaces DS on the grid.**

It's Sunday night. I did all my prep work for class yesterday, so that I could take the train to London tonight and see *Wicked* at the Apollo…

> *Click. A few thrilling bars of "Defying Gravity." Click to stop.*

…The last performance of the original London cast. The guy who took my ticket said I was in for a treat. The show was amazing, obviously. But my favorite parts were these moments when the actors would mess with each other. Fuck with the props, or give different lines and force the rest of the cast to just go with it. Or during the big numbers when characters would go their separate ways and you could feel something … I don't know … a little more real in the way they said goodbye to each other.

I go to London as often as I can. Every weekend, at least. It's only about 25 minutes from here by train. I feel like the more often I go, the more London will respect me. Like if I keep digging at it, following it in, it'll realize I'm serious and let me make the switch from tourist to local. Maybe share a few secrets or something. Little ones. I just need to give it time, so I always take the latest possible train back here.

> *Adam crosses behind Box 1 and pushes it 1 space DS on the grid. He clicks the button and the lights shift again, further transforming the space.*

(*Looking around*) This is Hadley train station. Graffiti all over the rail bed
    (*Seeing it*)—"Jenni sux monster cocks!" Jenni with an I. Sux with an X.
    (*Indicating various areas of the stage*) Puke stain … Puke stain … Pee puddle … Condom…
    It's after midnight. Twelve fourteen. So, Monday morning really. Not exactly the wee hours, but the train I just got off—that was the last one until something like six a.m. No one but me ever gets off the last train of the night in Hadley Cross. This place is locked up tight by 10:30. A glass of water on the night stand and a cigarette in the bed sheets.

Unit Three—Getting Settled

By now, I've been in England for about a year. I interviewed for the job back in Newfoundland—by phone. Got the call at a little past two p.m. on a Thursday and took it sitting in the hallway outside my senior seminar on Quantifiable Teaching.

Did you know that a properly designed multiple choice question should have no more than five possible answers—all of them plausible. No discernable patterns. Compound answers should be avoided whenever possible. Both A and B, Both B and D, All of the Above, None of the Above. Stuff like that. The objective, after all, is to test students. To teach, rather than to confuse or trick them.

So I interviewed on a Thursday, and by Friday I had it. Wasn't even finished with my degree yet but, "Splendid!" they said. "Marvellous!" Just in case it mattered, I told them I use a manual wheelchair. "Not to worry, they said. The school is fully up to code ... Just out of curiosity, can you do the ... what do they call them?... 'Wheelies' is it? Can you do wheelies?"

Please.

Adam pops a few flashy wheelies in answer.

"Wonderful!" they said. "The students will love that!" So, satisfied with my wheelies, they told me all about the school. Accessible washrooms, huge central elevator, extra-wide doorways. Smart-boards in every classroom and a computer for every student. I looked them up online—bright-eyed kids in blazers and ties with great knots, hands straight up in the air.

Admin even offered me this really cool place on the school property. I'm the English teacher who lives in the little red brick house ... There's a ramp up to the door because it's where they used to store all the really heavy AV equipment before I came along. And there's this...

Adam holds up the button.

It does some other things too, but mostly it's a door-opener. My house is close enough to the school that I can push the button in the parking lot and have my front door open by the time I get to the top of the ramp. So, I've got the work visa, I've got the job, I've got the house with the ramp and the magical button that opens the front door. I'm all set!

I showed up the week before start of term, right? Just to get settled. Start steeping myself in the local culture. Maybe dive into a plate of bangers and mash. Get used to calling my pants trousers and my underwear pants.

I flew into Heathrow late afternoon, took a cab to Liverpool Station—which, to avoid confusion, is in London, not Liverpool—and then hopped my first train to Hadley.

I wanted to stick around London that first night—launch into the city. But I came straight here because I felt like this was where everything would start. Train pulled in. I got out onto the platform. It was full dark by then, but I didn't care. "Students of Hadley Cross! Your teacher is here! Let the learning begin!"

I looked around. I saw the corner of the roof of my state-of-the-art school. The one with the smart boards and the extra wide doorways and the private wheelchair accessible bathrooms, and the kids with their hands dead straight in the air. I saw my whole *Dead Poets Society, Dangerous Minds, Renaissance Man, Mr. Holland's Opus* career waiting inside. I did not see an elevator at the station.

Unit Four—Pardeep

But there, God bless his cotton socks, was Pardeep. He's the station manager.

The night guy.

Adam CLICKS his button and a special comes up on Box 1.

When I got off the train that first time, Pardeep was, like, furiously scrubbing at a big graffiti dick on the door of his office. He kind of looked at me, then looked away like he was afraid I'd catch him staring. He looked at me. Then he looked away. Then he looked again and took a step closer. Looked at me … looked away … looked at me … looked away…

I know that dance.

"I wanna help him. But I don't wanna offend him … I wanna help him. But I don't wanna offend him … Help him!… Offend him!… Help him!… Offend him! …"

When someone starts that dance, it's usually up to me to stop them.

So I introduced myself: "Hey. I'm Adam. How's it going?"

"All right," he said. "Can … Can I help you?"

So I explained. I told Pardeep that I was about to start teaching English at the college. I told him I can walk up the stairs. That all he had to do was carry my chair across the bridge and leave it on the other platform. I'd get there in my own time.

Another click and the special on "the office" goes down.

You know what's great? With Pardeep there's no negotiation. He doesn't want to carry my chair across and then come back and carry *me*. He doesn't bend down and offer a piggyback ride, or explain how it's okay because he's got a cousin in a wheelchair—twice my size and he gives that guy piggybacks all the time. And once he finally understood that I can walk, Pardeep didn't insist on walking beside me on the bridge, just in case I fell. I asked Pardeep to carry my chair over the bridge and that's what he did. What he's been doing for almost a year since the day we met.

He was the new guy then, too. It took him maybe three months worth of late-night trains from London to start walking my chair across with me.

Adam crosses behind Boxes 2 and 3 and pushes them each 1 space DS on the grid.

Three months to realize that, here at Hadley station, the only things that the night manager actually manages are huge, enormous, massive expanses of silence. So when there's someone to talk to—about anything—Pardeep talks. And if it means he has to spend a little more time carrying my chair, that's fine.

In our journeys across the bridge together I've learned, for example, that Pardeep has a vast and varied porn collection. Because he never knows what he'll be in the mood for. He's currently exploring an interest in Asian twins.

I also know that he has a brother. But that Pardeep is the hands-down favorite. He said he wouldn't mind so much except that his mother actually *tells* everybody that he's the favorite.

Last week Pardeep mentioned that tonight is his mother's birthday. That he'd be taking the night off to go hang out with her in Colchester. Because if Pardeep hangs out with his mother in Colchester on her birthday, then Pardeep's brother doesn't have to. And if Pardeep's brother doesn't have to hang out with his mother in Colchester on her birthday, then that means that, for the rest of the year, Pardeep's brother doesn't give Pardeep half as much of a hard time about being the favorite.

Most nights though, Pardeep just kind of fills the silence with random questions for me.

How are my classes? Fine.
How are my legs? Fine.
Do they hurt today? No.
Do they ever hurt? No.
Really? Yes.
Do I have a girlfriend back home? Yep.
Is she in a wheelchair too? Nope.
Really? Yep.
Is she hot? Yes.
Do I miss her?
Oh! Wait. Hold on.

Unit Five—Melissa

Adam clicks again. A special comes up DSL. Adam crosses to it and pulls out an old-school cell phone. Maybe a clamshell or an old UK-style "candybar." Whatever it is, it's definitely not of the smartphone era. He dials.

It's just … Wait … What is it. It's an insane number of numbers. I never call her from the phone. Okay.

(Into phone) Hello? … Hey! Are you—where are you? Are you on your way to work? … Okay, cool, I won't keep you long. I'm just doing a thing and I thought it'd be kind of cool to bring you in. Check it out.

Adam holds the phone out toward the audience.

Everyone say hi to Melissa!

(If the audience plays along:)

Cool, huh? ...No, they're great. They seem really into it...

(If they don't:)

Aw, they're shy ... No. I swear to God there are actual people here ... like, more than two.

Yeah, no. It's totally solid. *(Thumping a fist against the bridge)* I just need to, you know, figure out how it all goes together ... Yeah ... How's work? ... Ha! I still love that they bow to you ... No, you deserve it ... Yeah, well, I mean they don't bow to me or anything, but they're pretty awesome ... Okay, me too ... Hey, wouldn't it be cool if you were actually here in the audience and you said hello when I got to this part in the show? It would be like talking to yourself, except you're not really there, so ... Right. I love you too. Have fun.

> *He hangs up. Another click of the button, and the special goes down as Adam moves to DSC.*

Melissa. My girlfriend. She's the one who found the ad online. One of those teach abroad things. We were doing some research in the library and she sent me *(taking in the station)* ... this. The posting for this job with nothing in the body of the email except a string of question marks and a little colon-bracket smiley face thing. We talked it over that night. She'd found a posting in Korea for herself, and this one for me. So we decided that we'll both apply, potentially spend a year apart. Then come back and compare notes. She got her job, I got mine. Eventually we'll settle on one of the two—either Korea, or here—and come back together.

It's actually been kind of great. We talk almost every day. Skype mostly, since I never remember to buy calling cards. I'm just getting up and she's getting ready for bed. She showers at night and I know when I've timed my call correctly because she doesn't turn on the video feed right away. "Hang on," she says. "I'm in a towel!" And I'm all like, "I don't believe you. I think I need some proof!" So she turns the video feed on and she's naked. "I was lying," she says.

I mean, we make more time on the weekends. Sit down with a cup of tea and half the planet between us. Regale each other with tales of the week's adventures.

Like, last weekend Mel told me about this crazy little club in Seoul that's pretty much made of plastic weather sheeting and old newspaper clippings. Each table has its own set of miniature beer taps, and the DJ dresses like a turtle.

Not to be outdone, I told Mel about my travels on The Tube. Last weekend, I rode around under London for a whole day with my copy of *Neverwhere*. It's an, I guess an urban fantasy novel by Neil Gaiman where the whole London Underground is this other world full of secrets and magic. But the stations and the stairs and the spaces underneath are all exactly where he says they are. So you can't help believing that all the magic might actually be there. I read the book and rode the tube. Got off at all the stations in the story—Earl's Court, Blackfriars, Angel, all of them—and I went looking for the magic.

I told Pardeep too. About the magic. He just laughed and asked me if I had anything better to do with my time.

Unit Six—Tony

So, but Pardeep is off hanging out with his mother tonight, remember? ... The guy in the office—his name's Tony.

> *Click. A special on "Tony in the office"—as earlier with "Pardeep in the office."*

I'd never met Tony before tonight. So, when I saw him on the platform, I introduced myself:

"Hey. I'm Adam. How's it going?"

"All right," he said.

Then I explained. I told Tony that I teach English at the college. I told him I can walk up the stairs. That all he had to do was carry my chair across the bridge and leave it on the other platform. I'd get there in my own time.

I waited for the negotiation. For Tony to want to carry my chair across and then come back and carry *me*. To bend down and offer a piggyback ride, or explain how it's okay because he's got a cousin in a wheelchair—twice my size and he gives that guy piggybacks all the time. And once he understood that I can walk, I waited for Tony to insist on walking beside me on the bridge, just in case I fell.

But Tony didn't do any of that. I asked Tony to carry my chair and please leave it on the other platform. And Tony said no.

> *Click. Tony's special goes down.*

I laughed. I couldn't help myself. But Tony was serious. Tony said that, no, he was not going to carry my chair over the bridge tonight because it's not something he's supposed to do. He explained that, if *he* were to fall and, say, break his leg while carrying my chair across the bridge, then his benefits wouldn't cover it. He'd be off work and the medical bills would come right out of his pocket.

(Gesturing off) My place is about five minutes that way. I can see the edge of the roof from here. I don't know, maybe I can even open the door.

> *Adam points the button off, in the general direction of his house. CLICK. The WIND comes back, full force. CLICK. The RAIN torrents. CLICK. They vanish. Adam considers the button. Looks for a moment like he's going to chuck it. Carefully, he collects and continues.*

When I asked Tony how I'm supposed to get from here to there, he said that wasn't his problem. That I should've thought about that earlier, and that I'd have to figure it out for myself. Then he went into the office. He hasn't come out since.

So here we are. Pardeep at his mother's, the whole town in bed. No more trains until 6 a.m.

What to do. What to do. What to do…

> *Quietly, with no prompting from Adam or his button, a SOUND rises here. At first, it's almost below the level of hearing—a rumble that's felt more than anything else. It grows throughout the next unit…*

Unit Seven—Triumphant

I have my phone. Still plenty of battery. I'm sure I could call someone from the school. The head of the English Department, he lives up in Clackton. Great guy. I'm sure I can give him a call and explain the situation. He'd be happy to come down here and give me a hand. I can buy him a round next Friday to say thanks. He's always first to the pub on Fridays. And Thursdays. And Wednesdays too, really. I could give him a call, but he's probably not in any shape to drive.

Whatever. I'll call Colchester for a cab, right? Get the cabbie out to handle my chair and have him *drive* me the actual, literal one-minute ride from here to my house. No. That's just stupid.

Besides, Tony told me to figure it out for myself.

> *The sound is clear now, still growing: the rumble of a train on tracks, but deeper. Stretched out and made somehow out of sync with itself.*
>
> *Adam takes in the set. Deciding, he pushes the DS staircase all the way US. He crosses in front of the remaining pieces and moves BOX 1 one space US on the grid. Now, with the three bridge blocks in the middle and two staircases, one at either end, five of the seven set pieces have come together to form a complete bridge lengthwise across Centre.*
>
> *Adam crosses to the SR side.*
>
> *He removes the velcro strap that holds his feet in place.*
>
> *Gets out of his chair and sits on the stairs.*
>
> *He begins methodically breaking down his chair.*
>
> *takes the rear wheels off and holds them together with one of the axle pins;*
>
> *folds down the seat back; hefts the frame and takes a moment to consider the pieces on the ground.*
>
> *He carries the pieces across the bridge,*
>
> *making as many trips as it takes.*
>
> *Once he's got all the pieces on the other side, he reassembles his chair,*
>
> *Gets back in.*
>
> *Secures his feet with the strap.*
>
> *He finds his button and clicks it again. The strange rumble of the train disappears instantly.*
>
> *And Adam speaks, still catching his breath.*

And that, ladies and gentlemen, is how one young crippled man triumphed despite overwhelming odds, in a kicked-in, fucked-up, pissed-on Essex train station. And that young man went on to have a full and satisfying career as a high school English teacher. He never failed a student because he believed that success was something unique and individual. He never raised his voice. And, in time, his students came to see him as a quiet example of what it meant to treat each day as a victory. The End.

> *Silence. A palpable shift in tone. Nothing for a long time, and then …*
> *A light on the other flight of stairs. Back where Adam started. He hasn't*
> *touched the button. He clicks it. The light stays lit. He tries again. Again.*
> *Finally, he addresses whatever it is that's taken control from him.*

Come on!

Nothing changes. Short-cutting in front of the bridge, Adam crosses to sit in the light, back where he started.

Fine.

Unit Eight—Lies

> *Throughout this unit, Adam fiddles almost unconsciously with the*
> *button. He clicks it, taps it, manipulates it. It does nothing.*

2007. Essex. English teacher. Distant girlfriend. Absolutely. But, it isn't December. It's June. One of those days when the heat makes everything smell like pavement and metal. Almost too hot to go out during the day. But at night, right now, it's perfect. No snow. No fat stupid raindrops blowing into the side of my fucking head and sticking to my skin. It's actually a beautiful night for a walk. Only there's never anywhere to go.

Except London. The whole of London, half an hour that way. *(gesturing)* Or that way. *(gesturing)* I really don't know. I'm not so good with directions.

That really is where I'm coming from, but I didn't get tickets to *Wicked*. I checked it out, but I couldn't really afford them. Even though I work for the school, Admin charges me full rent on my little red brick house. All three floors, even though it's just me in there. Even though half the rooms are locked. Full of old student transcripts and final exams. I swear to God, I'm going to wake up one morning, try the front door and find out I can't use that one either. I guess I like to get out while I can.

To Liverpool Station—which, to avoid confusion, really is in London; not Liverpool. The old streets—the ones with all the side doors and the stairways and the magic at the end. I tried a few of those back in my first couple of months here. I tried to follow them in so that London would know I'm serious. So it would respect me. All London did was turn me around, get me lost, take my money, and make me miss the last train of the night back to Hadley. So now, when I go to London, I don't go much farther than the Starbucks right next to the station.

I took some marking with me tonight. Not much though. Earlier in the year, I would sit at that Starbucks and write feedback until my hand hurt. Always in green ink because the current thinking is that feedback given in green ink fosters a desire in the student—to expand and improve, rather than just correct mistakes. Even if all I got were a few lines when I assigned a whole essay for homework, I'd still take out my green pen and write each student their own little outline. Here's what you can do next time. This is how it goes. Just this past Friday I was collecting the homework from Wednesday night: "With specific reference to the author's use of figurative language, discuss the treatment of war in Wilfred Owen's 'Dulce et Decorum Est.'" Two out of twenty-two kids handed something in. One was a copy-pasted Wikipedia article on the poem, with the hyperlinks still in it. The other was a crumpled sheet of paper with the words "War sucks" written at the top. I watched the kid write it about three minutes before the bell, and I asked him when I can expect the rest.

"That's it," he said. "And I already knew that. You didn't teach us anything. All you do is sit up there and do tricks."

Yeah. At first, I used them as a kind of reward. Someone replaces the comma in a run-on sentence with a period. *(Adam pops a wheelie)* Someone correctly identifies an example of foreshadowing. *(Adam slides into a wheelie-catch)* Someone points out a common theme between two separate pieces of writing, both of which they've read all the way to the end… *(Adam drops the wheelie he's been holding)* Well, no one's done that yet.

So, when they got tired of the basic tricks and didn't want to do the work it took to unlock the rest, I started doing stuff just to keep them watching.

> *Adam CLICKS the button toward the sound booth. There may be a couple of "mis-cues" here, but eventually things land on Entry of the Gladiators. The song gets louder.*

Then, when they weren't interested in watching the same little tricks, I threw in some bigger ones…

> *Adam psyches up, tricking all over the stage, whooping and hollering in time with the tune. He chains tricks: Two sets of catches, at SL and SR; one hand, other hand, no hands at DSC… A spin at Centre. Slow first, then faster and faster…*

Do you like this? Is this good? I bet you like this! Wait. I can go faster!

> *Faster! Until he falls. The music keeps going. Hurting, Adam fumbles for the button. Looks until he finds it. When he does, he CLICKS to turn off the music. It doesn't work at first. He CLICKS until it does. Then, as he rights himself:*

No. Sit down. I'm fine. Don't—I said I'm fine. I don't need the nurse. Go back to your seat. Sit—No, sit … I said (bellowing) SIT DOWN!

> *Adam gets back in his chair. He takes in the set and is suddenly livid with anger. He shoves the centre block all the way to the back of the grid. It hits the stage wall. He shoves each of the remaining pieces of the bridge to the periphery and they do the same. By the time he reaches the last piece, his anger has become a kind of resignation.*

Unit Nine—The Truth About Melissa

Crossing to the USR staircase, Adam retrieves a laptop and ear buds from the steps and crosses with them to the USL staircase. He puts the laptop on that staircase, opens it, and puts the buds in his ears.

"Hey ... Hello? No, I'm here. Okay. No, hang on. I'll move into the kitchen. I think it's closer to the router ..."

He pushes everything, stairs and laptop, all the way to its previous DSL location.

Okay. Are you there?... Okay. How was your day?
   What? ... No, how was your day? How ... was...
   I'm not yelling. This connection is shit. I just ... I need to—
   What?
   Okay. I'll call you back. Hang on.
   No. I'll ... Just wait. Five minutes ... No. Fuck ... Three minutes. Just please wait! I'll call ... What?
   Oh. Okay. We'll try again later then.
   All right. Have a good time ... Me too. Yeah. Bye.

Adam shuts the laptop.

I swear to God, the night I moved in, the Wi-Fi connection was perfect. I Skyped Melissa and we talked until, like, stupid o'clock in the morning. I carried my laptop all around the house—even across the parking lot so she could see the school. "This is where I'll be," I said. Then I took the computer back inside and sat in my bedroom with her. She turned her laptop in one slow circle and showed me her whole little apartment in Korea. Then she carried it into her bathroom and put it on the edge of the sink. Left the door open to cut down the steam and told me how amazing Seoul is while she undressed and took a shower. There was none of that stuff with the towel. I don't know why I said all that. This was better.

   Maybe we just wore out the Wi-Fi after that first conversation. Because now, whenever we manage to find some time that works for both of us, it's like trying to talk to the other side of the world with a tin cup and some string. On the scattered days when the wireless does decide to work properly, the pauses don't go away. Like neither of us wants to invest in a real conversation because we're both afraid that the call will suddenly drop, or the video will freeze and we'll be left talking to a picture without realizing that the other person isn't there anymore.

   Whenever I can't take that chance, I call her on the phone instead. I get maybe five minutes worth of talk time from England to Korea, cell-to-cell before that fucking stupid British robot voice interrupts to tell me that our minutes have run out. The conversations are all the same but at least the pauses are gone.

Unit Ten—Jack

Adam produces his phone. Dials; into phone:

"Hi! Are you busy? … Okay, I… Me? I'm—I'm just on my way home from the station. Oh, no, nothing. It's just … It's kind of funny, you know. There's this kid in my class. Jack … No, I know. I won't keep you. It's just—God, he's a fucking ninth-grader, you know? And he says all I do are wheelie tricks and that I don't teach them anything. And—but he's the one who comes up behind me in the halls and, like, pushes me. Pushes my chair. Sound effects and all. 'Vroom! Vroom! Here we go, sir! Goin' for a ride! Hang on tight! *Vrooom*!' Jesus …"

…Yeah. Today … today he actually did it in class. He just jumped up and started making his fucking engine sounds. And when I gave him detention for it, all I got was this stupid smarmy smile. "Gotta catch me first!" Then he ran out of the room … What? … No, of course not. You think he'd give a shit if I did? … It doesn't matter where he went. He wasn't where he was supposed to be … I'm not … I'm not yelling … Yes. He does it all the time … I've called them. No one ever answers. It just rings and rings. But, whatever. He always comes back for detention anyway … I don't know. Maybe he doesn't have anywhere better to be.

…Just Jack and this one other kid. Wiry little redhead guy. As if they don't see each other enough in class during the day. I don't know why they don't just put them in different classes or something. Anyway, this other kid … I don't know! … The redhead … The one who isn't Jack! I'm not yelling. Hello? …This other kid just sits there and stares at his notebook, I've tried everything I can think of to get him to do something. Any actual work, but it's like he's afraid to pick up his pen. And today it's just the three of us in there, you know. And Jack is staring right into the other kid. Like daring him to pick up his pen. So he does. The little redhead guy puts, like, the first letter of his name on the paper, and Jack fucking pipes up. "Look! Look! He's writing his name! The retard knows his name! Go on retard! You can do it!"… What? No I don't know his name. He only got the first letter out before he … snapped.

…I don't know. Jack is all "retard—retard—retard—retard—retard!"—

Gradually, Adam forgets the phone and the story grows outward toward the audience instead.

…and before I even know what the fuck is happening, Jack's out of his seat and across the room and he's got the little kid's hand covered in his big fucking paw, and Jack is, like, forcing it across the paper. Forcing this kid to make the letters in his name.

And the kid, he just goes postal. Like, ape shit. He swings at Jack with his free hand. Gets him solid on the ear. Jack goes down, and the little redhead starts kicking him. He gets a good one in and Jack's head sort of bounces against the leg of the desk. Now there's blood on Jack's face, and there's blood on the little kid's shoe, so I shove my way between the rows. I'm knocking desks over, and I'm trying to pull the little guy off of Jack. And I can feel him pulling against me, like he's going to pull me right out of my chair and onto the floor with them, and all I can think is that I'm not going to let this little red-headed shit get me out of my chair because I'm his teacher and I'll be goddamned if I can't hold on to one stupid kid.

So I brace myself and I get him around the middle. Pin his arms to his sides and now I've got this kid in a bear hug in my lap. And I can't see anything except the back of his shirt, and I can't move without letting him go. So we just sit there and wait. And after maybe about five minutes someone in the hallway looks in at all the desks knocked over and opens the door to see what's going on, and I don't fucking know…

The light shifts back. Adam returns to the phone.

What? Sorry. How was your day?

Hello? …Mel? *(to audience)* Time's up.

Adam leaves the phone on the USR stairs and crosses DSL.

After a year's worth of shitty internet connections and five-minute telephone conversations about how little my students care about anything I have to teach them. Or how much time I spend yelling at them. Or how fucking cruel they can be to each other and how they don't want my help. After a year's worth of all that, I called Mel to tell her about that long second when I thought I might just go ahead and let that redhead kid keep kicking Jack. But before I could get to that part, Mel told me that she needed some time to be in love with Korea, and that she didn't necessarily like the person I've become. My minutes were about to run out, but I had just enough time to agree.

Unit Eleven—The Button

When I was little—maybe about six years old—my father took me to see a specialist. One of the "foremost Canadian authorities" on child development and disability.

I usually took the bus home. Not the regular one. The small one with the wheelchair ramp in the side. The short bus. It would be there waiting for me after school, and the driver would take me right to my door. But on that day, my Dad was waiting instead. I asked him where we were going and he told me we were headed to the hospital. He did that sometimes, waited to spring surgeries or overnights on me so I'd have less time to dwell on them.

But when we got there, we didn't go through admitting like usual. We didn't even park in the regular lot. There was a separate one around back. We stopped there and went in a whole different entrance.

I'd never been in this part of the hospital before. Somewhere behind all the rainbows, and beach balls, and teddy bears painted on the walls. This was a place that smelled like industrial carpet and furniture polish, and coffee.

We ended up at the end of a long hallway. I remember a room with the size and the … I don't know … the heft of a lecture hall. But I'm pretty sure it was just a regular classroom. A semi-circle of folding metal chairs, with room in the middle for the doctor. I expected him to be on some kind of stage or something. Wondered if he was going to examine me with all these people around. But he was just there standing in the middle of the floor, in a really ugly sweater and running shoes.

My dad wasn't taking me to see the doctor. He was taking me to hear him speak.

The room turned out to be full of new parents. Parents whose kids had recently been diagnosed with Cerebral Palsy. My dad was the only one who thought to bring his actual kid with him. It's funny. I remember the doctor seemed to go on forever, but I can't recall much of what he talked about. Once I realized I wasn't going to be checking in for the weekend, I think I was more concerned about making it home in time to catch the latest episode of He-Man. Who was awesome because, when he wasn't He-Man, he was Prince Adam. Anyway, I do remember one thing:

The doctor had a button.

Adam looks at his own button.

I remember him asking the parents to imagine they had Cerebral Palsy. Then he asked for a show of hands. If these new parents could push this button and take their disabilities away, would they push it? I didn't raise my hand. I'm still not sure if that was because I didn't want to, or because I thought maybe the doctor wasn't asking me since I wasn't a parent and so I didn't count, or because I knew my father was watching to see what I would do. All I know is that this hour at this station—this was the first time I wished for a button to push. Which amounts to absolutely nothing, because all this button does is open the front door of a house that's roughly ten years and 7,600 kilometers from here. Now. Or, that's what it would do… *(Opening the back of the battery compartment)* … if it had any batteries.

Adam leaves the button on the USC block. Crosses DSC.

Unit Twelve—Front and Centre

Almost ten years ago, my girlfriend broke up with me over Skype because we couldn't seem to have a conversation that lasted more than five minutes and wasn't about how much I wanted to physically attack several of my students. How I sometimes wanted to give in to that impulse and was *not* worried about losing my job or getting sued, but instead about doing it in some way or other that didn't make me look weak in front of a bunch of ninth graders.

That night—this night—after the unceremonious end of me and Mel, I went to London, because most of the doors in my house were locked and sometimes I felt like I couldn't get out. I sat at Starbucks and graded papers because it's what I was paid to do. But it didn't take me very long because damned if I was going to give my students any more time than they gave me.

Marking finished, I rode the Tube with a book full of magic. But I didn't get off the Tube, because most of the magical places in the book don't have elevators out here in the real world. And because, as much as I felt like I couldn't get out of my house sometimes, getting off the Tube at the wrong time in the wrong place meant that I wouldn't make it back before the last train of the night leaves Liverpool Station for Hadley. So I got on the Tube and I rode it in circles.

I went from the Tube to the train. And it had to be the last train, because I hated Hadley Cross in ways that I've never hated a place before or since. Coming back to Hadley meant coming back to all of the things I couldn't do: teach, manage a relationship, walk up a flight of stairs without help from Pardeep. I didn't know a thing about Pardeep, by the way. Nothing except his name. And even that wasn't because he told me what it was. I saw it on his name tag. *Tony* has always been "the guy who said no when I asked for help." I guess I just wanted Pardeep to be a little bit more than the guy who said yes.

The train station: There was no graffiti. No kicked-in ticket machines. No naked light bulbs dangling from exposed wires. No beer cans or puke stains or anything like that. In fact, Hadley Town Council had just had the whole station redone with touch screen ticket machines and energy efficient lighting. Still no elevator. But the whole place smelled like fresh paint. I guess I just thought a story like mine would be easier to tell in a place where people expect things like that to happen.

I want to do that thing with my chair again. Take it apart and carry it across the bridge in pieces. Put it back together on the other side. I want to do the thing I said I did, and I want to keep doing that all night. Once for every time in the last ten years when I lied about what happened—to anyone who would sit still long enough for me to tell the story. Or maybe I can just do it a few times in front of, like, a whole bunch of people at once. Bulk apology. Easy way out.

I think that's the thing though. Even the easy way out is still a way out. Yeah, I could've called someone from the school. I could've called a cab down from Colchester. That's true, but I didn't think of those things until afterwards. On that night, on the steps at the station, I couldn't think of anything except how fucking stuck I was. In this little fishbowl of a town where my students didn't give a shit about anything I had to say, half a world away from a beautiful woman who was having an amazing time without me. And I swear this was the first time I'd ever wished for that magic button to make it so I could walk right out of there, right that second. And, oh God, I was only twenty-three, that meant that I would probably make that very same wish again and again and again between twenty-three and kingdom come. More than anything else, that scared the shit out of me.

So I sat there on the steps. Didn't move an inch. And, about fifteen minutes in, I had to use the bathroom. Most of the bigger stations have bathrooms, but not this little guy. And me? I've got a spastic bladder to go with all of my other spastic parts. That just means I gotta go when I gotta go. And when there isn't anywhere to go, that's when I really gotta go. And the very thing that makes my bladder spasm when I need to use the bathroom, it makes my legs spasm too. So if I try to stand up or kneel up or do anything that isn't sitting square on the can, I fall over and everything goes everywhere.

So I managed to hold it for about ten minutes. And then I couldn't hold it anymore. So, I pissed my pants, and then I sat there wondering whether or not someone helpful would come along before sunrise.

Someone came along. Just over an hour later. Maybe the only other person in Hadley Cross who was restless enough to be out and about after 10:30 without a real reason.

Jack. I don't know what Jack planned to do at the station close to two in the morning, but part of me hopes that he was out to vandalize with youthful abandon. Take some of the shine off the place. Jack showed up over there. He saw me over here. And he yelled across:

"You need some help, sir?"

And I told him I did.

So Jack came over and I explained. I told him I can walk up the stairs. All he had to do was carry my chair over and leave it on the other platform. I'd get there in my own time. And I know he saw me. He saw me because there were brand new energy efficient lights and no shadows to hide in. But he didn't say anything about any of that. He just picked up my chair, carried it to the other platform and left it for me. He was gone by the time I got to it, so I didn't get to say thank you. I'm not sure I would have said it then anyway. I was too busy building my lie, and by the time I'd made that five minute walk from the station to my little red brick house, I was ready to tell it.

Only Jack never said anything about it the next day. Or any day after that. And a few weeks later the school year ended—and I left. It wasn't until I got home to St. John's—sorry, Mount Pearl—when people started asking me what I did for a whole year in England, that I realized I had almost nothing to tell them, except a story about this one night in a train station when there wasn't anyone else around. When I took my chair apart, carried the pieces across a bridge and put them back together again. God it was a hell of a story, and folks loved to hear it.

Last week, after that lesson on semicolons—the one at the school in Richmond where my student blew in, hugged me stupid and then blew out again—I was taking the train back to Vancouver and the elevator at my home station was busted. I asked the SkyTrain attendant on the platform if he wouldn't mind carrying my chair up the stairs. They're not supposed to do that, but he didn't mind. He waited with my chair at the top and held it for me while I got back in.

"That was easy," he said. "You must've done that a few times before."

"Yeah," I said. "The last time I pissed my pants first."

(Adam exits DSL. Hold on the empty platform. Lights fade to black.)

End of play.

PART TWO

Past Is Present

The Last Reading of Charlotte Cushman

CAROLYN GAGE

In 1869, the American actress Charlotte Cushman was arguably the most famous performer of male and female roles. She embarked on a farewell tour of America after her breast cancer diagnosis.[1] When her farewell tour was finished, she went on a reading tour. It is impossible to determine how many members of Cushman's audience knew of her breast cancer diagnosis, or to determine precisely how the pain associated with that diagnosis affected (or did not affect) her farewell tour and her reading tour. It is possible to verify, however, that neither tour diminished her reputation as a performer. During her farewell ceremony after her death, thousands of her fans walked the streets of New York City, keeping a candlelit vigil for her.[2]

Perhaps it is unsurprising that Cushman chose to continue touring despite—or in defiance of—her physical pain. A "butch" lesbian performer who openly embraced that identity in both her public and her private life, Cushman defied gender roles and the idealization of heterosexual romantic pairings in her stage work. She played more than thirty masculine roles in her career, including playing Romeo to her sister Susan's Juliet. According to contemporary accounts, her portrayals of dashing male heroes thrilled her fans, especially the female ones. After attending a performance during Cushman's first British season, one female admirer reportedly coyly remarked, "Miss Cushman is a dangerous young man."[3] Audience members and friends tacitly understood that Charlotte was modeling the idea that romantic love between women belonged onstage and offstage. Cushman's friends referred to her real-life partner, Emma Stebbins, as her Juliet.

By proudly performing her "butch" identity onstage and in life, Cushman provided a role model for nineteenth century women who were dissatisfied with feminine gender norms of the nineteenth century and/or experienced same sex attractions. Cushman didn't just celebrate her "butch" physicality. She performed her roles so skillfully that theatre critics relished it too. In 1860, after watching Cushman play Romeo, a theatre critic for *The New York Times* wrote that "There is in the delicacy of Romeo's character something which requires a woman to represent it, and unfits almost every man for its impersonation."[4] For this reviewer, at least, Cushman was better suited to the role of Romeo than any male actor. When critics praised Cushman in her male roles, they were celebrating the presence of a "butch" lesbian in a public space, even if they were not aware that was what they were doing.

Charlotte Cushman in costume as Romeo, c. 1850, photo by Charles D. Fredricks & Co. (New York Public Library Digital Collections, Billy Rose Theatre Division).

Of course, neither Cushman nor any of her nineteenth century contemporaries would have viewed gender and sexuality through the lenses used now; there is no record of her referring to herself as "butch." In Carolyn Gage's *The Last Reading of Charlotte Cushman*, contemporary audiences are invited to examine a particular moment in the life of a celebrated public figure with a contemporary appreciation for how her example has influenced gender fluid performers. Gage's Cushman speaks when her biologically female body, which she had formerly re-presented so successfully onstage, is rebelling against her. Unlike her gender and her sexual identity, Cushman's breast cancer is not something she can choose how to physically represent to an audience. When she is in pain, she may hesitate or wince, even if the hero or heroine she is playing would not do so. Gage understands that a contemporary audience will welcome Cushman's confrontation of her physical limitations, just as nineteenth century audiences welcomed her confrontations of nineteenth century gender norms, onstage and offstage. Her magnetic stage presence can captivate any audience, in any age.

—Jill Summerville

NOTES

1. "Charlotte Cushman: Cross-Dressing Tragedienne of the Nineteenth Century," Boston: New England Historical Society, 2018; October 8, 2019.

2. *Ibid.*

3. Lisa Merrill, *When Romeo Was a Woman: Charlotte Cushman and Her Circle of Female Spectators* (Ann Arbor: University of Michigan Press, 1999), 114.

4. *Ibid.*, 128.

The Last Reading of Charlotte Cushman

Famed nineteenth century actress Charlotte Cushman was American's first native-born star of the stage. Her career included such highlights as playing a very celebrated Romeo opposite her sister as Juliet, playing Lady Macbeth opposite the famed William Charles Macready, and performing for President Abraham Lincoln. Just as lasting is her fame as a proudly "out" lesbian. She regularly played "breeches" roles onstage and often wore masculine clothes off; she had a number of romantic relationships with women about which, though described by historians for decades as her "friends," she was quite open. She helped establish an artists' group while in Rome that was openly inviting to lesbian artists, and she proudly called a woman her wife. Her acting legacy paved the way for strong tragedian actresses to come, and the stories of her personal life—after decades of enforced obscurity—are once again in the light.—Eds.

Author's Note: *The Last Reading of Charlotte Cushman* is a play about the lesbian actress Charlotte Cushman, who had been very, very famous and powerful in the nineteenth century. In my play, she is on her final tour, struggling against the cancer that will kill her.

Facing a diagnosis of permanent disability, I wanted to write about coming to terms with disease and mortality. I wanted to write about a woman who was saying goodbye to her life in the theatre.

The play was also an act of revenge against an industry that had treated lesbians and masculine women like freaks and outcasts. Here was a fierce, fat, "bull dyke" who, notwithstanding, had been the greatest English-speaking actress on two continents in the nineteenth century! It was empowering to bring her to life, and, through her, to get in touch with my anger and contempt for the kind of colonized female roles that are the staple in mainstream theatre—roles that relegate women like myself to positions as stagehands or character actors.

The heroic performer who defies death to keep the curtain up is theatrical cliché, but I didn't mind exploiting it, because the real drama of the play lay not in the plot, but in the celebration of butch sexuality that was represented by Cushman. The real Cushman had been a major womanizer, right up to the last years of her life.

This was the Cushman I wanted to celebrate—the scoundrel, the roué. I wanted to show my audiences the special charisma of the swashbuckling butch. As Cushman says in the play, "I have always maintained that only a woman can play Romeo with any credibility." The challenge of this play was to write a fascinating, funny, tragic, charming, rollicking, rant-and-roar, tear-jerking evening of theatre based on this larger-than-life theatrical legend.

CAST OF CHARACTERS
STAGE MANAGER: A man or woman of any age.
CHARLOTTE CUSHMAN: A large woman, masculine in appearance, late 50s.
Scene
The scene for the reading is the actual theatre where the play is being produced.
Time
The present.
The Last Reading of Charlotte Cushman © Carolyn Gage, all rights reserved.

* * *

ACT ONE

Lighting is set at pre-show levels. An antique table and chair are center stage. On the table is a pitcher of water with a glass, and next to them is a stack of old books with markers in them. An elegant vase with an arrangement of flowers graces the table.

STAGE MANAGER *enters, uncomfortable to be addressing an audience.*

STAGE MANAGER: Could I have your attention please? I've been asked to announce that the reading tonight has been cancelled. It seems that the performer is ill, and she won't be able to appear—

CHARLOTTE: *(From the wings.)* Just a minute! Just a minute! *(CHARLOTTE CUSHMAN enters. She is a tall, white-haired woman in her late fifties. She is masculine in appearance and comportment, and she wears her hair pulled back off her forehead. Her outfit is unorthodox, but it suits her well. She wears a man's tailored jacket and tie from the 1870s over a long, full skirt of dark color. CHARLOTTE is a proud woman, fiercely in control of her own destiny. Her life has been the theatre, and her relationship with her public has always taken precedence over her relationships with lovers or friends. She is dying, and she knows it. This will be her last stand, and she pulls all the stops. She enters, out of breath.)* What do you think you're doing?

STAGE MANAGER: *(Turning in surprise.)* Miss Cushman—

CHARLOTTE: Who told you to cancel my reading?

STAGE MANAGER: They said you had collapsed in the dressing room.

CHARLOTTE: *(Enraged.)* Yes, and I have expanded again. I want to know whose idea it was to cancel the reading.

STAGE MANAGER: It was Miss Stebbins, your … your…

CHARLOTTE: *(A challenge.)* My wife? *(Enraged, she turns toward the wings to confront Emma.)* Yes, well, Emma tends to overreact sometimes. *(To Emma.)* Don't you? *(To STAGE MANAGER.)* I'm sure Emma told you all about my cancer, didn't she? My *breast* cancer? *(To Emma.)* Yes. *(To STAGE MANAGER.)* And did Miss Stebbins tell you that it was my cancer that brought me out of retirement four years ago? And did Miss Stebbins tell you that in these four years of touring, I have performed hundreds of readings and plays? *(To Emma.)* No? *(To STAGE MANAGER.)* And did Miss Stebbins tell you that in all these years, I have never missed a single performance? *Never?* *(To Emma.)* No? *(To STAGE MANAGER.)* But, if you and Emma feel that it would be better for me not to go on, I will be happy to withdraw… *(Scooping up her books.)* … after I have collected my full fee, of course.

STAGE MANAGER: *(An agonizing pause, during which the STAGE MANAGER turns first to Emma and then back to CHARLOTTE.)* Miss Cushman, if you're willing to—

CHARLOTTE: *(Dropping the books.)* Thank you, I am. Now, if you'll just introduce me, I think we can get on with our evening. *(She hands her/him a card and turns her back.)*

STAGE MANAGER: *(Glancing in Emma's direction before reading the card.)* "Ladies and gentlemen, it is my privilege tonight to present the greatest English-speaking actress of two continents, a performer who has entertained for three presidents and the crowned heads of Europe, an American artist whose interpretations of Shakespeare's tragic heroines are legendary, and a leading lady for four decades…" *(With a flourish.)* … Ladies and gentlemen— Miss Charlotte Cushman! *(The STAGE MANAGER exits, and the lights come up on the set. CHARLOTTE turns to acknowledge the applause. She is still stung by Emma's interference.)*

CHARLOTTE: Well… *(Picking up the books.)* I was preparing to read a little Tennyson for you … and a little Bobby Burns … and some of Mrs. Browning's poetry tonight, but since Miss Stebbins has taken it upon herself to select a theme for this evening—death—I am afraid that the readings I had prepared are no longer suited to the occasion. Well… *(Pushing the books to one side.)* I shall just have to improvise. Death… *(She crosses to the table and takes a drink of water.)* The first time I encountered death, I was twenty-three years old and in bed with a prostitute. *(Sitting, she turns to the audience.)* That got your attention, didn't it? *(Turning toward Emma in the wings.)* See what you've started? *(To audience.)* This is all Emma's fault. *(A long look at Emma before she turns back to the audience.)* So—where was I? Ah. In bed with a prostitute.

Well, I was twenty-three years old and living in New York. I was what they called a "walking lady," which is the actor who takes the roles too large for the chorus and too small for the leads. This was at the Park Theatre. And it was excellent training, too. Everything was repertory in those days, and during my three years as a "walking lady," I performed over a hundred and twenty different roles. But what does this have to do with a prostitute?

I'm getting to it. The Park Theatre was managed by one Stephen Price, and it is an understatement to say that Mr. Price and I did not get along. You see, Mr. Price resented any actor who was more handsome than himself. *(She laughs.)* He saw it as his personal mission in life to drive me out of the company, and in February of 1839, it looked as if he just might succeed.

The Park Theatre was going to produce *Oliver Twist*, and there is a part of a prostitute in the play, Nancy Sikes. Well, in my day, no actress with any kind of reputation would touch a role like that, and Stephen Price knew it. So, naturally, he assigned it to me. If I took the part, I would be professionally ruined, and if I refused, I would be fired. Yes, Mr. Price finally had me where he wanted me.

And to tell you the truth, I considered quitting. It was quite an insult to be cast as a prostitute, and of course, he had done it in front of the whole company. But I had seen too many talented women lose out to temperament in this game, and I was determined not to be outmaneuvered. If there was a way to play Nancy Sikes without damaging my reputation, I was going to find it. And I was equally determined to see Stephen Price hoist on his own… *(Pausing to consider.)* … *tiny* petard. *(Laughing, she rises.)* So I accepted the part—graciously. And then I took myself down to Five Points. That was the area just east of Broadway—the worst slum in New York. And I rented myself a room at Mother Hennessey's, which was the cheapest and dirtiest rooming house I could find. That was where the streetwalkers and the drunks stayed, when they could afford a roof for the night. And it was there, at Mother Hennessey's, that I began to study the role of Nancy Sikes.

During the day, I went out on the street and watched the old women pick through the garbage, and then I watched the young women pick through the old men. I watched their hands, their hips, their elbows, their mouths, their teeth, their eyebrows. I watched them flirt, I watched them joke, I watched them steal—I watched the things that no one else was watching. And at night, I went to the saloons, and I studied the women there. *(Smiling.)* And sometimes the women studied me. On the third night, a young prostitute came into the bar. She was very sick, shaking all over, and she asked for water. They gave her a glass of whiskey, and she got sick all over the floor. The men thought this was funny. *(A long pause.)*

I went to help her, and it turned out she didn't have any place to stay for the night, so I took her up to my room at Mother Hennessey's, I undressed her, I helped her to bed… *(Pausing.)* And then she died. *(She sits.)*

That's it. That's the story. No last words, no touching prayers, no anxious faces hovering over the bed, no final embrace. A convulsion and she died. That was it. *(Reflecting.)*

"…Out, out, brief candle!
Life's but a walking shadow, a poor player,
That struts and frets his hour upon the stage,
And then is heard no more. It is a tale
Told by an idiot, full of sound and fury,
Signifying nothing."

What did I do? I took her clothes. *(Rising with mock indifference.)* Of course, I took her clothes. I had a show to open, and they fit me… *(With anger.)* And then I went back to the Park Theatre, and I gave them Nancy Sikes. Oh, yes, I gave them Nancy Sikes. Not the whore with the heart of gold, not the feisty little spitfire from the wrong side of town—oh, no—I gave them a prostitute the likes of which they had never seen on a New York stage, even though they passed a dozen girls just like her on the way to the theatre—even though half the men would go home with one of these girls on their arm.

But I gave them a prostitute they could see, not just look at—but really see. I gave them a prostitute that made them weep the tears that no one shed that night at Mother Hennessey's. And weep they did. You see, real life is too painful for most people. That's why they come to the theatre.

So—would you like to see Nancy? You would? All right. This is from the third act, where the boy Oliver has been kidnapped by Nancy's pimp, Fagin. Her boyfriend, Bill, is threatening to turn his dog loose on Oliver, and Nancy is determined to stop him. Here's Bill… *(Turning away to get in character as Bill Sikes.)* "I'll teach the boy a lesson. The dog's outside the door—"

(As Nancy.) "Bill, no! He'll tear the boy to pieces."

(As Bill.) "Stand off from me or I'll split your skull against the wall!"

(As Nancy.) "I don't care for that, Bill. The child shan't be hurt by the dog unless you first kill me."

(As Bill.) "Shan't he? I'll soon do that if you don't keep off."

And here comes Fagin: *(As Fagin.)* "What's the matter here?"

(As Bill.) "The girl's gone mad."

(As Nancy.) "No, she hasn't."

(As Bill.) "Then keep quiet."

(As Nancy.) "No, I won't … Now, strike the boy, if you dare—any of you! Don't 'dear' me! I won't stand by and see it done! You have got the boy, and what more would you have? Let him be then, or I will put that mark on you that will bring me to the gallows before my time! Oh, yes, I know who I am and what I am. I know all about it—well—well! God help me! And I wish I had been struck dead in the streets before I had lent a hand in bringing him to where he is. Ah, me! He's a thief from this night forth—and isn't that enough without any more cruelty? Civil words, Fagin? Do you deserve them from me? Who taught me to pilfer and to steal, when I was a child not half so old as this?—You! I have been in the trade and in your service twelve years since, and you know it well—you know you do! And, yes, it is my living! and the cold, wet, dirty streets are my home! and you are the wretch who drove me to 'em long ago, and that'll keep me there until I die—" *(She lunges, as if to strike Fagin.)* "Devil!"

> *(The gesture tears open CHARLOTTE's mastectomy scars, and she freezes in pain, her hand covering the place. Glancing toward the wings, CHARLOTTE holds up her hand to prevent Emma coming onto the stage.)*

No! I'm all right, Emma. I'll be fine—*(Turning her attention toward the table.)* I just need a little water … and I'll be fine. *(Sitting, she concentrates on pouring the water. She gestures toward the wings, in order to divert attention from her condition.)* Emma. Emma Stebbins, my wife. *(CHARLOTTE forces a laugh.)* Emma and I have been together—what?—twenty years now? *(She looks toward the wings, in need of Emma's support.)* Nineteen? *(Relieved at Emma's response, she turns to the audience.)* Nineteen years. Emma's counting. Emma Stebbins, the world-renowned sculptor. We met in Rome. Emma was living with Harriet Hosmer—*(She turns toward the wings. Emma has apparently said something.)* What? Oh, it's all right. They don't care. *(To audience.)* Do you? I didn't think so. *(To Emma.)* See? They don't care. *(To audience.)* Emma was living with Harriet Hosmer. She is a sculptor, too. An excellent sculptor. Harriet Hosmer—Hatty. *(To Emma.)* May I tell them about Hatty? I know they want to hear about her. Everybody wants to hear about Hatty. May I? *(Emma has said something.)* What? *(Defensive.)* What about Rosalie? *(Pause.)* All right, I will … *after* I tell them about you and Hatty. *(To audience.)* Emma's a little touchy about Hatty.

Well—Hatty Hosmer. Hatty's not speaking to me now.

Something about our hunt club in Rome. Hatty didn't think it was fair that they never gave the tail—the fox tail—to the Americans. Of course, she's talking about herself. Hatty's always talking about herself. But I have to admit, she can ride the pantaloons off the Italians. But there was no need to blow the whole thing into an international incident, which is what she did. Well, apparently she felt I didn't give enough support to her cause. So now she's not speaking.

But it's not really about fox tails. It's about death. I know Hatty. She lost practically her whole family before she was twelve. Her mother died when Hatty was six, and then she lost her two brothers, and then her sister. I just don't think she can take anyone else dying on her. So, you see, she's decided to kill the friendship instead.

But you want to hear the scandal. Well, I met Hatty Hosmer in 1851. I was thirty-five, and she—bless her heart—was just twenty-one. And a cuter little tomboy you never saw. Oh, she was a wild thing! Reminded me of myself. Anyway, I was touring in Boston, and she had just come back from medical school. She had been taking anatomy courses for her sculpting. Of course, she was the only woman they let in the school. That was Hatty. *(Rising.)* Well, she came backstage to see me, and, frankly, she was quite smitten. And, to tell the truth, I was rather dashing in those days—prancing around in tunics and tights … I had good legs. Still do. *(She shows us.)* Anyway, Hatty started coming backstage after every performance—and bringing me flowers. *(She shakes her head at the memory.)* It was very sweet.

But I was married at the time—to Matilda Hays, and Matilda did not think it was so sweet. Matilda and I were having some problems. Oh, Matilda… *(She sits.)* She had shown up at my door in London—not unlike the way Hatty was showing up in Boston—asking me for acting lessons. It has always amazed me how many young women seem to be in need of my instruction.

Well, as luck would have it, I had just lost my touring partner, and I was in the market for a new Juliet for my Romeo. How's that for a line? *(Laughing.)* Worked, too. Matilda auditioned for me, and I cast her, and we became lovers on and off the stage. It was all very daring and very romantic, and we were so pleased with ourselves, we got married. That's right. We had a ceremony and exchanged vows of celibacy—referring to men, of course—and promised to be faithful for eternity. *(Laughing.)* And it *was* an eternity. *(Another burst of laughter.)*

It turned out that Matilda was not really up to the demands of a touring performer, and she retired from her public role as Juliet, but she continued to accompany me as my wife. She told me she was happy, and I believed her. I have never understood a woman who is actively miserable and not doing anything about it—but that was Matilda. And such was the state of our affairs when Hatty Hosmer knocked on my stage door in Boston. *(She is about to proceed with more confidences, when she sees Emma give her "the look." She assumes an air of wounded dignity.)* But there's no point in boring you with the details. One thing just led to another, and the next thing you know, Hatty was joining Matilda and myself in Rome that winter—*(To Emma.)* To study sculpting. *(To the audience.)* The whole thing was very innocent. *(Protesting to Emma, who has said something.)* It was! *(She starts to speak to the audience but turns back to Emma.)* How would you know? You weren't even there! *(She rises, laughing. The joke has been on Emma.)*

Where was I? Rome … Yes, well, there had been one slight obstacle. Hatty's father, Hiram—but we all called him "Elizabeth." I can't remember now why we did that. *(Laughing.)* Well, anyway, "Elizabeth" was terrified at the thought of his daughter leaving him. I never met a more possessive man in my life. He had even built a little studio on the back of his house, just so that Hatty could stay home and be a little "sculptress." *(Soberly.)* Don't ever call Hatty a sculptress. *(She laughs.)*

Well, her father made us all promise that we would send Hatty back at the end of a year. That was twenty-five years ago, and Hatty is still in Rome. Well, Hiram had a fit and he cut off all the money. But Hatty had her revenge. Oh, yes, she had her revenge.

What she did was, she designed a monument in honor of a girl who had murdered her father—Beatrice Cenci. You don't know who that is, but, believe me, everybody in Rome knew about Beatrice Cenci. Her father had locked her up and raped and beaten her for years, and then she finally hired someone to murder him. Well, they arrested her, of course, and sentenced her to die— she was only seventeen—and the whole city was in an uproar, especially the women.

Well, Hatty's statue of Beatrice was something else. It was the most exquisitely beautiful female form I have ever seen—and I've seen a few. She has the girl lying on the stone slab of her prison cell, looking for all the world like an angel on a cloud—sleeping unmolested at last. And she has the sweetest little smile on her face. Hatty's statue of Beatrice has gone around the world now. Yes, it even went back to Boston, where Elizabeth could see it. Oh, yes, Hatty had the last word. She always does … She always does. *(Rallying.)* But the point of this whole story is how I met Emma. *(Turning toward the wings.)* You were hoping I'd forget. *(To audience.)* So, anyway, Matilda and Hatty and I moved to Rome. And then Hatty did what most young women do to older women who have helped them unstintingly and from the pure goodness of their hearts—she dumped me. And didn't Matilda just love that! Poor Matilda. She never could do anything on her own. She had to let Hatty use her in order to hurt me. So the two of them got together to act out their little melodrama for my benefit. *(Reflecting.)*

I have a horror of amateur theatricals, and so I booked a tour of England, leaving my little semi-retired Juliet to her understudy of a Romeo back in Italy. And, of course, after I left, there wasn't much point in the whole thing for Hatty, so she dumped Matilda. And then Matilda came running up to London, her little tail tucked between her legs, to see if I would take her back. I did, of course, but nothing could be the same between us—thanks to Hatty. But I had my revenge—*(Toward the wings.)* Didn't I? *(To audience.)* This is the good part.

Emma came over from the States to study sculpting, and of course, she met Hatty. Everybody who came to Rome had to see the Pope and Hatty. Not necessarily in that order. So, Emma met Hatty, and Hatty can be very persuasive when she wants to be. She talked Emma into living with her, and the next thing you know she was going all over Rome introducing Emma as her wife. Her wife! Hatty was about as domestic as her horse. But she made the fatal mistake of introducing Emma to me, and as Rosalind would say: *(Crossing seductively toward Emma.)*

No sooner met, but they look'd; no sooner look'd but they lov'd; no sooner lov'd but they sigh'd; no sooner sigh'd but they asked one another the reason; no sooner knew the reason but they sought the remedy.

That was twenty years ago—*(To Emma.)* Excuse me, Emma—nineteen… *(To audience)* And she is still with me.

Poor Hatty … But we're all friends now. Hatty even came and lived with us for six years. *(To Emma.)* Yes, we're all friends now… *(To audience.)* Except now, of course, with this death business.

Funny how everyone else is more upset about it than I am. They should know better. The only thing that kills an actor is a bad review. Audiences will forgive you if you die, but they will never forget a bad performance.

No, I have already died once in this lifetime, and once is enough, thank you. It was in New Orleans, the winter of 1835. I died every day for five months. Every single day. I'll never forget it. Nineteen years old, away from home for the first time—singing opera. You didn't know that, did you? Well, that's how I got started—and nearly how I got finished.

Yes, I was an opera singer. And I could have been a very good one, too, if my teacher hadn't insisted I sing soprano when it should have been obvious I was a natural contralto.

Well, the critics were brutal. Absolutely brutal. Would you like to hear what they said? Of course you would.

There are few things in this life which give us as much pleasure as other people's bad reviews. Well, let's see… "Seldom in tune, she possesses neither taste nor skill." You like that? Or "…we would as soon hear a peacock attempt the carols of a nightingale as to listen to her squalling caricature of singing…?"

Oh, I died a thousand deaths that winter. A thousand deaths. I had left Boston with such high hopes, and now it looked as if my life was over before it even started. I would go back to Boston, back to my mother's wretched little rooming house, back to a life of drudgery, back to Charlie Wiggins—the driveling little store clerk who was always pestering me to marry him. And wouldn't Mother have loved that! Yes, my life was over. *(As Wolsey.)*

"Farewell? a long farewell to all my greatness!
This is the state of man: to-day he puts forth
The tender leaves of hopes, to-morrow blossoms,
And bears his blushing honours thick upon him;
The third day comes a frost, a killing frost,
And when he thinks, good easy man, full surely
His greatness is a-ripening, nips his root,
And then he falls, as I do. I have ventur'd,
Like little wanton boys that swim on bladders,
This many summers in a sea of glory,
But far beyond my depth. My high-blown pride
At length broke under me, and now has left me,
Weary and old with service, to the mercy
Of a rude stream, that must forever hide me."

Cardinal Wolsey, *Henry VIII*. Charlotte Cushman, New Orleans.

But I never gave up. As long as I was still under contract, I would perform—no matter how vicious the critics, no matter how rude the audiences, no matter how unkind my fellow performers. No, when that curtain went up, I was always in my place. Dying every second, but *in my place*.

Well, finally, one of the critics took pity on me. He suggested that I might be successful in a non-singing role. That was it. That was my break.

I took the notice to the manager of the company, and I begged him to give me a speaking part. Well, he didn't have much to lose, because I was still under contract for another month, and, heaven knows, my notices certainly couldn't be any worse. So he told me the role of Lady Macbeth was mine if I wanted it. I wanted it.

Lady Macbeth. In two weeks. Now, bear in mind I was still just nineteen years old, and I had never performed a play in my life—much less a Shakespearean play, much less a lead role. But this was it—my one chance, and *I could not fail*.

What did I do? I made a plan. I would impersonate a famous actor who had been a success in the role. Not a bad plan—except that the actor I chose was Sarah Siddons. Sarah Siddons. "The" Sarah Siddons. England's greatest tragedienne. Lovely Sarah Siddons. Petite Sarah Siddons. Charming, seductive, gracious, vivacious, flirtatious, *feminine* Sarah Siddons. *(She nods.)* Yes, Sarah Siddons… *(A damsel in distress, veddy proper accent.)*

Alack, I am afraid they have awak'd,
And 'tis not done; th' attempt, and not the deed,
Confounds us. Hark! I laid their daggers ready,
He could not miss 'em. Had he not resembled
My father as he slept, I had done't.

(She laughs.) The director was concerned. He told me to be more passionate. *(Properly petulant.)*

"…Go get some water,
And wash this filthy witness from your hand.
Why did you bring these daggers from the place?
They must lie there. Go carry them, and smear
The sleepy grooms with blood …"
Oh!

> *(CHARLOTTE gives a feminine cry of exasperation.)*

…Infirm of purpose!
Give me the daggers!

(A long pause.) We were days from opening. The director was tearing his hair out. Finally he stopped the rehearsal. He told me I had no talent, that I was wasting my time, that I would never have a career on the stage, and that all my dreams were ridiculous.

Well, I might have accepted that I couldn't act. I might even have accepted that I didn't have a future—but that my dreams were ridiculous…? What did he know about the dreams of a nineteen-year-old girl? What did he know about my wanting to hold another woman in my arms, to feel her soft breasts pressed against mine, to kiss her on the lips, to wake up in the morning with her head resting tenderly on my shoulder? What did he know about my dreams of having enough money so that the woman I loved could live with me for the rest of my life, so that I could travel anywhere I wanted, dress any way I pleased, do anything I liked with anyone I chose? Ridiculous? No, my dreams were not ridiculous. They were beautiful, and this man had no right to make fun of them.

What did I do? I reared up on my hind legs like a beast who has been cornered. I showed him my fangs, and I showed him my claws. I backed that poor fellow into a wall, my fists waving in his face, and I tore into him. I let him know exactly what I thought of his arrogance, of his conceit, and of his "Shakespe-ah." I don't know what all I said, but I know that I said it. And when I was all through, shaking from head to toe, tears running down my face, waiting for him to fire me—do you know what he did? He clapped. The son-of-a-bitch stood there and clapped. And then he said: *(Whispering.)* "Do it just like that." *(Smiling.)* And I did. *(She turns her back, for a moment to get into character. During this speech, CHARLOTTE directs rage toward her body and the disease which is ravaging it—alluding to the mastectomy at the end.)*

…The raven himself is hoarse
That croaks the fatal entrance of Duncan
Under my battlements. Come, you spirits
That tend on mortal thoughts, unsex me here,

>   *(CHARLOTTE clutches her breast.)*

And fill me from the crown to the toe top-full
Of direst cruelty! Make thick my blood,
Stop up th' access and passage to remorse,
That no compunctious visitings of nature
Shake my fell purpose, nor keep peace between
Th' effect and it! Come to my woman's breasts,
And take my milk for gall, you murth'ring ministers,
Wherever in your sightless substances
You wait on nature's mischief! Come, thick night,
And pall thee in the dunnest smoke of hell,
That my keen knife see not the wound it makes
Nor heaven peep through the blanket of the dark
To cry, "Hold, hold!"

(She collapses in the chair, out of breath and panting.) I stopped the show … Stopped it cold… *(Struggling for breath.)* They loved me … They loved me! *(Unable to rally, she signals toward the wings.)* I think this would be a good time … for us to take a break… *(Lights fade, as CHARLOTTE rises with extreme difficulty to exit. Blackout.)*

End of Act One

ACT TWO

>   Lights come up on the same set. CHARLOTTE enters. She has rallied during the intermission, and she paces the stage like an animal in a cage. Conscious that her time is running out, CHARLOTTE plays with a feverish energy bordering on delirium.

CHARLOTTE:
'Tis now the very witching time of night,
When churchyards yawn and hell itself breathes out
Contagion to this world. Now could I drink hot blood,
And do such bitter business as the day
Would quake to look on.

(Smiling.) Hamlet ... Emma didn't think I'd make it back for the second half. *(To Emma.)* Did you? *(To audience.)* She didn't think I'd recover from my surgery either. I had a breast removed four years ago. One of the first operations of its kind ever performed... *(Pausing.)* A distinction which was not without disadvantages. *But*, I survived. *(To Emma.)* Didn't I? *(To audience.)* And here I am.

(Turning suddenly to Emma.) I'll tell you what, Emma—I'll make a bet with you. If I don't finish the show tonight, I'll cancel the rest of the tour and go home with you. How's that? *(To the audience.)* She likes that. *(To Emma.)* *But*, you have to agree, if I *do* finish the show, you will go with me to San Francisco. *(To the audience.)* I've always wanted to go there. They'd love me in San Francisco, don't you think? *(To Emma.)* Well, what do you say? Is it a deal? *(Rallying, she turns to the audience.)* You are the witnesses! Miss Emma Stebbins has just agreed to accompany Miss Charlotte Cushman on a tour to California and points west.

(Turning toward Emma, who has apparently interrupted her.) What? *(Irritated.)* Of course, I'm going to tell them about Rosalie. I said I would, didn't I? *(To the audience.)* You want to hear about my first girlfriend, don't you? I thought so.

Rosalie ... Rosalie Sully. I was twenty-six and she was twenty-two. Would you like to know how I seduced her? Well, I sat absolutely motionless for hours at a time and never said a word. You don't believe me? Her father was painting my portrait. *(She laughs.)* Rosalie Sully... *(Sitting.)* Well, Mother thought the whole thing was disgusting. She presented me with an ultimatum: Give up Rosalie or move out of the house... *(Defensive.)* What could I do? I was young, and I had no one to advise me. I did what I thought was the right thing. I felt I had no choice at the time... *(With mock contrition.)* I rented an apartment, so Rosie could sleep with me. *(Laughing heartily, she rises and crosses downstage.)* Oh, we were in love. We were so in love—and I had waited so long! Is there anything like that first girlfriend? It was sweet and tender and passionate and everything I had ever dreamed it would be. And more. And better. Rosalie Sully. My Rose. She died while I was over in England. Died at twenty-six ... Beautiful Rose.

(Changing the subject abruptly.) But that reminds me—we were doing death this evening, weren't we? I suppose you want to see me die. That's what they pay me for. So—what's your pleasure? Suicide? Sword wound? Musket ball...? How about poison? Poison is good.

This is Hamlet's mother, Gertrude. She has to die in front of both her husband and her son, but without upstaging either one of them. Needless to say, this is a role which presents a challenge for many women.

> *(CHARLOTTE, a vapid expression on her face, lifts the glass and sips from it as if it were wine. She suppresses a series of coughs, rises in alarm, only to lose her balance, and waves to Claudius to indicate that he is not to worry. Attempting to sit, she falls out of the chair and lies*

panting on the floor, but still indicates that there is nothing wrong. Pulling at the neck of her dress and gasping for air, she crawls painfully toward the front of the stage. She rejects an offer of help:)

No, no…

(Gesturing toward the table.)

…the drink, the drink—O my dear Hamlet—
The drink, the drink! I am pois'ned.

(A final suppressed gasp—and a wave to her husband to indicate that he is not to worry—and Gertrude expires.)

And then there's Queen Katharine. She dies of a broken heart. Henry the Eighth has divorced her, and this is her way of getting even. It takes her eight pages to die. *(Moving the chair center stage.)* I'll just hit the highlights. *(She positions herself by the chair.)*

My legs like loaden branches bow to th' earth,
Willing to leave their burthen…

(Snapping her fingers.)

…Reach a chair.

(She sits.)

So; now, methinks, I feel a little ease.

(She begins to sink, but rouses herself, irritably snapping her fingers.)

Patience—

(Coming out of character.) Patience is her maid.

(Katharine again, snapping again.)

Patience, be near me still, and set me lower;
I have not long to trouble thee…

(Rousing herself and snapping her fingers.)

Cause the musicians play me that sad note
I nam'd my knell, whilst I sit meditating
On that celestial harmony I go to.

(She sinks, but, irritated, she rallies for another snap.)

…Bid the music leave,
They are harsh and heavy to me
(Coming out of character and rising.) Here's Patience:

(A long scream.)

…How pale she looks,
And of an earthy cold … Mark her eyes!

(Another scream, and then she is Katharine again, rolling her eyes. She starts to die, but rallies.)

…Patience, is that letter
I caus'd you write yet sent away?…

…Sir, I most humbly pray you to deliver
This to my lord the King…
…Say his long trouble now is passing
Out of this world; tell him in death I blest him,
(For so I will.) Mine eyes grow dim. Farewell…

> *(Rallying.)*

…Nay, Patience,
You must not leave me yet. I must to bed…

> *(She rises and falls back.)*

Call in more women…
…Embalm me,
Then lay me forth. Although unqueen'd, yet like
A queen, and a daughter to a king, inter me.

> *("To hell with it.")*

I can no more.
(Katharine dies, and CHARLOTTE rises to replace the chair.) Needless to say, Henry had the rest of his wives beheaded.

But you want to know about my most famous dying scene, don't you? It was in *Guy Mannering*. You've never heard of it, of course. One of those Sir Walter Scott potboilers.

I played Meg Merrilies, Queen of the Gypsies. And do you know my whole part was less than twenty minutes long—*and* at the end of the last act—and *still* this is the role everyone remembers? Not Lady Macbeth. Not Rosalind. Not Gertrude. No, Meg Merrilies, Queen of the Gypsies. It is one of the cruel ironies of the theatre, that an actress who has distinguished herself in some of the greatest classical roles in dramatic literature, can go down in history for twenty minutes of the worst applesauce ever written. Well, I have no intention of doing Meg Merrilies here tonight… *(She begins to thumb through one of the books.)* Still … she *did* sell out every performance… *(Still thumbing.)* And that was even during the war… *(More thumbing.)* Lines all the way around the block… *(Looking up suddenly.)* But you don't want to see it, do you? You do…? All right, but don't say I didn't warn you.

> *(She turns her back, musses up her hair, and whirls around with a wild leap. This speech is delivered with a thick Scottish burr. A critic of her day described this scene thus: "…she stood like one great withered tree, her arms stretched out, her white locks flying, her eyes blazing under their shaggy brows. She was not like a creature of this world, but like some mad, majestic wanderer from the spirit-land.")*

"The tree is withered now, never to be green again; and old Meg Merrilies will never sing blithe songs more. But I charge you … that you tell him not to forget Meg Merrilies, but to build up the old walls in the glen for her sake, and let those that live there be too good to fear the beings of another world; for if ever the dead come back among the living, I will be seen in that glen many a night after these crazed bones are whitened in the mouldering grave!"

(Jumping back to play the villain.) "Hark ye, Meg, we must speak plain to you! My friend Dirk Hatterick and I, have made up our minds about this youngster, and it signifies nothing talking, unless you have a mind to share his fate. You were as deep as we in the whole business."

(As Meg.) "'Tis false! You forced me to consent that you should hurry him away, kidnap him, plunder him; but to murder him was your own device! Yours! and it has thriven you well!"

(As the villain.) "The old hag has croaked nothing but evil bodings these twenty years; she has been a rock ahead to me all my life."

(As Meg.) "I, a rock ahead! The gallows is *your* rock ahead!"

(As the villain, pulling an imaginary gun.) "Gallows! You hag of Satan, the hemp is not sown that shall hang me."

(As Meg.) "It is sown and it is grown, and hackled and twisted—"

> *(She is indicating a noose, when suddenly she makes the sound of a pistol shot and clutches her heart. A critic of her day has described her death in these words: "When Hatterick's fatal bullet entered her body, and she came staggering down the stage, her terrible shriek, so wild and piercing, so full of agony and yet of the triumph she had given her life to gain, told the whole story of her love and revenge." She screams and staggers downstage.)*

"I knew it would be like this!" *(Collapsing on the floor, she crawls the entire length of the stage to snatch victory from the jaws of defeat. She speaks her dying words to Dirk.)* "It has ended as it ought."

(After dying a lugubrious death, CHARLOTTE rises and dusts herself off.) Meg Merrilies, Queen of the Gypsies ... But I didn't just play queens. I played princes and kings, too. Breeches parts. That's what they called it when we took the men's roles. And why shouldn't we? They had all the lines.

I played Aladdin, and Oberon—King of the Fairies ... And two cardinals—Richelieu and Cardinal Wolsey. I was the first woman to play Cardinal Wolsey. And, of course, Hamlet. I borrowed Edwin Booth's costume. *(Remembering.)* Filled it out better than he did, too. *(She laughs.)* But my most famous breeches part was Romeo. Oh, Romeo! How I loved to play that boy! Mad, passionate, tempestuous Romeo. I loved him! I *was* Romeo! *(Shaking her head.)* All those years of pent-up passion for my girlfriends ... All those long nights of fantasy—and frustration! I felt as if I had been rehearsing for Romeo all my life.

And Susan was my first Juliet. My baby sister Susan. You didn't know that, did you? Yes, my sister and I acted together for ten years. And those were the best years of my life. Especially, *Romeo and Juliet*, and especially when we took the play to London. Yes, Susan and I were a team. Top billing: "Charlotte Cushman and her sister."

Well, Mother had a fit. It was bad enough that *I* was in the theatre, but Susan! Oh, no, not Susan!—not her precious, little, blue-eyed, baby girl! No,

Mother had it all planned out that her *beautiful* daughter was going to marry a rich man, and that he was going to support the whole family, and then she and Susan would never have to work again. *(A bitter laugh.)* And Mother was in such a hurry to spare Susan a life of drudgery, she forced her into marriage at the age of thirteen. Thirteen. How did she get Susan to go along with it? Well, she told her that the man was sick and going to die soon—which is what he had told Mother—and that the whole thing was just a legal formality so that Susan could inherit his property. Well, needless to say, the scoundrel was lying about the state of his finances—*and* his health! One year later, there was Susan, my baby sister, fourteen-year-old Susan—pregnant, abandoned, and being hounded by an army of creditors. Well, I came to the rescue, of course. I was already supporting Mother and both my brothers.

But I'll tell you something—the day—the very *day* that baby was weaned, I marched Susan down to the Park Theatre and got her an audition. My baby sister was *never* going to have to depend on a man again—not if I could help it!

Well, they cast her, and then Susan and I started working together. You know, the women didn't usually team up—but *we* did. We knew each other's timing, we knew each other's business—There was no one in the theatre who could beat us! And we played everything—*everything*: Mistress Page and Mistress Ford in *Merry Wives*, Gertrude and Ophelia in *Hamlet*, Oberon and Helena in *Midsummer Night's Dream*, Lydia Languish and Lucy in *The Rivals,* Desdemona and Emilia in *Othello*, Lady Macbeth and Lady Macduff, and then—our most daring—*Romeo and Juliet!*

In 1846 we took the show to London. Oh, that was a story! But first we thought it would be a good idea to try it out in Scotland. Well, we managed to scandalize the entire population of Edinburgh. For weeks rumors were flying that Susan was an unwed mother, and that I was … well, what I am!

Of course, none of this would hurt our reputations in London. No, what almost stopped us there was a dead actor. That's right, a dead actor. His name was David Garrick.

It seems that Mr. Garrick had taken it upon himself to improve on Shakespeare's plays—which meant, of course, writing longer scenes for himself and cutting the women's lines. Oh, do I know David Garrick! He may have died before I was born, but I know him. I have been sharing the stage now for forty years with the David Garricks of this world, and they are no different now than they were a hundred years ago.

Well, Mr. Garrick had done such an excellent job of promoting himself, that his version of *Romeo and Juliet* had become more popular than Shakespeare's. When Susan and I got to London to rehearse with the company at the Haymarket, there was not a single actor who knew the original version. Furthermore, they absolutely refused to learn it. No, they were not about to let two Americans teach them their Shakespeare—much less two women, much less a woman who intended to dress like a man and make love to her sister! *(Laughing.)* Well,

Susan and I had no intention of performing the Garrick butchery—so there we were, on the verge of an actors' strike. Then, at the eleventh hour, the manager of the Haymarket stepped in. He posted a modest notice in the Green Room, to the effect that any actor who was not willing to cooperate with the Misses Cushman would be free to seek employment elsewhere.

And so we opened. December 30, 1846. And we were an immediate sensation. I have always maintained that only a woman can play Romeo with any credibility. The male actors with the maturity and experience to handle the role are obviously too old to be boys. On the other hand, an experienced actress can impersonate a young man well into her forties—provided, of course, she has the right "attitude." *(To Emma.)* Then, too, there are those things that only a woman can know about what pleases a woman. *(To the audience.)* Apparently the critics agreed. They wrote that I put their gender to shame with my lovemaking. Yes, rumor had it that "Miss Cushman was a very dangerous young man." *(Laughing.)* So, Susan and I were a sensation. We ran for eighty consecutive performances at the Haymarket—which was a record. And then we went on tour to the provinces. And then Susan had to go and ruin it all. She got married ... again! *(CHARLOTTE begins to pace.)* Helena, *Midsummer Night's Dream.*

> *Injurious Hermia, most ungrateful maid!*
> *Have you conspir'd, have you with these contriv'd*
> *To bait me with this foul derision?*
> *Is all the counsel that we two have shar'd,*
> *The sisters' vows, the hours that we have spent,*
> *When we have chid the hasty-footed time*
> *For parting us—O, is all forgot?*
> *All school-days friendship, childhood innocence?*
> *We, Hermia, like two artificial gods,*
> *Have with our needles created both one flower,*
> *Both on one sampler, sitting on one cushion,*
> *Both warbling of one song, both in one key;*
> *As if our hands, our sides, voices, and minds*
> *Had been incorporate. So we grew together,*
> *Like a double cherry, seeming parted,*
> *But yet an union in partition,*
> *Two lovely berries molded on one stem;*
> *So, with two seeming bodies, but one heart...*

>   *(With sudden fury.)*

> *...And will you rent our ancient love asunder,*
> *To join with men in scorning your poor friend?*
> *It is not friendly, 'tis not maidenly.*
> *Our sex, as well as I, may chide you for it,*
> *Though I alone do feel the injury.*

Yes, Susan got married. She got married and gave up acting. Or I should say, she gave up the stage. Her whole marriage was a performance, if you ask me. We were never close again after that. *(Agitated by her memories.)* Yes, Susan betrayed me. Just like Matilda. Just like Hatty. Just like all the women I have tried to love—they always leave me. I don't understand it. I have never abandoned a woman in my life. *(Turning with irritation toward Emma who has interrupted her.)* What? *(In a threatening tone.)* What about Rosalie? *(Pause.)* I told them she died. *(Bullying the audience.)* Didn't I? I told you she died while I was in England, didn't I? *(To Emma.)* See? I told them… *(She starts to address the audience but turns back to Emma with sudden ferocity.)* But you want me to say I murdered her, don't you? Stuck a knife in her heart like Iago—don't you? That I betrayed her, because I told her I would only be gone for six months, and instead, I stayed in England for three years.

(With rising anger.) Yes, I did stay. Because for the first time in my life I was a leading lady. For the first time in my life the managers were coming to *me*. And for the first time in my life, money—*real* money—was finally coming in. And wasn't that the whole point? To make enough money so that Rosie and I could live together for the rest of our lives? Yes, I stayed, and I would do it again.

(To Emma.) But you want me to say that I killed her. *(To audience.)* Do you know that Rosalie wrote to me every single day of those three years? Every single day—and sometimes twice a day! What was I supposed to do with all those letters? Drop everything to answer them? Was I supposed to apologize to her, because my life was full of excitement and glamour, while she had nothing better to do than clean her father's paintbrushes—and write me those interminable letters? Was that my fault? Was I supposed to give up my life and live hers, because she couldn't live mine? *(Enraged, she turns toward Emma.)* Is that what I was supposed to do? If Rosie killed herself, it wasn't my fault!

> *(Turning back to the audience with manic intensity.)*

So—would you like to see some of my Romeo? Let's see … This is the scene at the end of the play where Romeo is entering the vault of Juliet's tomb. He thinks she has died, but she is really just asleep—and he is going there to kill himself.

> *(She attacks the scene with Romeo's frenzied desperation.)*

Give me the light. Upon thy life I charge thee,
What e'er thou hearest or seest, stand all aloof,
And do not interrupt me in my course.
Why I descend into this bed of death
Is partly to behold my lady's face,
But chiefly to take thence from her dead finger
A precious ring—a ring that I must use
In dear employment—therefore hence be gone.
But if thou, jealous, dost return to pry
In what I farther shall intend to do,

By heaven, I will tear thee joint by joint,
And strew this hungry churchyard with thy limbs.
The time and my intents are savage-wild,
More fierce and more inexorable far
Than empty tigers or the roaring sea…

>   (*Turning suddenly, she confronts the body of Juliet. Exhausted,*
>   *CHARLOTTE drives herself to finish the monologue.*)

…O my love, my wife,
Death, that hath suck'd the honey of thy breath,
Hath had no power yet upon thy beauty:
Thou art not conquer'd, beauty's ensign yet
Is crimson in thy lips and in thy cheeks,
And death's pale flag is not advanced there…
…Ah, dear Juliet,
Why art thou yet so fair? Shall I believe
That unsubstantial Death is amorous,
And that the lean abhorred monster keeps
Thee here in dark to be his paramour?
For fear of that, I still will stay with thee,
And never from this palace of dim night
Depart again. Here…

>   (*She falters.*)

…here will I remain
With worms that are thy chambermaids;
O, here…

>   (*She falters again.*)

Will I set up my everlasting rest,
And shake the yoke of inauspicious stars
From this world-wearied flesh…

>   (*She has difficulty going on.*)

…Eyes, look your last!
Arms…

>   (*Faltering.*)

Arms, take your last embrace!
(*As she reaches out her arms for Juliet, she breaks down and turns her back to the audience. Racked with sobs, she collapses in the chair, her face in her hands.*) I'm sorry. I can't finish it. (*She takes out a handkerchief, breaks down again, and then collects herself.*) I'm sorry … his has never happened before. I… was just … remembering Rosalie.

(*Taking another moment.*) Yes, I did betray Rosie. There was another woman. Of course there was another woman. I was only thirty, and I was the toast of London. Of course there was another woman. I know Rosalie heard the rumors. Mother would have told her. *(Weary, but without bitterness.)* Yes, Mother would have enjoyed that.

And Rosie began writing me desperate letters. And I wrote angry letters back, denying everything. So then, of course, she knew. The truth was, I had outgrown Rosalie. How could I tell her that? But I never should have lied to her. That was the betrayal. Rosie deserved the truth. We all deserve the truth.

(Looking at Emma.) Well, Emma … it looks like you've won the bet. *(She begins to gather the books.)* You know, the great tragedy of *Romeo and Juliet* is that Romeo doesn't know that Juliet is still alive. He puts himself through all that agony for nothing. All the time Juliet is just waiting for him … waiting for him, and he doesn't have the sense to know it.

(A long look at Emma.) Well—*(She rises. This is her farewell to forty years in the theatre.)*

Our revels now are ended. These our actors
(As foretold you) were all spirits, and
Are melted into air, into thin air,
And, like the baseless fabric of this vision,
The cloud-capp'd tow'rs, the gorgeous palaces,
The solemn temples, the great globe itself,
Yea, all which it inherit, shall dissolve,
And like this insubstantial pageant faded
Leave not a rack behind. We are such stuff
As dreams are made on; and our little life…

   (Pausing to smile.)

…Is rounded with a sleep.

(To Emma.) Let's go home, Emma. I'm tired. *(To the audience.)* Goodnight. *(Exiting with tremendous dignity. Blackout.)*

End of play.

Tales of My Uncle

MONICA RAYMOND

It may seem counterintuitive that some in Disability activism and Critical Disability Studies will regularly include geriatric impairments in statistical calculations of disability—as social barriers do negatively affect them—and yet will hold the same people, illnesses, and disabilities at arm's length. Ann Leahy notes,

> Approaching the issue of ageing together with that of impairment and disability involves reckoning with paradox. Despite impairment often being considered a social norm of ageing, or perhaps because of it, older people with impairments are rarely regarded as "disabled" in quite the same way as children, or younger adults might be. This is so, even though disabled people age, and most people who are ageing will experience disability (barring premature death).[1]

This expectation of geriatric disability as a social norm collides with the reception of other disabilities as social abnormalities. In her influential article "Unhealthy Disabled: Treating Chronic Illnesses as Disabilities," Susan Wendell offers distinctions which help explain some of this paradox:

> [M]odern movements for the rights of people with disabilities have fought the identification of disability with illness, and for good reasons. This identification contributes to the medicalization of disability, in which disability is regarded as an individual misfortune, and people with disabilities are assumed to suffer primarily from physical and or/mental abnormalities that medicine can and should treat, cure, or at least prevent.[2]

Although Critical Disability Studies is beginning to broaden with recognizing the limitations of a purely social model approach, the social constructionist analysis remains a foundational principle. "Disability," within the theoretical framework, is not an individual condition, but rather a discriminatory social system which allows obstacles in transportation, employment, and architecture, coupled with "prejudiced attitudes, discrimination, cultural misrepresentation, and other social injustices."[3]

193

This approach is built on an assumption of pride in self and community, yet in so much of western society, aging is seen as a negative; something to be avoided. Geriatric impairments are so often viewed as steps toward death, and, perhaps worse in a youth-obsessed culture, obsolescence. So often, these changes with age are framed purely within the medical model and treated as a sign of the body "breaking down." Despite the fact that most people will, one day, reach old age, much of Western civilization—and particularly the United States—lacks a widespread, mainstream movement focused on Senior Identity Pride.

In her article "Linking Aging Theory and Disability Models," Michelle Putnam points to the cold calculation that often lies just below these prejudices. Discussing J. Dowd's social exchange theory and its examination of "the cost-benefit relationship between the individual and society," she notes that, "when applied to aging, the assumption is that the cost-benefit ratio falls out of balance [...] therefore, the costs associated with interacting with the older adult often outweigh the benefits."[4] Critiquing this model of commodifying human life and social interaction, of course, parallels goals within Critical Disability Studies and similar commodification in labor and "normative" design standards. Despite this, there remains a chasm. "Some unhealthy disabled people, as well as some healthy people with disabilities," writes Wendell, "experience physical or psychological burdens that no amount of social justice can eliminate. Therefore, some very much want to have their bodies cured, not as a substitute for curing ableism, but in addition to it."

Mort Silk at two stages of life (playwright's collection).

There is a danger that acknowledging these facts might provide support for those who prefer the individualized, medicalized picture of disability. Thus, in promoting the liberatory vision of social constructionism, it is safer and more comfortable for disability activism to focus on people who are healthy disabled.[5]

As noted in this collection's introduction, the editors of this project felt strongly that limiting our understanding of disability in this way was not useful to our goals, nor did it match our personal experiences. Indeed, two-thirds of the editorial staff would be categorized as "unhealthy" disabled. Few outside of the most stringent Disability activists will view this as controversial; in the years since Susan Wendell's article became a must-read and widely cited landmark, an awareness and acceptance of chronic illness as disability has spread within Critical Disability Studies, and most theorists now attempt a more nuanced view of the social model. Despite this, Geriatric Studies and Critical Disability Studies remain, at best, distantly acquainted. Whether this is a marker of the reach of medical model assumptions, a reflection of societal prejudice, internalized ableism, or, extending Wendell's argument, the problematic effect of inviting "unwelcome" impairment into pride-oriented, identity-driven disability activism, similar challenges around inaccessibility, employment, and governmental policy continue to adversely affect both groups.

—**John Michael Sefel**

NOTES

1. Hamish Robertson, Ashton Applewhite, and Susan Macaulay, "Paradoxically Thinking: Ageing with Disability, Disability with Ageing: INCG," International Network for Critical Gerontology, March 2, 2018, https://criticalgerontology.com/paradoxically-ageing-disability/.

2. Susan Wendell, "Unhealthy Disabled: Treating Chronic Illnesses as Disabilities," *The Disability Studies Reader*, Lennard J. Davis, ed. (New York: Routledge, Taylor & Francis Group, 2017), 160.

3. *Ibid.*, 161.

4. Michelle Putnam, "Linking Aging Theory and Disability Models: Increasing the Potential to Explore Aging With Physical Impairment," *The Gerontologist*, Vol. 42, Issue 6, 1 (December 2002), 799–806, https://doi.org/10.1093/geront/42.6.799.

5. Wendell, 161.

Tales of My Uncle

Monica Raymond's uncle, Mort Silk, lived all his life in New York City, where he acted, directed, and taught English and served as an assistant principal in the NYC public schools. His long and creative retirement was full of travel, relationships, painting and photography. He died at home in June 2018 at the age of 96.

Tales of My Uncle was originally written for the New Masculinities Festival at the NYC Gay and Lesbian Center and performed there on October 20, 2018.

Tales of My Uncle © Monica Raymond, ALL RIGHTS RESERVED.

* * *

RING

This is my uncle's ring. You can't see it from where you're sitting, but it has the iconic theatre masks, one smiling and one frowning, cast in silver. I adopted it after he died this past June. He was 96. If he'd made it to August 4, he would've been 97.

I wear it on my ring finger, where you'd wear a wedding ring. Wedded to the theatre?—Hmm, I don't know about that.

BEDBOUND

The last year of his life, he was in home hospice. Bedbound. He couldn't get out of bed, couldn't even fully sit up. The most he could manage was an angle of about 35 percent.

His head was clear, though.

HOLIDAY DINNER

I first knew my Uncle Mort, my mother's younger brother, when he would come to holiday meals, which involved lots of passing dishes down a long table, lots of grabbing and yelling, lots of gravy and spilling. He was impeccable and imperturbable, our bachelor uncle. He cut his turkey into bite-size morsels, dabbed at his lips with a napkin, crossed his knife and fork on his plate and said it had all been delicious.

I had the impression my mother's meals were tastier than the bland bachelor fare he made for himself, the skin crisper, the flavors sparkier. It was delicious, but he could only take so much of it. He dabbed his lips with a napkin, crossed his knife and fork on his plate, said it had been delicious, and always left early.

He was always the first to go.

THE LAST TO GO

When he died, he was actually the last to go. The last of that generation. My mother, my father, my father's young brother (my uncle on my father's side), all of them had gone before.

ASSISTANT PRINCIPAL

He was an assistant principal at a junior high school in the Bronx. His smooth surface, like a stone smoothed by the ocean, a tool for ironing out quarrels.

He was an assistant principal, and it was easy to imagine being sent to his office for some infraction or other.

POO

I learned Mort was gay when he began to bring Michael with him to holiday meals. Michael was my age, thirty years younger than Mort. But he seemed even younger than that, a kind of *puer aeternus*—maybe that was why Mort nicknamed him, fondly, "Poo." Poo was almost as wide as he was tall and wore his sloshy billowing fat under loose light-colored T-shirts. He was blind, with tiny perpetually closed eyes in deep-set dolphin eye sockets. And he had the wide, face-splitting crease of a dolphin smile.

MORT AND MICHAEL

Michael was everything my uncle was not—round where my uncle was upright, sloppy where my uncle was neat, opinionated and argumentative where my uncle was dignified and discrete, crazy for '50s rock 'n' roll where my uncle practiced Mozart, goyish where my uncle was Jewish, boyish where my uncle was—well, avuncular.

They lived together for twenty years.

A DREAM

Mort is 96, going on 97. He wakes up from a dream. In order to pass to the next level, they're telling him he has to sleep with a woman. But he doesn't want to sleep with just any woman.

"Doesn't Adele count?" I ask.

A GIRLFRIEND

"I had a girlfriend," he tells me.

"You did? When?"

"At the Dramatic Workshop."

The Dramatic Workshop, where Mort studied acting on the GI Bill after he got out of the army, alongside Walter Matthau, Bea Arthur and Harry Belafonte, was one of the high points of his life.

"Naomi Feigenbaum," he says. "It means 'fig tree.'"

Now he wonders if he was unfair to her, Naomi Feigenbaum with whom he broke up over seventy years ago. She was Israeli, and he wonders if the things he was critical of her for were just a result of her coming from a different culture.

"We had a sexual relationship," he tells me, with a kind of wonder.

"It was satisfying."

ADELE

"Doesn't Adele count?" I had asked.

Adele was Adele Sicular. I'm not sure if I ever actually met her. In the photos of them together, she's a tough, voluptuous, intellectual-looking NY woman in her 50s, then 60s, with a crisp ruff of white hair. Next to her stands my uncle, hair black and sleek, long eyelashes, even oval face. Handsome, boyish, something deferential, held-back, a courtier.

She had been his psychiatrist. That was her specialty, in the 1950s, young gay men who wished not to be, as almost all of them at that time were. She was married when he first came to her as a patient. When her husband died, they moved closer. First separate apartments in the same building. Then they moved in together.

He lived with her till she died in 1976. She was 78, and he was 55, still with a good chunk of life ahead of him.

So that's where he'd been returning to, all those Rosh Hashanahs and Thanksgivings; my bachelor uncle, as patient, as smooth, as un-disclosing as a stone.

A GOOD MAN

"Your uncle was a good man," they told me at the funeral. His caretaker, Maria, said "An educated man, he never made me feel less."

Among his belongings, I found a plaque from a teacher he'd supervised. "You saw the good in me," it said, "even when I couldn't see it in myself."

One time, in the last year of his life, when he was flat on his back in bed, I asked if I could get him something from the outside world. I meant some little treat, but he thought for a while.

Then "Make it a happier place," he said.

MY UNCLE'S JOURNAL

My uncle left a journal he kept for just a year and a half of his life, from 1989–91, when he was pushing 70, about the same age as I am now. It begins out of nowhere, when Michael steps in cat vomit, and ends just as arbitrarily.

He was living with one man and in love with another, with all the predictable joy, angst, and sense of not-enough that that implies.

HE KEPT BUSY

In one three-month period, he volunteered for the AIDS dinner at the synagogue, filed and took photos for the American Theatre Wing, took the cat to the vet, and read to the blind at the Lighthouse. He went to the Prime-Timers group at the Gay and Lesbian Center, practiced The Sunken Cathedral and maintained an affectionate flirtation with David, his piano teacher. He took in a play, ballet, or concert almost every night, and visited Stockbridge, Tanglewood, and the historic homes of Mark Twain, Edith Wharton and Harriet Beecher Stowe.

He also found time for friendly casual sex with Tony, Felix, Bob, and Joe. And he took in the occasional porno flick.

A JOURNAL ENTRY

Here is a part of a journal entry for July 17, 1989.

"I went to a porno movie at the Adonis. I had sex with Steve Keitel, a closeted man of 49. We chatted and will probably get together over coffee to chat. He never heard of the Gay and Lesbian Center!" (followed by one of his rare exclamation points) "I urged him to get some information about its services …"

Ah, Mort! Ever the educator!

THE LAST MORNING

The last morning of his life he asked me, "Is there any candy around here?" I found one of those Dove chocolate squares in the fridge and broke it into tiny pieces on his tongue.

"Good," he said. And "thank you."

RING

This is his ring.
This is his belt.
This is his hat.
I take off the hat and bow to the audience.

End of play.

Gramp

Mandy Fox

Based on the recordings of William Earl Murdock

Though radically different plays in form and tone, *Tales of My Uncle* and *Gramp* share a great deal in common. Certainly, on a surface level, both plays are remembrances of deceased, older males by their professional theatre artist female relatives, and both plays feature men with a background in professional performance (one in theatre, the other in music).

There is far more, however, just beneath the surface. Both of these plays, for example, consider these men at a time when they require growing levels of palliative care and attention, a status which carries its own stigmas, especially among men of mid-twentieth century America. Both plays follow men who occupy a gray land between familial unity and estrangement; they are certainly connected to and, it seems clear, loving toward their families—and yet they are apart from them as well, with secrets and compartmentalized lives containing their true, daily experiences.

The most important tie between these plays, however, exists beyond the text, though alluded to by their titles. *Nihil de nobis, sine nobis* (nothing about us without us) has become a cornerstone axiom of Disability Rights activism,[1] and presenting yet another example of an able-bodied person "imagining" life as a disabled person is not what this collection is about. Although our original call prioritized Disabled voices, we allowed that disability-adjacent voices would be considered under certain limitations. Despite a great number of submissions that fell into this latter category, Monica Raymond and Mandy Fox were the only such voices to be included, in large part because they avoided most of the problematic aspects of the rest of the stack. Monica Raymond's play makes no effort to "imagine" how her uncle felt; it is a series of facts and reflections on her part—the closest she comes to attempting to speak in his voice is when she pulls directly from his own writing. Meanwhile, after speaking with Mandy Fox extensively, it became clear how thoroughly she based the play on family memories and her grandfather's own recorded words, the *vast* majority of the lines being verbatim from inherited reel-to-reel tapes. Both plays deal with mortality, and yet avoid the sort of *Tuesdays with Morrie* themes that so often accompany such works. Furthermore, both plays engage with somatic impairments without once attempting to turn them into metaphors or, worse, "cure" them.

What we appreciated most of all, however, were the titles that each author chose for their works. Both *Tales of My Uncle* and *Gramp* alert the audience to the authors' own biased and potentially error-prone place in the storytelling. These are not "truth"—they are the stories of an uncle and a great-grandfather, as understood by a niece and a great-granddaughter. The humility in realizing the difference is a rare and desperately needed commodity in works about disability, and therefore one we thought deserved attention.

William Earl Murdock, photographer unknown (playwright's collection).

I don't claim to have the knowledge or authority to state these plays represent the *right* way for able-bodied artists to write about disability, but based on so many examples from history and from a disappointing number of the submissions we received for this collection, I can at least say that these two works avoid many examples of the *wrong* way. That, in and of itself, feels like a useful addition to this complex cultural and literary debate.

—**John Michael Sefel**

NOTES

1. Its origins as connected to Disability Rights, let alone as a term in general, remain controversial. I had long understood it to have originated in the 1988 "Deaf President Now" student protest at Gallaudet University in Washington, D.C., yet in his 1998 work, *Nothing About Us Without Us: Disability Oppression and Empowerment*, James Charlton traces its use among Disability Activists to a few years prior to that, among activists in South Africa. Meanwhile, its use as a statement against oppressive conditions goes back far earlier, with historian Frank Golding finding evidence at least as far back as sixteenth-century Poland.

Gramp

AUTHOR'S NOTE: This play was constructed verbatim from reel-to-reel audiotapes containing "letters" from my great-grandfather to my grandmother throughout the early 1960s, which I inherited in 2004. Over fifteen years I transcribed, categorized, contextualized, and shaped those tapes and his words into this stage play. These are his words, his music, and his life.

William Earl Murdock, known primarily as "Earl," was born blind in Ironton, Ohio, in 1886. Taught to read Braille at the age of six by his Aunt Mary (who had no experience teaching students without sight), at sixteen Earl became the first blind student to attend the Jacob Tome Institute in Port Deposit, MD. He held a number of jobs, from farming to working on a road gang with the WPA, but for most of his life Earl worked as a musician and piano tuner. Success brought high-profile jobs, such as tuning Liberace's piano in advance of a highly anticipated concert tour. But his primary clientele was local schools, churches, and private families. In addition to a $12 tuning fee, he was provided with a ride to and from the location and a meal—this last even spurring a local rivalry as to which customer claimed to make the best creamed onions for lunch.

With the advent of the phonograph, Earl bought a music store where he delighted costumers with elaborate window displays of suspended dolls, dancing along to the latest hits on demonstration phonographs.

In addition to the piano, Earl also played the clarinet, saxophone, accordion, Clavietta, and Solovox, and was employed as the calliope player on the *Homer Smith*, an Ohio River excursion boat. He and his wife Ethel Henry had one daughter. After Ethel's death in 1958, Earl lived alone until his early 80s. He passed away in 1971, shortly after meeting his six-month old great-granddaughter.

CAST:
GRAMP—80s, blind, piano player and tuner, funny, resourceful, handy, widower, also called Earl.
CLAUDE / CLAUDETTE—30s–60s, male or female, sibling of Gramp's bartender-friend.
PUCKER—40s–50s, male, Gramp's closest friend, police officer, checks on Gramp daily.
Note: CLAUDE and PUCKER could be played by the same male actor.
SETTING:
Thanksgiving Day, 1964, Ironton, Ohio, late afternoon.
Gramp © Mandy Fox, all rights reserved. Companies interested in producing *Gramp* may contact the author at fox.393@osu.edu.

* * *

An efficiency apartment in government-subsidized housing.

An upright piano.

A bare bulb in the center of the room, very few wall hangings, if any.

A couple of dirty windows with open sheers and yellowed roller shades.

A kitchen area with a refrigerator, stove, sink, and cabinets.

A 1950s, chrome and Formica table with two chairs.

A Queen Anne style chair adjacent to a free-standing ashtray.

A hallway leading to the bathroom and bedroom.

The front door is just offstage, suggesting a modest vestibule.

A console television.

Stacks of *Reader's Digest* magazines written in Braille.

A reel-to-reel recorder and a typewriter, both circa 1964 or earlier.

In general, it's a bit of a mess, the bachelor pad of a blind widower.

Lights up on Gramp's apartment. We hear keys rattling and the front door open. We might see GRAMP, but not the SUPER.

GRAMP

I apologize for the inconvenience. I sure do appreciate you coming out, especially with it being a holiday and all. I could'a sworn I put m'keys in m'pocket before I left the Moose last night, but then again, we had quite a few 807's. Ha! You know what an 807 is, don't'cha? It Ham Radio speak for beer. It seems the FCC duddn't look with too much favor on the word "beer." Later, Pucker's gonna' come by and we're gonna' have ourselves some … Yea, ok. Well, I'll be seein' ya'

> *The SUPER slams the door abruptly. GRAMP enters in a rumpled suit, carrying a take-out container. He removes his suit jacket and throws his coat on the chair. He wears a short-sleeved dress shirt. He places the take-out container in the refrigerator, opens a bottle of beer, and drinks deeply.*

GRAMP

Speaking of 807.

> *He speaks to the audience.*

I don't think that ol' boy was too happy with me draggin' him out on a holiday.

I prob'ly pulled him away from his family and all that.

Course lots of fella's prob'ly lookin' fer an excuse to get away.

Take a breather.

Maybe I did the ol' boy a favor.

> *The clock chimes: Westminster Bells and 4 chimes.*

That's ol' Matilda striking, there.

She's doin' good business.

4:00.

Ooo-wee, that was a long night.

We were up at the Moose Lodge in Huntington last night.
Played from 4:00 to 7:30
Then jumped in the car
And come on down here to play the Ironton Moose
From 9:00 until … unconscious.
We made about thirty bucks, which is not bad.
When we got through, we had played eight or nine hours.
I'm not exactly give-out, but I'm pretty tired.
Neither one of those piana's were any good.
That's what tires a fella out more than anything else,
These ol' broken-down piana's.
And I'm thinking what a poor salesman I am,
Not to have those things tuned up and in good shape.
I get back here, only to discover,
I've locked myself out.
Had to go to the hotel.
Super didn't seem particularly sympathetic to my plight.
I tell you, if it ain't one end, it's the other.
I guess be all right.

> *He exits to the bathroom and returns swigging on a bottle of antacid.*
> *He belches occasionally and says "Excuse me" most of the time.*

I went down to Stone's and had my Thanksgiving dinner.
   Boy, it was a nice one.
   $1.75 with tax.
   You couldn't by any stretch of the imagination have dinner at home for that price,
   Except some of those frozen things.
   I had tomato juice…
   And what, to me, tasted like turkey soup…
   Turkey, Dressing, Sweet potatoes.
   Oh the sweet potatoes were just perfect!
   Peas…
   And then of course, had a plate with olives and celery and radishes…
   Pumpkin pie and coffee.
   But I brought the pumpkin pie home.
   Brought a piece for Pucker when he comes by later.
   We're gonna' have us a little Thanksgiving: little pie, little 807.
   Got it in the ice box there, waitin' for us.
   Pro'lly watch a little football on the television.
   It's pretty nice to live downtown where I live, ya' know.
   All I have to do is walk out three steps and there I am at Stone's with the big turkey dinner.
   Now that's something to be grateful for!

> *He accidentally knocks over his bottle of beer, which breaks on the floor.*

Whup. Whup.
  Shoot.
  There goes my 807…

> *He mops up the spill with a dishtowel. He picks up a broom and starts sweeping and generally cleaning up as he talks.*

Well, I was out in the country the other day.
  Gee that air out there smells good.
  Well, I worked out there on this ol' piana.'
  Turned out pretty good.
  Had a nice lunch.
  Normal operating procedure is: I tune the piana' and play a little concert,
  The owner pays me for the tuning,
  Provides round-trip transportation, and a home-cooked meal.
  Well not *always* a meal, but…
  Most a' the time.
  And creamed onions are usually involved.
  Apparently, word has got around
  That I appreciate well prepared creamed onions.
  So the last several times I have tuned piana's in town,
  The lady of the house has prepared some sort of creamed onions.
  Oh, I've had little pearl onions and sliced onions and sweet onions.
  I've had 'em with parmesan and swiss and rosemary and thyme.
  Even had one batch with a little cooking Sherry in there.
  Boy they's good.
  Pretty nice, huh?
  Ta' have ladies competing with one another over my taste buds.
  It would seem that I am the winner in this scenario.
  These folks who live out in the country,
  I tuned for the other day, ya' know,
  Boy, they had a nice car.
  You know what else:
  They did a Hamm Radio outfit in their car!
  It's called a mobile (pronounced MO-beal).
  We was talking back and forth to a fella out in St. Alamo, in California!
  He sent us a "73": that's Hamm Speak for "Best Wishes."
  We was talking back and forth, while we were driving along the road!
  We could make out what he was saying pretty good, but…
  Ya' know, a fella has a thing like that in his car,
  Seems like it'd be dangerous,
  Distract his attention off the road.
  Another thing, it keeps him more or less out of talkin' with his family

And the kids would have to keep quiet and all that kinda' stuff.

Why, I don't know whether I'd like that 'er not.

Well, these people don't have kids anyway.

Imagine about twelve years and none showed up yet.

I told her to keep tryin'. Ha!

You might know when there's good ballgames on hand, why…

People want their piana's tuned.

Well, the lady was nice enough to get out a transistor radio and I heard most of it.

The station interrupted to report on that astronaut business.

That seems kinda' unusual situation,

To have an astronaut in the air and an exciting ball game on at the same time.

I wouldn't want to listen to that astronaut business all day long anyway.

Ol' boys have my best wishes.

Ya' know Buzz Aldrin and … oh, Lovell's his last name.

Ooo-wee! It'll take all the king's horses and all the king's men

To put Humpty Dumpty together again.

Boy, that is the biggest waste 'a time and money that was ever heard of…

> *He freezes. He hears something. He slowly raises the broom then beats the floor violently.*

Doggone roaches.

I can hear em, see.

I hear 'em clickin' around.

This is what comes with living on top of a bar and grill.

Stone's is a very fine establishment, but the bugs come with the territory.

The upside is, the air always smells like delicious hamburgers.

> *He freezes. He listens.*

(Hushing his voice) I hear that old lady next door.

Got her radio going now.

She sent me over a bowl of beans the other day.

You know, navy beans just cooked in greasy water.

That's all right, they's good.

I've had two meals off of them,

Now I think I got enough for a third.

See now, I put up with her radio all day long and I play one song on the piana' after ten o'clock in the evening and I'm written up.

Someone filed a complaint with the Superintendent of the building.

Can you believe that!?

I guess there's worse things could happen.

> *He puts the broom away. He fetches his typewriter and places it on the kitchen table.*

I'm due to send off a letter today.

My typewriter broke down.

I can write long-hand, but it ain't pretty.
You know that tape, 'er ribbon, 'er whatever you call it,
maybe it's a steel tape…
Anyhow, it pulls the carriage to the left
And without it yur' hopelessly sunk.
Unless you've got somebody to stand around and push on it while you type,
Which I haven't got.
Doggone thing broke in two.

> *He drops a chunk of bees wax in a small saucepan, places on the
> stove, and turns the burner on.*

Pucker took a look at it.
Said it looked like it could be opened up.
So he's gonna' bring me some tape he cut out of the ends,
Ya' know, where it's hooked onto the machine.
I'm gonna' fuse it together with a thin layer of bees wax and see if that holds.
He was supposed to be by yesterday, but he got tied up with work, I guess.
He'll be by in a little while.
We'll have ourselves a couple of 807's and a bit a' pie.
Perhaps some football.
Yes sir!

> *He begins to disassemble the typewriter.*

Well, the air seems better now in here than it did before.
I'd rather tune two piana's than do housework.
That stuff's hard on your back.
'Nother thing I'm thankful for:
I'm thankful I'm able to get around and do those chores.
Poor 'ol Nellie Fannin.
She's got arthritis real bad.
She can hardly drag herself out to get somethin' ta' eat!
She just stays in the house,
Doesn't go anywhere,
Doesn't have anyone to help her.
Doctor says her muscles just sort a…
Not petrified,
Ostrafied.
Or what is it?
Retrograded?
Aw heck, you furnish me a word.
Well, that's something I can be thankful for.
I've been feeling right good lately.
Still take my blood pressure medicine.
Seems to be effective.
Fixing what is ailing me.

If we knew how many people are not able to get the proper medical attention,
Just because they don't have the money to pay for it.
That's just downright cruel.
It seems to me were gonna' have to have some kind of a deal with the doctors.
  Americans are going to have to do something about it sometime,
  But our government's so doggone big with so many units,
  It's practically impossible to get 'em to do anything.

> *A train whistles. The tracks are a short walk from his door.*

Well, that Doc Black is good for something anyhow.
  He's still fat as a hog.
  I don't see how he can be that way and preach diets,
  Ya' know, reducing diets to his patients.
  Hey, that reminds me!
  I got some candy in the mail yesterday.

> *He rushes to the back room and returns with a half-eaten box of candy. He eats a piece as he talks.*

I don't know who it's from.
  Might be Sister Ella, down in Charlotte.
  She sends me up some occasionally, but she usually sends me chocolate covered nuts.
  These'r creams, caramels, and, I believe, nougat.
  I saved the paper off it so I could show somebody,
  See who it came from.
  Maybe I'll have Pucker take a look at it when he gets here.
  It'd be a joke on me if it belongs ta' somebody else, wouldn't it?
  Once in a while I *do* get a letter 'er something in my box that belongs ta' the people next door.
  Hm.

> *He is about to pop one more into his mouth, thinks better of it, and places it back in the box. He sits at the table and takes off his shoes.*

Well, I ordered a few groceries.
  It seems as though I have to have something to eat.
  It's been three weeks since I got groceries.
  I think it was before my typewriter broke-down.
  Course I have to coordinate the grocery and the milkman,
  And the laundry and so on,
  With my off-time.
  Did you know the milkman don't bring milk on Saturday anymore!?
  Boys are getting lazier and lazier.
  I swear I never saw anything like it!
  Now me, I'd tune a piana' anytime.
  3 o'clock in the morning if necessary.

I'd think nothing of it.
But boy, those fellas on a reg'lar salary,
If you need them out at three in the morning that would just be too bad.
They wouldn't show up.
And my doggone groceries!
I like to eat a boiled potato just like an apple.
Ya' know, peeling and all.
I didn't realize 'till I got cooking for myself
How much difference there could be in potater's.
I can't tell too much about them, of course, but b'the *feel* of 'em.
I suppose you can tell by the *looks* of the potato if it's what you want 'er not,
But I can't so I just have ta' take what they send me.
I usually get ten pounds at a crack,
In these mesh bags, ya' know.
I had an idea that potatoes were graded for size,
But evidently they are not.
There may be three or four big ones on top,
And the rest of them are just mediocre like.
I'm gonna' talk to them about that.
Oh, you probably don't give a darn about potatoes.

> *He crosses to the chair and picks up a* Readers Digest *written in braille. He sits. He grimaces and reaches toward the cushion below him. He finds his missing keys and shakes them in celebration.*

Ha! Found my keys!

> *He places the* Reader's Digest *on his chest/stomach and moves his fingers across the page.*

November 26.
  Hm.
  I read here in *The Readers Digest* that Franklin Roosevelt took the liberty to change Thanksgiving to the 4th Thursday instead of the last Thursday.
  Made quite a difference, ya' know.
  It's raining outside.
  Bad ol' day for any football games that are scheduled.
  I s'pose they'll carry on no matter what.
  Y'now, I get surprised a lot of times.
  I go out and it's pourin' rain.
  It's awful hard to hear rain in this place.
  The roofs are not metal, ya' know, they're tar.
  Course if it's blowing or the rain has a piece of ice in it,
  I can hear that on the windows back there by my bed.
  Otherwise I'm pretty well...
  I'm not cooped up.
  Just ... insulated.

I hear the neighbor's radio again.
I'm not sure whether you'd hear it 'er not.

> *He freezes and listens for several seconds.*

Oh, and I've been reading about the colored people demonstrating.
We don't have any protestations around here yet.
You never can tell, might break out any minute.
But this town is pretty thoroughly integrated.
On occasion colored folks come into Stone's to eat,
And they serve them without question.
I have sympathy with the way that they're going about it to get what they
want.

> *He fetches his reel-to-reel recorder and places it on the table, next to*
> *the typewriter, which is now in pieces.*

It occurs to me, that if I'm going to write a letter today,
I better see to this little problem with my recorder.
I tape-record my letters,
For obvious reasons.
This here is the Silvertone, Monaural Tape Recorder,
Model number two-three-zero.

> *He holds up the tapes and box.*

These little tapes come in this little box.
An' this little box comes with a little spot for the address on there.
I type out said address,
Glue it on said box,
Put my tape inside,
Give it to Pucker, and he mails it for me.
If Pucker's already come by,
I can take it down to Stone's and they'll send it out.
But I usually just wait for Pucker.
Pretty nice to have somebody to do things for you,
Like mail a letter.

> *The clock chimes. A "quarter after the hour" chime.*

Pucker'll be here before I know it,
So I better get this letter goin'.
My recorder's been actin' up.
It got some sticky stuff in it somehow
And when it would sit for a minute 'er two,
It'd run real slow.
So I put some, uh, what'dy-call-it…
Lighter fluid on it.
Doggone if that didn't clean it out.
It's not quite up to the speed it was when I first got it, though.

It's about a quarter of a tone off.
Henry Lee said he'd bring me over a little watch oil.
Lessen the drag on the belt a little bit.
Ya' know, Henry said that watch oil costs 10 thousand dollars a gallon.
How 'bout that?
I supposed it's probably on the order of some sort of penetrating oil.
I have that, uh, what's it called?

> *He fetches the bottle from under the sink. He puts a bit in a glass and dips a small brush in it.*

Liquid Wrench!
It's not a petroleum product.
It's just a phenol product.

> *He smells it and recoils. He brushes a bit onto the recorder.*

Ooo-wee! One thing, oh, it smells terrible! Ha, ha!
But it helps me tune an' ol' piana' lot's a times without breakin' strings, ya know.
Take a little brush and put that on the strings up there by the top,
With the sliding of the pressure bar, ya' know.

> *He sniffs it again, recoils, and replaces the lid. He has been setting up his reel to reel during the previous conversation. He begins recording. He's proud to demonstrate this high-tech machine for us.*

Ooo-wee! Wow, that smells terrible! Ha, ha!
Let's see if we can record here.
Hello test.
One, two, three.
Hello test.
Greetings and salutations!
Happy Thanksgiving one and all!
Hope you all are doing well and enjoying your Thanksgiving Dinner,
But knowing you all as I do,
I doubt very much whether you got around to all that yet.
Ha!
As for me, I just finished m'dinner.
Had a very fine feast down ta' Stone's, as usual.
This is, of course, just another day in a way.
Some people have to work, I guess.
Like Pucker's gotta' work today.
The cook and the waitress at Stone's,
Anybody in the food or entertainment business,
The holiday comes up, that's their biggest time usually.
Yea, Everybody has his own work ta' do.
Hey, 'fore I forget, regarding my 'lectric bill:
The 'lectric man blamed it on the window fan.

He said I use about 5 kilowatts a day.

Well, I sure don't.

Recorder don't take anything much.

Neither do the radio and I don't use the television very often.

Frigidaire, of course been pretty hard-pressed to keep things cool, but
It don't run all the time.

So I guess I'm gonna' have to wait till the next bill comes around to see what happens.

It was about $4 more than it was the other time.

So he could be right, it could be the window fan.

I layed it in to complaint just the same, by gosh.

Well, they got the place all decorated up here in the streets.

So you'll get to see it all "duded up" when ya' come.

I'm anticipating your visit and praying that you'll have decent weather ta' come in.

Just a little rain won't hurt anything, but...

'Bout a foot a snow out and it'd just be too bad, wouldn't it?

You know, they got the strike on up at the South Ordinance Plant,

Wait, no, they changed the name to the Nitrogen Division.

Well, It seems that anybody that's *in* the plant can't come *out*, and if they *come* out, they can't go *back* in.

They've done all kinds of things up there.

They cut the telephone wires, put boulders on the switch strikes,

And I don't know what all.

Anyhow, Pucker has a son-in-law up there and he has trouble with, uh...

Oh, what are they called...

HEMORRHOIDS!

Well, seems as though they come back on him while he was in there and they have to get him out.

So yesterday, they was supposed to...

Helicopter down in there and put him on it.

Poor fella' must have some fairly...

Disturbing hemorrhoids to be helicoptered out.

I don't know whether they did it or not.

B'Boy that's going a' settlin'!

I don't know what they're after, but whatever it is, they're sure after it strong!

> *He gets a cigarette and a lighter from a kitchen drawer. He lights it and sits in the chair adjacent to the ashtray.*

I don't know whether I told you or not, but I've made an upside down resolution for the coming new year.

I resolved to start smoking.

How 'bout that?

So I've been smoking a few cigarettes here and there.

That famous cigarette that travels the smoke further,
In an', through an', out an' around, over an'…
Extra fine tobacca,' ya' know,
Pall Mall or Pell-Mell.
So we shall see what we shall see.

>   *He has a coughing fit. He picks up the glass with the Liquid Wrench,*
>   *intentionally sniffs it, and recoils. He finds another glass with fluid, sniffs*
>   *it, and drinks. After he recovers, he speaks.*

I'm liable to quit again anytime.
   I did pretty good though.
   I was quit for a year and half.
   I don't know yet whether I'll quit smoking or drinking during Lent next year.
   Maybe both.
   Seems as though that's the only time I do anything for the Lord.
   I get into quite a number of churches, but not for the purpose of worshiping.
   Y'know, I'm there for tuning and such.
   We try to do a good job, As good as we can.
   Maybe I'll get credit for that.
   Yes, sir, this tobacco's mighty fine.

>   *He coughs again, though less than before.*

I better go easy on this stuff nowadays, though.
   I think I'm getting' a little too old to mess around with too much of it.
   Hey! You know what?
   I'm getting a "too old" complex.
   Hm. I don't want to do that!
   No, boy! That would be rough!

>   *The phone rings loudly. Earl is both alarmed and excited.*

Hang on! I gotta' go to the phone!

>   *He answers the phone.*

Yello'?…
   Yes…
   You doin' all right?
   I think it was Mon-dee, 'er, uh…
   No, was Tues-dee 'cause Pucker was over ta' the…
   Okay…
   I'll talk to ya'…
   Yes, I'll talk to ya' later…
   Yeah, I'm writing a letter…
   She's doin' fine…
   Yes, they're fine too,
   They're growing like weeds…
   Yes, all right…

Happy Thanksgiving.
Sure will…
Ya'll take care…
All right…
Oh…
Oh, okay…
Bye…
Ok, bye…
Oh, ok…
Bye, bye…
Ya'll take care…
Bye.

He hangs up the phone and continues talking to the tape recorder.

Well … Friendly Weatherspoon was just talking on the telephone.
I swear!
She done nothing but a'yak yak yak all day long.
You can hear her all over the building.
Well that's all she's got to do I guess.
That and look after her baby.
Nellie says that Friendly told Pucker that Richie,
That's her "baby" you know.
Friendly told Pucker that Richie is 11 years old in the sixth grade,
But *we* are of the opinion that he must be close 14.
Y'know, he was kind of retarded there for a while.
I don't know how he's doing now,
But he seems to me like he could learn pretty good.

He drinks more of the antacid. He belches from time to time.

I think the better part of valor for me is to eat and drink less.
I think that's where my salvation lies.
I just took a dose of medicine,
Not a big one, just a little one.
That dressing and stuff is trying to backfire on me a little bit.
I don't know whether it's good for that or not, but I imagine it is.
Well if it don't help, I'll just get me some good ol' soda.
I'spect I better not go to bed tonight till around midnight.
My stomach will still be rolling around and trying to grind up some of that junk and I'll be trying to sleep.
Ha!
I don't know which one will win out.
Great world, isn't it, if you don't weaken.
You know, i'changes a person's outlook on life a little bit
When you get to my age and you don't have any assurance you're going to wake up in the morning.

See here in a year or two,
Some little bug gonna' get me.
But I might be able to stay a while.
I hope I don't get so I tell the same story over and over like Pop did.
Or George Struthers.
'An Jimmy Handshaw.
'An Ernie Lee.
'An Freddy Thompson.
'An Gertie Emerick.
Gettin' to the point, they bend boys out lowfully.

     A train whistles.

There goes the ol' DT&I trainline.
    Detroit, Toledo, and Ironton.
    Carryin' that ol' pig ir'n (iron) back and forth.
    Yes, sir. She's doin' good business.
    Oh, I meant to tell you,
    The insurance lady asked me to get dark glasses.
    She had a word in there,
    Was part of the description of the frames,
    I couldn't make it out because the braille got mashed down somehow.
    So I wrote her letter and asked her about it.
    But the other night I was in the Bonanza store down here
    And they had some heavy, dark glasses for 88 cents,
    So I bought me a pair and put 'em on!
    I don't know whether it's worth the trouble to fool with them or not.
    Maybe I didn't get the right kind.
    Hey, they finally changed my numbers on my door.
    My apartment numbers, ya' know.
    They changed them to raised wooden numbers,
    Like you'd see on the exterior of buildings.
    I can feel 'em better than painted numbers.
    Hopefully I won't end up in anyone else's apartment again.
    Believe me, no one was more surprised than me.
    Both times!
    I don't want to do that no more.
    Ooo-wee!
    Get written up again.
    Work myself right outta' a place to live.
    Nope. Nope. Nope.
    Oh, I meant ta' tell ya', my typewriter's still broke down,
    So if you see long-hand on this thing don't get scared.
    Ha! A fine thing to tell ya' when you won't hear that till after you got the thing.
    You know that tape, 'er ribbon, er whatever you want to call it…

His thought is interrupted by the recorder making a noise. It may or may not be audible to the audience.

Whup. Whup.

Recorder is making that froggy noise again.

I don't like that.

I'll have ta' get in there and put something else on the belt, I guess.

Put a little powder on there…

A loud knock on the door. He is both startled and excited.

Hang on. I gotta' get the door!

GRAMP shuts off the tape. We hear the door open, and the following conversation. We don't see CLAUDE.

Hello! What can I do fer' ya'?

CLAUDE

You Earl?

GRAMP

I am. Do I know you?

CLAUDE

I'm Quarter's brother, Claude.

GRAMP

Claude Justice?

CLAUDE

Yea. Well, Quarter wants you to come up to Colgrove to Thanksgiving dinner tonight.

GRAMP

Really!? Aw shoot. I can't. Pucker said he was comin' by and I promised him I'd be here. Aw shoot.

CLAUDE

Well, lemme' bring ya' some. Ya' didn't have any fruit salad?

GRAMP

No.

CLAUDE

No green salad?

GRAMP

No.

CLAUDE

Well, lemme' bring ya' some a' that. In the meantime, I gotta' go on up to Huntington, but I'll be back after while.

GRAMP

Well, ok. We'll be here. Happy Thanksgiving to ya's!

CLAUDE

Happy Thanksgiving. I'll be back after while

> *We hear the door close and GRAMP enters. He speaks to the audience.*

I don't look for him back with any of that.
   That's Quarter's brother, Claude Justice.
   Quarter is the daytime bartender down t'Stone's.
   She's a very nice lady, seems to be.
   I had a peculiar experience down ta' Stone's the other day.
   I come in and order six bottles of beer in a sack,
   You know, to bring home.
   And then I get a big glass of draft to drink sitting there at the bar.

> *As he speaks, he retrieves some sort of powder from the kitchen and crosses to the tape recorder. Throughout the following section removes the reels carefully, expertly unscrews the cover, and applies the powder to the belt inside the recorder.*

After while, Quarter, she comes up and says, "Here's ya' another beer
   A fella sent up, sitting down the bar there"
   I says, "Who is it?"
   She says, "I don't know, he's a stranger to me"
   I says, "Go ask."
   She goes up and asks him and he says, "I'm stranger here. I'm from Michigan."
   Then he gives Quarter a dollar and ten cents for me to pay for my six beers I bought.
   Then after little while he comes up and sits down beside me
   and we talk for about five or ten minutes, I guess.

He buys me another beer and tells me he's a truck driver.
Tells me 'bout driving these trucks, hauling this big machinery.
Just all by hisself and he's gonna' eat a steak.
He just must enjoy spending money.
Of course I enjoyed him spending it on me. Yes sir!
But boy, a fellow doesn't have that happen to him very often, ya' know.
Least I don't.
Looky there! All the more to be thankful for!

> *He holds his stomach and belches now and again. Perhaps swigging more antacid.*

Oh man!
Excuse me.
I'm not used to eating real heavy like that,
Like I did in days gone by, you know.
Believe it's a whole lot better for a fella if he duddn't.
Oh like today, once in a while, it doesn't hurt anything.
But golly, where I eat one sandwich now,
I used to eat two or three when mother was living.
Yes sir she really knew how to feed ya', I'll say that.
I enjoyed a very plentiful supply of vittles for 46 years.
I sure did.
In a few weeks here…
Would'a been our forty-ninth wedding anniversary
It's a shame she couldn't stay with me till fifty.
Just to commemorate that, a little bit,
I'll play a few bars of The Anniversary Song, huh?

> *He sits at the piano and plays. When the song is done, the clock chimes. A "thirty minutes after the hour" chime.*

I suspect that ol'clock or be here when I'm gone.
Mmm-hmm.

> *He has reassembled the tape recorder. He resumes recording.*

Greetings and salutations! Again!
Well, I got ta' send my payment in tomorrow on the recorder.
Eight dollars.
That's all right.
That's something to be grateful for:
Those time-payment-deals.
Although it cost you a little more,
You can have the thing you want
And still not deplete your resources to the danger point.
The only thing you have to watch out for
Is that you don't get too many of the doggone things.
Yeah that's the pitfall, I guess you'd call that.

It's nice though that the merchants are prosperous enough to allow us to do that.

That they can carry us along, you know.

Well, I sure know from experience how much money it takes

To finance those deals and how much it hurts when one of 'em goes bad on ya'.

'Course I was just a tiny guy in the business,

It was a kind of a touch-and-go thing for me.

I sure got mine, huh?

I haven't got ta' tune for any of the big boys this year.

Course it was all on account of Floyd Hune that I got ta' tune those.

I don't remember when that was I tuned for Liberace.

Could look it up, I guess.

Floyd was learning to ta' tune last time I talked to him.

Maybe that he's got good enough to handle it himself.

One thing's sure, didn't have anything else to do.

I was up there at the ol' music store,

There was hardly a person came in the place.

Gosh, when we owned it, we used to have customers!

Came in for records and strings and reeds and things like that.

But they don't seem ta'…

Course we had 'lot a' hours in the afternoon,

Hot, summer afternoons

An' no one come in.

'Course long about that time, I'd sit down at the piana'

And start playing some tunes, ya' know, loud as I could.

'Fore ya' knew it, here come somebody,

Just pulled in by the music, ya' know.

I'm not sure that would work anymore.

Seems like everything now is guitars

Or if they do have a keyboard it's

An organ or a … accordion.

I was tellin' Ernie Lee about that recently.

He was over the other night.

We ate several cheese sandwiches and drank several beers.

Then we go over to The Sand Bar.

Oh boy! What music they got!

They got a tenor sax, an organ, accordion, and drums.

This woman playing the organ, she just pulled out all the stops and let her go.

Loud as it would go!

Ooo-wee!

(a sudden reversal) I didn't like it.

Poor ol' Ernie, he still couldn't hear real well.

I'm blind and he's deaf, how 'bout that!?

Music's not what it used to be…
Tony, You know, he's the accordion player over there?
His last name is Combo: Tony Combo.
Can you imagine that?
That's what he plays in: "The Combo"!
Ha!
He really plays that accordion with dexterity,
Except when it comes to chords. Ha!
Oh boy! No wonder I can't play the accordion
'Cause I try to put in a chord that I would do on the piano,
But if I just used common ordinary cords like he did I believe I could.
You know those hillbilly tunes he plays use just common, ordinary chords,
You know, like C, G, F.
Oh, once in a while they get a D, D7,
But very seldom in a minor key.
Music's not what it used to be.
'Course the long-haired concert pianists,
They still play the old masters music you know.
I reckon that stuf'll last forever.
The piano has fast lost its prestige in the shuffle.
Everything is guitars.
Ernie and his group are playing down at The Eagles now on Sunday nights.
Boy, Ernie's sure got a nice car.
Pontiac.
Main feature about it is he has an air conditioning system.
Terrific.
You can cool with it.
Heat with it.
Or ventilate without heating or cooling, either one.
Oh, it's just a real outfit, that's all.
I don't know what the darn thing cost him.
I 'spect it cost him, oh, close to $4000.
But it sure runs nice. Boy!
What'll they come up with next, I wonder.
Yes sirree, there's no stoppin' progress.
The hands of time march on…
Hey, ya' know one nice thing about a tape recorder?
You can "Sit Right Down and Write Yourself a Letter"!
Ha! How 'bout that!?

> He sits at the piano and plays a peppy version of I'm Gonna' Sit Right
> Down and Write Myself a Letter.
> We see smoke billowing from the stovetop. He stops abruptly and
> sniffs the air. He realizes there is a fire, jumps up, and heads toward the
> bedroom. He crosses back to the tape to stop recording.

Whup. Whup. Shoot! Shoot!

> *He proceeds to the bedroom as the smoke thickens. He returns with a bedpan, which he dumps on the stove. He pulls a bag of flour from a cabinet and dumps it on the stove. He picks up a throw rug from the floor and beats the stove until he is sure he has extinguished the fire. Everything is a mess, including him. He is tired, frightened, and covered in flour. He wipes his hands and face on a dishtowel and crosses to rest in his chair. The phone rings before he can sit. He answers it.*

Yello?

Yes, who's this?

Oh…

Oh, are you Winnie's cousin?

Winnie Stagatt?

Stagatt?

Well…

Oh…

Nevermind.

No, I don't believe I have his number.

Yes.

Yes, saw him down ta' Stone's.

Oh, it must'a been two weeks now…

Hello?

> *She hung up on him. He hangs up the phone.*

I just had a caller on the telephone.

One of them females that lives up front there.

I don't know what her name is.

She calls up here about once a week wantin' to know something.

A'Yak, yak, yak.

Don't s'pose she's sweet on me, do ya'?

Naw!

Not inner'sted (*interested*).

It would appear that I've made quite a mess.

Worse things could'a happened I guess.

Hey, you know what?

There's something to be grateful for:

I'm grateful I didn't burn my apartment down.

How 'bout that?

Pretty nice ta' live downtown where the action is.

Stone's next door,

Bank across the street,

Grocery, laundry, and milk delivered.

Pucker comes by nearly every day.

Yes, Sir, I got everything a feller could need.

Doin' good business.

He starts recording again.

Hello again.
Turning out to be a fairly eventful day here.
Phone calls and visitors.
Pretty nice to live right in the middle of town where the action is.
He deliberately omits any mention of the fire.

I want'd tell ya',
I locked myself out again last night.
I think I told ya', I was goin' up ta' the Moose at Huntington to play from 4:00–7:30
Then back to the Ironton Moose ta' play 9:00 to whenever.
Pretty unusual to have two gigs in one night.
Anyhow, Al Pierce brought me down from Huntington,
Stayed to watch me play and brought me home about 2:00 a.m.
By the time I got upstairs and realized I'd locked myself out,
Pierce was prob'ly halfway back ta' Huntington.
Course there's no one around the building office at that hour.
So I stumble down 5th street to the Wayfairer and rent a room for the night.
Cost me most of my proceeds from the entire evening's work.
I'm gonna' put a key down at Stone's now.
They're gonna keep it there in the register.
Just as a sort of fail-safe.
A back-up plan.

The clock chimes and he opens his wristwatch and feels the clock-face. A "45 minutes after the hour" chime.

Mm-hm.
My wristwatch is doin' good business.
Well, it's good to have a day like today at least once a year.
Lets a'person consider for a time,
All the blessings he's had.
One of them that *you* can be thankful for is that you were able t' land you a job.
When women get up into their 40s, y'know,
It's pretty hard to get anything that's any good.
Glad everything is going as well as can be expected.
Y'know, another blessing you've got, and boy, I mean it's a big one,
Are those two kids.
If you didn't have them you'd be lost.
Lost!
I'd kind of like to see you snap out of the doldrums you said you had there.
Maybe you have, I don't know.
I hope so.
Well, th' other day, Handshaw was George came down.

Course I wasn't participating in their activities.
I drunk about 6 'er 8 bottles a' pop though.
Had the hiccups when I woke up the next mornin' too.
That stuff's as hard on ya' as beer.
But it doesn't disturb your heart like beer does.

> *He lights a cigarette and coughs.*

I guess what disturbs your heart the most is a cigarette.
Anyhow, my ol' heart works like an ol' grandfather's clock.

> *He freezes to feel his pulse.*

Well, I was just trying to feel my pulse.
Can't hardly feel it.
Maybe it's gonna' quit, I don't know.
Be all right.
Yea, ol' Puckers going to be Sanny' Claus over at Romers.
Imagine that!
They're having a kind a' open house tomorrow night
And everybody that comes in has to have an invitation.
Can you believe that?!
The former manager of Romers,
He was an awful nice fella.'
He gave me a watch chain on my last birthday.
I guess he didn't know what else to do with it. Ha!

> *He unbuttons his shirt. He is wearing a white, tank undershirt.*

Anyhow he got involved with his drinking, you know.
Maybe unlock the store and get the girls started working,
And they wouldn't see him the rest the day.
And so he proceeded to get himself fired.
Handshaw was over here, oh, Saturday last,
An' we went down ta' Stone's 4:30, somethin' like that,
And Ernie Williams was in there
And he guzzled that beer till after 12:00.
I had to go off and leave him.
I got tired.
I can't understand how a person could do that.
There's no such thing as *having* to drink.
They claim that there is such a thing, but I don't.
If you've got important stuff to do, you're not going to drink.
I don't think anyway.
You've certainly got plenty of important things to do, don't 'cha.
You, of course, have your parental responsibilities.
And an exciting new job...
To keep you occupied...

He takes off his over-shirt and drapes it on something in the living room. He has a large bruise on his arm. Perhaps from falling. At some point he gets his robe from somewhere and puts it on.

Ol' Handshaw gets a few beers in 'im and he's hard to understand you know,
Slurs his words up.
    We get along pretty good though.
    No arguments.
    He says to me, "Earl would you ever like to own a beer joint?"
    Well, it didn't take me long to answer that,
    "No I wouldn't have one of those doggone things if it took in $1000 a day!"
    I like a cool beer as well as the next fella,'
    But too much'a the stuff…
    Just like poison to ya'.
    Poisons your life, in a manner of speaking.
    Like last Sunday, Pucker was up here and he was drinking beer and I wasn't.
    I was drinking buttermilk.
    Well now, a few days later I was drinking beer and he wasn't.

        He wears an open robe over his white, tank undershirt, suit pants and stocking feet.

Occasionally, Pucker takes a notion now to lay off for a week or two.
    Every now and then I do as well.
    Just get tired of the stuff.
    After a while doesn't seem to have any…
    Inebriating effect on either one of us.
    Just like drinking coffee or water.
    Hey, *you* might consider taking a break every now and again.
    Might do you good.
    Help with the doldrums maybe…

        Pause. A train whistles.

Say, I did a thing,
    I imagine you'll approve of it, I don't know.
    I gave Pucker a key to my apartment.
    'Cause he's all the time worrying about me
    An' can't find where I am.
    So I, (*choking back his sadness*) doggone it!
    He'll have a key,
    Can open my door and look in.
    If there really is something the matter with me,
    I'll be fine because he's about the only fella' I can depend on.
    See him every day or so anyhow.
    I'm sure I haven't got anything he'd want y'know.
    I know damn well he'd never take any money if he found it.
    You get as old as I am, see,

Libel to have something happen.

Fall down.

Break a hip,

Break an ankle,

Something like that.

Maybe hit my head, knock myself out,

Set my apartment on fire *(an inside joke with the audience)*.

Oh, there's hundreds of things could happened to ya'.

When you get old, why, things don't wait around 'bout hittin' ya'.

They just get you right now.

Yes sir!

So I think I can pretty much count on

Him dropping by on me every day.

I told you I went to Pete Peters funeral.

Al Lillian took care of him,

Which is very nice for him to do and I appreciate it a whole lot.

Notice of the funeral in the paper said private

So they didn't have very many there.

The Rev. Rupp was the minister.

His remarks were short but appropriate.

He recited the words of rock of ages—one verse and no music.

We went out to the cemetery.

So, good old boy that I've known all m' life

Will not come up to see me anymore.

I just couldn't help thinking that it won't be long till I'll be the chief attraction

At one of those gatherings maybe.

I'm serious about it because you get up my age

And you don't know whether you're going wake up alive or dead in the morning.

Pete wadn't sick at all.

He just went out in the yard an … took a little situation.

Out there ten or fifteen minutes and he came in,

Sit down, and all the sudden,

Pete noticed there's something wrong with him.

Call the ambulance right quick and the hospital.

I guess 'for they got there he was dead.

He'a good ol' boy.

He wadn't any saint, I guess.

He wadn't any devil either.

Hope I get to see him again sometime.

None 'a my whole crowd left, ya' know.

Ol' Pete Peters was the last one of 'em.

Maybe Emerson Lucas is still living.

Stanley Lee, ya' know, used to be in my quartet?

He died way back in, oh heavens…
I believe it was 1908.
Golly, that's been a while ago, hadn't it?
Hey, there's something to be grateful for:
Waking up in the morning!
Well, did I tell you they're tearing down the old bank building?
It'll look different around here when they get this building out-of-the-way.
They're really going after it.
They're not trying to salvage anything you know just tear, smash, bang!
Throw it on trucks and get it out of the way.
Out with the old, in with the new!
I think that's a darn shame.
'Course if you keep the old stuff around, why…
There wouldn't be any room for the new stuff.
I bet it's going to look pretty nice because they're going to a lot of expense.
One thing sure, I still won't have to go far to bank my money.
Yeah, I'm beginning to feel like as if I live on Wall Street.
Pretty nice, huh?
Hey, you know what else I'm grateful for?
This recorder.
Really makes life worth living.
I'm not kidding.
I get a lot a' fun out of it.

> *He gets the pumpkin pie from the refrigerator and a fork from the kitchen drawer. He eats as he talks.*

'Course you don't listen like I do 'cause you got work all day,
  Where I don't have,
  Not every day at least.
  Handshaw was telling me he's gottta' friend who's a jeweler, up in Dayton.
  He's a Frenchman and everybody calls him Frenchy.
  An' ol' Frenchy was telling Jimmy,
  When he got ta' feeling kind of low-bad,
  He had an' old parchment in his pocket that he take out and read,
  Made him feel so much better.
  Handshaw says, "Let's see it" so he pulled out this thing
  And it was the Gettysburg address by Abraham Lincoln, ya' know.
  Remember him?
  It had Lincoln's signature on it
  And they conceived the idea that this was an extremely valuable document,
see?
  They took it to the library there in Dayton
  And the woman said there's no doubt about it
  That's Lincoln signature.

They took it several places and there was no question about it.
It was the real thing.

> *The lights blink off. The early-evening light coming through the window.*

Whup.
I think I heard my bulb burn out again.
Must be a short in that fixture somewhere.
I didn't even know they was on.
I guess we musta' left it on when we left for Huntington last night.

> *He retrieves a bulb from the kitchen, drags a chair to the center of the room, climbs it, and replaces the bulb.*

Well, he finally sent it off to Washington.
About a month later, he heard back.
Turned out it was just another old parchment.
So I guess Handshaw went over to Dayton today
To give old Frenchy the bad news.
Guess he'll give him something to be *ungrateful* for.
Though, it's nice for something like that to pop up in the fella's life y'know,
Least it gives him a few days of a thrilling period of time.
It's something like if I'd hear that somebody left me 1 million dollars.
I get a kick out of that,
Till I found there was nothing to it.
Mother used to say that the Henry's own the land
Where the Queens Palace in England is situated.
She said they all went down together,
Sent some guy over there to see about it,
And he never returned.

> *The new bulb flashes and burns out. GRAMP falls. We hear the chair slip and he hits the floor hard. He is still. The tape runs off the reel and flaps wildly. He starts to move gradually. He is on the floor with broken glass and other debris spread around him.*

Whup, whup, whup.
Oh, shoot.

> *He is hurt, but mobile. He makes it to his feet slowly, wades through the mess on the floor, and switches the tape to the second side. He takes a breath and resumes talking into the recorder.*

GRAMP

Ok.
This is side two.
I hope the birthday went off in good shape.
Thought about you many times yesterday.

The night you were born, old Doc Marshall, ya' know,
Took care of the process.
Me an', I believe, Mabel Ketter was there,
Yea I'm sure she was,
and your Aunt Bertha was there.
She and I sat down there in the dining room.
While it was closed in stairway that went upstairs,
We left the door open so we could hear what was going on, ya' know.
Mother was moaning and going on.
The next thing we knew, "Waaaaa!"
An ol' Bertha says, "Little Vera."
You know we talked about calling you Vera for a while?
Oh boy! That was a joyful moment for me.
And I'm glad to say that joy hasn't turned to sorrow.
We had our first frost on the night you were born.
I went out and got some roasting ears
They were slightly frostbitten, but they were still all right.
Alice Pruce was cooking for us you know.
She couldn't move around the kitchen much faster than I did.
One of the slowest cooks I ever saw, but it was good.
Golly those days just seem like yesterday, or something like that.
The figures don't lie.
You know only thing I can't figure out is how these 48 years went by in such a hurry.
My goodness!

The light changes as the sun sets.

When I think about what a long life I've had an…
Well, the money that I've had…
An think a' what I got now…
When I think a' the places I've been,
And the tunes I've played,
And the people I've played with…
Gee.
I don't think there's a person living that hasn't had their share of sorrows.
Course it seems sometimes that your share is a little bigger than the other fella's. I guess it's evened up pretty well.
Course my life is been a little different from yours or most people's,
But it seems I've come through pretty well.
Hey you know you were talking about on your last tape,
Me bringing you up to be a baby then going off and leaving you.
You know the only reason I did that is because I loved you so much.
I just couldn't help… (*he cries*)
It's no disgrace to cry a few tears once in a while.

That's why we're equipped with … a crying apparatus.
Course I don't like to see a person too sentimental.
Neither do I like to see a person be all self-sufficient,
And not affected by any memories or anything that's gone by in their life.
Pretty hard to strike a happy medium, but I have an idea *you've* come close
to it.
I can't stop few tears once in a while,
Certain kinds of music,
Certain thoughts that I have.
I'm not ashamed of it.
Course there's no question in my mind I'll see the folks before you do.
That is if all things we have been taught from childhood on up
Pan-out to be like they say they were.
But if the Seventh Day Adventist's have their way
We'll all go to heaven at the same time.
Nobody goes there, according to them, until the resurrection morning,
When they'll hear Christ's voice and the voice of the trumpet.
And out they come. Yes sir!
But I don't know which is correct.
Regarding what you said on your tape:
You know if I needed you, I'd call.
When Mother was sick,
I didn't call you as soon as I should've.
I thought I was able to do more than I was.
I'd never be that way anymore.
You know, that I've got plenty a' people lookin' in on me.
Handshaw and Pucker.
Pete Peters… *(He remembers that Pete has died)*
Hey I saw George Struthers last week.
He's 81.
Seems to be in pretty good condition.
Other than his vision.
Doctor says there's nothing he can do for him.
He comes up here and we didn't have a light on,
Ya' know, don't need it.
And when he goes to go home,
He goes down these side steps,
And out in that bright light and…
He could see just fine.
Lasted about thirty seconds.

> *Pucker enters, lit by an almost-blinding side-light coming from the hallway. He wears a police uniform. GRAMP freezes.*

PUCKER

What ya' doin? You doin' a letter?

GRAMP

Pucker! Hey, Pucker! Happy Thanksgiving!

PUCKER

Same to ya's. You's doin' all right?

> *GRAMP shifts into host-mode, turning on the television, opening the icebox, etc.*

GRAMP

Hey, I got some pumpkin pie in the … well, I already ate my piece, but I still got yurs. I got a couple of 807's in the icebox fer' us. C'mon in!

PUCKER

I can't today, Earl.

GRAMP

I'm just finishing this up. C'mon in. Have a seat. Ball game's on. You wanna' 807?

PUCKER

I can't today. Nancy and the kids is at her mother's house waitin' on me. Naw, I'll be back tomorrow. We'll celebrate tomorrow, Buddy. Bye, bye.

GRAMP

(*perhaps overlapping*) Wuh … I…Happy Thanksgivi…

> *The door slams shut. The clock chimes. Westminster Bells and five chimes. A moment of stillness. The light changes as the sunset grows in intensity.*

Ya' know, this tape recorder's been a wonderful comfort to me.
    And I hope you've enjoyed it too.
    'Cause I don't feel like you've been away like you have, ya' know.
    I feel like I've been with ya'.
    Course I haven't…
    Gives me the illusion though.

Ya' know how I told ya' I got written up for playing the piano so late at night?

And remember when I had that trouble identifying which apartment was mine … twice?

And, of course, you remember that very small kitchen fire I had last summer, which will … never happen again, of course.

Well I received a letter late last week informing me that the landlord has kept a detailed tally of my missteps and plans on not renewing my lease unless I have someone who can be held accountable for my hijinks and any reparations that may be necessary. I'm quite sure he won't take too kindly when he hears I locked myself out again early this morning.

Aw, Honey, I'monna' need you ta' come down here and help me.

They're gonna' kick me out if I don't have a co-signer on my lease.

I got a "Mayday." SOS. CQD.

Hey, you know what that means, don't 'cha? Means "Come quick danger."

Seems I'm gonna' need a little assistance.

I wouldn't ask if it wasn't absolutely necessary.

> *Earl makes his way to his feet and shuffles to the piano. He might have broken a rib or two. He's definitely bruised.*

How 'bout a little music, huh?

This was one of Mother's favorites.

> *He plays a bit of "September Song." He pauses.*

When I quit my letter and the tape runs off and I quit talkin'.

Don't pay attention to it,

Whether I've said goodbye 'er not.

Cause that…

That don't mean nothin'.

So, y'all take care 'a yourselves for me now, will ya'?

Happy Thanksgiving.

Lights fade as he continues to play.

End of play.

Dyscalculia

KATRINA HALL

In Season 3, Episode 6, of her cable television program, *Crazy Ex-Girlfriend*, U.S. comedian and singer Rachel Bloom is seen by a hospital psychiatrist after attempting suicide. Bloom, who regularly tackles difficult subjects through comedy, sings with excitement, hoping that a diagnosis will finally provide the "fix" for her struggles. "For almost 30 years," she sings, "I've known something was wrong, but Mom said weakness causes bloating, so I tried to be strong." She sings about the various over-the-counter pills, meditations, affirmations, and other "solutions" she's tried unsuccessfully through the years. Now, however, she believes that this psychiatrist will be able to solve her lonely battle.

> THERE'S NO NEED FOR REGRET
> 'CAUSE I'M ABOUT TO GET
> A DIAGNOSIS!
> A DIAGNOSIS!
> DON'T TELL ME "NO, SIS—
> —TER, YOU DON'T FIT IN"
> DOC, PRESCRIBE ME MY TRIBE, GIVE ME MY THRONG
> TELL ME THAT THIS WHOLE TIME, I'VE BELONGED
> WITH THOSE OTHER PEOPLE WHO SHARE
> MY DIAGNOSIS

Bloom comedically emphasizes what Katrina Hall so painfully shows: not having a name for one's reality can be a lonely and frustrating experience, filled with self-critique and doubt. This is not, of course, to suggest a diagnosis is some form of miracle—certainly not in the way that Bloom's character hopes it will be. The medical model assumption that a person is somehow incomplete until given a label through diagnosis is not only offensive, but dangerous[1] and historically oppressive.[2] Recognizing this, however, should not invalidate the many people for whom a diagnosis can make a tangible difference, whether in accessing care, creating a greater sense of control, or letting go of past feelings of shame.[3] At the very least, in an ableist world which is quick to disbelieve and ignore individual experience, some see a diagnosis as a sort of social lubricant, granting an official "certification" to their claim and helping ward off the questions of "are you sure it's not just your imagination?" and "you don't *look* sick."[4] In Katrina Hall's case, as explored in her autobiographical play *Dyscalculia*, a diagnosis was the first step to a new approach to life and self-care.

While her late diagnosis is ultimately a positive experience, the decades it took to arrive can't be ignored. Consider her words during the final moments of the show:

> KATRINA (current day): [...] I don't resent any of it that came before. What'd be the point? The path back from your life now won't ever lead to who you never were. This is a good now, so resentment isn't an option. But while I don't resent, I do, on occasion, sometimes, just in passing, wonder what maybe, possibly, could have potentially might have been.[5]

Although late diagnoses and negligent schooling can happen to anyone, race, class, and gender have historically played a substantial role. Even today, with contemporary, post ADA, IDEA, and FAPE implementation, inequitable standards and availability remain ongoing problems in many urban and rural areas.[6] Katrina Hall's dive into educational and class inequities in *Dyscalculia* gives a painful reminder of how lonely a learning disability or neurodiversity can be when misunderstood, undiagnosed, or treated as a character defect.

—John Michael Sefel

Notes

1. Sheila Jones and Morten Hesse, "Adolescents With ADHD: Experiences of Having an ADHD Diagnosis and Negotiations of Self-Image and Identity," *Journal of Attention Disorders* 22 (1), 2014: 92–102. https://doi.org/10.1177/1087054714522513.

2. Janette Y. Taylor, "Colonizing Images and Diagnostic Labels: Oppressive Mechanisms for African American Women's Health," *Advances in Nursing Science* 21 (3), 1999: 32–45, https://journals.lww.com/advancesinnursingscience/Abstract/1999/03000/Colonizing_Images_and_Diagnostic_Labels_.6.aspx.

3. Philip Wylie, Wendy Lawson, and Luke Beardon, *The Nine Degrees of Autism: A Developmental Model for the Alignment and Reconciliation of Hidden Neurological Conditions* (Hove, East Sussex: Routledge, 2015), 105.

4. *Ibid.*, 103.

5. See the play, following.

6. L. Bueso. "Challenging Objectives: A Legal and Empirical Analysis of the Substantive FAPE Standard After Endrew F. *UCLA*. iii," 2019, ProQuest ID: Bueso_ucla_0031D_18122; Merritt ID: ark:/13030/m58w8fvf. Retrieved from https://escholarship.org/uc/item/6pv5p6sb.

Dyscalculia

Throughout the play, Katrina Current Day speaks directly to the audience, existing outside of the scenes. All other Katrina ages (and all other characters) exist within memories, staged as fourth wall realism, with the notable exception of the court. Katrina Current Day is able to walk in and out of these scenes at will.

Dyscalculia © Katrina Hall, all rights reserved. Those interested in producing this work may contact the author at Katrina.Hall.Plays@gmail.com.

* * *

ACT ONE, SCENE ONE

> *KATRINA CURRENT DAY stands on stage with one male, STUDENT 1, and one female, STUDENT 2, seated behind her. A third chair is unoccupied.*

KATRINA CURRENT DAY: (*To Audience*) 8:45 a.m., Fredrick Douglas Elementary School. Fourth grade, 1976.

> *KATRINA AGE 10, backpack in tow, slumps toward the empty chair, but is cut off by STUDENT 1.*

STUDENT 1: 'Sup Orca? (*Poke*) I said what's up, Orca?! (*Poke*) What'ya got in my bag?

KATRINA AGE 10: Leave me alone.

STUDENT 1: Gimme my bag then!

STUDENT 2: Oh my God, that ain't your bag! Quit it!

STUDENT 1 (*To STUDENT 2*): Shut your black ass up! Ain't nobody sayin' shit to you! Mind your business! (*To KATRINA AGE 10.*) See that fat ass? Got fat mouth over there talkin' like my bag ain't my bag. Gimme!

> *KATRINA AGE 10 barely manages to hang on to her bag during the tussle.*

STUDENT 2: Stop! Boy stop! Stop! (*Runs to door*) I'ma tell, quit it! I'ma get the teacher! (*Yelling*) Hey! They fightin' in here!

STUDENT 1: Yo, sit your ass down somewhere! I said ain't nobody talkin' to you! Need to mind your ol' peasy-head business!

> *TEACHER 1 enters as KATRINA AGE 10 and STUDENT 1 scramble to their seats.*

TEACHER 1: Good morning class! Does everyone remember yesterday's lesson? We learned map reading, right? There're treats for anyone who remembers!

> *Students affirm they remember.*

Outstanding! Now, I'm going to give each of you a map, and when I say "Go!," I want you to open them, find where it says the treasure is, and all you find you get to keep. Okay?

> *TEACHER 1 hands each student a brightly colored map.*

Ready? Go!

> *Seconds after the hunt begins, STUDENT 2 finds a Snickers Bar and holds it up for the rest of the class to see.*

KATRINA CURRENT DAY: (*To Audience*) My God. This teacher, this angel come down straight from Heaven-on-high, has seeded this entire classroom with regulation 1976 sized Snickers Bars! What's a "fun size?" It's 1976! We don't know! Oh my God. You know what? These fools—Look, all these fools need to keep out of my way!

> *Begin film projection of a rudimentary treasure map showing the confused path and footsteps of the following monologue.*

KATRINA AGE 10 (*To Self*) Okay. This is north up here … Wait … No. It looks like the desk … The desk … the desk is east, but, that makes, that makes. That way north, but then it don't—It don't match this north thing on here. She balls up map in frustration as projected map is simultaneously scrawled over. (*To Self*) I don't understand. (*To TEACHER 1's back*) I don't understand.

TEACHER 1: Nice job everyone! (*School bell rings.*) Okay, that's recess! Everyone back in twenty minutes!

> *All exit while KATRINA AGE 10 remains puzzling over her map. Enter STUDENT 2. KATRINA AGE 10 stuffs map in her pocket.*

STUDENT 2: Hey, how many you find?

KATRINA CURRENT DAY: (*To Audience*) I am Snickers-less, but I am proud.

KATRINA AGE 10: (*To STUDENT 2*) Four.

STUDENT 2: Where they at?

KATRINA AGE 10: I ate 'em! Dag!

> *STUDENT 2 methodically chews a Snickers while very deliberately scrutinizing KATRINA AGE 10 face.*

STUDENT 2: You ain't find shit you fat dummy!

KATRINA AGE 10: Ain't nobody thinkin' about you!

STUDENT 2: Shut up! That's why you fat and stupid!

> *STUDENT 2 storms toward exit, pauses, then walks back, Snickers bar in hand.*

STUDENT 2 Here bighead.

> *KATRINA AGE 10 ignores her.*

Hurry up! You takin' up all my recess!

> *KATRINA AGE 10 accepts candy.*

KATRINA AGE 10: Thanks.

STUDENT 2: You still stupid, dummy!

> *Exit STUDENT 2*

KATRINA CURRENT DAY: (*To Audience*) That was fourth grade. Biweekly fist fights for having the extreme bad manners to be a short, fat, weirdo, and not understanding why I couldn't read a map—Wait. Who likes Snickers? (*Katrina hands candy to nearest audience member who wants it.*) I'm here for the Jolly Ranchers these days.

> *BLACKOUT.*

ACT ONE, SCENE TWO

> *Lights up on KATRINA AGE 11, alone at her desk. Enter TEACHER 2 with an armful of folders.*

TEACHER 2: Did you finish the chapters from last night?

KATRINA AGE 11: Yes! Mostly. All except the last pages. Of the beginning. Of the first half.

TEACHER 2: (*Impassive.*) Why didn't you finish? Was there something you didn't understand?

KATRINA AGE 11: Okay, yeah, ummm, I understood what everything said, but the longer I was reading, the longer I was reading. I can't read too long 'cause if I do, I understand less than I do if I didn't. I mean, the less I read at a time the night before, the more it sounds like I read more when you ask the next day. Like today.

> *TEACHER 2 stares.*

Yes, no I didn't finish.

TEACHER 2: (*Canned enthusiasm*) We'll begin with reading then!

KATRINA AGE 11: Yeah. Okay.

TEACHER 2: All right, let's begin.

> *TEACHER 2 passes folders one at a time as KATRINA AGE 11 places each on the desk after inspecting it and saying "check." This sequence, except where indicated, should move at as quick a pace as the performers can manage.*

TEACHER 2: Reading folder A!

KATRINA AGE 11: Check!

TEACHER 2: B!

KATRINA AGE 11: Check!

TEACHER 2: C!

KATRINA AGE 11: Check!

TEACHER 2: D!

KATRINA AGE 11: Check!

TEACHER 2: E!

KATRINA AGE 11: Check!

TEACHER 2: Math folder 1!

KATRINA AGE 11: Check!

TEACHER 2: Reading folder F!

KATRINA AGE 11: Check!

TEACHER 2: G!

KATRINA AGE 11: Check!

TEACHER 2: H!

KATRINA AGE 11: Check!

TEACHER 2: Math folder 2!

KATRINA AGE 11: Check!

TEACHER 2: Reading folder I!

KATRINA AGE 11: Check!

TEACHER 2: Math folder 3!

> *KATRINA AGE 11 holds, stares uncomprehendingly, then passes the folder back.*

TEACHER 2: Reading folder J!

KATRINA AGE 11: Check!

TEACHER 2: K!

KATRINA AGE 11: Check!

TEACHER 2: L!

KATRINA AGE 11: Check!

TEACHER 2: Math folder 3!

> *KATRINA AGE 11: hands back immediately.*

TEACHER 2: Reading folder M!

KATRINA AGE 11: Check!

TEACHER 2: Math folder 3!

> *KATRINA AGE 11 Hands folder back.*

Math 3!

> *KATRINA AGE 11: Hands folder back.*

Math 3!

> *KATRINA AGE 11: Hands folder back.*

Math 3!

KATRINA AGE 11: Wait! (*Hands folder back*).

TEACHER 2: Math 3!

KATRINA AGE 11: I don't… (*Hands folder back*) I have a question!

TEACHER 2: No, you don't! (*Hands folder back*) It's fine!

KATRINA AGE 11: I don't understand! (*Hands folder back*)

TEACHER 2: (*pause*) Well of course you don't, but it's not as if I can do anything about that. Look at you. Why would you understand?

> *School bell rings.*

Done for the day! (*Gathers folders*) If you're worried about flunking, don't. You'll pass. Why not?!

> *Exit TEACHER 2*

ACT ONE, SCENE THREE

KATRINA CURRENT DAY: (*to Audience*) I was done with school after that, but it'd be another year and a half before I gave up pretending. I "passed" fifth grade with the barest understanding of long division. By the sixth, I was cutting for weeks at a time, and by the seventh, I'd put it behind me entirely.

> *She extracts hip waders from her backpack and proceeds to put them on.*

What I did instead was spend most of my days either at the arcade or the movies. From the '70s to the mid–'80s, there was some weird zoning thing in Center City that resulted in Market and Chestnut, starting from City Hall to blocks and blocks down either street, mostly being made up of video arcades and movie theatres. The Market theatres were exclusively porno. That part of Market was also the one location with a McDonald's, so if I wanted breakfast, my only option as a thirteen-year-old girl cutting school at 8 a.m. was to wade through The River Semen.

> *PREDATOR 1 watches, unnoticed, as KATRINA AGE 13 painstakingly wades through the verbal gauntlet. Prerecorded, overlapping catcalling of multiple Predators' voices alternate the following:*
> *[PRE-RECORDED PREDATOR VOICES]: Hey pretty. Hey. Where you goin'? Can I come? Can I talk to you for a minute? Can I have a smile? Come on back here girl. I wanna tell you somethin'… somethin' to show you. What'ya got under there? Somethin' pretty? What'ya savin' it for … do you right baby girl…*
> *PREDATOR 1 emerges and begins trailing KATRINA AGE 13. As he speaks, her wading becomes more desperate and labored.*

PREDATOR 1: Hi. Hello? Baby girl. I said HELLO. Oh, you gonna act like you don't hear nothin', right? You too good to speak? Your fat ass too good to speak?! Bitch, fuck you! You ain't shit! Fuckin' dyke ass bitch! Let me catch your dyke ass out here tomorrow! See if I ain't got somethin' for that ass!

> *Exit PREDATOR 1. Scene becomes McDonald's*

KATRINA CURRENT DAY: (*to audience*) Unfortunately, making it into McDonald's wasn't always a guarantee of getting a few minutes' break before having to walk out and go through some version of the whole mess all over again.

> *Enter PREDATOR 2*

PREDATOR 2: (*To KATRINA AGE 13*) Baby girl? You wanna go in the alley out back and do this cocaine with me?

> *KATRINA AGE 13 stares straight ahead. Exit PREDATOR 2. Enter McDonald's Clerk who hands KATRINA AGE 13 a to-go order. Exit McDonald's Clerk.*

KATRINA CURRENT DAY: (*to audience)* The McDonald's thing was just to kill an hour. Really, I was just waiting around for nine o'clock, because that's when the regular theatres on Chestnut Street would open.

> *Begin slide projection of still pictures of The Goldman Theatre.*

The Goldman was my favorite. Two screens, two movies per screen, and a staff that couldn't give two shits about an underage girl coming in at 9 a.m. on a school day.

> *She heads to theatre seats and begins removing waders.*

You'd pay for one double, then sneak into the other after the first one was done. For three dollars, you could watch movies from 9 to 5, and be back home before your mom got home from work at 6.

> *Lights do a movie theatre fade. The sound of a reel-to-reel begins and is heard throughout the following sequence until the sound of PREDA-TOR 1's breathing stops. The film's audio begins and indicates KATRINA AGE 13 is watching a martial arts movie where the fighter is female. The audio is a bit too loud. Enter PREDATOR 1 who sits one seat away from KATRINA AGE 13. The film audio begins lowering as the volume of PREDATOR 1's breathing rises. KATRINA AGE 13 sits paralyzed as PREDATOR 1's groans become incorporated into, then reach parity with the film's audio. The film audio continues to lower until it disappears entirely. PREDATOR 1's sounds grow quicker and more urgent until, at climax...*
> *BLACKOUT.*

ACT ONE, SCENE FOUR

> *LIGHTS UP. KATRINA CURRENT DAY IN THE GOLDMAN rises and composes herself.*

KATRINA CURRENT DAY: (*to audience*) What was I saying? (*Beat*) Oh. Math. Right. (*Beat*) I spent two years acquiring an education in Blaxploitation and Shaw Brothers movies, at the expense of proper book learning. It was easy. My father was gone, and my MOTHER was negligent to the point of never bothering to ask why it'd been years since she'd had to sign a single report card.

Enter MOTHER and TRUANT OFFICER 1.

As it turned out, I'd been one at least on person's radar for months.

MOTHER: (*To KATRINA AGE 15*) Get you ass over here.

> *KATRINA AGE 15 approaches but stops just outside of striking distance.*

TRUANT OFFICER 1: (*To MOTHER*) Mrs. Hall, we've been mailing you for months. We have no record...

MOTHER: (*To KATRINA AGE 15)* Been makin' sure you got to the mail first, right?

TRUANT OFFICER 1: (*To MOTHER*) ... no record of Katrina having set foot in class since just before seventh grade. Are you aware you're legally accountable...

> *MOTHER steps toward KATRINA AGE 15. KATRINA AGE 15 simultaneously steps away.*

MOTHER: You need to tell me how you got a truant officer comin' up in my house.

TRUANT OFFICER 1: (*To MOTHER*) Can you explain?

MOTHER: (*To KATRINA AGE 15*) You best believe you need to explain!

KATRINA AGE 15: (*To TRUANT OFFICER 1*) I can explain!

MOTHER (*To KATRINA AGE 15*). There ain't no way to explain!

KATRINA CURRENT DAY: (*To Audience*) I cannot explain this.

TRUANT OFFICER 1: Look, Mrs. Hall, I need you to please listen. You're legally responsible for your daughter's truancy. In this case, there might potentially be penalties involved. Financial ones.

MOTHER: (*Impassive*) Yeah, let me ask you. You the point person for any questions about this mess. You the one?

TRUANT OFFICER 1: For now, yes. Anything further...

MOTHER: Okay.

> *MOTHER takes KATRINA AGE 15 by the arm and leads her toward the door.*

Go on and leave your card or whatever.

> *MOTHER opens door. TRUANT OFFICER 1 extends card toward MOTHER, who makes no move to take it. They hand it to KATRINA AGE 15 instead.*

TRUANT OFFICER 1: (*To MOTHER*) I'm available by phone between nine and three every Monday through Thursday. (*To KATRINA AGE 15.*) That goes for you too. You understand?

MOTHER: She ain't stupid. She a lyin' sneak, not a stupid one though.

> *TRUANT OFFICER 1 attempts to say something, before Mother cuts them off.*

MOTHER: No need. I got everything I need to know.

> *TRUANT OFFICER 1 makes a second attempt to speak.*

MOTHER: What you gonna do besides repeat yourself?

> *Exit TRUANT OFFICER 1.*
> *KATRINA AGE 15 attempts to escape MOTHER's grip as soon as the door closes.*

MOTHER *(tightens grip)*: You stay your ass right here.

> *KATRINA AGE 15 reflexively pulls away.*

MOTHER Right here. Do not fucking move. If you make me chase you, I'll never get tired of hurting you.

> *MOTHER removes the belt from around her waist, then wraps it around her hand so it'll strike buckle first. KATRINA AGE 15 breaks paralysis and runs out the door. MOTHER goes after her. From offstage, the whip-crack jangle of metal striking flesh is heard.*

MOTHER: What did I fucking say?! What?! Did I?! Fucking say?!

> *BLACKOUT.*

ACT ONE, SCENE FIVE

> *LIGHTS UP ON: KATRINA AGE 15 SITTING ALONE.*

KATRINA CURRENT DAY: After. Patchy. It's still patchy. I forgot … I just remember—Something's wrong.

> *Enter TEACHER 3. KATRINA AGE 15 rises and begins pacing.*

TEACHER 3: How are you today Miss?

> *TEACHER 3 begins to mime writing on a blackboard. Begin video of multicolored jumble of numbers morphing and crashing into one another.*

KATRINA AGE 15: I'm kinda tense and stomach-achy the way I always get when math's around. I feel like I should understand it; I mean, I think I should understand it at least some, 'cause everything that ain't math comes so easy. I mean, there's something not right about that. It feels like something's wrong. Right? You think maybe? That sounds, like, not right. Right?

TEACHER 3: Sit down. We need to start working on some problems.

KATRINA AGE 15: I don't feel like sitting.

TEACHER 3: Sit or stand, we're doing these today.

KATRINA AGE 15: But…

TEACHER 3: I'm not for your fuckery today Miss.

> *KATRINA AGE 15 attempts to distract and amuse as she snakes to the floor, lies on her back, and stamps her feet.*

KATRINA AGE 15: No! Nooooooo! No! No! No! No! No!

TEACHER 3: Nobody cares.

KATRINA AGE 15: No?

> *KATRINA AGE 15 rises and composes herself.*

KATRINA AGE 15: I never, never know what you're talking about! It's like, every time you … It's like all the time when you start talking about fractions or whatever—

TEACHER 3: (*As if she hadn't heard.*) We're doing fractions today. Since you won't have a seat, we'll go over these up here at the board. Show me the common denominators.

> *KATRINA AGE 15 stares blankly.*

TEACHER 3: Oh girl, please. We've been over this! To find the common denominator, you—

> *Fade in audio of the following sounds as described. As TEACHER 3 mouths the instructions, KATRINA AGE 15 hears audio of an old television test pattern rolling into white noise, followed by the sound of a fax machine failing to connect.*

KATRINA AGE 15: Umm, wait. That's, that's…

> *Fade in audio of the following sounds as described. KATRINA AGE 15 mouths perfectly in time to the audio of an old television test pattern rolling into white noise, followed by the sound of a fax machine failing to connect.*

KATRINA AGE 15: … like that. Like that?

TEACHER 3: You know damn well that's not what I said, and you're not going to joke your way out of doing these.

KATRINA AGE 15: That is what you said! (*Beat.*) That's not what you said? (*Beat.*) That's what it sounded like you said. (*To self*) Why can't I understand what you said?

TEACHER 3: All this wasting time just because you don't like math stops today.

KATRINA AGE 15: (*Distracted*). I don't understand.

TEACHER 3: Don't like. Don't understand. Same difference.

KATRINA AGE 15: Oh my God, how is that the same?

TEACHER 3: What did I just say?

> *KATRINA AGE 15 mimes writing on a blackboard as the jumble of numbers playing on the video become more nonsensical. TEACHER 3 sits and marks papers.*

KATRINA CURRENT DAY: (*To Audience*) When you tell people you don't understand math, they never think you mean exactly what you say. That you're being literal. They think saying you don't understand is synonymous with saying you find it difficult. But that's not the same thing at all really, is it? (*To TEACHER 3*) Guess it's easier going around flipping your tits over how I'm lazy and lack focus, than it is to consider there's something profoundly wrong with the degree to which I just cannot fucking count.

TEACHER 3 looks up to find KATRINA AGE 15 staring at her.

TEACHER 3: Done? *KATRINA AGE 15 makes affirmative noise. TEACHER 3 inspects the nonsense passing for answers.* What the shit is this?! We just, literally just went over all of this. You know, it takes just as much energy to pretend to listen as it does to actually listen! All right. Let's go over it. Again. You have got to get over this I-hate-math-therefore-I-can't-do-it foolishness.

KATRINA AGE 15: I don't hate math! I mean, I don't like it or nothin', I just can't ever tell … When you be tryin' to tell me how to do stuff it don't sound like nothin'!

TEACHER 3: Take a seat.

KATRINA AGE 15: Okay, listen, I'm tryin' to tell you…

TEACHER 3: I mean it. (*KATRINA AGE 15 sits.*) Now, concentrate!

KATRINA AGE 15 listens as TEACHER 3 mouths instructions that sound like test patterns, white noise, and fax machines as the lights slowly dim.

ACT ONE, SCENE SIX

LIGHTS UP ON: A VIDEO ARCADE.

KATRINA CURRENT DAY: It's Arcade Day! A.k.a, any day there aren't any movies I want to see because I've seen all of them five times already. I'm 15, playing *Tempest*, and I'm very, very good at it. So good, I'll be able to play another 5 or 6 hours, and still have enough cash left over to buy a dusty meatball sandwich from my favorite street vendor to eat on the walk home.

TRUANT OFFICER 2 enters and approaches KATRINA AGE 15.

TRUANT OFFICER 2: What's your name?

KATRINA AGE 15 turns to him, then immediately turns back to her game.

KATRINA AGE 15: Outta my face Mr. White Folks.

TRUANT OFFICER 2: Not in your best interest to make me ask again.

KATRINA AGE 15: (*Leery*) Kysha

TRUANT OFFICER 2: How old are you "Kysha"?

KATRINA CURRENT DAY: (*To Audience*) Well shit. It's a truant officer.

KATRINA AGE 15: (*To TRUANT OFFICER 2*) Seventeen.

TRUANT OFFICER 2: You don't look seventeen.

KATRINA AGE 15: I ain't from around here. We ain't from Philly. Me and my parents ain't from Philly. We came—we came to Philly for the weekend, to visit my grandparents. To visit daddy's, dad's, parents. We stayed later than we thought we was gonna, so, dad umm—Dad said we should just, take the day off and leave later. Later on today. And I'm seventeen.

KATRINA CURRENT DAY (*To Audience*) It's good, right? I was ridiculously proud of myself!

TRUANT OFFICER 2: Yeah. Come with me.

> *TRUANT OFFICER 2 grabs KATRINA AGE 15 and begins dragging her toward exit.*

KATRINA AGE 15: Hey!

> *KATRINA AGE 15 resists to the point of having to be dragged out by her heels.*
> *BLACKOUT.*

ACT ONE, SCENE SEVEN

> *LIGHTS SLOWLY UP ON: A SWEATBOX INSIDE THE POLICE ROUNDHOUSE AT EIGHT AND RACE.*

TRUANT OFFICER 2: What's your real name?

KATRINA AGE 15: (*Silence.*)

TRUANT OFFICER 2: Your mom at work? Where does she work? She home? I need a number.

KATRINA AGE 15: (*Silence*)

TRUANT OFFICER 2: Nah? Nothing? (*He takes a cigarette from his pocket*) All right "Kysha." You be ready to tell me what I need to know when I get back. That ain't a request.

> *Exit TRUANT OFFICER 2*

KATRINA CURRENT DAY: (*To Audience*) Four years of cutting and I couldn't tell you what a truant officer even was. Now? They're every-goddamn-where! They call these rooms sweatboxes. The sweat's all psychological though. Psychic perspiration. It's still better than having my mother find out. Not a hope in hell of keeping this from her though, because in spite of being in constant trouble, I don't have any street smarts worth mentioning. Dude clocked this immediately, because, oh my God, the white foolishness he's about to spit when he gets back is something he knew could only work on someone who didn't have the start of a hint to the beginnings of a goddamn clue!

> *Re-enter TRUANT OFFICER 2.*

TRUANT OFFICER 2: Ready with that name? Yours? Mom's?

KATRINA AGE 15: (*Silence*)

TRUANT OFFICER 2: All right, That's cool. Here's how it's gonna go. It's two thirty now, past lunch, so you're gonna have to wait till about five o'clock for something to eat. We'll get you a cheeseburger from McDonald's. Then we're gonna all go home for the evening, and you're gonna spend the night here. By yourself. When we get back in the morning, we're gonna put you in a foster home and leave you there for as long as it takes to find out who you are.

KATRINA AGE 15: My mommy works for Penn Mutual!

TRUANT OFFICER 2: Good start. That's a start.

KATRINA CURRENT DAY: (*To Audience*) I became expert at spotting T.O.'s after my bust and was able to cut in peace for a good while after that. Inevitably though, The City of Philadelphia decided it'd had just about enough of my shit.

ACT ONE, SCENE EIGHT

> *Family courtroom at the Philadelphia Courthouse. Enter JUDGE.*

JUDGE: Good afternoon, Grace.

LAWYER: Afternoon, Judge.

JUDGE: Your boy's going overseas? That right?

LAWYER: That's right. Yes.

JUDGE: Congratulations to both of you. Wish him good luck from me.

LAWYER: Will do. He'll appreciate that.

KATRINA CURRENT DAY: (*To Audience*) He seems okay. I mean, he's talking to other white folks and, you know, y'all are always all nice to each other and shit. Definitely rather be at The Goldman though. And oh listen, mother's making sure to keep the focus on what really matters.

MOTHER: (*To LAWYER*) It's not my fault!

KATRINA AGE 15: (*To LAWYER, who doesn't hear*) Yes it is.

LAWYER: (*To MOTHER*) I know.

KATRINA AGE 15 (*To LAWYER, who doesn't hear*) No you don't. (*LAWYER turns attention to KATRINA AGE 15. KATRINA AGE 15 To LAWYER.*) Hey, there was a crazy amount of guards when we came in. Is it always like that? Why they need all that for family court?

LAWYER: Never mind.

KATRINA AGE 15: They all had rifles. Why they need sidearms and rifles? That's weird, right? Seems like, overkill kinda.

JUDGE: Are the parents present?

KATRINA AGE 15: (*To LAWYER*) "Parents"? Plural "parents?" Why'd he say it like that?

> *Enter KATRINA'S FATHER dressed in prison uniform, flanked by a GUARD.*

KATRINA AGE 15: (*Unashamed*) Oh. Hi pop.

FATHER: Hey baby.

> *A scrim is place onstage and the GUARD places FATHER behind it. FATHER pantomimes his crimes as they're read aloud. LAWYER hands KATRINA CURRENT DAY a portfolio.*

KATRINA CURRENT DAY (*To Audience*) Five Fast Facts about my Father: From the case law file of the Commonwealth Court of Pennsylvania, and a report from the *Philadelphia Inquirer*. (*She reads from portfolio.*) After having served three of a possible twenty-one-year sentence for burglary, larceny, and receiving stolen property, Donald Hall was released on probation on January 19, 1981. Two months later, on March 10, 1981, Hall pistol whipped and robbed furniture store salesman, Harry Feldman, in the 1500 block of West Diamond Street.

GUARD: (*To Audience*) Two months after that, on May 20, 1981, Donald Hall was apprehended and formally charged with the murders of criminal associates Richard Mayberry and George Ellerbee.

LAWYER: (*To Audience*) Mr. Hall had been arrested and charged with the shootings after having already been formally arrested and charged with holding up the Central Penn National Bank, at Seventh and Chestnut Streets, some days earlier.

KATRINA CURRENT DAY: (*To Audience*) In addition to receiving forty-plus years for the assault on Feldman and the bank robbery, Dad was also sentenced to a death penalty for each of his first-degree murder convictions for Mayberry and Ellerbee.

> *Scrim is removed, and GUARD escorts FATHER back where they started.*

JUDGE (*To Audience*) Mr. Hall made legal history by becoming the first inmate in Pennsylvania to have his double death sentence commuted to life in prison as the result of being re-sentenced.

KATRINA CURRENT DAY (*To Audience*) My father was incomprehensibly dangerous. He only got permission to be here because the state agreed to pay for the extra security. And yet…

JUDGE: Is there anything the parents would like to say?

MOTHER: No.

JUDGE: Mr. Hall?

FATHER: Whatever's gonna make it all right for her. Just so she's okay.

JUDGE: I have all your scores here. There's nothing indicating you can't succeed in school. Katrina, if I let you go right now, will you go to class?

KATRINA AGE 15: (*Beat*) No.

MOTHER: Dumbass!

KATRINA AGE 15: I will never be smarter than I am this second you outpatient!

JUDGE: (*Long-suffering*) Grace, please calm your client.

MOTHER: You're a dumbass you fat ox! All you had to do was say yeah! Now they gonna put you in some home! What'ya gonna do now fatass?! Fuckin' ox!

JUDGE: You've got one last time to test me Mrs. Hall.

KATRINA AGE 15: Shit, wait. What? Shit. Shit!

JUDGE: (*To LAWYER*) There's an opening at Carson Valley?

LAWYER: There will be next week. She'll have the summer to acclimate before starting classes in the fall.

KATRINA AGE 15: Oh my God, what? What?

JUDGE: All right Miss Hall, that's the end of our business. Good luck to you.

KATRINA AGE 15: Judgeithinkimadeamistake...

JUDGE: Mr. Hall? I'm sure your daughter's grateful you're here to support her, but after today you're never to come into my courtroom again. You're too much trouble. Adjourned!

> *LAWYER leads KATRINA AGE 15 toward one exit as GUARD escorts FATHER toward another.*

KATRINA AGE 15: Dad?!

> *FATHER starts to speak but is forced out of exit before he's able. KATRINA AGE 15 exits simultaneously. LAWYER returns and comforts MOTHER as lights fade.*
> **End of Act One**
> *Intermission*

ACT TWO, SCENE ONE

> *The scene opens in silence and in the dark. While the lights are still down, a litany of voices begin speaking various racist, bigoted words and phrases. As the lights come up, we see KATRINA CURRENT DAY laying on her back on the floor as the words wash over her. As they finally fade to nothing, she rises to her feet, and begins to speak.*

KATRINA CURRENT DAY (*To Audience*) I'd been sentenced to the suburbs.

> *Begin projecting still images of Carson Valley School.*

Carson Valley School was—is, just outside of Chestnut Hill, but really, it was another country. It was a residential program where kids like me could attempt to get our high school degrees in between tennis matches and excursions to Plymouth Meeting Mall. You were tracked for either a GED or, in my case, a diploma from Springfield High School.

> *Enter STUDENT 3 who walks right into KATRINA AGE 18 as if she doesn't exist.*

KATRINA CURRENT DAY: Watch it!

> *STUDENT 3 looks through her and keeps walking.*

KATRINA CURRENT DAY: Springfield was the first time I'd been plunked down into a never ending wave after wave of white faces for hours on end. It was also where my lexicon of bigoted, racist slurs expanded exponentially.

> *Enter STUDENT 3 and STUDENT 4. Their exchange is perfectly amiable and has the cadence of everyday speech.*

STUDENT 4: Nigger fuck-cunt, wop wog spook.

STUDENT 3: Chinky Chinaman hymie heeb. Right? Coon kike silver back.

STUDENT 4: Towel-headed moon cricket. Porch monkey dago beaner.

STUDENT 3: Camel jockey. Tar baby spics, zipperhead Sambo.

STUDENT 4: You coming to practice?

STUDENT 3: Yup. Later man!

> *Exit STUDENT 3 and STUDENT 4. Enter STUDENT 5.*

KATRINA AGE 18 (*To STUDENT 5*) Did you hear them? You believe that shit?

STUDENT 5: Yeah, that's fucked up for you. But check it out, right, my family's lived here all my life, so my blackness is mostly ignored. If I hang around you Carson blacks, they'll treat me like you Carson blacks. Seriously, don't talk to me.

> *Exit STUDENT 5. Enter STUDENT 6.*

STUDENT 6 (*To KATRINA AGE 18.*) I want to seem nice for self-serving reasons, so I'm going to ask if you're okay.

KATRINA AGE 18: What if I'm not?

STUDENT 6: Doesn't matter since I'm not actually being nice to you.

KATRINA AGE 18: No?

STUDENT 6: No. I'm being nice for me, on the strength of my muddled, aggressively opaque understanding of karma!

KATRINA AGE 18: You all suck entire ass and this place is starting to harden me!

STUDENT 6: Let's talk again the next time I decide it'll benefit me!

> *Exit STUDENT 6*

KATRINA CURRENT DAY: (*To Audience.*) The only thing Springfield motivated me to do was spend all my time cutting in the cafeteria, so I ended up getting my GED and, miraculously, into college.

> *The sound of a stadium sized crowd chanting is heard: "Here we go Lions! Here we go! Here we go Lions! Here we go!"*

KATRINA CURRENT DAY (*cont., yelling over the cheer*) Carson must have pulled some strings! Somehow, in spite of scoring in the thirteenth percentile in math, I got into Penn State! University Park! During my first go 'round as a freshman!

> *Chanting stops. STUDENT 7 enters and hands KATRINA CURRENT DAY a family size bag of chips.*

KATRINA CURRENT DAY: (*Intermittently stuffing face*) Oh my God, how?! You know what? It doesn't matter, because all I did was skip class, avoid football games, and eat myself into a thirty pound weight gain.

> *Enter STUDENT 8 who unintentionally makes eye contact with KATRINA AGE 18.*

STUDENT 8: Hello, far-too-unambiguously-black-to-cause-me-anything-except-free-floating discomfort female. I'd've blown right by you, but since we've made eye contact, I feel that weird impulse that sometimes overwhelms us to show that I'm one of the "good" ones. I will now proceed to be overly chatty while speaking in tones all slopping over with artificial sweetener, which I assume, based on your density of melanin per square inch, you aren't nuanced enough to find infantilizing.

KATRINA CURRENT DAY: Hi suck ass who I'd've had much more respect for if you'd've just blown right by me. But no, instead you opted to burden me with your neurosis, social anxiety, and knee jerk tendency to other anyone who doesn't look like you. It's multiple encounters like this that cement my belief college ain't for me; at least, not now. I'm thinking I need another quarter century or thereabouts before I make another attempt. Yeah, twenty-five years sound right somehow. I will not miss you.

STUDENT 8: Oh same! Same!

> In the following dual dialogue, "Take care!" and "it'll be as if we've never met" must sync up.

KATRINA AGE 18: This is where I tell you "Take care!," mainly because it's what people say in polite society when they want there to be no mistake that an encounter, especially one as pointlessly shallow as this, has concluded, and after, blessedly, it'll be as if we've never met.

STUDENT 8: I'll depart by saying "Take care!," but we both know it's just one of those ritual phrases that helps grease the wheels of escape, completely devoid of any authentic concern for your well-being, and as soon as you're out of my field of vision, it'll be as if we've never met.

> Exit STUDENT 8. Enter MOTHER who snatches chips from KATRINA AGE 18.

KATRINA CURRENT DAY: After Penn State invited me to leave, there was no job and no Carson to fall back on. I'd had that one summer job shelving books at Penn State's main library, but what the hell was I gonna do with that? The only option was to live with my MOTHER.

MOTHER: You best be tryin' to find yourself a job.

KATRINA AGE 20: I know.

MOTHER: Ain't nobody trying to support some grown ass woman.

KATRINA AGE 20: Yeah. Yeah, I know.

> Exit MOTHER.

KATRINA CURRENT DAY: (To Audience) I'd make daily pilgrimages to Center City, job hunting.

> Enter SUPERVISOR.

SUPERVISOR (To KATRINA AGE 20) Thank you for applying!

They hand KATRINA AGE 20 a folder.

SUPERVISOR: The last step in the applications process is this test in basic English and math. You have an hour to complete it. Nice meeting you and looking forward to working with you!

Exit SUPERVISOR.

KATRINA CURRENT DAY: (*To Audience*) Lots of entry level clerk positions in Center City used to require these pathetic tests in order to get in the door. They were laughable except for the math. The math kept them from being funny.

BLACKOUT

ACT TWO, SCENE TWO

KATRINA CURRENT DAY sits in the living room, watching and listening intently to commercials for computer training and truck driving schools. Enter MOTHER who doesn't hear any of KATRINA CURRENT DAY's response during this scene.

MOTHER: You find anything yet?

KATRINA CURRENT DAY: Your loathing has nothing to do with my past truancy or current unemployment.

MOTHER: Shit, you even lookin'?

KATRINA CURRENT DAY: It has to do with neither of us being enough to keep dad in line.

MOTHER: Lord, I don't know how you're gonna get hired.

KATRINA CURRENT DAY: Not pretty enough by half and too fat by far to be the child of someone with a malignant attachment to surfaces.

MOTHER: Too fat to fit into a decent outfit.

KATRINA CURRENT DAY: I aged you. You'll go to your grave resenting me for being the reason people can guess how old you are. You were always so proud of not looking your age.

MOTHER: Nobody asked for you, you know.

KATRINA AGE 20: This is where I tell you, take care…

MOTHER: Just suckin' up food and heat!

KATRINA AGE 20: … because it's what people say to grease the wheels of escape…

MOTHER: He the one wanted to keep you.

KATRINA AGE 20: … from a connection as pointlessly shallow as this…

MOTHER: Turned out to be not worth a damn.

KATRINA AGE 20: … and after you leave my field of vision…

MOTHER: Just like him.

KATRINA AGE 20: … it'll be as if we've never met.

> *BLACKOUT.*

ACT TWO, SCENE THREE

> *LIGHTS UP ON: KATRINA CURRENT DAY LEANING ON A LIBRARY CART.*

KATRINA CURRENT DAY: (*To Audience*) I was able to move not long after, because I found a job. No math required! (*Begin projecting stills of various library stacks*) That one summer job I had at Penn State's library turned out to be my life line. Unlike now, if you wanted an entry level library gig back then, you'd be competing against maybe twelve other people at most, and ten of them would be deejays! (*She takes her cart and begins traveling the stage as she mimes shelving books*) I went from one academic library to the next, working my way up until I settled at the Law Library at Rutgers Camden. Good benefits like free classes.

Not that that mattered, because but how was I gonna pass college math? So for fifteen years, that's what I did. Not take classes.

> *Beat*

Then I started taking classes.

> *Beat*

I know there should be some sort of revelatory transition there, but that ain't what happened. It just turned on a dime one day.

> *She begins using the cart as a desk and mimes stamping books.*

My intention was to major in Art History, earn a library degree, then parlay that into a premeditated, first degree murder.

> *Beat*

I wouldn't have a choice! The only way I'd land my dream job as Head Archivist at the Philadelphia Museum of Art would be by sawing the current archivist's head clean off. See? I didn't need a revelation. I had a plan! I'd deal with the math when I'd have to deal with the math.

> *Transition directly into:*

ACT TWO, SCENE FOUR

KATRINA CURRENT DAY (*To Audience, cont*) Immediately Art History turned out to be a bust, culminating in one online professor challenging me to a fist fight. *Long story.* No time for that now!

(*Whirling around the room*) I don't have a major; I'm registering late, and the only available gen-ed classes that fit my schedule are Play Reading Analysis and Acting I.

Christ, seriously?

KATRINA AGE 46 stops dead at the entrance to Acting I being blocked by ACTING PROF

ACTING PROF: We're full up!

KATRINA AGE 46: Can I do stuff anyway?

ACTING PROF: Okay. Welcome home!

KATRINA CURRENT DAY: (*To Audience*) So I majored in theatre, which started out as a means to an end, but morphed into an end in itself. I committed to the new path I'd carved, and grew surer that it'd been right to do so, and I put off the math as long as I could. Right up to the day I couldn't.

Transition directly to:

ACT TWO, SCENE FIVE

KATRINA AGE 49, STUDENT 9, STUDENT 10, and TEACHER 4 in math class.

KATRINA 49: (*To Audience*) I don't have to be stellar. I just have to pass.

TEACHER 4: Questions about last night's homework before moving on?

Everyone raises their hand.

TEACHER 4: (To STUDENT 9) Yes?

STUDENT 9: Can you go over the last two problems?

TEACHER 4: Sure. In the first one, you have three radical two, plus five radical seven, plus eight radical two, plus three radical seven. These are like terms; so since the radical two is the same, you can add the three and eight. Three and eight is eleven, so it's eleven root two. These two are also like terms. You can add the five and the three to give you an eight, so it's eight and seven. In the next one, five x plus four x? Those are considered like terms. Whenever you have like terms, you're allowed to add the coefficients. Five plus four is nine, so five x plus four x is unkindness of one. Now, say you have another Elvis coffee?

STUDENT 10: Divide trunk secret girl by all the ghosts?

TEACHER 4: You can't plus maybe air can't I litigation.

KATRINA AGE 49: What?!

STUDENT 10: Okay!

TEACHER 4: Moving on. Add truth in exit back to knot, no jumpty. Posture changes and five folded flowers. Preen playing that won't hurry, we've plenty of a bouquet, and over the kitchen is not to seduce the sink. Playing the enters brilliant attending brillish.

STUDENT 9: He bellish against the would like to smile, freen up.

STUDENT 10: And apartmenters brush themselvet curtainst risent?

TEACHER: 4 Yes!

KATRINA AGE 49: No!

TEACHER 4: Doesn't forted verts . Did, bee hers afters. How splendor esser sufferwas of afted vet of make the sice. Seendid, devotherty? Noblender two to my two my blend. Quite sight it ally bellie, reakfaster. Well? About are dreakfastench, which mothen couple of could conderlying up. Slight reakfaster and breally, wither and lancerniff. Holded in, we've them is Themsens rish.

KATRINA AGE 49: Hey! Hey! This is worse than before! Listen, please! Listen, okay, I thought—I thought math was just … I thought it was just … I thought it wouldn't be like before, but it's worse. I don't understand you! I don't! Goddamnit…

> *KATRINA AGE 49 flees from class and into COUNSELOR'S office.*

KATRINA AGE 49: Can I arrange math classes online at another university?

COUNSELOR: You'd need permission from the Dean and the head of the math department.

KATRINA AGE 49: How do I get that?

COUNSELOR: Just put it in writing.

KATRINA AGE 49: I put it in writing, then get permission. Got it!

> *KATRINA AGE 49 rushes to exit*

COUNSELOR: Oh no. No, that's never happening.

KATRINA AGE 49: (*Whipping back around*) I am not going to let you make me crazy!

COUNSELOR: You won't get permission because you're asking for the same reason everyone who request that asks. So you can pay someone to take the classes for you.

KATRINA AGE 49: How very dare you! I just would … Never! (*Beat. Then contrite*) Thank you for your time.

> *She turns to leave.*

COUNSELOR Have you been to The Learning Center?

KATRINA AGE 49: What? No.

COUNSELOR: If you're having trouble, make an appointment. Ask for Tim.

> *Exit COUNSELOR. Enter TIM.*

TIM: Katrina? Tim. What can I do…

KATRINA AGE 49: I need you to listen to exactly what I'm saying. I mean word for word what I'm about to say. No euphemisms are about to come out of my face, okay? I mean, exactly, exactly, what I'm about to say. I need you to listen, okay? I don't understand math. I'm not saying it's hard. I'm saying it's impossible. Whenever anyone tries to explain it, I literally, I mean I literally can't recognize what they're saying as English. I know what plus, and minus, and multiply mean, but I don't understand them. They just—it's impossible, and I haven't said anything else but exactly that for decades, and nobody'll fucking—Okay, I am sorry, but I can't say it any plainer than I've been saying it the whole time. I cannot pass the math requirement. Man, shit—Okay, I'm sorry. I'm sorry. Okay. I've wasted a shit-ton of time.

TIM: (*Even*) Can you read an analogue clock?

KATRINA AGE 49: (*Exasperated*) What are you—Yes. Yeah.

TIM: Can you figure out the tip at a restaurant?

KATRINA AGE 49: If I round up to tens, yes. (*Beat*) I'm sorry, but is this pertinent? I'm going to be late for work. (*Rises to leave*) I'll reschedule...

TIM: Can you read a map?

> She stops dead, then sits down.

KATRINA AGE 49: Not at all. Not ever.

TIM: What about graphs? Any issues with those?

KATRINA AGE 49: I can't read them. I've never told anyone, but no. I can't understand them.

TIM: Mm-hmm. Any other problems? Trouble with comprehension?

KATRINA AGE 49: No. Well, no. Never mind. No.

TIM: What is it?

KATRINA AGE 49: It's not comprehension. I can't—I have to learn everything in fifteen minutes. (*Beat*) I mean, I can't do anything, read, for longer than fifteen minutes.

TIM: What do you mean, "anything?"

KATRINA AGE 49: I mean, as far as school goes, I can barely finish the reading, and I haven't ever finished a paper.

TIM: You can't focus on anything for longer than fifteen minutes at a time.

KATRINA AGE 49: That's it. If I can't learn something in fifteen minutes, I never will.

TIM: Mmph.

KATRINA AGE 49: Yeah?

TIM: From the sound of it—I need you to make an appointment with Student Health. Make an appointment for testing.

KATRINA AGE 49: For what? I mean for what specifically?

TIM: For one, ADHD.

KATRINA AGE 49: Oh please!

TIM: Says the woman who can only concentrate in fifteen-minute intervals.

KATRINA AGE 49: That doesn't—Does that mean—Hold it, that always meant...

TIM: Very likely yes.

KATRINA AGE 49: Huh. What else?

TIM: No need to speculate at this point. Tell the people at Student Health I sent you. They'll know what to look for. If you need any help with classes in the meantime, make an appointment here. Just let us know.

KATRINA AGE 49: (*Beat*) I said a thing and you heard me.

TIM: Of course. Keep me posted, all right?

KATRINA AGE 49: Yes. Thank you.

> *Direct transition to:*

ACT TWO, SCENE SIX

KATRINA CURRENT DAY: (*To Audience*) The ADHD diagnosis was confirmed immediately, and I was given the first iteration of my medication. It made me low key speedy. And I had this focus! And, oh honey! (*Music begins playing*) First normally, then intermittently out of sync. Too fast at some points, too slowly at others.

> *As KATRINA AGE 49 dances along with the music, she makes sporadic eye contact with a random MARK in the Audience. Her agitation increases with each glance as the music warps in and out of time. She dances unsteadily over to the MARK.*

KATRINA CURRENT DAY: (*To the MARK, with escalating hostility*) Something you need to get off your chest? I mean, you keep looking at me like I took your ice cream, so I thought I should ask. Sitting there minding your business like you own the place!

> (*To Audience*) They keep eyeballing me... (*Pointing at the MARK.*) ... like I shoulda, maybe, more than glanced, at the list of side effects of the shit I'm taking!

> *Recording of a commercial quality voice-over fills the room.*

COMMERCIAL VOICE: This mediation is available by prescription only. Please contact your doctor immediately if you experience any of the following: Headache. Nausea. Joint pain. Rapid breathing. Increased heart rate. Inability to prevent yourself from screaming into a stranger's face.

KATRINA CURRENT DAY: Oh, no...

COMMERCIAL VOICE: Are you really trying to knuckle up in here? Girl seriously, stand down! It's not that serious. Stop acting like you're brand new. You know it ain't that type of party!

KATRINA CURRENT DAY: (*To the MARK*) Oh wow. That is shit embarrassing. I promise, I am so, so, sorry. I can't even—It just made sense at the time. (*Patting pockets*) I wish I had something...

> *STUDENT 2 bursts into the room.*

STUDENT 2: Bell's in five minutes! (*She sprints toward KATRINA CURRENT DAY*). Here!

STUDENT 2 spikes a full-size Snickers onto the floor, then sprints back out the door. KATRINA CURRENT DAY picks up the candy, gives it to the MARK, and thanks them.
Direct transition to:

ACT TWO, SCENE SEVEN

At the doctor's office.

DOCTOR 1: How are you dealing with the new prescription?

KATRINA AGE 49: Fine! Probably. I don't know. I'm still trying to gauge. I don't feel differently except for those time when I don't feel the same.

DOCTOR 2: I see. There's time. We'll see what things are like down the road a bit. In the meantime, let's go over your test results.

DOCTOR 1 and DOCTOR 2 begin reading their clipboards at a normal pace, progressively pacing up until finally culminating at the speed of an Olympic ping pong match.

DOCTOR 1: ADHD?

DOCTOR 2: Addressed.

DOCTOR 1: Reading folder difficulty?

DOCTOR 2: Slight, yes.

DOCTOR 1: Dyslexia?

DOCTOR 2: No.

DOCTOR 1: Nonspecific.

DOCTOR 2: Non-debilitating.

DOCTOR 1: No impediment?

DOCTOR 2: No.

DOCTOR 1: Dysgraphia?

DOCTOR 2: Not indicated.

DOCTOR 1: Analog comprehension?

DOCTOR 2: Yes.

DOCTOR 1: Left from right?

DOCTOR 2: Poor recognition.

DOCTOR 1: Directions?

DOCTOR 2: Difficult.

DOCTOR 1: Yes.

DOCTOR 2: Visualizing?

DOCTOR 1: Which?

DOCTOR 2: Numbers.

DOCTOR 1: Meaningless.

DOCTOR 2: Nonsensical?

DOCTOR 1: Muddled.

DOCTOR 2: Concepts?

DOCTOR 1: Counting?

DOCTOR 2: Grasping.

DOCTOR 1: No.

DOCTOR 2: Inability...

DOCTOR 1: ... impossibility...

DOCTOR 2: ... addition...

DOCTOR 1: ... subtraction...

DOCTOR 2: ... division...

DOCTOR 1: ... formula...

DOCTOR 2: ... value...

DOCTOR 1: ... sequence...

DOCTOR 2: ... arrhythmic...

DOCTOR 1: ... numerical...

DOCTOR 2: ... arithmetic.

DOCTOR 1: Dyscalculia!

DOCTOR 2: Dyscalculia!

KATRINA AGE 49: Discalclea?

DOCTOR 1: Dyscalculia!

DOCTOR 2: Dyscalculia!

KATRINA AGE 49: *(Beat)* Tell me.

DOCTOR 2: Two things. First? We have news. After? We have good news.

DOCTOR 1: First. In your case, the condition appears to be developmental.

KATRINA AGE 49: As in born with it?

DOCTOR 1: Exactly.

DOCTOR 2: It's your parietal lobe.

DOCTOR 1: There's an impairment.

DOCTOR 2: ADHD increases the risk of being affected.

KATRINA AGE 49: The reason I can't understand a map...

DOCTOR 2: ... the inability to understand or retain math, yes. All of it.

DOCTOR 1: That's first. That's the news.

KATRINA AGE 49: You said there was good news.

DOCTOR 2: Yes.

KATRINA AGE 49: And that is?

DOCTOR 1: Now you know!

KATRINA AGE 49: All this time?

DOCTOR 2: Yes.

KATRINA AGE 49: (*To Doctors*) Dyscalculia?

DOCTOR 1: Dyscalculia!

DOCTOR 2: Dyscalculia!

KATRINA CURRENT DAY: (*To Audience*) Dyscalculia.

> *Direct transition to:*

ACT TWO, SCENE EIGHT

KATRINA CURRENT DAY: (*To Audience*) It's all still in progress. I can focus my thoughts often enough, for long enough, that I'm able to do something like write a play.

I mean, I wrote a play!

But I'm still learning how to be more gentle with myself when the dyscalculia simply won't allow some concepts to yield. I'm allowed to take math substitution courses to meet my requirement, and as suspected, they're still pretty damned mathy, but doable. That's all that matters. I don't resent any of it that came before. What'd be the point? The path back from your life now won't ever lead to who you never were. This is a good now, so resentment isn't an option.

> *Enter TEACHER 1*

But while I don't resent, I do, on occasion, sometimes, just in passing, wonder what maybe, possibly, could have potentially might have been.

> *KATRINA AGE 10 takes the map from her pocket and exams it, confused and uncomprehending.*

KATRINA AGE 10: (*To Self*) I don't understand. (*To TEACHER 1's back*) I don't understand.

TEACHER 1 (*Turning to KATRINA AGE 10.*) Did you say something?

KATRINA AGE 10: (*Extending map*) I don't understand.

TEACHER 1: No? Well…

> *TEACHER 1 retrieves two chairs and sets them facing each other.*

TEACHER 1: … let's see if we can try and figure it out.

> *Lights fade as they sit facing each other, head to head, and begin trying to make sense of it all.*

> *End of play.*

PART THREE

Alone, Together

The Brechtones

Billy Butler

In his 2016 article for *Jstor Daily*, "Stage Death: From Offstage to in Your Face," Michael Lueger argues that any staged death is "a means to force us to confront ugly truths about our society that we might choose to avoid [.]"[1] However, unlike an actor in television or film, a stage actor performing a stage death has to experience that death at the same time that an audience does. Further, as the late theatre director Herbert Blau points out, watching theatre is confronting the fact that, "he who is performing can die there in front of your eyes; is in fact doing so. Of all the performing arts, theatre stinks most of mortality."[2] A film or television actor does not have to relive his performance every time an audience watches it, but a theatre actor does. Even if he does not die in a particular play, he will be a little closer to death when he finishes the play than he was when he started, simply because he is living real hours in his real life. Sometimes, dying in front of an audience becomes, not just a possibility evoked by an enacted stage death, but an actuality. The seventeenth century French playwright, Moliére, collapsed onstage during a performance of his 1673 play, *The Imaginary Invalid*, and he died hours later.[3]

In most cases though, stage deaths are scripted, and a curtain call is a reassuring reminder to an audience that it is a character, not an actor, who has died. In some scripts, the actor is more comparable to a poet-speaker or a songwriter-speaker, someone for whom the demarcation between author and narrator has collapsed. For example, we do not know for certain whether or not the first person narrator of Robert Frost's poems is Frost himself, but his narrators are given no distinguishing features of their own. The stage death of a performer-narrator, a persona whose identity is conflated with that of a performer, does not carry the same reassurance for an audience. The persona is not the performer, but he/she/they could be. The conflation of the performer-narrator's identity with the performer's becomes more complicated if he/she/they is performing a death that is self-inflicted. Is such an onstage death merely an emotional moment in a script, or is it akin to a confession in a psychologist's office?

Of course, in order to accurately answer that question, it is necessary to analyze what a particular death means in a particular play. To be fair, literary analysis is subjective. However, the dramatic structure of a play can provide guidance regarding how its dramatic arc should be analyzed. For example: Robert Gordon claims in his 2017 article, "Brecht, Interruptions, and Epic Theatre," that twentieth century German writer, director, dramaturg, and theatre theorist Bertolt Brecht's plays for his Epic Theatre were "self-consciously retelling a story, rather than realistically embodying the events of a narrative."[4] Brecht wanted his audience to focus on his play's narratives, not the emotions the events of the plot aroused in his characters or in the audience members themselves. According to Gordon, Brecht's plays, "[supplement] the core drama of human relationships with information [...in order to] make the dramatic structure itself an instrument for analyzing social reality and promoting change."[5] In a play adhering to Brecht's rules for dramatic structure, then, an individual character's death should be analyzed for its personal, sociopolitical, and sociocultural significance. In a Brechtian play, a self-inflicted death could be analyzed as an individual's plea for help, but it could also be used as a site of inquiry to critique any sociopolitical or sociocultural institutions that might have failed that individual. To be fair, many analytical lenses may be applied to any dramatic structure. The sociocultural significance of an individual death may be important in a psychological realist play, and a death in a Brechtian play may have an important emotional significance in the plot—think of the deaths of Willy Loman in Arthur Miller's 1949 play, *Death of a Salesman*, and Katrina's death in Bertolt Brecht's 1939 play, *Mother Courage and her Children*.

In *The Brechtones*, Billy Bitter, the onstage persona of playwright, performer, and musician Billy Butler, is dependent on pills and alcohol. However, different substances serve different functions in the play. When he drinks, he conforms to the stereotype of a tormented musician. His history of alcoholism also functions as a narrative device. Because he has blacked out frequently, he learns a secret from his past at the same time that the audience does. Unlike the alcohol Bitter uses to self-medicate for his depression, the pills he takes throughout the show are prescription medication. The pills are a symbol of his impending death, the only "cure" for his isolation that he can imagine. Of course, prescription medication can sometimes mitigate a person's depression by changing that person's relationship to his/her/their psychological and emotional experiences, but no medication will bring the kind of cure that Bitter seeks. Sometimes, medication can provide increased stability. Death brings not stability, but stasis. Only addressing the symbolic significance of medication within the narrative would be doing this play a disservice. This is a Brechtian play, so we should also address how Bitter's relationship to medication reveals how medication is marketed to consumers in the real world and how that marketing is potentially harmful to them. The manner of Bitter's death may be unique to him, but his viewing medication as a panacea is not. In fact, drug companies tacitly urge consumers to view medication that way.

According to Joanne Kauffman's 2017 article in *The New York Times*, "Think You're Seeing More Drug Ads on TV? You Are, and Here's Why,"[6] 771,368 ads for prescription medication ran on American television in 2016, the last year for which data was available. In ads for prescription medications, people with various physical, emotional, and psychological conditions have physical, emotional, and psychological experiences associated with those conditions—experiences the voice-over actor calls symptoms—that impede their ability to enjoy their personal lives. A medication that treats those symptoms, a medication with side effects that scroll down the screen too quickly for viewers to read, restores their quality of life.

Billy Butler in Brechtian make-up, taken through textured glass (© David Mendelsohn).

Though the ads representing prescription medication as a panacea are unquestionably hyperbolic, medication can provide a valuable link between the medical model of disability and the social model of disability. According to the medical model of disability, the disabled body should be corrected through medical intervention to allow an individual to successfully participate in community life. The body is an aberration that needs to be fixed. The social model of disability arose in the twentieth century as a critique of the medical model. According to the social model, it is a society's attitudinal, physical, and social barriers that prevent an individual with a disability from successfully participating in community life. Bitter's experience with prescription medication shows that the benefits of medication can be costly. Since it is marketed as a panacea, someone for whom it is not immediately physically, emotionally, or psychologically effective may experience more intense feelings of loneliness than he/she/they experienced before using the medication. Since dependency on medication can carry a considerable stigma, Bitter's experience is a complication of the social model. Ideally, Bitter's medication would help him more fully participate in his society, but his dependency on that medication makes him increasingly socially isolated.

In any play wherein an overdose's primary significance is how starkly it reveals the social reality that made death possible or desirable for a particular character, the audience is directly or tacitly being asked to imagine how the social reality of the play is similar to the social reality of the real world. If the social reality of the play is similar to the social reality of the real world, then an audience must decide which, if any, social changes could prevent a death in the real world. Watching the death of a performer-narrator reminds an audience that, although a fictional character's fate may be predetermined, no one else's is.

—Jill Summerville

Notes

1. Michael Lueger, "Stage Death: From Offstage to in Your Face," *Jstor Daily*, September 21, 2016.

2. Herbert Blau, *Take Up The Bodies: Theatre at the Vanishing Point* (Chicago: University of Illinois Press, 1982), 83.

3. Will G. Moore and Ronald W. Tobin, *Encyclopedia Britannica*, 16th ed., s.v. "Moliére: French Dramatist." Chicago: Encyclopedia Britannica, 2017, https://www.britannica.com/biography/Moliere-French-dramatist/Scandals-and-successes

4. Robert Gordon, "Discovering Literature: Brecht, Interruptions, and Epic Theatre," London: The British Library, September 7, 2017.

5. *Ibid.*

6. Joanne Kauffman. "Think You're Seeing More Drug Ads on TV? You Are, and Here's Why," *The New York Times*, December 24, 2017.

The Brechtones

TIME: Present
PLACE: A dive bar, anywhere, USA.

Note: *the show is performed on an actual bar stage, with the actor playing "Death" truly serving as a bartender throughout. The crowd is welcome to come and go just as they would at any bar show.*

CHARACTERS:

The Brechtones: An aging house band consisting of drums, guitar, bass, and maybe a horn or two. They change depending on who is available or better yet, willing.

Billy Bitter: a middle-age troubadour on his last leg, figuratively and literally. He kicked heroin years ago but has taken the edge off with whiskey. The pills are from a prescription because of a physical injury, or so he says. Tom Waits meets Joe Strummer.

Penny Diver: Early twenties. She is a cross between Amy Winehouse and Billie Holiday. Punk style with a turn of the twentieth century aesthetic. She is inspired by Jenny Diver/Pirate Jenny from *Three Penny Opera*.

Death: A Bartender. Typical death. Tends the bar.

Guest Poets: These truly are "Guest Artists," and change nightly.

The Brechtones premiered in 2018 at the Players' Ring, Portsmouth, New Hampshire.

The Brechtones © 2018 Billy Butler, all rights reserved

* * *

As the audience arrives: a sign, written in chalk, has any drink/dinner specials, as well as, "Beat-Nite with The Brechtones!"

The setting is an old towny bar, cheap hotel meets tenement apartment. Dirty, sticky, a thick haze of who knows what. There is a stage with an Afghan rug and microphone center. This is the poet "mic." There is some sort of lounge chair to one side for guest poets and squeezed in there somewhere is the band. The stage is surrounded by cocktail tables with a bar on one side. The bartender greats people as they are seated and serves drinks.

The band, "The Brechtones" wander on to the stage. They sip their drinks as they get settled. They are older musicians—worn but not weak and good at what they do. They look as if they were caught in the crossed streams of 1920 and 2020. They play an instrumental version of "It's a Crying Shame."

When they finish the song one of them leans into a mic.

A BRECHTONE: Guys and gals, Billy Bitter.

> *He counts them into the next number. BILLY BITTER enters with a violin case under his arm and sets it on top of the piano. He is 40s-50s with a bit of slouch. He wears a bowler or something of the sort. He sits and plays. Music begins for "LOSS"*

BILLY: YEAH, THEY SAY I'M A BARROOM FLUNKY
PILL POPPIN' TEETH ROTTEN DRUNKEN JUNKY
MAKE NO EXCUSES FOR ALL MY ABUSES
I CHOOSES AND LOSES ALL ON MY OWN
WANDERED AND SQUANDERED AND LIVED ON THE STREET
SHARED MY WARES WITH ANY HEPCAT I'D MEET
MADE SOME NOISE AND A LITTLE BIT OF FOLD
AND I'LL KEEP ON KEEPIN' ON TIL IT GETS OLD
LOSS, HOSS, THIS IS A STORY 'BOUT LOSS
LOSS, HOSS, THIS IS A STORY 'BOUT LOSS

> *Band solos.*

I LIVE ON THE ROAD, BOOZE, AND BAR FOOD
SLEEP IN MY CAR WHEN I CAN'T FIND A ROOF
ANSWER TO NO ONE AND OWE NO ONE NOTHIN'
NO BAR TAB, NO SCAR, SCAB GETS UNDER MY SKIN
THEY SAY I AM JUST CHEATING DEATH
DOWN TO COUNTING EACH AND EVERY BREATH
WHEN I'M DONE AND SHE'S READY TO COME
WON'T FIND SURPRISE OR DISAPPOINTMENT IN MY EYES
LOSS, HOSS, THIS IS A STORY 'BOUT
LOSS, HOSS, THIS IS A STORY 'BOUT LOSS

> *On the applause he drinks.*

Give it up for the Brechtones.

> *As the audience applauds, he takes a haul from his vaporizer and then turns to a member of the audience*

Vape? No? You know we can talk, right? This isn't a play.

> *Takes another big haul*

They banned smoking a while back. I've been sucking on this machine since. I feel like fucking Darth Douchebag, but what am I going to do? I like my chemicals. They say this is better for me. The other "they" say it is just as bad if not worse. Fuck it.

(*To the Brechtones*) Guys, this one is a vape-y barroom feel.

> *Taking another long haul, Billy starts speaking in rhythm, like a beat poet, a rapper, hipster patter-song. The band jams as he speaks.*

I played this club in Chicago once in the early aughts.

You know, just another faux rock joint shit-hole.

There was a sudden waft of years of spilled drinks and hastily mopped up vomit as I broke the threshold.

"No smoking!" the bartender cried from the dark.

I drop my dog-end in a half-filled Natty Light.

I remember when the smell of stale cigarettes was a warm welcome. Sure, we were all in a blue haze of second-hand cancer on the fast track to an iron lung, But at least we had couth. And sometimes we'd open a window or a door.

I get making laws against poisoning ourselves, but it seems disproportionate. Beer, booze, fatty fast foods, greasy spoons.

Oh, but smoking is bad for you,

Yeah, smoking is bad for you. I had to take so many breaks I couldn't get through a set.

All I could think about was my next cigarette.

My eye was on the clock more often than not,

Waiting for the next break so I can shake away the shake of my body informing me of another shot of carcinogen.

Addiction is a powerfully cruel landlord. Turning on the heat so high that you could put your head in the oven for relief.

Or making it so cold you swallow cubes off ice to warm up.

And now I vape, bra, I vape now, bra.

DEATH: Oh, you vape, bra? I'm muthafuckin ethereal!

BILLY: They made a machine that delivers all the chemicals I need through steam. Isn't that amazing? They'll really impress me When they figure out how to vape whiskey.

Until then I got my hunger suppression, to wall off depression, keep me thin raise my heart rate and keep me sedated. That's important for a musical vagrant like me. Because this vape ape no longer needs a break I can now play for days. Just keep bringing me bourbon and pretzels.

Because I can vape, bra. And I still tell the young

Do as I say, not as I do. Smoking is bad for you,

Booze is bad for you,

Drugs are bad for you, Vaping is bad for you.

Shit, I'm am too. Thank, you.

> *The band ends the jam. He crosses to the piano for his drink.*

They say count your blessings, right? Like some god gave you extra attention, like you're special or some shit.

"I'm so blessed!" "I got that promotion, I passed that class, I'm a fucking gluten-free vegan douche-loofa! Hashtag—'So blessed!'" Please, go on and tell me how god has picked you. Tell me all the fucking things you got because you are a god's favorite child. Look, I understand, nice things happen. But to think that there is some almighty power giving you special treatment while some teenage junkie OD's on bath salts is delusional and dangerous.

> *He sits at the piano.*

No. There is no god. At least not the thousands-year-old cave-dwelling scribed kind. Who am I to say. All I know is God would not give two shits about you or your hashtags. So, no, you're not blessed, you're fucked in the head with deep-seeded daddy issues.

> *He begins playing "I Got That Going for Me."*

Being thankful is something completely different. It's humble, reflective, and trust me, I know all about being humble. I humiliate myself every chance I get. I am grateful, though.

> *Sings*

I CAN PLAY PIANO AND THE GUITAR
DRIVE A BOX-TRUCK AND A STICK-SHIFT CAR
I GOT THAT GOING FOR ME
I CAN SING AND DANCE, ACT LIKE A FOOL
BUILD YOU A SCENE WITH A POWER TOOL
I GOT THAT GOING FOR ME
TAKE YOU HIGHER THAN YOU'LL EVER KNOW
AND BRING YOU DOWN WITH ME IF YOU DON'T LET GO
GONNA HOLD ON TO WHAT I GOT
TILL I'M GONE
TILL I'M GONE
I'M GONE
LOYAL TO A FAULT UNTIL YOU'RE NOT
TEAR YOU TO RIBBONS WHEN YOU GET CAUGHT
I GOT THAT GOING FOR ME
I'M AN EMPATH, STONER, DROPOUT, AND MANIC BOUTS
OF JOY, GRIEF, AND CRIPPLING PANIC
I GOT THAT GOING FOR ME
THINGS AREN'T SO BAD, I GOT TODAY
A ROOF, A MEAL, AND MUSIC TO PLAY
I GOT THAT GOING FOR ME
I GOT THAT GOING FOR ME
GONNA HOLD ON TO WHAT I GOT
TILL I'M GONE
TILL I'M GONE
I'M GONE
I CAN SORT OF MAKE A COUPLET RHYME
WATCH WHAT YOU SAY I MIGHT MENTION YOU SOMETIME

> *On the applause he gets a tumbler of whiskey from the bartender*

Any celebrities here tonight?

> *To audience member*

Hi, there. You somebody famous? What's your name?

> *(Aud: Bob.)*

Where are you from, Bob?

>   (*Aud: Boston.*)

I'm Sorry?

>   (*Aud: Boston.*)

No, I heard you, I'm just sorry.

>   *He crosses to the bar.*

I've had a few celebrities in my audience here and there. Tom Cruise once ate at a joint I played. It was a month after the gig but still, cool, right?

DEATH: Do you know what the most ironic thing Jesus ever said was? "It took being crucified for me to get nailed."

BILLY: Hey, you know why the kids don't like playing hide and seek with Jesus?

>   *They both put their hands over their eyes*

He cheats. "I can still see you!"

So, I was playing this LA thing, can't remember where exactly, but I had just closed out the night with a cover of "Ol' 55" when lo and behold guess who is there at the bar; ol' Mumbles himself. I wanted to shake his hand and tell him how much I admire him. But I just had to get high first. I just had to be stoned to meet Tom. So, I ducked out back, sniffed whatever was in my pocket and headed back to the bar. I guess I took too long, he didn't stick around. Only thing left was his glass. So, I finished off the last of his back-wash.

>   *Takes a swig from his glass*

Tommmm Waits tastes fine.

>   *He crosses to the poet mic.*

This one is called, "A Lobotomized Comparison."
>   (*To the Brechtones*) Something Waits-ian.

>   *The band plays "Tom Waits for None."*
>   *Spoken*

The whiskey is gone and the ice has melted into watered down syrup
   And as the chord changes to a minor I'm reminded of the growler, drunken poet, dramatist, musicist
   Am I a man or am I just the outline of a man?
   Smoking too many cigarettes while pining the lost virtues of generation ×
and blaming a new generation for their lack of vision, work ethic, and taste
   Back in my day we had rocks, and we liked it, damn it
   Get off my lawn with that commercial shit
   Pop rock is a candy you suck on when you need a fake and sudden rush
   You gotta sing like Louis Armstrong fucking Ethel Merman in hell to know
what's really real

>   *Sings*

TOM WAITS FOR NONE

TOM WAITS FOR NO ONE
TOM WAITS FOR NONE
HE DOESN'T CARE
HE'S NOT THERE

Iconoclast, iconograph. The last of the Weillians grinding out my own plays and saying my own lines Marginalized, criticized, vocalized, soberized, romanticized, aggrandized, immortalized. Skidrow Romeo on the forefront of obscurity. I'm the coolest muthafucking balladeer anywhere

Don't care what you want I make my own for myself and my friends

A problem child, an impossible adult, difficult to work with, a bulldozer, a tornado, angry, bitter, hollow, and definitely hard to swallow. Banging on an upright with a dogend perched on chapped lips like a homeless Hoagy Carmichael. On the fringe, the tinge, the fridge, bridge, verse, chorus

TOM WAITS FOR NONE
TOM WAITS FOR NO ONE
TOM WAITS FOR NONE
HE DOESN'T CARE
HE'S NOT THERE

An eccentric Ziegpunk cabaret jazzed up vaudevillian. Born from everything touched, seen, and breathed. Meme-ed and meme-ed and meme-ed

Dad was dark like me in the unlit corner of a bar sucking on regret and envy Striking matches for no other reason than to make a fire. Bang those rocks together folks because a noise can turn into a melody. Doesn't have to be pretty, in fact, most prefer it ugly. We only get one trip, it's up to us to make it worth it. As life moves on so does music, art, theatre.

The rest is silence.

TOM WAITS FOR NONE
TOM WAITS FOR NO ONE
TOM WAITS FOR NONE
HE DOESN'T CARE
TOM WAITS FOR NONE
TOM WAITS FOR NO ONE
TOM WAITS FOR NONE
HE DOESN'T CARE
CAUSE HE AIN'T THERE
NO HE AIN'T THERE

Song ends

And now my hepcat hipsters, it is time for the participation part of our program. Let's bring up some of our guest poets. Please welcome to the stage... (*ad lib*)

> *This is the first of four guest poet spots in the show. Poems should be no more than three or four minutes. Can be any kind, rhyming, spoken word, rap, etc. They should have a musical theme in mind, ie; slow*

summery feel, mad blues, etc. Band jams under them all. First theme is "family." Once the first poet is done:

Thank you, (*ad lib*)

> *First poet exits.*

And now our featured poet. Please welcome, Miss Penny Diver!

> *PENNY DIVER, early 20s heads to the mic. She looks like she just walked off a 1980s punk rock video shoot in 1925. Maybe dreadlocks, a mohawk, blue hair, tattoos. The band jams as she reads from a small notebook.*

PENNY: I met my dad tonight.
He was hiding behind a piano.
I don't imagine he was expecting me,
But here I am pops, flesh and blood, family
DNA, what can I say, you gonna be ok?
I have so much to tell you.
My childhood was hell,
you should know I survived a junkie mom,
junkie mom's boyfriends,
whiskey and pills,
no food, no school,
it's a wonder I'm alive.
And then mama made that final dive.
I didn't tell anyone for days.
'Cause facedown was a familiar sight,
just about every other night.
Her eyes would glaze and she would
fall and sleep wherever she'd lay.
I think I knew anyway. But it was nice and quiet;
still, suspended state.
I enjoyed the silence and the wait,
not a breath, not a sound, almost meditate.
When they finally came for her, nobody saw me.
Maybe I was dead too, you know, a ghost
Or maybe a demon.
This was my fault and I was trapped in a sort of limbo.
I stood in the hallway of a baby boomer tenement still a baby myself and watched as they carried her sheet covered plank down the stairs.
Neighbors shook their heads and rolled their eyes, saying they weren't surprised, because of all the loser guys who went in and out and out in all hours of the day and night.
"She lived alone" I heard them say.
I wanted to tell them who I was but I didn't have the voice to speak, I then sat in that flat on the couch for a week.

Beyond that is a blur.

My teens were the streets, shelters, floors of people I'd meet.

Junkies, cokeheads, meth-heads, trippies, hippies, ravers, cruisers, slavers, bruisers, pimps, chimps, Johns, and cons.

Busked from dusk to dawn. Begging for dollars, quarters, and nickels. I've killed myself for a Benjamin a hundred times.

Crossed the country with these two thumbs,

Hitched a ride on a boxcar with a bindle like a bum.

I then realized I was searching for something.

I knew I needed to find you

The only thing left of mum was a book of poems she wrote

And a note about the loner vagrant musicmaking daddy sperm donor

It read…

    She reads a letter

"One stretch below 14th street

I met a man who wore a heart on his sleeve.

He sang about pang, lust, and disgust,

He was the only man I'd ever trust.

He was my Billy who wrote me a love song.

But of course as always there was something wrong.

I was knocked up and strung out on junk,

He was too high or sleeping or drunk.

So, I left him there passed out in that bed

Figuring he thought I was just dead.

I tried and tried almost as hard as I cried

To kick, cold turkey, get back on the wagon

But nothing can stop you when you're chasing the dragon.

I'm sorry child; you were never planned

If you live long enough I hope you understand

I am damaged and broken beyond all repair

No love for the likes of me, not even you should care"

    She closes the letter

Mama, the junkie nut didn't fall far from the tree.

Now, I'm complete. You, daddy, and me.

    She closes her notebook.

Thank, you.

BILLY: Big hand for our poets. And how about that Miss Penny Diver. Ain't she something.

    The booze is now kicking in. He is really feeling the effects and moves almost in slow motion. He opens his violin case and it is set up like a medicine-meets-liquor cabinet. He pulls out a medicine bottle.

Papa needs his medicine. Before you get all judgy and shit, I have a 'scrip, a doctor's note, and a damn good excuse. I got this back thing, maybe from sitting at this piano for long stretches, but I imagine mostly due to the short way down a set of long stairs during a bender. The junk really does the trick but makes me completely useless. I kicked a few years ago. I don't like to say "I quit," no one likes a quitter. I'm—in between hits. They say that booze numbs the pain, I find it does quite the opposite. That's why I drink, a lot. Trying to stay in the real feels. At the moment I just need to perform.

He opens the Viagra bottle

Oops, the little blue ones, that is whole different kind of performance. I don't really need them anyway. Here we go, these babies pick me right up. Adderall. The middle-class meth.

He pops a few in his mouth and then pulls out a different bottle

These here are for sleeping. Ambien. The shut down for a few hours kind or the long cold sleep version. Depends the dosage, or your mood I suppose.

Yet another bottle

Oxys are for pain. Mostly physical pain.

Another, this one unopened and quite full

Serotonin will make you happy. Notice how full it is.

He pulls out a black bottle.

This is the one that can really end it all. I had three of them at one point but have been slowly carving away at them for a while now. Just a little slice and it makes everything so nice.

Looks at the label

"Euphorica. Take only as directed. Do not drink alcohol or operate heavy machinery …" I fail these tests every time. And I've always wondered why they say "heavy machinery," what about light machinery? And shouldn't it be "any" machinery. Are we not machines?

Living, breathing meat-machines.

We drive and operate these things like we know what we're doing and get especially bold when chemicals are introduced. Should be a big red warning label on us.

The uppers are now taking affect.
Billy begins to play "A Whiskey, An Oxy, and a Couple of Percs"

EVERYBODY'S GOT THEIR STUFF
WHEN LIFE GETS A LITTLE TOO ROUGH
THEN WE LOOK FOR ESCAPE
SO WE SELF-MEDICATE
IT ISN'T PAIN THAT'S ALWAYS THE ILL
SOMETIMES IT'S JUST TOO MUCH TIME TO KILL
MOSTLY IT'S ABOUT FEELING A FEEL

BLURRING THE LINE OF WHAT'S REALLY REAL
AND WHEN THAT SINKING FEELING LURKS
THE ONLY THING THAT REALLY WORKS IS
A WHISKEY, AN OXY, AND A COUPLE OF PERCS
A WHISKEY, AN OXY, AND A COUPLE OF PERCS
IF YOU'VE GOT NATURAL TALENT
YOU JUST MIGHT BE IMBALANCED
OTHERS ARE SIMPLY BAKED AND BURNED-OUT DISEASED, HOOKED,
DIRTY AND STRUNG OUT
GOT ME A CASE OF THE ME'S
IT'S LIKE A MOBIUS STRIP TEASE
WHEN YOU'RE AN ADDICT
SIMPLY ROUTINE BECOMES HABIT
I ALWAYS END UP FEELING WORSE
THERE'S JUST ONE CURE THAT KILLS THAT CURSE
A WHISKEY, AN OXY, AND A COUPLE OF PERCS
A WHISKEY, AN OXY, AND A COUPLE OF PERCS
IF YOU WANNA BE CLEAN
GOTTA BACK TO THE BEGINNING
BUT ALL YOU ARE IS SOBER AND THEN
THE WHOLE THING STARTS ALL OVER AGAIN
NOTHING GOOD EVER LASTS
BIG BRIGHT STARS BURN OUT SO FAST
MAYBE THAT'S WHY I'M STILL ALIVE
I'M JUST GOOD ENOUGH TO GET BY
MY BONES ARE CRACKING, BRAIN IS TOO
JAW'S SO STIFF CAN BARELY SING TO YOU
I DON'T CARE WHAT I HAVE TO TAKE
I'LL SWALLOW THE MOON TO STOP THE ACHE
WHAT DO YOU WHEN EVERYTHING HURTS?
FIND YOURSELF A REALLY GOOD NURSE WITH
A WHISKEY, AN OXY, AND A COUPLE OF PERCS
A WHISKEY, AN OXY, AND A COUPLE OF PERCS
A WHISKEY, AN OXY, AND A COUPLE OF PERCS

Billy crosses to the bar.

Women. Man ... I keep my distance, emotionally anyway. I'm no good for them.

Death pours him a drink.

I did have one somewhat lasting relationship with a woman twenty-mmm years ago. We were around the same age. A ginger junkie. I've always been a sucker for a red-headed basket case. Rare breed indeed. She came to a handful of gigs. Then started to follow me around like I was the fucking Grateful Dead. Wasn't the greatest lay but I liked her enough to let her in. She called me daddy. I fucking hated that. Not because it's creepy, that part I like, but I always wanted to be a dad and whenever she called me daddy I felt like the universe was mocking me.

He takes a shot

One night after a sweaty bout of booze, sex, and debauchery in New Orleans, I told her I thought we should go exclusive. You know, just the two us, like the Cunninghams, or even better for the worse, the Huxtables. She smiled, lit a cigarette, and said, "Sure honey. We should get married, find a nice little house, pump out some puppies." We fell asleep puzzled together like two spoons dreaming of white picket fences, fake sugar, and fucking PTA meetings. When I woke up she was gone. I figured she went for smokes, or coffee, or more junk.

Never saw her again.

That was the last meaningful relationship I ever had. I've even tried to make a go of it with men. Yeah, spoiler, I like the peen. That was even worse. It's true what they say, you know, all men think about is their cock. Don't get me wrong, that's not necessarily a bad thing, but once in a while it's nice to just sit and be quiet. Talk about the beauty of a well-cooked meal or how the tree in the yard catches the breeze, the sky, the sun. Getting high seemed to always be the trick. I could get all that beauty from a healthy dose.

So, out of fucking nowhere comes this girl. It's possible. The timing is right, and her facts are close. Close enough. Maybe it's a sign. Maybe the universe is telling me something. Maybe I'm insane. No, that is a fact.

Who the fuck am I kidding?

To Penny

If you hadn't said you were my kid, I would have tried to, you know…

I'm better off alone. Shit, you all are better off if I am alone. Just don't call me daddy.

He begins to play "Daddy Issues"

PENNY: HE SAID DON'T CALL HIM DADDY WELL,
   WHAT ELSE COULD HE BE?
   WHEN HE'S TWENTY-MMMM YEARS
   OLDER THAN ME
   ISN'T THAT EVERY MAN'S FANTASY? DADDY
   MOTHER WAS A REVOLVING DOOR
   NEVER A LACK OF MEN FOR SURE
   IN AND OUT, IN AND OUT, IN AND OUT,
   IN AND OUT—CONSTANTLY
   I KNOW ALL ABOUT "MASCULINITY"
   A LITTLE BIT OLDER, WITH A SPECKLE OF GRAY HAIR
   LINES ON THE FACE, A SAG HERE AND THERE
   WHAT DO YOU CARE? IT DOESN'T AFFECT YOU

UNLESS YOU'RE OVER FORTY-TWO
FRESH OFF THE PRESS, FRONT PAGE NEWS
I GOT BIG TIME DADDY ISSUES
IT'S NOT TOO HARD TOO UNDERSTAND
I NEED A MAN WITH A CALLOUSED HAND
TALL OR SHORT, RICH OR POOR DON'T MATTER MUCH
ALL IT TAKES IS A WELL-BRED TOUCH
A SEASONED SOUL WITH A CHIN OF STONE
BEEN IN A FIGHT, BROKE A BONE
I LIKE MINE GROWN, BRUISED, AND RIPE
YEAH, YOU KNOW THE TYPE
THE ONES WITH REALLY BIG SHOES
A HEALTHY DOSE OF DADDY ISSUES
YOU AIN'T GOT NO CLUE
WHERE I BEEN OR WHAT I'VE BEEN THRU
KNOW WHAT I WANT AND KNOW HOW TO GET IT
AND DON'T TELL ME HOW MUCH I'M GONNA REGRET IT
IF YOU'RE STILL HUNG UP ON YOUR MAMA
AND YOUR TOYS
GOT NO TIME FOR THAT, NO, NO, NO,
FUCK THAT NOISE
DON'T EVEN BOTHER, DON'T WASTE MY TIME
I'M GONNA FIND ME A FELLA PAST HIS PRIME
I DID MY TIME AND PAID MY DUES
I'LL INDULGE ALL I WANT IN MY DADDY ISSUES
GOT THEM DEEP SEEDED
FULLY ROOTED
BORDERLINE
TEXTBOOK DEFINITION
POSTER CHILD
MINT CONDITION
CLASSIC CASE OF DADDY ISSUES

> *On the applause Death enters. Literally. Dressed in a black robe with a hood that covers his head and face. He joins Billy at the piano. He sits, then pulls out a bottle and pours both of them a drink. Billy plays 'Stoned on 42nd Street' during the scene.*

BILLY: A conversation with death … What makes you come?

DEATH: I only go where I am wanted. It isn't really up to me to decide your ending. It just kind of happens. It's up to the person dying, really. If people actually had an inkling of the true consequences of their actions, lineage, and the chaotic nature of the universe, they might have an idea of how and when I might come.

BILLY: Is there really a list of those whose life is done?

DEATH: Yes.

BILLY: Tell me about a famous one.

DEATH: Like who?

BILLY: Warhol, Kerouac, Bowie, no—Attila the Hun.

DEATH: All very good deaths. Attila, knowing he wouldn't join the divine, begged and begged for more time. By the way he wasn't poisoned, it was too much wine and his liver blew up. Alcoholism was a thing even then.

I know, it's a lot less exciting. History changes things a lot. He does that.

BILLY: Who?

DEATH: History. A sort of Greek god type. Yeah, it's a male. His-story.

BILLY: I see what you did there.

DEATH: Human history is a set of rules that people have agreed upon. You people can't handle the truth. You want to feel safe and secure, so you tell yourselves stories to feel better.

BILLY: I'd rather forget. I just try to focus on getting through the day.

DEATH: Yeah, the whole one day at a time thing.

BILLY: And the future means nothing to me.

DEATH: The only thing you have is the future.

BILLY: Not this ape, I'm of the punk generation, no future.

DEATH: Punk is dead. Trust me, I know. He just cut my lawn.

BILLY: Punk is dad.

DEATH: If punk is dad, then death is apparent. Look, death isn't about you, it doesn't happen to you. It happens to those left behind.

BILLY: Bullshit.

DEATH: Serious shit. (*To the crowd*) Drink up folks, happy hour is almost over. (*To Billy*) Don't worry, I got your tab.

> *Death crosses back to the bar. Billy intros the second guest poet spot. The theme is "life."*

BILLY: All right, let's bring up another poet. Please give a warm welcome to… (*ad lib*)

> *Second poet does their three minutes. When the poet finishes…*

BILLY: (*ad libs, then*) …please give a big loud welcome to the ever popular, Miss Penny Diver!

> *Penny heads to the mic. Billy and band start to play "ANOTHER DARK DAY"*

PENNY: AFTERNOON'S TURNED TO NIGHT
CAN'T SEE WITHOUT A LIGHT
IT'S ANOTHER DARK DAY
NO BRIGHT YELLOW THINGS

NO HAPPY SONGS TO SINGS
IT'S ANOTHER DARK DAY
STUBBED MY TOE ON THE COFFEE TABLE
NOTHING COLORFUL TO SAY
EVERYTHING'S A TOUCH OF GRAY
IT'S ANOTHER DARK DAY
PULLED BACK THE CURTAIN
JUST TO MAKE CERTAIN
YEAH, IT'S ANOTHER DARK DAY
TRY AND HIDE IN A SHADE OF BLUE
CAN'T ESCAPE THE CLOUDS THAT COVER YOU
SO YOU JUST SIT AND WAIT
FOR THE FICKLE FINGER OF FATE

> *Band instrument solo.*

PENNY (cont'd, spoken): They say nearly all bridge jumpers change their minds halfway down, "Oh, my God, what have I done? Everything in my life that I thought was unfixable is fixable, except this." Then splat and that's that.

I've tried to kill myself countless times.
I'm not dead yet,
Let me tell you why.
It's that ancient instinct to survive.
When your every thought, action, and motivation
Is informed by that satiation.
All your choices come back to one thing and one thing only,
Filling that void.
Doesn't matter who you are or where you walk in the world.
There is only joy
When it is in you
And then You become a passenger,
Lose control,
Kidnapped and Stockholmed.
You're not in charge anymore.
The urge is and you are now at the bottom of the pole.

> *Sings*

THE DAY IS OVER NOW
I FOUND MY OUT WAY SOMEHOW
FROM ANOTHER DARK DAY
GRAY FADES TO BLACK
AND THE NIGHT'S COME BACK
FROM ANOTHER DARK DAY
I TURNED ON THE LIGHT
SO I COULD SEE MY WAY
THROUGH ANOTHER DARK DARK DAY

EVEN WITH THE SUN UP HIGH
STILL CAN'T FIND I IN THIS DARK DAY

> *On the applause Penny heads to the bar as Billy steps up to the poet mic. The band plays a death note.*

BILLY: And now, Death tells a joke.

DEATH: As a bar tender, I've started really appreciating the finer things. Like the single malt. Led to my fifty-seventh divorce. Brenda number three once asked why I don't look at or hold her the same way I do the Scotch. Hush baby, I think this single malt is older than you.

> *Drum hit. Billy takes the mic from the stand and sits on a stool.*

BILLY: Once upon a time this rock outfit from Scranton, PA, asked me to be the supporting act for their European tour. For you straights, that means the opening band. What a fucking nightmare. This band recorded really well but were terrible live. Like The Shaggs but without the talent. We didn't get along well. Anyway, I got lost in Paris shame-walking at dawn after an after-after-party. Missed bus call, and the bus left without me. Sixteen hours and a thousand euros later, I arrive in Valencia, Spain by cab. I missed load-in and sound check but got to the venue just in time for my set. I was a mess. I hadn't bathed in two days and the only thing I had consumed the entire time was wine so I'm sure smelled like the worst of them. After my set, which I killed by the way, the headliner's singer calls me a hippy and tells me to "wash my ass." Apparently, I said, "Go fuck yourself, you fucking Joey Ramone wannabe." Or something, something … Living in a cab makes you a little edgy, you know? This guy. Late twenties, could barely carry a note, but knew all the best Green Day chords on his credit card bought guitar, spent most of his time staring into any and all reflective surfaces. Making sure his hair was perfect. Well, after I insulted him, he laid into me. Huge blow out, things were thrown, more names were called, shit met fan. They played their set, terribly I might add. Loaded out, and on the bus they decide to tell me I'm booted from the tour as they pull up to the curb of some random train platform in the south of Spain.

> *He returns the mic to the stand.*

This one is called, "On a Train to Madrid." (*To the Brechtones*) Something Spain-ish.

> *He steps up to the poet mic as the band plays, Spain-ish Jam.*

On a train to Madrid.
Never did get a chance to see Alicante.
Spent the last of my time trying to fix what went wrong.
Now, I don't care because you just stood there
With that blank stare.
Should have listened to my gut like I never do.
Dragging my ass, my bags, and my pride across the platform,
Trying to disassociate my anger and hate

As my arms fall off from the weight.
I feel queasy until I look out across the rails.
This train is my horse and I am Cervantes.
Limping away from a battle lost fighting windmills
And dragons.
On a train to Madrid
I make music
You comb your hair
Everywhere.
Doesn't matter how you feel, how you play, or where you're booked,
All that matters is how you looked.
And you look maaahvelous, daaahling!
This mirror goes to eleven.
Sitting on my ass
In first class
On a train to Madrid.
Feeling relieved to put kilometers between us
As you speed away in your autobus.
Be careful with that axe,
It may come down when you're not looking
You don't see shit kid.
And you still don't know what you did
And all I have left to say Is learn to play.
Thank.

> *Band ends the jam and segues right into the next song. Penny takes the stage. Billy joins in on piano singing backup. They begin "Nobody Wants to Deal with Your Shit"*

PENNY: WE'RE BREAKING UP MY INSPIRATION'S DEAD
MY BLEEDING HEART IS BLED

BOTH: ALL THE ROLES ALL THE ROLES,
HAVE BEEN PLAYED

PENNY: THE INS AND OUTS, THE UPS AND DOWNS
TOO MANY POETS, PREACHERS AND CLOWNS

BOTH: I'M TIRED AND I WANNA GET PAID
YOU CAN DANCE THE WAY YOU WANT
BUT DON'T BULLY YOUR WAY THROUGH THE PIT
KEEP IT ONE STEP, ONE STEP BEYOND 'CAUSE
NOBODY WANTS TO DEAL WITH YOUR SHIT
NO MORE
NO, NOBODY WANTS TO DEAL WITH YOUR SHIT
NO, NO, NO
NOBODY WANTS TO DEAL WITH YOUR SHIT

NO MORE
NOBODY WANTS TO DEAL WITH YOU

PENNY: YOUR MEDIOCRITY IS EASY TO SEE,
PRACTICED AT PROCRASTINATION
EMBRACING ALIENATION

BOTH: COLLABORATION AIN'T A SOLO YOU KNOW

PENNY: YOU BLUR THE LINE OF
EGO AND PASSION
YOU WEAR YOUR COSTUME LIKE
RUNWAY FASHION

BOTH: YOU'RE PRECIOUS, YOU'RE PRECIOUS,
A BEDAZZLED STONE

PENNY: YOU CAN DANCE THE WAY WANT
BUT DON'T BULLY YOUR WAY THROUGH THE PIT
KEEP IT ONE STEP, ONE STEP BEYOND 'CAUSE

BOTH: NOBODY WANTS TO DEAL WITH YOUR SHIT
NO MORE
NO, NOBODY WANTS TO DEAL WITH YOUR SHIT
NO, NO, NO
NOBODY WANTS TO DEAL WITH YOUR SHIT
NO MORE
NOBODY WANTS TO DEAL WITH YOU
I'M STANDING IN MY OWN LIGHT
I SEE MY SHADOW ON THE FLOOR
GIMME MY 15 MINUTES
AND I'LL BE OUT THAT DOOR

Billy grabs his "violin case" and heads out the door.

PENNY: WHERE DO YOU THINK YOU'RE GOING,
IS THIS SOME MYSTIC PATH YOU'RE CARVING?
IT LOOKS LIKE YOUR SOUL IS STARVING
CAUSE YOUR EYES ARE BLOODY RED
I ACT MY WAY THROUGH YOUR FICTION,
LIKE I'VE DONE A MILLION TIMES
BUT CAN'T REMEMBER THE LINES
'CAUSE MY BRAIN FELL OUT OF MY HEAD
YOU CAN DANCE THE WAY WANT
BUT DON'T BULLY YOUR WAY THROUGH THE PIT
KEEP IT ONE STEP, ONE STEP BEYOND
'CAUSE NOBODY WANTS TO DEAL WITH YOUR SHIT
NO MORE
NO, NOBODY WANTS TO DEAL WITH YOUR SHIT NO, NO, NO

NOBODY WANTS TO DEAL WITH YOUR SHIT NO MORE
NOBODY WANTS TO DEAL WITH YOU

On the applause the third guest poet takes the stage. Theme is "facade."

PENNY: Thank you, very much. I think that is about enough of my shit. Let's do another poet.

    Please welcome to the mic… *(ad libs)*

Third poet does their bit and when finished…

PENNY: *(To the Brechtones)* Fellas, gimme a back-beat.

    Band plays Poseur Jam.

You ain't punk rock you bubble-gum pop.
Trying to be visible
And totally original.
Center of the conversation
Without invitation or humiliation indignation, manipulation
That's your reputation.
A big fish in a small pond
Got'em all conned
Oh look you did a thing,
And take the credit for everything.
You suffer 'cause
You had it tougher, cuz
No one can struggle like you does
Show them what really you got
Something you're really not.
A tool,
A fool,
An insufferable bore.
A Gansta,
A Hipster,
A rancid trendwhore.
Addicted to race, hooked on sadness, madness, outrage, inrage,
Style, linage, status,
Culture, schooling, sass, and class.
Oh, you hate Star Wars, huh?
Doctor Who, superheroes, awkwards and weirdos?
Facespace fury for everyone.
Defined by who you vote for but you're still broke you're
So annoyed you scream into the void.
But no one is listening. No one cares.
There's no more discourse or culpability,
Remorse or accountability,
Sense and sensibility.

We talk over each other, louder and louder until it turns into a literal laundry list of useless shit.

> *Band ends. Dissonance.*

BILLY: (*Echoing from offstage*) Dissonance.

PENNY: Cognitive dissonance.

> (*Echo*)
> *Billy enters to the bar. He looks a little worse than when we last saw him. What did he take?*

BILLY: What if I told you everything you think is real, everything you know, all you were taught is a lie? You would tell me to prove it, right?

PENNY: Right.

BILLY: Now, suppose I had empirical evidence, would you accept it?

PENNY: No. So even though you know deep in your soul, that everything you do to yourself is wrong…

BILLY: I still do it.

PENNY: Why?

BILLY: Because I like it. I'm used to it. It is the only thing I know I can be truly loyal to. At least I am in control of something. I wanna be someone different, useful, happy.

> *He sets his "violin case" on top of the piano. Penny tries to take it, he holds it close.*

Hey, the FDA says it's ok.
These were created to ease, to please, fight disease
And for small fees, they'll prescribe whatever fills your needs.

PENNY: (*Pissed*) Dissonance.

BILLY: Dissonance.
> (*echo*)

PENNY: Cognitive dissonance.
> (*echo*)

BILLY: A belief so resigned, even a god couldn't change your mind.
Jesus himself could walk into this room and tell us all he wasn't a son but a daughter,
but we'd all just laugh say he drank too much water.
I've seen it, happens all the time. Or maybe it was the wine.

> *They stare at each other for a moment. She is trying to get through to him.*

How about you just sing another fucking song?

> *He sits and plays the band joins him on "Take Me Now." Penny crosses to the mic.*

PENNY: ALL I WANT IS SOME AFFECTION
  IT DOESN'T HAVE TO BE MOTIVATED
  ALL IT TAKES IS ALL YOUR ATTENTION
  I DON'T THINK THAT'S TOO COMPLICATED
  SO HOLD ME, SQUEEZE ME
  LOVE ME, TEASE ME
  TAKE ME NOW, BEFORE I CHANGE MY MOOD
  I GET THE SHIVERS WHEN YOU TOUCH ME
  MY EYES GROW HEAVY FROM YOUR CHEAP PERFUME
  AND WHEN YOU START TO PET ME
  IT MAKES MY HEART GO BOOM, BOOM, BOOM
  I DON'T THINK THAT'S TOO COMPLICATED
  SO HOLD ME, SQUEEZE ME
  LOVE ME, TEASE ME
  TAKE ME NOW, BEFORE I CHANGE MY MOOD

> *Band jams a solo, during which Billy grabs the bottle of Euphorica while still playing and pops a pill. Was it by accident? After the solo Penny speaks while the band jams.*

I speak from my scars, not from my wounds.
I've already given everything I'm not.
There wasn't ever an explanation,
Not that I remember, but I may have forgot.
Looking back there was motivation
But I didn't know I would end up here,
Now, time is going a million miles a minute,
Days go by year by year.
Pain will hurt you
But pain will also change you.
Not everything is roses, butterflies, and rainbows.
In fact, the universe is dangerous and dark.
Your bias toward all things bright beautiful
Makes you an easy mark.
They say that balance is the key to true happiness.
I am still wondering who this "they" may be.
I'm not trying to turn you into a cynic or shit all over your happy-time reality,
But oh, my lord what fools we mortals be.

> *(Sings)*

I KNOW A DARK AND PRIVATE PLACE WE CAN GO
IN THE BACK OF MY OLDS' FOGGIN' UP THE WINDOWS
OR WE CAN FIND ANOTHER PARTY
BOY OR GIRL THERE AIN'T NO SHAME
'CAUSE A BODY IS A BODY
AND IN THE DARK WE ALL FEEL THE SAME

SO HOLD ME, SQUEEZE ME
LOVE ME, TEASE ME
TAKE ME NOW, BEFORE I CHANGE MY MOOD
HOLD ME, SQUEEZE ME
LOVE ME, TEASE ME
TAKE ME NOW, BEFORE I CHANGE MY MOOD
TAKE ME NOW, BEFORE I CHANGE MY MOOD
TAKE ME NOW, BEFORE I CHANGE MY MOOD

> *She exits on the applause, the band segues right into the next tune, "The Longest Suicide in History." Billy is almost slumped completely over the piano. Yet, he can still churn out this tune.*

BILLY: THERE'S A SEDUCTION IN SELF DESTRUCTION
THE HIGH OF GOODBYE
EVERY LINE IS BLURRED
EVERYONE'S ABSURD
NO WHEREFORE OR WHY
THAT MONKEY GOT HER HOOKS IN ME
THE FUTURE IS WRITTEN FOR ME
ADDICTED, THE LONGEST SUICIDE IN HISTORY

> *Something clearly isn't right with him, he is slurring and his playing is more sloppy than usual.*

OH MY GOD YOU CAN BET
IT'S BETTER THAN SEX
NO, I AIN'T LYIN
DON'T CARE WHAT YOU GOT
SNORTED, SMOKED, POPPED, OR SHOT
WHATEVER, I'M BUYIN'
THERE'S NO MAGIC OR MYSTERY
JUST A SLIGHT CASE OF PTSD
ADDICTED, THE LONGEST SUICIDE IN HISTORY
I SWEAR, I'M GONNA STOP, I'M DONE WITH THIS SHIT
ONE MORE HIT AND I'M DONE

> *Billy plays a short solo on the piano. Sax takes over the jam. Billy gets up to leave. Death reminds him he forgot something. Billy goes back to the piano for his "violin case" then exits.*

PENNY: HE NEVER CAME BACK
THAT WAS THE LAST
ANYONE SAW HIM
NOBODY CRIED
NOT EVEN I MOURNED HIM
IS THERE HOPE FOR A DOPE OF A PUNK LIKE ME?
THE NUT DON'T FALL FAR FROM THE TREE
ADDICTED, THE LONGEST SUICIDE IN HISTORY

The band jams. She goes to the chalk board and erases "Billy Bitter" and writes her own name in his place. She introduces the last of the poets. The theme is "death."

Welcome everyone to beat-night. Here, we celebrate words, music, and life. Please welcome to the mic… (*ad lib*)

   Poet does their bit.

PENNY: Thank you (*ad lib*)
   A eulogy for the living…
   Remember tomorrow and reflect on what may come.
   What has been has been and did done.
   Look back forward.
   History is for repeating.
   The future is now. Now, and now. The future is now.

      (*She sings*)

WHAT GOOD IS ALL THAT DOOM AND DREAD,
NOW THAT YOU'RE DEAD?
WHERE HAS THAT WOE IS ME GOTTEN YOU LATELY?
YOU REACHED TOO HIGH FOR THAT HIGH WAY UP HIGH
YOU PLAYED THE FOOL, THE POET, VAGABOND KING
BALLADS AND TALES ABOUT
EVERYTHING AND NOTHING
RANTING AND RAVING TO ANYONE LISTENING
NO, IT WAS NEVER CHARMING OR COOL,
THE ONLY ONE FOOLED WAS YOU
YOU'RE TO BLAME
IT'S A CRYING SHAME
I'LL SAY IT AGAIN
IT'S A CRYING SHAME
JUST TO SHOW US ALL
HOW FUCKED UP YOU REALLY WERE
YOU HAD TO PUSH IT A LITTLE BIT FURTHER, DIDN'T YA?
GUESS THERE WAS FINALLY ENOUGH
PILLS, JUNK, AND LIQUOR
THE REAL TRAGEDY IS HOW YOU'D REFUSE TO BE
ANYTHING BUT CATASTROPHE
AND LITTLE REMAINS
IT'S A CRYING SHAME
I'LL SAY IT AGAIN
SUCH A CRYING SHAME
      Instrument solo.
      Speaking

He was found
In a shit hole downtown.

Surrounded by notebooks of stories and tunes strewn all across his motel room.

They say that he od'd, Propped up staring at the TV.

I imagine that's how he'd wanted it to be, But really?

If you could have sobered up even just for a minute,

Maybe you wouldn't have to be six feet deep in it.

There was a small mention in the Times.

A few short sweet lines somewhere buried behind small crimes.

      Sings

SOMETIMES THE HERO NEVER SHOWS

YOU END UP FIGHTING ALL THE FOES, ALONE

YOU CAN SAVE YOURSELF, YOU KNOW

BUT NOW YOU'RE GONE AND NOTHING'S LEFT 'CEPT ME

IS THIS REALLY HOW YOU WANTED IT TO BE?

ALL IN VAIN

IT'S A CRYING SHAME

SMALL TOWN FAME

IT'S A CRYING SHAME

BET YOU'D SAY THE SAME

IT'S A CRYING SHAME

      FIN

      ****Bows/Encore****

      "TOO MANY VAMPIRES"

PENNY (*cont'd*):

I'M LEAVING, I'M MOVING, THE FOG IS TOO THICK

I CAN HEAR THEM,

THE BAD THINGS SINGING BEHIND THE BRICK

THEY COME FOR BLOOD AND YOUR SOUL AND IMMORTALITY

EAT YOUR FLESH AND FUCK YOUR GUTS,

IMMORALITY

WHAT GOOD ARE THEY TO ANYONE,

WHAT PURPOSE DO THEY SERVE?

SUCK THE LIFE OUT OF EVERYTHING

JUST TO SELF-PRESERVE

THE PSYCHOPATH KNOWS ITS MATH, PLANS EVERY PLAY

ROLL YOU UP AND SMOKE YOU IF YOU GET IN THE WAY

THERE'S TOO MANY VAMPIRES

TOO MANY VAMPIRES

TOO MANY VAMPIRES

ALL OVER ROME

YES, THEY WALK AMONG US, EVEN IN THE SUN

FEED ON GREED, FEAR, AND HATE,

THEIR FANGS DEEP DUG IN EVERYONE

MANIPULATING PEOPLE LIKE PUPPETS ON A STRING
TOYING WITH EMOTIONS LIKE A PLAYTHING
THERE'S NO HOLY WATER, CRUCIFIX, OR TRINITY
THAT CAN SAVE YOU FROM THIS DEVIL'S MORBID MINISTRY
SO PEACE, I'M OUT, FUCK THIS PLACE,
YOU'VE ALL LOST YOUR HEADS
SUCKED DRY OF HUMANITY ALL THE BLOOD IS BLED
THERE'S TOO MANY VAMPIRES
TOO MANY VAMPIRES
TOO MANY VAMPIRES
ALL OVER ROME
MAKE SURE YOU STAY AWAKE AND
ALWAYS CARRY A HAMMER AND STAKE
BE READY WITH A TORCH AND SPADE
DEMONS DON'T LIKE A SHALLOW GRAVE

     Instrumental

THERE'S TOO MANY VAMPIRES
TOO MANY VAMPIRES
TOO MANY VAMPIRES
ALL OVER ROME

                                                End of play.

Hiccups

Ben Rosenblatt

In his 2017 Netflix special, *3 Mics*, Neal Brennan tells the audience that in some of his jokes, he will have a girlfriend, and in others he will not.[1] While speaking with Jerry Seinfeld during his appearance on Seinfeld's Netflix series, *Comedians in Cars Getting Coffee*,[2] Brennan admits he is subverting a comedic tradition by admitting while onstage that his jokes are deliberately crafted, and he may present details from his life that are not actually true. He admits that revealing a truth—even if that truth is that he will sometimes tell untruths for the sake of his punchlines—might create a candid moment of pathos not usually associated with stand-up comedy. Traditionally, a comedian is not seeking empathy from an audience. If audience members empathized too closely with a man slipping on a banana peel, for example, they might become so concerned about the possibility of his injuring himself that his fall would not make them laugh. If audience members could laugh at him, their laughter would be due to two factors. First, he would not express pain, either physical or emotional, in a way that elicited empathy. Second, audience members would be aware that his actions were staged. He might slip on a banana peel, but he would not actually hurt himself.

To be fair, an audience might laugh if the man slipped accidentally, provided he did not seriously hurt himself. In that case, the audience would be laughing at the lack of self-awareness that led to his fall.[3] For a moment, imagine another, less familiar scenario: What if the man slipped and fell for a reason he could not help? The third scenario provides a possible framework for the work of a comedian or comedic actor with a visible or apparent condition. A successful comedian must not elicit empathy, because empathy might prevent an audience from laughing at him, but how can he make an audience laugh at a physical, emotional, or psychological trait beyond his control?

There are two ways he could make effective comedy. First, he could feign a lack of self-awareness about how his physical, emotional, or psychological traits appear to an audience. In this case, his persona differs from, say, Charlie Chaplin's, in only one respect. While Chaplin feigns both his difficulties and his lack of self-awareness in regard to them, a performer with a visible or apparent physical, emotional, or psychological condition only feigns the latter. Second, he could indicate to the audience that he either could overcome or has overcome the immediate physical, emotional, or psychological difficulty audience members are witnessing, even if he could not overcome his visible or apparent condition. This comedic choice does not require that the performer present himself as lacking in self-awareness. Therefore, it increases the possibility that an audience may empathize with him, since he is both admitting his own difficulty and admitting that that difficulty is not of his own making.

His very presence, then, is a potential complication of traditional comedic structure. Audience members might empathize with him even while they laugh at him. Of course, like any comedian or comedic actor, he can make specific physical and vocal choices to make an audience laugh. It will be harder to make sure an audience does not empathize with him. If he chooses not to feign a lack of self-awareness about his own physical, emotional, or psychological difficulties, he is also admitting that those difficulties are not always entirely under his control.

By contrast, how he represents or re-presents them onstage is entirely under his control. A performer onstage is deliberately encountering his audience. Even if he cannot control every detail of that encounter, he is still controlling the performer/audience dynamic of the onstage world, and his control of that dynamic is a humorous reversal of the ablebodied/disabled power dynamic of the real world. Traditionally, comedy is the art of re-presenting a familiar physical, ideological, or emotional struggle so compellingly that an audience laughs. A comedian or comedic actor with a visible or apparent condition can present his unfamiliar struggle so compellingly that an audience momentarily sees that struggle as he does, and it joins him in laughing about it.

However, the re-presentation of an identity is only possible if a performer is comfortable with the assertion that that identity consistently represents him. In Ben Rosenblatt's play, Rosenblatt's persona becomes increasingly comfortable with his disability identity. Yet we also meet characters for whom disability identity and sexual identity are ambiguous. This ambiguity is best exemplified by Rosenblatt's questioning of his sexuality. When he wonders, sometimes agonizes, over his repeated questioning of whether or not he is gay, he illustrates that one's relationship to an identity is not always consistent. Rosenblatt questions to what degree his sexuality is influenced by public perceptions of that identity, his own actions, and his own self-identification. Disability, or any other identity, could be subject to the same analysis. By talking to an audience about his disability, Rosenblatt shows that audience how a performer can deliberately represent and re-present an identity onstage. However, he also shows how intersectionality, simultaneous identification with multiple minority identities, functions in the real world. The process of questioning his sexuality is also a process of exploring the boundaries of his disability identity. Is he experiencing genuine homosexual desires that recur because he is repressing them, or is his returning to the *thought* of having homosexual desires a manifestation of an obsessive compulsion? In the real world, intersectional identities can never be completely separated. It is impossible to entirely control how someone perceives a particular identity, or even how one feels about it oneself. Rosenblatt stages the real-world experience of living with intersectional identities (disability and sexuality). In other words, he stages the experience of living, with all of its unexpected vulnerabilities.

—**Jill Summerville**

NOTES

1. Neal Brennan, *3 Mics*, Script, September 28, 2017, https://scrapsfromtheloft.com/2017/09/28/neal-brennan-3-mics-2017-full-transcript/.

2. Jerry Seinfeld and Neal Brennan, *Comedians in Cars Getting Coffee*, Season 10, Episode 8, YouTube, https://www.metacritic.com/tv/comedians-in-cars-getting-coffee/season-10/episode-8-neal-brennan-red-bottom-shoes-equals-fantastic-babies.

3. In his 1900 essay, "On Laughter," the French philosopher Henri Bergson argues that it is a comedian's physical and intellectual rigidity that makes his actions elicit laughter. In the case of the man slipping on a banana peel, then, his slip is funny because he should have altered his physicality to adjust for the presence of the banana peel, and he did not. Bergson's analysis of comedy is predicated on the presence of an able-bodied performer.

Hiccups

A note about this play:

All characters are to be played by one actor. Characters should be delineated by the actor's embodiments and vocal choices alone and not with any added costumes, etc. All are based on real people and real stories. Some of the dialogue is taken verbatim from interviews, some from memory, and some fictionalized.

* * *

Lights up and Ben enters. He checks that his props are in place. He pulls out a cheap, portable Casio keyboard and plunks out a few notes to ensure the batteries are working. Then he builds and suspends a dark, ominous, dissonant chord, using the organ sound. After a few beats, silence.

BEN: (*To himself*) Buzzzzzzzz. Bzz. Bzzzzz. Bzz. Bz. Ok…

He walks center and takes in his audience. A deep exhalation.

Ok. Hi everyone. Thanks for coming. My name's Ben, for those of you who don't know me. Um-oh! I'm supposed to tell you that emergency exits are there and there [*he points*]. And if you wouldn't mind shutting off your cell phones and stuff like that, that'd be great. Thanks.

What else? Is there anything else? That's it, I guess. I guess I just start.

Long pause.

All right, I'm starting. Here goes—

Hold on. Wait. I'm just gonna try to tell the truth? Like the truth-truth. Ya know, like the 100 percent indisputable, unchanging objective truth that leaves no wiggle room for questioning or doubt? That deeply satisfying, pure and perfect level of truth that doesn't really exist? That's what I'm aiming for here. Ok? Certainty. Ok…

Pause.

Ok, 'cause for me … well, above all I'm a truth seeker. The most important thing in all of life is that I'm living my own truth. Sometimes I feel like I'm in one of those old cartoons where there's a devil on one shoulder and an angel on the other. And my devil is spewing terrible thoughts; all doubt, lies, negativity, self-loathing, worst-case scenarios. Whereas the angel is reality … well, I don't know, who knows for sure what reality is? But it's a more realistic sense of things, I think. Only the devil has perfected the art of convincing me that the angel is the liar and that if I'm listening to the angel then I'm just lying to myself, which to me is like … completely unacceptable. So I have to do what the devil tells me to.

Ok. So. Ok.

The truth. The truth. The truth. Here goes…

> *Ben clumsily moves a chair from one side of the stage to the other, an attempt to establish a sense of place. He becomes Dr. Carter.*

DR. CARTER: Hi, Ben? Hi, have a seat. Welcome to the Center for Cognitive Behavioral Psychotherapy. I'm Laura Carter.

BEN: Hi. I just want to make sure, they told me fees are dependent on a sliding scale, Dr. Carter?

DR. CARTER: Actually, it's not "Doctor" yet. I'm finishing up my pre-doctoral fellowship here at the Center. You can call me Laura.

BEN: Ok…

DR. CARTER: And yes. The sliding scale payment structure does apply.

BEN: Good, 'cause I'm an actor, so, ha.

DR. CARTER: We can start one of two ways. You can either tell me what's on your mind, why you chose to come in, or if you prefer, I can ask you some questions and we can get at it that way.

BEN: Umm, I can just talk, I guess. Umm, I can't tell if I'm going crazy or if I'm some kind of human anomaly or if I've been so deeply in denial of my true self my whole life that everything I've ever thought and felt is a lie. One night, I canceled plans with a friend last minute and felt really badly about it. I was worried he was upset with me or didn't want to be my friend anymore, which is stupid but anyway. I was anxious about it and suddenly I was struck with this random thought that if I care that much about what he thinks of me … that … I must be gay?

And at first I thought it was kind of ridiculous because my whole life, I've only been attracted, emotionally and physically to women. Like I can remember having crushes on girls as early as second grade and being a horny lunatic all through middle school and high school and even still, lusting over women all the time and never over guys, ever. Not one instance that I can even think of. Except the thought kept coming back over and over, making me really anxious, and suddenly it started to make me believe that somehow all of my experiences were lies, or that somehow my memory wasn't allowing me to recall the truth, or that I was in a deep denial that was somehow blocking all of my real, natural homosexual urges, while creating this false arousal and emotional connection to women … and that if I would only admit the real me to myself, I'd realize the truth, that I'm a gay man, and suddenly I'd be attracted to men and not women anymore.

So I've tried to just admit it, accept it. I broke up with Susan, my girlfriend of three years, and it devastated her, only making things worse. I even tried coming out to my parents to see if telling someone would help it stick in my head, but that didn't work. Cause I'm not gay, I don't think. But even as I say that, something keeps telling me that I am.

And now, my whole life, every waking moment, is consumed with answering this question of whether I'm gay or not. Every single person I pass on the street, man or woman, I'm trying to gauge my attraction to, and if I look at a sexy woman and I don't instantly have a raging hard-on, somehow that's definite proof that I'm gay. Or I'll see a guy and my mind will just bombard me with images I don't want to see. Like a big 20-inch penis or like [*sighs*] me jiggling his balls and I'll be highly scrutinizing the sensations in my, uhh, in my "groinal area" and it'll feel … like I don't know, like maybe something moved down there!

So then I go to the internet and I start searching through people's coming out stories, trying to find a story that's similar to mine, but I can't find anything even close. Everyone talks about knowing it on some level from a young age … and then I remember the time I kissed Danny Barnes on the cheek in elementary school and somehow that nullifies my entire history and my fulfilling three-year relationship with Sue—who I miss desperately but can't talk to without almost having a panic attack—and becomes the sole determining factor of my real sexuality, which is obviously nonsense, but something must be up if I'm so fucking anxious about it constantly. I mean, I can't even eat a hot dog without … so I don't anymore. I avoid eating hot dogs, sausages, which sucks because I love sausage! And now I just said "I love sausage" and I can't help but think maybe it's my subconscious trying to tell me something.

So finally after more days and days of endless googling, I ended up on this web site for people with Obsessive Compulsive Disorder. A message board where people share their stories and there was this whole section of people talking about OCD as it relates to their sexuality, which is apparently quite common.

And there I started seeing tons of stories that looked like mine, except now, I was taking the smallest discrepancies and saying "Oh nope, that's not me, I must be gay." And then I came upon one where a guy said his OCD latched onto the idea that he might be a woman trapped in a man's body? And I instantly started panicking about that thought as well. And I became certain that that was true for me too! And I was freaking out, but it was also kind of a relief because it made me realize that something must be up. That people who really deal with that issue, deal with it their most of their lives and don't just pick it up off something they read and instantly feel like they need to resolve it.

And so anyway, now I'm thinking maybe I have OCD but I'm also still thinking maybe that's a bullshit lie I'm telling myself to remain in denial of my true self cause if I'm not really gay I must be crazy and why am I obsessing about this in the first place cause I have lots of gay friends who I love dearly and I don't know why it would matter to me if I was or not. I mean dealing with coming out might be really hard, but at least I'd be sure of my authentic self. But I'd never be able to be with Sue again and I love Sue—but maybe I don't and never really have. And I know I've just rambled on forever and yeah. That's why I'm here.

He exhales deeply.

Do you know the answer?

DR. CARTER: Thank you for sharing all of that, Ben. I know it's not easy, and I'm sorry that you're struggling. When you say you get anxious, how would you describe your physical experience?

BEN: My heart rate skyrockets, tightness in my chest, racing thoughts … I do a lot of pacing around, fidgeting. Am I gay or is it OCD?

DR. CARTER: Do you know what we do here, Ben?

BEN: I read that you specialize in anxiety disorders, including OCD, and do Exposure and Response Prevention technique or ERP or whatever it's called. Can you answer my question, please?

DR. CARTER: If I do, do you think it will stop you from obsessing?

BEN: I don't know. Probably not, but I'd really like to know what you think.

DR. CARTER: I'll say this only once, because it's important in therapy that we break the habit of your compulsive reassurance seeking, ok? No more after this. Can we make that deal? I don't think you're gay. What you're dealing with is Obsessive Compulsive Disorder, not a sexuality crisis. OCD is a disorder characterized by obsessions and compulsions. Obsessions being defined as intrusive thoughts, meaning that they are unwanted, repetitive and often distressing. And a compulsion is a behavior that one engages in to neutralize the distress brought on by the obsession. This is exactly what you described.

BEN: Why this particular obsession, then?

DR. CARTER: In Cognitive Behavioral Therapy, we've realized that understanding why you have a particular obsession is not relevant to feeling better about it or being able to manage it better or being able to resolve the OCD crisis. The content of the obsession is irrelevant, like mental garbage. They're the same types of thoughts that occasionally float through almost all our minds, usually unnoticed, but a misfire in the panic center of your brain, the amygdala, sets off an alarm that can't be turned off.

BEN: Ok. But if you saw how much of a mess my room is, you'd never suspect me of OCD.

DR. CARTER: Well, that's a common misconception of OCD. Many people do have observable compulsions, like keeping their space clean, but I'd say for the vast majority of people I work with, their compulsions are mental and take place only in their minds. Like all the ruminating you do about your past.

BEN: Well isn't that consistent with what someone who was dealing with a sexuality crisis might experience? A lot of questioning and reassessing of their past?

DR. CARTER: Sure. The difference lies in the reasons behind it. Someone with a lifelong history of sexual and romantic proclivity for women, if faced with a real reason to question their sexuality, might consider the idea that they're bisexual. There is a vast spectrum of sexuality. Your black and white thinking on the issue is a hallmark of OCD. And the desperate need to solve this immediately and your belief that having an answer will bring about long-lasting relief to your anxiety? Another clear indicator of OCD.

BEN: How can I be sure you know what you're talking about? I feel like if you really knew how to listen for the right clues, there's no way you'd think I'm not gay. I mean you're the therapist they gave me 'cause I could only afford fifty-five bucks a session! …Sorry.

DR. CARTER: It's ok. Mental garbage, remember? The answer is: You don't know. I worked with a patient whose obsessions focused on existential questions. One of his fears was "How can I know I'm not a robot." Truly, how do we know we're not very sophisticated machines created by someone that's hiding behind a curtain somewhere? Most obsessions are about things that one cannot be one hundred percent certain of: We can never be one hundred percent certain that God approves of us. We can never be one hundred percent certain that we don't have hidden pedophiliac desires … or that we're not lying to ourselves. Now I can waste your time answering "How do I know this and how do I know that" and lead you round and round the same thought cycles you experience on your own, or we can make use of your fifty-five bucks by beginning to work on embracing the uncertainty. You might be a giant liar in denial. You might be a fraud. You might be missing out on the chance to have the great love that awaits you if you could really accept yourself. Living with that doubt should be your new goal. Are you ready to begin working on that?

Ben breaks from the scene and speaks to the audience.

BEN: This first meeting with Laura provided relief … for approximately four seconds before the "What ifs" began to swirl about my brain.

What if I only picked her office for therapy because I knew she'd have an OCD agenda and that she'd tell me it's OCD no matter what, so I could continue living in denial?

What if I unconsciously wove subtle lies and ambiguous phrasing into my story, so she'd give me the answer I wanted to hear?

I raced home, grinding my teeth and fretfully fidgeting my fingers. Unable to squelch my compulsive need for greater certainty, I hopped on my laptop as soon as I walked in the door. There was a great OCD message board at healthboards.com. The majority of posts on the first page were all about my exact kind of OCD (And they still are. I'm serious. Go to the page when you get home—healthboards.com—and you'll see post after post from people struggling with what they call SO-OCD or Sexual Orientation Obsessive Compulsive Disorder. It's by far the most talked about spike theme. There are even some who have it in reverse; those who've long accepted their homosexuality agonizing that they might unfortunately be straight.)

But still, the "what ifs"…

What if the people posting about having gay obsessions were secretly Christian missionaries trying to convert self-loathing closet cases?

All the "what ifs" in life kill me. For example, relationships. Can you—if you're in a relationship can you raise your hands? All the couples? Yeah, please raise your hands. Don't be shy. Go ahead. Thank you.

Ok. So there are 7.6 billion people in the world. *[Singling out one couple]* Even if you're only looking at half the population, the chances that she's your best possible match are still over 422 times less likely than you being struck by lightning … twice. What if you meet someone better? What if you settled?

Sorry, that's actually none of my business. Don't listen to me. What do I know? You probably did find the one. I'm just, you know, just like "what if?"

Or rather, here. It's like this: You were all given a piece of paper and a pencil when you walked in, yeah? Anyone not get one? Ok good, so…

I'd like you all to write a list of four names: First, write the name of the person who's been the most generous to you throughout your life.

    He waits a moment for his audience to write

Got it? Ok, second, write the name of the person who relies on you most. This could be a child, an elderly relative, maybe a friend who's been in need this year. Ok? #3! The person who you enjoy spending time with most. Your favorite companion. Quick quick quick, write it down. Good? And finally, #4, write down the name of a person you came here with tonight. Only one, though, your favorite of the group. Don't worry, you don't have to show it to anyone. Done?

Ok. Now I'd like you to write, beneath your list, that you hope they die.

    Beat.

Why are you hesitating? Nothing's going to happen to them as a result. But what if it does?

Anyway, online. The message board. It served as a great meeting place. I received support from sufferers all across the country, and I'm honored that some of the folks I met have agreed to share their voices here tonight to help illustrate the diverse array of OCD experiences. So, without further ado, let me introduce them!

First meet Jess, 27 from Los Angeles, CA…

    Ben plays a few chords on the Casio, introduction music, punctuated by a sweeping "welcome" gesture toward stage right, as though someone is about to enter. When no one does, he sidesteps into position and transforms into Jess.

JESS: Horses are my favorite animal. When I was a kid I always wanted a little horsey, errrr pony, whatever. 'Cause they're so stately and masculine, yet also graceful and a little stupid and doofy at the same time. So Cute. When you see 'em on TV you just want to nuzzle 'em and you're like "awwwww." But then in person they have, like, straw in their hair and they smell and you're like "blech!"

BEN: Matt, 56, from Geneva, IL…

> *Intro chords, "welcome" gesture, transformation.*

MATT: (*Showing a photo in his wallet*) Yeah, those are my babies. Well, they're not babies anymore, but to me? Of course. Always. They were just perfect. I mean they still are perfect, but then they were little angels. Now? Heh, well…

BEN: And Ramon, 19, from Doral, FL…

> *Same drill.*

RAMON: Hellooooooooo! My name is Ramon!

> *Ramon waves. Beat.*

JESS: There was a commercial that explained my OCD perfectly. It wasn't intending to, but it did. It showed a man's feet walking up to a baby. Like the guy gets home at night and he walks up to a baby. And it's fine but then it rewinds and it shows he walks through a mud puddle and he was in the city and walked on garbage and was in the city and on the train and every place his shoes have been that day. And that's how my mind works. It will just backtrack and say this thing touched this thing and touched this other thing and it will just keep going until I'm like "Ok I'm not clean I need to wash." That's kind of how it goes for me. This weird backward process. My mind goes where no one else's would possibly go. Like "Oh the mailman handed me this mail." But for me it's like "Where was the mailman, did the mailman wash his hands after he went to the bathroom and before he was in that bathroom who else was in there?" And it's usually only a few steps before I'm like "Ok I need to wash."

MATT: I feel like OCD roots out the most important thing in your life and makes you unable to enjoy it. In my life that thing has always been family. In regard to my Harm OCD—my fear that I'm going to unexpectedly hurt someone physically, or that I already have without realizing it—it's a lot of thinking. Thinking and thinking and thinking and thinking the last thought meant something more than the previous thought, or … thinking the last thought felt more real or pure or crucial. Thinking that thought mattered and deeming it fact.

RAMON: Ayayay, I've had all of them! I've obsessed that I've had Cancer, AIDS, mouth disease, that I was in love with my sister—hehe, that one was crazy—that I was going to kill my sister … [*sigh*]

JESS: My mom's actually a school psychologist and she's asked me several times "What's going to happen if you don't do it" and I don't know. I just have this ever-present nagging feeling that something's "not right." And I need to do whatever I can to make it right, but nothing works. It's an all-consuming mental discomfort, and if I just let it go it won't stop. And if I really let it go I'll have a panic attack.

RAMON: I've had OCD for as long as I can remember. I'd usually have it really bad for about six to seven months and then it would go away for two or three years and then come back with a different theme. Well, it would never go away but it would be manageable. But this latest obsession, that I like to call "butt-brain," I've had for two years straight. It won't go away. It's going to sound weird but I constantly obsess on my tailbone. There is always something there and usually I'm convinced I can actually feel it.

Turning and feeling his tailbone.

Like it feels like there's a bump that's different than it felt yesterday. It's shifting, I think. And I also feel phantom pain from it sometimes. The brain is crazy what it can make you think. I don't know how to explain it so good. But it's always there from the moment I wake up to the moment I fall asleep. It's this feeling. Like now. I'm feeling it but I can't tell if there's something there or not. And the worst part is, even after hours and hours of endless searching on the internet, I haven't heard any stories of anyone else having this exact kind of OCD, so it makes me doubt that it's OCD even more and that it must be some kind of actual physical condition. But the truth is I have had OCD all my life so it must be it.

I ask people all the time if they see or feel anything there and they always say no. But I think they could just be lying and saying that 'cause they don't want to tell me that I have a weird—and who knows, potentially dangerous—growth on my tailbone. Here. Put your finger here. Do you feel anything there or is it just my OCD?

MATT: A disturbing thought will pop into my head. I'll see a knife, or something, and instantly my mind goes to envisioning me stabbing my—a loved one, and … so anyway, then I'll switch it in my head? I'll imagine giving her flowers instead? I'll switch out or like try to blank out the negative thought for the positive one. Usually that just makes it come back stronger or with greater anxiety—ya know, the violent thought—and so I think of the flowers again. It can really be a war between the two for hours.

JESS: Hand washing is a big part of it. If I touched a carton of milk that I had gotten from the grocery store, then the person that put it on the shelf touched it, the cashier touched it, so I'd pour it and wash my hands then touch the next thing and wash my hands.

I'd get up sometimes, on really bad days I'd spend time washing my hands no matter what I was doing. I'd just get up from the sofa and start washing my hands. And my hands um up to my wrists were just red all the time. They were just bright red and they stung. And they were cracking and bleeding because I washed my hands and used sanitizer so often that I was just destroying my skin. I would be washing them with such hot water so often all the time that they were just bright red. It was like I was wearing gloves.

Ben speaks to the audience.

BEN: I have to admit, I find myself thinking, even now, "What if this whole play is just another way of me trying to convince myself that I have OCD when I really don't?" Ya know? It might just be another ego-concocted scheme to fortify my self-delusion. Here I am lumping myself in with these other people who really have OCD, to avoid facing the reality that I've been lying to myself all these years. It's a possibility…

> *Lights and sound again take us back in time.*

DR. CARTER: So how about it, Ben? Were you able to come up with any ideas for low level exposures?

BEN: I don't know, not really.

DR. CARTER: Ben, I know it's very difficult work but if you want to find your way through this you have to commit to it. Today, as hard as it may be, we are going to compose a hierarchy. We'll develop a list of situations that will challenge the fear caused by your obsession and rank them in order from easiest to most difficult. So let's talk about some of your triggers.

BEN: Half the time I'm not even sure what the trigger is. My whole life just feels like this jumbled web of intrusive thoughts, rumination and anxiety.

DR. CARTER: That's because every time you respond to an unwanted thought by reassuring yourself with your past experiences, checking your arousal level, comparing your story to others, or avoiding sausages it's reinforced and becomes more likely to be activated again in the future. You're preventing the occurrence of natural corrective learning experiences that would ultimately cause your unwanted thoughts to decrease in frequency and intensity.

It's as though there's a bumblebee flying around you. Swat at it, it's sure to attack. With Exposure and Response Prevention we're going to habituate your fear system to the supposed threatening situation. So tell me, what's a good trigger?

BEN: Just waking up in the morning is a trigger.

DR. CARTER: What happens?

BEN: Umm, I guess, like, well … ya know, often times when I wake up in the morning, I'll have, ya know … like…

DR. CARTER: An erection?

BEN: Mhm. And then I'll just get bombarded with, like, thoughts I don't want to be having. Like images of attractive men, I guess.

DR. CARTER: Ok and what do these dream men look like? These attractive guys. Describe them, physically. What's your type?

BEN: Ummmmmmm.

DR. CARTER: Go ahead, tell me, what's your ideal man? Muscular and athletic? Artistic and sensitive?

BEN: *(Blushing)* I don't know. A combination maybe. Like Antonio Banderas.

DR. CARTER: And why him?

BEN: Because he's like dark and strong and mysterious but also passionate and sensitive and multi-talented.

DR. CARTER: *(Playfully…)* I see.

BEN: Oh my god.

DR. CARTER: So on a scale of 1–10, where is your anxiety right now?

BEN: 6ish, maybe, 7?

DR. CARTER: Ok, that's a good place to start. So let's say for one of your low-level exposures you're going to go on-line, find a sexy picture of Antonio Banderas, print it out and carry it in your pocket. Every hour, on the hour, you're going to look at it. And you are going to try your absolute hardest to ignore the pull to ruminate about whether or not you're attracted to him or if there's evidence as to whether you're gay or not. You'll do nothing to mitigate the anxiety. Instead you're to relish in it and then go on thinking about whatever it is you want to think of. What do you enjoy, Ben?

BEN: Music, songwriting, um, baseball. I'm a huge Yankees fan.

DR. CARTER: Great! Then say to your OCD, "Thank you for trying to help figure this out, but right now I'm going to think about last night's Yankee game!" And then do it!

BEN: Ok…

DR. CARTER: And each time you do this, Ben, you're going to mark down your anxiety level. So let's say the first time it's a 7. Write that down. And hopefully as the week or weeks go on, we'll see that number begin to drop. Ok? But remember, the trick is not to avoid the anxiety. It's to encourage it! Now, what are some other low-level exposures? Hmm. You're a music lover … are there any particular songs that you think of as gay?

BEN: Oh my god, yes! Wait … how's it go? *[hums lightly to himself]* You know that George Michael tune?

> *He begins to sing* Wake Me Up Before You Go Go *by Wham!* Dr. Carter cuts him off within the first few words

DR. CARTER: Great! That's going to be your new ringtone.

BEN: I can't. That song is terrible. All my friends would know something was up because that song is out of the realm of anything even remotely listenable. That's just … no.

DR. CARTER: Ok, we'll save that for more of a high-level exposure.

> *A shift in lights and sound.*

RAMON: The worst episode? Um … When I was 11 years old my OCD got focused on my swallowing. I was worried if I wasn't constantly focused on my swallowing that I would choke on my own saliva. On the day of my sister's Quinceañera it was real bad, and I was supposed to be part of the 15-candles ceremony, which is a big deal, but I was scared that when I got called up I would get too distracted and not be able to focus enough on my swallowing that I'd choke to death. So I went to the bathroom and locked myself in the stall and put my feet up so no one could find me and I heard them calling my name over the microphone over and over but I didn't come out until like 2 hours later. Ayayay. My mother yelled at me real bad, but what could I do? It felt like life or death, hehehe.

JESS: When I took the subway for the first time by myself in New York. Mhm. I had my first panic attack. And I thought I was dying. And I collapsed on the floor of the subway station in the corner, which is disgusting and obviously didn't help anything. It made it worse. I thought I was gonna have a heart attack, and then I blacked out.

MATT: Well, the uh, the intensity of my obsession greatly increased after the birth of my second child, my son? I had thoughts that … I would throw him out the window. Oh my god, you're gonna put that in there, aren't you? Ah well, yeah … I… I did, so I was scared of walking by his crib. I'd spend days hiding under my duvet. You can imagine my wife, Linda, loved that. She used to wear my shirts to put him to bed because supposedly they recognize the smell and it would remind him of me, but then I started to think that maybe I had unconsciously gotten some paint thinner on my shirt and that there could be lingering fumes so I wouldn't want her to do it. And one night it started a shouting match and I was thinking "God, I just want to smack her" which … ya know, I mean I never would, or at least—I don't know—I hope I wouldn't, but … and the sound of the baby crying in the other room just … well, everything heightened exponentially. And I thought "I'd rather kill myself than hurt my kid" so then I started to obsess that maybe I was suicidal and was gonna commit a big family murder-suicide.

>   *Shift in lights and sound.*

BEN: That's it, Laura, I give up! I'm done! I can't do it anymore! I need to just come out of the closet already!

DR. CARTER: Ok, slow down. What happened?

BEN: I was actually doing ok. The first week was awful. No progress. But the second week I was starting to see the tiniest glimmer of light. On Thursday I had, like, a thirty-minute stretch where I didn't have a single spike or rumination. I was completely able to focus on other things, like my songwriting, and had forgotten about all this crap. It was amazing! And I was doing my exposures and the anxiety would kick in, but I was mostly able to resist checking or reassuring. I had been marking down 7s and 8s and now they were down to 4s and 5s. So anyway, I'm at home over the weekend, just hanging out on my couch, watching the Yanks, and I've got my picture on the coffee table, occasionally glancing over at it. And I get up and go to the bathroom, and while I'm in there, my roommate comes home. The first thing he sees, sitting on the coffee table when he walks in is this!

>   *Ben pulls out a picture of a shirtless Antonio Banderas with hearts drawn around his nipples in bright pink lipstick.*

He didn't say anything, but I know he saw it and any progress I had made went straight to hell. I'm a fucking mess. Now just being in my apartment with my roommate is, like, a massive trigger. So I start desperately searching for reassurance again.

DR. CARTER: Ben…

BEN: I went to this gay message board online, and I started typing. Every slight sexual attraction I can recall from, like, my first erection to now. Every feeling. Every possible piece of evidence. Like I wrote about how I used to love wrestling as a kid and tack up pictures of the wrestlers on my wall, and that maybe I was unknowingly doing it cause I wanted to look at their bodies, but really most of the pictures I had of them were of their bloody faces, but there were occasionally some of just them posing and maybe that was my gay self trying to self-actualize. I wrote every single thing that I think might have the tiniest relevance to my sexuality.

DR. CARTER: Ben, hold on…

BEN: My post was 8 and a half pages long, and I asked them to tell me what they think. Am I gay or straight? I sat there refreshing the page every 45 seconds for like 6 hours and finally I had a response. Some nice guy, one of the forums leaders, named Bearhugger wrote to me and said:

DR. CARTER: Ben, it doesn't matter what he said…

BEN: He said "I remember when I was struggling to accept myself, I went to a therapist. He asked me three questions, which I answered, and told me I was gay. You answered all three questions in your post and you are straight as an arrow. I read every word you wrote, and none of your story is indicative of homosexuality. You are clearly very anxious. Get help."

DR. CARTER: Well…

BEN: But instead of relief, all I found was more doubt. Maybe I left something out! Maybe he accidentally skipped the part where I said such and such. What were the three questions I answered? What if I wasn't being completely honest in those sections?

DR. CARTER: Ben…

BEN: More checking, more researching, more agony, endless. Fuck this shit!

DR. CARTER: Listen to me. This is ok. It's actually good. You've made tremendous progress and setbacks will happen. How you respond is crucial. Here's a trick: Personify your anxiety and your OCD thoughts in your mind and talk to them. Think of them as separate. Encourage your anxiety to rage on. So say "Bring it on!" Try it. "Come on, anxiety, bring it on!"

BEN *(Reluctantly and unenthusiastically)*: Come on, anxiety, bring it on…

DR. CARTER: I'm serious. "Bring it on!"

BEN: Bring it on!

DR. CARTER: Learn to enjoy the anxiety, like the feeling you get on a roller coaster. It's scary but fun! See how bad you can spook yourself. And remember that the content of your OCD thoughts is irrelevant, so laugh at them! Like "Ha riiiiight, I looooove penis."

Ben is baffled.

DR. CARTER: (*cont.*) Go ahead.

BEN: Ha. I love penis…?

DR. CARTER: Yes! Now, is there a way, in your mind that the stereotypical gay person moves.

BEN: Ummm, I don't know, more feminine, kind of?

DR. CARTER: Do it! Prance around like your idea of a gay man, shouting how much you love penis.

BEN: Now? (*Awkwardly skipping, limp-wristed in a circle.*) Mmmmm I looooove penis! I looooove penis!

Silence as lights shift and Ben finds himself "caught" in front of his audience. He steps forward and speaks to the theatre:

Ok, everyone, listen. I swear I'm not a homophobe. I… this … I'm sorry, it's just … it was an important exercise for me. A response to mental garbage, not a real judgment. Or, I don't know, maybe that's a lie. No. Blame the OCD. It's the liar, not me. Well, ok, I lie sometimes, too, but we all do, right? Every single one of you does.

Singling someone out.

You really mean it every time you tell her (*pointing to the woman next to him*) she looks beautiful? You really wake up next to her every single morning, crust in her eyes, the smell of her shit emanating from the bathroom, without a single doubt that there's someone else in the world you'd rather be loving? Rather be fucking? Or is there just a tinge of resentment that you never share?

How, exactly, are you able to rationalize it, you lying piece of shit?

That was rude. I should apologize. I'm sorry.

Ok, when I just apologized, I wasn't actually sorry. I only did it to assuage my guilt. It's not working, though. Only when I've convinced myself that I'm actually sorry does the guilt subside.

It's ok. You'll forgive me, anyway.

Or you can carry around hatred for the rest of your life. Your choice.

Fuck. Ok. I'm just—I'm just gonna pretend I didn't do that and move on. Ya know, like you do with all the terrible things you do in life.

Lighting shift

MATT: I decided to commit to the work 'cause I was fed up. I was really determined. My hierarchy began with—I had to—I had to buy a knife set? I had thrown all mine out in favor of using plastic. I mean, seriously. Who does that?

Mid-level? More with knives. I had to sit and eat dinner with my kids around, using the stainless steel cutlery, using a steak knife. And I had to make sure I consistently hugged my kids. I hadn't been doing that cause um—I'd have images of strangling them. So, there was a while I was afraid to hug my kids. Afraid I was gonna, ya know … that those images were representative of my real desires, so. So anyway, yeah, I had to do that. Hug my kids, which I was terrified of. Awful.

I, uh … the high-level um … Ya know, it's—I feel like I'm, well I'm obviously so much better than I used to be. I'd say on a moment-to-moment, day-to-day basis I don't suffer anymore. It's always there, always gonna be there, but you, it's … it's um … there are still some things that I don't feel comfortable, you know, um … I think, well it's just really vulnerable to share what they were. So, if you don't mind I'd rather not—ya know, I think I'd rather just end the—yeah, just I think I'd like to move onto the next part of the conversation.

> *Lights and sound.*

DR. CARTER: So? How did it go this week? Tell me about your exposure. The date with Jenny. Were you able to have a good time?

BEN: I don't know. It was … She's not Sue.

DR. CARTER: I mean your anxiety. Did you mark down your progress?

BEN: I mean, I wrote numbers down. But what progress? And what for? I'm so tired. I just want to go to sleep and never wake up.

DR. CARTER: Ben, I know it may not feel like it, but you are making strides. This is the most difficult and most crucial stage. It's imperative that you stick with the exposures and record your experience so we can proceed accordingly. I promise you this works.

BEN: Well, that's great in theory, but I have to tell you something. I've been offered a yearlong fellowship with one of the leading Shakespeare companies in the country. I leave for Washington, D.C., in two weeks.

DR. CARTER: Ben, that's amazing! Congratulations!

BEN: Thanks. A little part of me is excited. But mostly I just keep thinking how anxious I'm going to be meeting so many new people, presenting myself as someone I'm not certain I am.

DR. CARTER: Think of it as more exposure. We can continue on the phone. I'll walk you through it.

BEN: The fellowship pays $150 per week. I can't afford therapy anymore.

> *Lights and sound. To audience…*

I moved to DC and was still just getting pummeled 24/7 by unrelenting OCD spikes. Depression gripped me, and—when I wasn't at the theatre—I spent most of my time drinking alone. But I was also trying to continue ERP on my own. I was making up my own exposures—like, I would watch weight lifting competitions on TV for all the muscly, oiled-up guys. Um, I bought popsicles and sucked on them as if … you know, I would … anyway. Then one day, I tried an exposure that spiked my anxiety to the max.

> *Lights shift, as Ben sits and opens up a laptop computer.*

I sat in my dingy DC apartment, pulled out my laptop, and entered a google search for…

> *Pause. He struggles to finish the sentence. He stares at the audience.*
> *He tries again.*

I sat in my dingy DC apartment, pulled out my laptop, and entered a google search for…

RAMON: Ummmm, excuse me, Ben?

BEN: (*Alarmed*) Uh, Ramon, we're in the middle of the play. What's up?

RAMON: I was thinking now might be a good time to try a little exercise with the audience.

BEN: What? No. I'm about to—I got this. Hold on … I sat in my dingy DC apartment, pulled out my laptop, and entered a google search for…

RAMON: Ben, I know you said the reason you put us other characters in this play was to "help illustrate the diverse array of OCD experiences," but admit it. There's a second reason.

BEN: A second reason?

RAMON: You feel insecure doing a play that's entirely about yourself, and you need somewhere to divert the attention when things get too vulnerable. So let us do our job.

BEN: O-ok. I, um … is that—

> *To audience.*

Do you guys mind if Ramon speaks to you for a bit?

RAMON: Of course they don't mind! I'm their favorite character!

> *To audience.*

Ummmm, hi everyone!

So you may have noticed that many of the OCD manifestations I experience are body focused. These are especially brutal because they involve ongoing bodily processes that are impossible to escape. It's like this … ready?

On three, I want you all not to think about the blinking of your eyes. Ok?
One, two, three!

No, I said not to think about your blinking. Try harder. How are you all doing with that? Still thinking about it? Now what if I told you you'd never be able to stop?

BEN: Ok. Thank you, Ramon. I'm ready to do this. Um, where was I? I'd just gotten to DC. I was making up my own exposures. Then one day, I tried an exposure that spiked my anxiety to the max.

Lights shift, as Ben sits and opens up a laptop computer.

I sat in my dingy DC apartment, pulled out my laptop, and entered a google search for … for gay porn.

After clicking the link for onlydudes.com, I instantly stood and started pacing back and forth. What if I—um … what if I… get hard? No no. Forget about the "what ifs." Don't ruminate. Ignore the pull to think about what it means. My heart rate began to soar.

Resolved to continue the exposure, I forced myself to sit back down. Filling my computer screen were the little previews of each video. White dicks, Black dicks, Asian dicks of of of *all* shapes and sizes. Buttholes too! Hairy and waxed and everything in between.

This alone would've been as intense an exposure as I was prepared to handle. But something within drove me to go further. Was it will or desire? Audacity or lust?

Clearly if I'm finding myself in this situation I must be gay, right? Yes. No. Yes. No. Yes. No. Stop!

I saw a video titled "Space Mission." I clicked.

Two recorded male voices are heard over the theatre speakers in a breathy, hypersexualized tone.

PORNO VOICE1: Three, two, one … ignition!

PORNO VOICE2: Aw, yeah … my rocket is headed straight for Uranus!

Suddenly we hear passionate moaning, grunting and other sex noises.

BEN: Oooooooooooooooooookay.

He clicks.

Three seconds of flesh on flesh and I paused the video. I'd done the exposure. The E. Now it was time for the RP: Response Prevention. No checking for any signs of what my sexuality might be. No answering any of the questions spinning in my brain. What'd Laura say? Think about the Yankees…

Ben covers his eyes, then speaks to himself, trying to redirect his thoughts.

BEN: Goddammit. Ok. Yankees. Yankees. Yankees. Jeter. Ohhhhh, you think Jeter's cute don't you? Don't answer that question. Yankees.

His cell phone begins to ring.

Yankees. We need to make some moves this off-season. Desperate for some pitching.

The phone still ringing, he pulls it from his pocket, checking to see who's calling. Without answering, he yells at his phone…

Goddammit, Sue, stop calling me!

Ben silences the call, then speaks to the audience.

It was crushing Sue. I was. And the more I was confronted with that the more anxious and obsessive I'd get. And I still—I still hurt people sometimes by not being totally certain of how I feel all the time. Or at least I have since. And it's—how do you live with yourself? How do you? (*pointing to individual audience members*) Or you? Or you? How do you live with yourselves? I don't know how anyone can both deeply know themselves and truly like themselves at the same time.

> *He clicks play on a new video.*

PORNO VOICE 3: Thanks for tuning in. Today, I had only one very specific goal; to get fucked by a dozen big beautiful cocks right in the ass! Here's the highlight reel!

> *Sudden sounds of sex. Moaning.*
> *Ben covers his face and again tries to keep from ruminating by shifting his thoughts, as the sound of the porn crescendos underneath…*

All time Yankee leader in hits is Jeter. All-time Yankee leader in RBIs: Gehrig. Homeruns: Ruth. ERA: Rivera. Wins: Ford. Stolen Bases: Henderson. Fielding Percentage: Mattingly. Mattingly was boring in Evansville, IN. Won rookie of the year in '85. Retired in '95. All-time Yankee leader in games played: Mantle. Rookie in '51. Won triple crown in '54. Hit his 500th homerun in '65. What? Yankees! Stop! Yankees, Rivera! The 2000 World Series, Rivera deals, the wind-up and the pitch … strike three, he strikes him out! The Yankees win! Oh my God!

> *He presses pause on the video. He breathes on a quiet stage. Standing, he builds a haunting and dissonant chord on the Casio, using the organ sound. The eerie sound underscores the following text, as Ben closes his eyes and explains…*

You see, an exposure is like spreading honey over every inch of your body and inviting the bees to swarm. The reflex is to swat them. But even if you catch one, there's hardly a moment of relief and they're back, more vicious than before. So you refrain. They come in greater number and with a nastier sting than you ever imagined possible. As the bees cover your body, crawl up your nose and buzz in your mouth, stinging your flesh from top to toe, you simply must wait … allow yourself to hurt … and then ask for more.

> *Silence again for a brief instant. Ben returns to his laptop and presses play.*

PORNO VOICE 3: That's right! Fill both my holes to the brim!!

BEN: (*To himself again, hand covering his face*) Ok. Ok. Ok.

> *The phone starts to ring, once more. Underneath the following words, the sound gets louder and faster, growing intense. The porno sounds, too, begin to crescendo with the telephone ringing to an absurd level, all rising and swirling together, a cacophony more reflective of Ben's internal experience than reality. We may even also hear some snippets of Ben's OCD-riddled internal monologue, his intrusive thoughts, added in the mix as well.*

Aboard about above across after against along among around at before behind below beneath beside between beyond by down during except for from in into like of off on onto over past since through throughout to toward under underneath until up upon with within without. Who? What? When? Where? Why? How? What am I doing? Thinking? Wanting? Needing? Huh? Wait. What?

> *As the sound reaches its peak, Ben finally slams the computer shut and impulsively, thoughtlessly, almost accidentally answers the phone, bringing all sound to a jarring halt. He speaks into it frantically…*

Hello? Sue! I—hey. I'm great but now's not a good time. Can't talk. I know I've been really busy. I know, I'm sorry. I can't give you the answer you're looking for. I can't be with you. I just can't. I gotta go. Please stop crying. Sue, I told you not to call me! Just because. Sue … Sue stop fucking calling me! I don't want to talk to you, ok? Jesus Christ!

> *He hangs up the phone and clutches it to his chest. To himself…*

I'm sorry, Suze.

(*To audience*) I opened my journal and marked down my anxiety level, like I was supposed to. On a scale of 1–10? 11.

> *Ben takes a long swig of booze. Lights shift.*

JESS: I'm pretty well-adjusted and don't mind telling people. Darren, my fiancée, knows about it and has been a huge help. My mom knows about it. But don't try to cure me. Don't tell me to stop washing my hands. Good friends would do that so often "You need germs for your immune system." Like I know that!

MATT: No one in my life knows about it other than Linda. No one. I wish I could share it more, but … well it's … I want to be able to explain to my kids why I wasn't a better father. And it's … how do you tell your kid "I wasn't there 'cause I worried I might kill you" without sounding like a total monster?

JESS: And I get really annoyed when people respond with their own like… (*valley girl*) "I'm SO OCD about that!" And then they laugh? I'm like 'no, OCD is a clinical diagnosis and if you have it that's fine but don't use it flippantly. A lot of terms are used flippantly now, like retarded, OCD. I'm tired of explaining that OCD doesn't mean someone is quirky.

RAMON: What do I care if people know? The way I see it, everyone has OCD at least a little bit. Everyone's gotten sick and gone onto WebMD to check their symptoms to make sure it wasn't some life-threatening disease and freaked out for a few hours. Now. Heighten the anxiety by about 5,000 percent and make it last every second of every day for four and a half years and (*snaps*) voila! That's OCD!

JESS: Plus, "I'm so OCD" doesn't even make sense, grammatically. You can't be a disorder. "I'm so epilepsy!" "I'm so cancer!" OCD is something I have, not something I am.

> *Lights and sound shift.*

BEN: Months continued to pass in DC, as I remained persistent in the exposure work. My anxiety levels were slowly decreasing, and I was drinking less. One night…

… one night…

Ok, one night…

JESS: (*Stepping forward, speaking to the audience*). Jess to the rescue!

BEN: Wait. One night…

JESS: Nope. My turn!

So. Here's what I'd like you all to do. Close your eyes. Imagine you have a terrible cold. Sneezing, sniffling, stuffy nose. Suddenly, a tissue appears in your hand. You blow your nose. A big honking trumpet of a blow. As you pull the soft cotton away from your face, you peer into it. Visualize the thick yellow mucus. A chunky booger or two. Some flaky nose crust. Maybe even a small streak of blood intermixed with germy phlegm. Really picture it in your mind's eye.

Now, keeping your eyes closed, imagine trading dirty tissues with the person next to you and using theirs to wipe your mouth. That's literally what it feels like just being in the same room with someone who sneezes.

BEN: One night! … I put on my sharpest clothes, slicked my hair back, spritzed myself with fine cologne and decided to hit the club. The gay club. Cobalt, it was called. I remember feeling excited, like it was gonna be a fun adventurous exposure, another sign that my steadfast adherence to daily ERP was paying dividends after all. When my cab pulled up to the club, I could feel the bass thumping in my chest, already. The upbeat techno house music that I typically couldn't stand, got me movin'!

Ben taps a button on the Casio, starting a cheesy samba drum beat. He dances, smiling, as he continues the story.

I paid my cover and danced my way into the overcrowded venue. My eyes darted from beefcake to beefcake. There was the strapping, tall blonde lumberjack type swaying far to my left, a slender rosy-cheeked and extraordinarily flexible young guy wearing a belly shirt grinding with a drag queen over against the wall, and a greased up dude in a leather vest and green spandex shorts gyrating just beside me. "Am I attracted to him?" my mind raced. Or him? Or him? As I gulped down my rising uneasiness, I suddenly locked eyes with a man across the dance floor. A man who looked just like a Desperado-era Antonio! A rush of excitement and dread washed over me, as I began to weave toward him through the crowd. Our piercing stares never wavered, and soon we were face to face, each pulsing to the beat. We danced silently for a few moments, before he smirked and shouted over the blaring music. "I'm Juan!" "I'm Howard," I lied for some reason.

One song morphed into the next and now his hands were all over me. Fuck. Am I leading him on? Would I be aroused if I wasn't so anxious? Ahhhh, my panic levels were soaring, but I'd learned by now to enjoy the feeling! Like a roller coaster, I remembered (*even though I fucking hate roller coasters*)! "It's time," I told myself. My mouth moved toward his. It lingered open for what seemed like an eternity. I tasted his breath for a moment. Then … we kissed!

>*The Casio beat stops.*

And I felt … I felt…

…not-outrageously-disgusted-so-does-that-mean-I-liked-it?!

I turned and bolted for the door, turning back once to check and see if maybe I found him attractive. "Don't!" I said to myself as I looked away again, reminding myself not to check or search for meaning. The whole way home it was:

Oh my god, oh my god, oh my god, oh my god, oh my god—

>*He pulls out his laptop, still repeating…*

oh my god, oh my god, oh my god … ok ok ok ok ok … Google…

>*Speaking the words he types…*

"Am I gay or is it OCD…"

>*…but before he hits enter…*

No. Don't check. Don't ruminate.

>*A deep exhalation. Ben stands. He closes his eyes, sustains the dissonant chord on his Casio, as in the earlier "Bee" section, and calmly explains to the audience, as he trains his mind…*

Here come the bees again. The goal is to let them land. On your arms, your neck, your face, everywhere. Let them crawl down your back. Enjoy the flutter of their wings against your eyelids. Let them be. Find peace with the bees. Learn to ignore them, or to love them, even, and eventually you'll stop noticing them. They might even fly away.

>*He opens his eyes. He calmly closes his laptop.*

I opened my journal and marked down my anxiety level: 6.5.

>*He pulls out a pad of paper and pencil and moves to the other side of the room, bringing his portable keyboard with him.*

With the slow but steady progress I was making, I finally found myself able to partake in some of my old hobbies again…

>*Opening his notepad to an empty page, Ben begins writing chords on his keyboard to the words he'd written, fumbling along the way.*

[*singing*] FOLLOW YOUR HEART THEY SAY
   BUT WHAT IF YOUR HEART TAKES A
   PATH OF TREACHERY AND SIN?
   AND YOUR BEST LAID PLANS
   AIN'T THOSE OF A MAN
   BUT THE DEVIL WHO LIVES WITHIN?
   AND ALL YOU THOUGHT THAT YOU KNEW

ALL YOU HOPED WOULD BE TRUE
IS A LIE YOU CHOSE TO BELIEVE?
WOULDN'T YOU HAVE TO EXPLORE IT?
OR COULD YOU—
(*spoken*) No …

      He crosses out a couple of lines and then goes back

COULD YOU LEARN TO IGNORE IT?
WOULDN'T YOU HAVE TO BE SURE OF IT?
WHICH ME AM I SUPPOSED TO BE?
(*spoken*) Ok, chorus …
NOW I'M NOT READY FOR YOU, LADY
'CAUSE I'M STILL TRYING TO TRUST MYSELF
BUT I'M NOT GONNA LOSE THIS FIGHT
THOUGH I'VE BEEN PUNCHED OUT TONIGHT
I'LL GET BACK ON MY FEET AGAIN

      Beat.

RAMON: Anyone still thinking about their blinking?

BEN: Ramon!

      Ben closes his notebook, moves downstage and confides…

I am a liar. I am a fraud. Sometimes. I mean, who isn't? But I can't see myself as a mostly honest person, who like every single other person in the history of human existence, occasionally lies. I'm honest or I'm a liar. Capital H or capital L.

But the truth isn't always 100 percent knowable, so it's tricky, ya know? Like a few years ago I admitted to a girl on the first date that she'd probably just end up another notch on my belt, cause … well, the devil told me to. It was saying "you're just gonna get sick of her and want to fuck around so end it now!" But I recently reconnected with the girl and she's amazing. All the qualities I'm looking for. Maybe if I'd lied we could have ended up happy together. But the millisecond it feels like there's the slightest lie, half-truth or omission, the anxiety kicks in and it can be unbearable.

One of the things I've been exploring with my current therapist, who takes a more Freudian approach, is the relationship between my anxiety and anger. She seems to think my anxiety is a cover for a "deep well of anger" I'm harboring toward my parents as a result of their divorce blah blah blah. Or that I'm protecting my relationship with my father somehow?

But I don't know. That probably has nothing to do with my OCD. I feel like it could, though. Or that it should? Or that there should be one thing—maybe that—which is behind all of my life struggles. And if I could just figure it out and address it then it would be solved and I could go on living a life free of anxiety and full of total certainty for the rest of eternity! No?

      Beat.

RAMON: I am superbly talkative and extroverted. Some of it is my OCD tendencies. If I'm sitting in a class and I feel like I have something to say, I won't back down and think "eh this isn't the most incredible contribution," I will get it out there! It's a huge piece of who I am and it's definitely caused some issues on the negative side like people tell me to shut up and when I was a kid I was disruptive in class but it has a great effect on my personal skills. If I go into an interview, I can talk to anyone.

JESS: I have always been a total perfectionist when it comes to my business proposals and such and I think that goes hand in hand cause I think perfectionism is a kind of compulsion itself. I don't know anything about the science behind it so I'm just gonna throw that out there, but I think those two things reside in the same part of the brain. And I think if I didn't have the tendency toward OCD I wouldn't have the tendency toward perfectionism and I wouldn't want to give that up.

MATT: My work—my life—is a product of the way my mind works and OCD is part of that. So yeah, I'd say it makes me the painter that I am and my work is amazing. Other than my family, it's the most valuable part of life. My everything. That said, I'd trade it in a heartbeat. Faster, even.

BEN: Almost a full year had passed since I left The Center for Cognitive Behavioral Therapy for the last time. But as the exposure work became a habitual part of my daily life, something Laura told me in one of my early sessions finally clicked...

DR. CARTER: With this work, you don't see a lot of gains at first. It can take some people a really long time. Then one day a patient will come in and say "I don't know why but my obsessions don't have as much of a hold on me." And I'll think "What do you mean you don't know why? You've been committed to ERP." But I think it can be confusing to associate something that makes you feel even more anxious with long term mental wellness. It's a clear sign, though, that they've reached a tipping point. Now they recognize the disconnect between their anxiety and the content of their thoughts and at that point they can really lean into the anxiety and make a lot of progress very quickly.

BEN: So on a Tuesday afternoon in early April, after a very enjoyable and mostly anxiety-free viewing of Brokeback Mountain, I was visited by some friends...

He plays the suspended "Bee chord" on the Casio.

BEN: But this time, as they landed on my every part, I smiled, buzzzzzzzzzzzzzed along with them, and within seconds, quite casually...

The chords stops.

...moved on.

Ben pulls out his phone, dials, waits, speaks.

BEN: Hey Suzie-Q, it's me. Hope you made it to work ok after I talked your ear off til 5 a.m. Thanks again for ... everything. Anyway, can't wait to finally see you next weekend. Just wanted to let you know, if you want to stay an extra day I got tickets to opening day at RFK for the Nationals. Nice day in the sun, a little baseball, couple beers, couple sausages [*smiles to himself*]. I think you should stay. Anyway, think about it. Byeee.

I opened my journal and marked down my anxiety: 2.5.

A realization—

Hey, wait a second. I just did that without … Matt, wasn't it your turn to swoop in with an exercise before the bees attacked?

MATT: You didn't need me.

BEN: I guess not.

MATT: But I do want to point something out to ya.

BEN Yeah?

MATT: Jess, Ramon, and I? There's a third reason you put us in this play. It's the same reason you sought us out on that message board to begin with. Reassurance. You trot us out here alongside you to corroborate your account of OCD, so you can remain confident you actually have it.

BEN: But—but what if without seeing the parallels between your stories and mine, all these people don't believe I have OCD? What if they think I'm lying?

MATT: What if they do? What if you are? (*shrugs*)

BEN: I guess that means I gotta ask you three to leave, huh? I gotta finish the last page-and-a-half on my own. Any final words?

JESS: Oh! Public bathrooms have always been a problem for me. Until last month I hadn't used one in well over a year. I'm probably gonna have horrible kidney disease when I'm older. It's hilarious. No. I'd work 16-hour days and I would not pee for 16 hours and I'd like be proud of myself that I could hold it for that long. I mean it's not something to be proud of, it's really bad for you, but I'd come home and be like "Yeah! I haven't peed since this morning!!" And Darren would be so mad at me like "You're gonna die. You're gonna give yourself like urine poisoning." And I'd be like "Nope. I'm awesome!"

MATT: I feel like OCD picks at the thing that is least likely to be true for someone and that's why it holds so much power. Because it takes away the things you love most. Speaking of which, I gotta wrap this up, anyway. Linda's coming by with the kids. My weekend.

RAMON: I used to be ashamed of the thoughts I was thinking. But remember, you know, it's just a hiccup in your brain, and you didn't choose to have it, and millions of people around the world suffer from it and there's no reason to feel any shame is very important, because… (*nods*)

BEN: (*Watches his friends "exit." Waving in an off-stage direction.*) Bye!

Facing the audience. Beat.

Eight years passed after finishing my fellowship in DC. The exposure work had become a habitual part of my everyday life, and the intrusive thoughts surrounding my sexuality reduced to a dull murmur. I got a great acting gig touring the world with an important piece of documentary theatre and saw immense power in the form. It got me thinking…

> *Lights and sound shift. Ben's cell phone rings. His ringtone is Wham's "Wake Me Up Before You Go Go." He does a little dance and sings along for a few lines before answering.*

Hello? Laura! Thanks for returning my call. I saw that you run your own center now.

That's awesome. Congratulations. It's basically just background noise at this point. Mmm, I'd say it's hovering at right about a 1. Never thought I'd be able to look back at that time and laugh, but here I am. I know there's no cure and I'll always have to manage it on some level, but thanks to you I have the tools to do so. Anyway, the reason I called is that I'm writing a play about OCD and I was wondering if you'd be willing to be interviewed for it. Indeed, it will be quite the exposure exercise. That would be fantastic! Now? Yeah, let's get started!

> *Lights and sound shift.*

Aaaand … that's it. The blood and guts of the doubting disease. Is that it? Yeah, that's it. I think. Who knows? Maybe I left something out. The one key piece of information that proves I'm just in denial, that I'm a total fraud. Maybe this is all a lie. Maybe it is.

Maybe…

Is that ok? Yes, right? Is it? I think so. Is it? Matt? Jess, Ramon? I think so…?

> *Lights fade.*

> *End of play.*

Ex/centric Fixations Project

Bree Hadley

"Who am I?" and "Who am I to you?" are two very different questions that could both yield equally complex answers. Further, the answers could vary from one day to the next, based on changes in the physical, psychological, and emotional state of the person posing the questions, as well as whether that person were in a public or private space. In her scholarship, Bree Hadley pays attention to people inhabiting public spaces. She also pays attention to the people who are watching people in public spaces—spectators, forming evaluative judgments based on what they think they see. "In the United States, United Kingdom, Europe and their colonies, imaginings of the disabled body have historically been dominated by a teratological impulse," writes Hadley by way of introduction to Disability Public Space Performance:

> Slimy Monsters. Medical specimens. Cripples. Charity cases. Inspirations. Though they differ across times, cultures and contexts, there can be no doubting that such personae—and the historical, social and symbolic meanings such personae are invested with—have a strong impact on a disabled person's status, identity and sense of self.[1]

As the title of her play, *The Ex/centric Fixations Project* suggests, a public interaction—particularly a public interaction between a someone with bodily differences and someone who may attempt to exert influence over that person—reveals the ethical complexities of spectatorship.[2] All an audience member knows about the protagonist of this play, who may or may not be named William Horatio Bates, is gleaned from existential details provided by multiple unidentified narrators. Audience members' knowledge of Bates (his physical injuries, his childhood memories, how he came to be in a medical setting) is based on their perceived knowledge of him, and an audience's perceptions may or may not be accurate. The psychologist who addresses Bates has medical knowledge, but even that does not necessarily help the psychologist to form accurate perceptions of who Bates *is*. Like all forms of expertise, medical expertise has its limitations. A psychologist who can classify all of the physical hardships Bates has endured does not necessarily have an intrinsic understanding of their why they are important

317

to Bates himself. If an audience perceives Bates as "eccentric," then it is only because that audience's evaluation of Bates is ex-centric, based on observations provided by outsiders instead of on a narrative provided by Bates himself. When outsiders determine the significance of events Bates has experienced based solely on their own observations, they make him an outsider in his own life.

Bates is a character in a play, and every character in a play is shaped by how a particular audience watching a particular performance on a particular night perceives and responds to that character's words and actions. In that sense, Bates is no different from any other character in any other play. Because this play is set in a medical facility where the person who would be physically positioned in the center of a hospital room, the patient, is disallowed to create his own narrative, it is impossible to read or see this play without considering the implications of robbing a patient of agency in a real world medical setting. If a patient's life is a narrative, a doctor or a psychologist may appear in that narrative as both an agent and an observer. A medical professional's initial perceptions about a patient may not be accurate. Treating those perceptions as universal "truths" about a patient instead of personal observations may cause a patient to be mistreated. For a patient, "mistreatment" could mean both misdiagnosis and dehumanizing treatment.

In *Ex/centric Fixations Project*, neither the nameless narrators nor the psychologist referenced in the text address their ethical obligations towards Bates as people who are observing him in a public space. For them, what is most important about Bates' narrative is how they present it for an audience, not how Bates perceives its significance. Yet the audience members, who are also observers forming their own perceptions of Bates, may learn from observing the dispassionate observers onstage that Bates deserves more compassion. They may analyze and critique their own perceptions of Bates and decide whether those perceptions are justified or unjustified. Better still, they may more carefully consider their own ethical responsibilities as observers when they interact in public spaces with people who have visible bodily differences.

—**Jill Summerville**

Notes

1. Bree Hadley, "Introduction," *Disability, Public Space Performance and Spectatorship: Unconscious Performers* (Basingstoke, Hampshire: Palgrave Macmillan, 2014), np.

2. For the fully analyzed text of the play, please see: Bree Hadley, "Practice as Method: The Ex/centric Fixations Project," in *Material Inventions: Applying Creative Arts Research*, ed. Estelle Barrett and Barbara Bolt (London: I.B.Tauris, 2014), 145–165.

Ex/centric Fixations Project

* * *

2 It begins with an ending.
1 You've got to start somewhere.
3 I don't think it's a secret.
1 Why don't you start with the last thing you remember before you found yourself.
3 Before it happened.
1 It's as good a place as any.
2 Tuesday 2nd September 2008, 2:52 p.m.
1 A little over a year ago now.
2 All I remember is feeling ill.
3 [*Simultaneously*] All I remember is feeling ill.
2 Nothing. It's nothing really. A late night, a lot of wine.
3 One eye open, red, and tingling.
2 I don't know how I got here.
3 [*Almost simultaneously*] I don't know how I got here.
2 Have you ever woken up and decided today is the day you're going to start on the right foot?
1 Right, then. The right foot.
2 You know, get things together.
1 Get some sunshine. Get some perspective. That's what you want to do.
2 No more distractions.
3 A smell. A sizzling smell. Like baking. Or burning. Or burning hair.
2 I want you know I'm not a bad person. It's just…
3 What's the word?
2 I wish I'd been born at a different time. One that wasn't so…
3 Wired.
1 The clock is ticking.
3 The whole world is ringing.
2 There aren't enough minutes in the hour, aren't enough hours in the day. Not enough time to waste on all the little obsessions I live for.
1 Baking? Burning?
3 An allergy, that's all. Running eyes, raw nose, lines looping slowly round the surveys of my skin.
1 3 o'clock. 6 o'clock. 9 o'clock. 12 o'clock.
2 TV. CD. DVD.
3 OCD.
2 An accumulation of facts, ideas, impulses.

1 A bright blur, black and blue and red.

2 It hurts a little.

1 It happens a lot.

2 More and more all the time.

3 My head pounds, my vision blurs, my ears ring, my chest heaves, my belly cramps, my hands begin to shake, my legs can't bear the weight.

2 It's true. I swear it's true.

3 It's nothing to worry about.

1 It's a well-known fact that the human body is not a perfect mechanism. Nature, in the evolution of the human tenement, has been guilty of some maladjustments. She has left some troublesome bits of scaffolding.

2 Most of the time, it's nothing to worry about.

3 The beat of my heart, the hitch of my breath, the bright halo of colors and chatter and footsteps closing in around me, making it harder to gather my thoughts.

2 No one is worried about it. Why should I be worried about it?

1 Saturday 6th September 2008, 11:51 p.m.

2 Saturday. It happened on a Saturday.

3 I think.

2 [*Overlaps*] I think.

3 This is hard. I don't know how to start.

1 Midnight.

2 It's as good a place as any.

1 As good a time as any.

3 I remember.

2 A maze. I remember a maze of sterile white walls, and windows, and glass.

3 The mindnumbing mundanities of therapeutic routine race a time-ravaged old clock around its preordained circuit. The impassive platoons of the caring profession lurch perfunctorily from one run-of-the-mill crisis to the next, their studied display of dispassionate care scant dressing for the cold hard core of loneliness at the heart of this harsh-lit space.

2 Flashes of movement. Faces hidden behind every corner.

1 We're ready for you.

3 Words from the wings.

2 I ought to be at home here.

3 Words from the wings, urging me on.

2 It's like I'm on display.

3 Noise, light, cold, discomfort.

2 It's like I'm on a stage. One sterile little stage amongst tens, or hundreds, or thousands, and I'm about to share my story with a room of half-seen, half-sensed strangers.

3 Unreal, and unrelenting. [*The pace quickens. 1 starts whistling*]

2 Room, after room, after room of half-seen strangers.

3 Overrun by halting pronouncements of disease, decay.

2 Screams from smiling mouths.

3 Disaster.

2 Watching me. Waiting for me.

3 The hard trills and hissing of hospital machinery, and the technicolor retchings of TV monitors. Fragmentary reminders of a world that offends the eye with its cacophony of demands.

2 Just beyond the reaches of what I can see.

3 Erratic relay of envelopes and specimens. Lashes flutter, lips race, heads body, shoulders swing. Blood runs down sweat-soaked heads, and arms, and hands and legs.

2 Fingers twist rings on worried hands. Worried hands wipe furrowed brows.

3 Bodies dance rapidly around solitary despair.

2 The scene is set.

3 The story begins.

2 The hem of the hospital gown against my hip. The chill of the stale, stagnant air closing in around me. Nauseating stench. My strength wavers. I clutch at a wall. My eyes narrow, as I think of the walk to come. I resist the temptation to close my eyes. To fall...

1 We're ready for you now.

2 A strangely melodious voice that might once have been my own interrupts my silent reveries.

1 [*Whistling rises again*]

3 Can I trust you? No, but can I really trust you?

2 I need to focus.

3 I have something to tell you.

2 The preliminaries are more important than the story itself.

3 I know this is a bit unconventional, but when you hear what I have to say, I think you'll understand.

2 I take a deep breath.

3 I need your help.

2 I don't want to leave my dignity on this cold and dirty floor.

1 [*Whistling stops*]

3 Monday 8th September 2008, 6:19 a.m.

1 Right then.

2 The scene is set.

3 Let me see if I can explain.

2 I pitch forward into the bright thronging blur, second thoughts cut short by the metallic clang of doors closing behind me. I press forward, forward into the corridor, plotting a course between wide set walls and doorways, punctuated by chairs and carts and faded propaganda a decade past done.

3 The medical merry-go-round, is that what they call it?

2 The truncated mechanical murmuring of talk on fast forward grows louder.

3 Whatever it is, it has taken me on quite a ride.

2 I spend my days pretending I have acclimatised to the pace of this amphetamine blur.

3 A billion little bubbles dance round the corner of my eye.

2 Alien. Aggressive. A maddening intrusion boring into my brain.

3 Bright, off-white bubbles, racing across the surface of things.

2 It's accelerating so fast now it puts my nerves on edge.

1 When everything starts with, "I know you're busy, but…" it's always a bad sign, right?

3 Black is for urgent. Blue is for really urgent. Red is for really really urgent.

1 A lot starts that way lately. A lot of bad signs lately.

2 If it were constant, I could learn to live with it.

3 But the world won't stop racing the clock towards the receding horizon of an unwanted future.

2 With the passing of days, and weeks, and months, it only gets worse.

3 The world gets fuller, and faster, and louder.

1 Just one step.

3 One more, and one more, and one more again.

2 Imperceptible beats of time lost, bleeding, between one moment and the next. Between hand and gesture, foot and floor, here and there, then and now.

1 Just on step. Just one more step.

2 Zeno's paradox. Whole world's existing in secret pockets of time.

1 It's time now.

3 Time.

2 Time.

3 The one thing this world steals away as soon as my mind is turned, as soon as my concentrations wavers.

1 Tuesday 9th September 2008, 3:08 a.m.

2 [*Overlaps, queryingly*] Tuesday 9th September 2008, 8:56 p.m.

3 [*Overlaps, queryingly*] Tuesday 9th September 2008, 11:26 p.m.

1 All right, then, let's take a look, see what we've got here. [*Consults casenotes, which indicate what was left in office after Bates' disappearance, what characterizes Bates' physical condition, etc.*]

3 Eyes raised, papers ruffled, they can't even meet my eyes.

2 You don't want to start with a story. You want to give them something they can see. Something physical. Here. Now. In the present.

1 Glasses. Keys. Teacup. Letters. Books. A lot of books.

3 All that was left behind.

2 Things that ought to be private, but aren't.

1 Does that mean anything to you?

2 The physicality is important.

3 I need to get their attention.

2 Its very important.

3 I need to choose my words wisely.

2 They watch. They like to watch.

1 Heavy-lidded eyes, high set ears, pursed lips.

3 Somewhere between a whistle and a sigh.

1 Sharp, pointed and severe.

2 If you listen, they'll tell you precisely what they want to see.

1 Cheeks patchy and pock-marked, with that every so slightly melted look, as
   though the invisible touch of once-loving fingertips was pulling them down.

3 A dark spot at the temple.

2 They'll tell you something about yourself.

1 There's something about you that puts me off. Nervous, and, well, scary-
   looking.

3 Something you didn't know.

2 Something you didn't want to see.

3 Light and shade and shadow morphing into one.

1 I can't help wondering if you've got something in the back of your mind,
   taking up all your attention.

3 Every conversation the same. Like I keep starting a sentence I can't finish.

1 Why don't you tell me about it?

2 It's complicated. It's really complicated.

3 Everything I've ever said. Everything I've ever done.

2 Fragments, flashing through my brain.

1 It's like you're piecing together things that don't quite fit, without any kind
   of pattern or plan.

2 I don't know what to say.

3 I forget.

2 I forget to move, or think, or breathe.

3 I have no life. I wake. I eat. I work. I sleep. I wake. I eat. I work. I sleep.
   [*Continues*]

2 I don't know why I do it.

3 I wake. I eat. I work. I sleep.

2 I sit for hours.

3 I'm on a deadline.

2 Just a little behind.

1 I think you're hiding from something.

2 The show must go on.

3 I'm fragile.

2 No, that's not true.

3 I'm built of bones that have already begun to dry up and turn to dust.

1 Well, something like that. A little like that.

3 I'm alone in two worlds, or three, or four.

2 No, that's not quite true either. It's a cliché.

1 You're filing a hole.

3 I do things the only way I know how.

2 I stay silent because I cannot fit your abstractions.

1 It's a stage.

3 I constantly recategorise things, trying to construct my own logic.

1 It's just a stage.

2 You cannot hear me.

3 I sing in the darkness.

2 I sing against death.

3 I'm a little obsessive about that.

2 More and more of my life disappearing into those secret pockets of time.

3 Nothing goes unnoticed, nothing goes astray.

2 No, that's a lie.

1 Retroactive diagnosis is a fool's game.

2 What else could explain the lost moments?

3 The pinging of a phone pregnant with new messages. The worrisome bulges in data sets that expand in the blink of an eye. The wear on new machinery that wasn't there but a moment before.

2 Just because I don't see it doesn't mean I don't sense it.

3 It sings strange tunes to me.

1 That's true.

2 [*Almost simultaneously*] That's true.

3 [*Overlaps*] That part, at least, I know is true.

1 Lie down, just lie down. Let me see if I can help you.

2 Wednesday 17th September 2008, 3:25 a.m.

1 Thursday 18th September 2008, 6:05 a.m.

3 [*Overlaps*] Thursday 25th September 2008, 3:29 p.m.

1 [*Overlaps more aggressively, trying to exercise some sort of control over the conversation*] Thursday 25th September 2008, 11:51 p.m.

2 Midnight. The mindnumbing mundanities of therapeutic routine race a time-ravaged old clock around its preordained circuit.

1 Name? [*Checking Bates' patient details. 2 and 3 overlap throughout this exchange, almost as though it's a competition over the "correct" answer*]

3 Bates.

2 William.

3 Horatio.

2 Bates.

1 Nationality?

3 American.

2 Originally.

3 American.

1 Address?

3 1*4 Stockport Road South.

2 Stockton Road South.

1 Phone?

3 467066058*.

2 234706605*.

1 Age.

3 20.

2 26.

3 46.

2 Married with a partner and two kids.

1 Marital status?

2 Nobody ever asks about that.

3 Nobody ever asks about that.

2 A truth is not strengthened by an accumulation of facts.

3 Life is full of stories that don't make sense.

2 They tell me it came upon me suddenly.

1 An accident?

3 I don't think so.

2 I saw the signs. For days, and weeks, and months beforehand.

1 Stress at home?

3 I don't think so.

1 Stress at work?

3 I don't think so.

1 Drugs?

3 I don't think so.

1 A debt? A threat?

3 I don't think so.

1 Someone made you do it, then?

2 Approximate answers.

1 [*As an aside*] I have to choose my words wisely.

3 Strange melodies.

2 Lies given in answer to a question never really asked.

1 [*As an aside*] No, that's not altogether true.

3 What else is there.

1 [*Starting to feel a sense of frustration*] Why then? Why? What was in it for you? There had to be something in it for you?

2 The devious impulse to make and manipulate and control worms its way into the core of my being.

1 Things happen. I know that. But if you keep it inside, I can't help you. You get that?

3 Yes. I get that. I get that now.

2 It wakens my senses to the smallest of possibilities.

3 I don't have much, but I have his words, and that's all it takes to make a world.

2 C'est tout. C'est tout quil me faut.

1 Monday 29th September 2008, 2:26 a.m.

2 A buzz.

3 [*Recalling prior doctor-patient encounters*]. "Hello dear, how are you today?" His greeting is always the same, always full of feigned life and light and like.

2 There's always a buzz in the background.

1 [*Trying to confirm control over the conversation, more for himself than for others*] I play the role of the respected eye doctor, efficiently dispatching the unending stream of patients with due ratio of sympathetic detachment. Engaging scholars who dare challenge my methods with due rigour of scholarly debate.

2 Its feint, but it's always there.

3 "Good thanks," I mumble, and manage a smile.

2 A bright blur.

1 A good impression. At times a great impression.

2 I want to find a way to crawl inside his skull.

3 "The pills are just for fun, then?"

2 I think it would be enlightening.

3 "Yes, well, except for the headache, good," I say. I smile. I think I smile. "That's okay, I'll be gone soon."

2 A beat.

3 A beat, and I've missed the joke.

1 All doctors, they say, are slightly insensitive. A self-defense strategy, perhaps, designed to protect them from the all-pervasive tide of human misery that presents itself daily for their inspection.

2 A relief.

3 I'm the only one who is aware of it.

2 I'm alone in two worlds, or three, or four.

3 Aware of it all the time.

2 I used to like putting on his masks.

3 He's always been good to me.

2 New language, new clothes, new identity.

1 I'm good at pretending. [*Some doubt is starting to creep into his self-description*]

3 [*Getting cynical when thinking of the "right" answers for this medical routine*] My nerves are much better now. I'm less shy. I never used to show that I was shy or that I lacked confidence.

2 That's not true.

3 It was hard, but now it's easy.

2 That's a lie too.

3 I pretend I'm interested in his stories. That way, I don't have to tell my own.

2 I have not life, but for this buzz. This constant, blinding, deafening buzz.

3 I don't think he minds. I'm good at getting him to the punchline. That's the main thing, yes?

2 No.

1 I don't think so.

3 The conversation almost flows.

1 Tuesday 30th September 2008, 9:13 p.m.

[Draws the letter Bates left behind from the casenotes]

2 I laboured over my words for months you know.

1 Trivia. Trouble.

2 I wrote in darkness. I wrote against depth.

1 Trauma.

2 I knew all along what I wanted to write.

3 I knew all along what I wanted to say.

2 I knew all along what had to be done.

3 Even if I didn't like it.

1 [*Reading 2's letter*] "Sorry it's taken so long to get back to you, my love."

2 [*Overlaps*] Sorry it's taken so long to get back to you, my love.

3 A cliché. Lies.

1 "It's been frantic, as it always is."

2 As it always is.

3 As it always is.

2 Things were bad between us then.

3 Fights. Silent screaming. Lies given in answer to questions never really
  asked.

1 "I'll tell you more about it when I'm back next week."

2 You used my words against me.

3 If you pay attention, they'd tell you precisely what they want to see.

1 "It's taken longer than I thought, but I understand it all now. No doubt about
  that."

2 You must have known.

3 No ad libbing.

1 "A week. Maybe two. And I'll be done."

2 You must have known I'd find out about it.

1 "It hasn't been all work and no play."

2 About what you did, and what you said, and what it meant.

1 "Shall I worry you with a few details of what I get up to when you're not
  around?"

2 Smiles. So they know its in jest.

3 I don't think you'd believe me if I told you.

2 Just because I can't see through your crowded maze of mirrored glass
  doesn't mean I don't know what is going on.

3 I don't want you to know.

2 I just don't want you to know that I know.

1 Wednesday 1st October 2008, 3:22 p.m.

3 Piecing together things that don't quite fit, without any pattern or plan.

2 A lot starts that way lately. A lot of bad signs lately.

1 I ought to be at home here. I ought to be in control. [*Increasingly doubting
  his control in the doctor-patient encounter*]

2 What you don't know can't hurt you.

3 Or so they say.

2 So they say.

1 Whose life am I talking about here anyway?
3 They watch, you know.
2 They like to watch.
1 Worlds that are not my own.
3 Or so you say.
1 Words that are not my own.
2 Or you say.
3 Zeno's paradox. Whole world's existing in secret pockets of time.
1 My concentration wavers.
2 Noise from the wings.
3 Faster, and fuller and louder.
1 This can't be me.
2 My head pounds, my vision blurs, my ears ring.
1 This can't be me.
2 Colors and chatter and footsteps closing in around me, making it harder to gather my thoughts.
1 I feel mute. Immobile. Exposed.
3 Saturday 4th October 2008, 12:15 a.m.
1 Wait, stop. Let me see if I can explain.
3 All doctors, they say, are slightly insensitive.
2 But willful blindness comes more slowly for some.
1 I was born into the word a bundle of questions. A bundle of questions waiting for answers which, I was to learn, would be a long time coming. [*Remembering*]
2 A very long time coming.
1 I inherited my father's propensity to take things hard.
3 To suspect the worst before the worst had come.
1 What I wanted, most of all, was to tear the façade from the surface of things and tinker with the plates and pulleys and cogs.
2 Prompts from the wings.
1 Creaking away behind the calming platitudes.
2 A heart attack, cancer, a stroke, cancer and a stroke.
1 At night, I would slip silently from beneath the sheets, sneaking barefoot down the corridors, the long arteries connecting the limbs of my family's compartmentalized home. I would seek out dark corners, where I would wait, and listen, and watch unseen behind windows and paper-thin walls.
2 A car crash, an accident, a collision at sea.
1 I worried I would be caught.
3 Worst case scenario.
2 Defeated by a constant, all-consuming anxiety.
    Drowned in the blackest depths of a desire I could not fathom.
1 I filled my mind with doubtful justifications for my night time drifting.
2 I want to go home.
3 That's all.

2 I want to go home.

3 It pops into my head all the time, you know.

2 I really want to go home.

1 You'd think it was simple, right.

2 Turn, and turn, and turn again and I'll get there.

3 I haven't the strength to haul myself through the muck of another Saturday night on Paine Street.

2 The street I first lived in. The house I first lived in. The room I first slept in.

1 My justifications wore thin.

2 The covers, worn flannel, starting to fray. The pillow stained green with troubled dreams, pliability lost over long years supporting my secret thoughts.

1 A thin as the walls through which I try to divine your world.

2 But I know the secret now.

3 That's not where home is.

1 Tuesday 7th October 2008, 12:16 a.m. [*Trying to pull back from the memories*]

3 You ever notice how it's always related to some past trauma you can't remember.

2 You'd be happier if you didn't feel the pain.

1 Same story, again and again and again.

3 Can't complain. I'd like to.

1 I can all too well imagine the blunt indictments that will spill forth from those secret pockets of time, bearing false and unfair witness to my failures.

2 I don't need to be like you.

1 I don't want to be like you.

3 Wednesday 8th October 2008, 4:16 p.m.

1 Stop. Stop. Let me start at the beginning.

2 Beneath, behind, below.

3 [*Prompts*] Once upon a time.

1 Once upon a time.

3 It was eight or ten months ago now.

2 Thursday 9th October 2008, 6:33 a.m.

1 Once upon a time I had a lot of dreams.

2 Big and dark and difficult.

3 Like a stone.

1 I lived by the water. Near enough to see the city lights. See them. Smell them. Taste them. Safer at a distance.

3 Yes, I remember.

2 Sights, sounds, tastes, smells.

3 The tick of a clock. The turn of a conversation.

1 It doesn't make a very good story.

2 Not near enough.

1 Not nearly enough.

2 I remember.

   [*Deliberately undecidable overlapping—1 remembers events from his childhood, 2 remembers events from just before the moment he disappeared, 3 oscillates between the two*]

1 One night.

2 A knock at the door.

3 it must have been the fourth or fifth time he returned to me safe, sound, but somehow different.

1 He found me nestled behind a door.

2 "Bates? Are you there Bates?"

3 He got angry. Startled, I think, by the way I caught his gaze. Clung to his gaze, as if trying to draw the memories from the deepest recesses of his soul.

2 A deep voice. Male.

3 Dishevelled brows dart together, bringing a brief flicker of life to his barren, ageless fact.

1 He asked the questions and gave the answers.

2 There? Yes. But not for much longer.

3 "A drink. A drink of water. Only a drink of water."

2 I hoped—feared—the revelation to come.

3 But the eyes that stared back at me stayed blank.

2 "Are you there? Are you there?"

3 There? Yes, but not for much longer.

1 Please don't come any closer.

2 The word were longer and longer in coming.

3 A stringy breath, a single bead of sweat snaking its way down the neck of his dressing gown, the only sign that he was even alive.

2 As the silences built, and built, I started to worry again.

3 His body hidden beneath heavy folds of flannel, it was only when I heard the metallic slap-scrape of his feet hitting the wooden floor that I realised he was moving towards me.

1 Go back to bed.

3 [*Almost simultaneously*] Go back to bed.

2 But I hear something more.

3 Something behind the silence.

2 Something in the back of his mind, taking up all his attention.

1 Noise, pain, cold, discomfort.

3 The soft click of a door finding its latches, and I was left squinting at a thin square of light around a solid barrier, hoping the sheer force of my scrunched up will could narrow my gaze long enough to get through.

2 The door stayed shut after that.

1 Or maybe I only remember it that way.

3 The door stayed shut, but I never forgot that scared, closed look I saw on his face. I know, then, there was a secret hidden in what I had seen.

2 A secret I could not remember or imagine.

1 Wednesday 5th November 2008, 7:35 a.m.

3 What? [*Roused from the rememberings*]

2 Wednesday 5th November 2008, 1:29 p.m.

1 [*Overlaps*] Wednesday 5th November 2008, 11:40 p.m.

3 He turns to meet my gaze. Smiles.

1 Please. I need you to take this seriously.

2 I told you a story once.

1 I think … I think I saw myself in you.

3 Not a stranger. A student. A student of mine, working here now.

2 I don't know if you remember.

1 I heard your name, and it called to me.

3 It was a long time ago now.

2 A lifetime ago.

3 Am I supposed to smile back?

1 I didn't mean it to be this way.

2 Short, sharp.

1 I thought I was doing the right thing.

2 Sometimes less words say more

3 Just because I can't tell you everything doesn't mean I don't tell you the important things.

2 Its what is between the words that counts.

3 Just because I don't tell you all the time doesn't mean I don't tell you when it is important.

1 I wasn't trying to get away from you.

3 I told you when it was important.

1 I never thought badly of you.

2 Lies.

1 I thought I was doing the right thing.

2 It's not worth getting emotionally involved.

1 Lies in answer to a question never really asked.

3 Most of the time, you didn't need to know. You didn't need to know, and you didn't want to know.

2 It's only a problem when you get emotionally involved.

3 Wednesday 12th November 2008, 9:25 p.m.

1 I was more careful after that. [*Remembering again*]

2 I would wait until morning before sneaking through those corridors, confident he would never catch me in daylight.

3 It all seemed so different.

2 The echoes, sounds and smells of the small cluttered rooms a false reminder.

3 Throwing me off the scent of what went on there.

1 I would close my eyes. I would close my eyes, and cup my hands over my temples, and try to recapture the moment.

3 Try to remember.

1 To imagine the secrets I had managed to miss in that shining square of light.

2 [*Almost simultaneously*] To imagine the secrets I had managed to miss in that shining square of light.

1 I would collect things.

3 If you can remember.

1 Little things.

3 The tick of a clock, a taste, or a smell.

1 Brown-tinged teaspoons still smelling sharply of bergamot.

2 Cardboard boxes, crumpled in the bin.

1 Bits of black hair, shiny, snaking their way across the carpet.

2 Needles and pins and pieces of tread from newly mended cloths.

1 Broken glass, refracting a dozen indefinable images from its tabled surface.

2 Glasses. Keys. Letters. Books. A lot of books.

3 Tissues.

2 Torn bits of tissue and bandages.

3 Then your mind is at rest.

2 Streaks or floating clouds of grey, flashes of light, patches of red, blue, green, yellow.

3 Your mind is at rest, and you'll see a perfect black when your eyes are closed and covered.

1 I hid them all away. I hid them all away in plastic bags in an old leather satchel beneath my bed, labelled with a day, and date, and time, and cryptic little notes confirming a significant I could not find words for.

2 Tuesday 18th November 2008, 5:01 a.m.

3 Patients assume I'm knowledgeable in my area.

1 I just don't understand what's wrong with them.

2 I'm always talking myself up.

3 A professional. Clear. Concise, helpful and informative.

2 I'm always catching myself up.

3 To make it as a doctor you have to be dedicated. Understanding. Compassionate.

1 It's as thought I've done something to them.

2 It never really exhausts me, you know.

1 I've never seen such energy for revenge.

2 Never enough to drown out all those voices and forget, just forget.

1 They take pleasure in it, that's why.

2 Prepared to argue the difficult cases before whichever registrar, or committee, or bureaucrat can make the cogs of the medical machine turn.

1 They make the cogs of the medical machine turn.

2 I want to dance. I want to sing. I want to speak.

3 Saturday 22nd November 2008, 11:59 a.m.

1 Midnight.

2 Saturday.

3 Again.

1 He presented with a significant history.

2 Muscle fatigue, malaise, headaches, nausea, numbness, night sweats, insomnia.

1 A lengthy list of complaints. Or so he claimed. So they all claim. Such cases could be multiplied indefinitely.

3 12 days. 14 days. 20 days.

1 The time-frame is ill defined.

2 It sneaks up on you.

3 I counter his superficial arguments with some facts of my own.

2 I tell myself it's nothing, in the hope I'll stop thinking about it.

1 There are marked abnormalities present. It suggests the presence of systemic involvement.

3 A smile, a blink, so I can't see behind his eyes. The conversation is over.

1 It's too soon to consider invasive measures. When the time comes, all the relevant factors will, of course, be taken into account.

2 Stare into the light long enough and you'll see the dark.

1 Friday 21st November 2008, 10:43 p.m.

3 Have you worked it out yet?

1 Fragments of what I wrote flash through my mind. [*Losing his equilibrium*]

2 It's taken longer than I thought, but I understand it all now. No doubt about that.

1 Everything I've ever said. Everything I've ever done.

2 Let me see if I can make sense of it for you.

1 I've deteriorated a lot lately. I can't do things for myself.

3 Might die.

2 It's quite obvious.

1 After two months waiting, watching, wanting, I should know.

2 I should know.

3 I don't know.

1 It's pretty serious.

3 A heart attack, cancer, a stroke, cancer combined with a stroke.

2 It's not cancer.

3 A car crash, an accident, a collision at sea.

1 It's an ugly situation

2 It's an ugly scene

3 I can't make the words say what I mean.

1 I grind my teeth, gnash my lips, bite my tongue. Loops of dull heat hook their way under my limbs. Little bits of my drift away.

2 I feel great. It's like I'm high. It's like nothing I've ever felt before.

1 It's not a pleasant feeling.

2 It's not an unpleasant feeling.

1 It's like I'm not myself.

2 I'm no longer myself.

1 It feels like the floor is starting to shrink beneath me, the boards drawing

back from their runners, sharp edges coming closer and closer, until I'm balanced precariously on a single plank running the length of the room.

3 We're stuck on this tightrope together, centrestage.

2 Just one step.

1 I'm acutely conscious of how protracted my steps must seem.

3 Just one more step.

1 Am I even moving?

2 I can go forwards.

3 I can go backwards.

1 But I can't go any other way. Not anymore.

3 One step. Just one more step.

1 I have to resist the temptation to run. I have to resist the temptation to turn my head, track their eyes, take everything in.

2 The mind is not a perfect mechanism.

3 I know—I think I have always known—that I will never be fast enough.

2 I will never catch the constant imperceptible signals that swirl around me, accusing me in the most unfriendly way.

3 Seeing me. Smiling at me. Judging me.

1 Memories cascading, leaving me cold.

3 Labelling me with a guilt I will never own.

2 But there's another space in this space.

1 Another time in this time.

3 Another self in this self.

2 My mind wanders.

1 There is no off switch.

3 I can stop the show, shut of the lights, but where does that leave me.

1 I can't stop seeing it. I can't stop hearing it.

2 [*Almost simultaneously*] I can't stop seeing it, I can't stop hearing it.

3 They're telling me pieces of my own past.

1 How did I come here.

2 His wasn't an auspicious entry into the world.

3 He didn't get on well with his father.

2 He didn't get on well with his mother.

3 He didn't get on well with his wife.

1 Like a past life coming back to me, in the blink of an eye.

3 You must remember.

2 Things happen. I know that. Things happen.

1 I remember…

2 But if you keep it all inside, I can't help you.

3 I remember the glint of steel.

1 It brings me back to myself.

2 Tuesday 25th November 2008, 5:17 a.m.

3 [*Overlaps*] Tuesday 25th November 2009 8:48 p.m.

2 I was more careful after that.

3 [*Simultaneously*] I was more careful after that.

2 I sat on the floor, alone at last.

1 Alone, still, and almost silent.

2 I started picking my way through the boxes and bills and papers and photos and trinkets.

1 The detritus of a life.

3 A life no longer my own.

1 All around me.

3 Bound and bundled together.

1 In hiding.

3 Seconds ticked into minutes, and minutes ticked into hours.

2 I steeled myself to my tasks.

3 Slowly, delicately, deliberately.

2 I broke the corpse apart, piece by weight piece, fingers trembling and the feel of jaundiced innards, I began to transform them, cocooning myself in comfortable piles and categories.

3 Smooth.

1 As plastic.

3 As metal.

1 As glass.

3 As bone.

2 And then, as I neared the bottom of the box I was taken aback.

3 An abrupt and sudden fear.

2 After all these years, I find myself looking into my own eyes.

1 Large, flat, and unblinking.

3 A surface for so long reflected the words and worst of me.

2 They seemed a strange little insect now, lilting slightly, legs skewed to one side, drawing back into themselves, in the dark, after a history of long and weary wear.

1 Dark.

2 Tracing the frames with my fingers, I felt their fragility, hinges creaking with the slightest urge to movement.

1 Not dead yet.

3 Not dead at all.

2 Specks of oil and grime and dust glistening in the half-light.

1 Lubricating blood just beginning to warm up.

3 A little insect longing to scratch me in my sleep.

2 The large, looping frames long since fallen out of fashion had always covered at least half my face.

1 Starting to spin a sticky web.

2 Capturing my hopes, my tears, my smiles. My all to infrequent smiles.

1 A trap.

2 How many times had I caught my own reflection.

1 How many times had I longed to scratch my way through those strong, thick shields, shattering the placid surface.

3 Not at all what it seems.

1 Not all is what it seems.

2 Longed to clear my way through with my spit and sweat and tears.

1 Turn back.

2 Turn back and look at life from the other side.

3 Again.

2 A dull plasticy thud and the prisms fold back into my hand, dark spots of blood blinding my eyes for ever.

3 My palm a forest populated by filaments piercing the surface of my skin.

1 The shady sleep-deprived eyes of a stranger stared back at me.

2 An unfamiliar smile found its way to my lips

3 Wednesday 26th November 2008, 4:15 p.m.

2 It wasn't long after that that the world behind the light-rimmed door went dark forever.

1 Wednesday 3rd December 2008, 11:36 p.m.

2 Midnight.

3 Midnight.

1 There was a point there.

3 A point.

2 [*Almost simultaneously*] A point

1 [*Almost simultaneously*] A point when things could've gone either way.

2 It wasn't the light, but the dark, that showed me the way.

1 Standing in front of the hospital. No idea how I got there. I just knew I wasn't going on that stage anymore. I wasn't even in the wings. And I wasn't ever going to be again.

2 It looked different now.

1 A maze, not just from the inside, but from the outside.

2 The medical merry-go-round, is that what they call it?

1 I used to call the tunes.

2 But it wasn't much fun.

1 Make the stage turn round its circuit.

2 It wasn't much fun at all.

1 Roads and ramps and welcoming artwork everywhere.

2 A thousand frozen faces. Smiling at me from inside a kiln-hardened moment of happiness.

1 Roads and ramps and welcoming artwork everywhere, but no way in.

2 No safe harbor beneath the eaves of this concrete monstrosity.

1 I left behind an outline of myself.

2 Saturday 7th November 2008, 12:03 a.m.

3 It was from others that I learned what came next.

2 Trivia. Trouble.

3 Trauma.

1 The detritus of a life.
2 A rock right in the middle of my stomach.
1 Warm, and hard, and hollow.
2 Weighing me down.
1 I know how it happened.
3 After an hour, two hours, three hours waiting.
1 I know how it works now.
2 Dragging me down.
1 My stories are starting to turn green.
3 It only took two minutes.
2 I'm trying not to get confused.
1 Dark, thick, green.
3 Off the tightrope. Off the tightrope and onto the cold and dirty floor.
2 It's muddy.
3 The clock is ticking.
2 It's muddy and muffled but it's getting clearer.
1 You start someplace, and by talking, and talking, and talking, you end up someplace else.
3 Won't be long til these dark green tendrils seep into every thing.
1 And that's how I knew it was over.
3 Over everything.
1 Plans got cancelled.
2 I left behind an outline of myself.
1 Tuesday 9th December 2008, 2:06 a.m.
2 [*Overlapping*] Tuesday 9th December 2008, 3:30 a.m.
3 [*Overlapping*] Wednesday 10th December 2008, 2:42 a.m.
2 [*Overlapping*] Wednesday 10th December 2008, 7:00 p.m.
1 [*Overlapping*] Thursday 11th December 2008, 4:04 p.m.
    [*The characters recount Bates' fugue days, before he was found again*]
2 I walked for hours.
1 The first drenching of a humid summer dulled the sound of leaf-litter underfoot.
2 The fickle pulse of citybound traffic underscored the rise-and-fall of a hundred human voices.
3 The inconsequential murmur of heedless conversation.
1 The city squalid, stagnant and oppressive.
3 Stripping me of every last piece of strength.
2 Waiting. Waiting for release.
1 I turned my face to the wall, took shelter in darkened buildings.
2 I ventured out only at night, into a city crowded with lights and sounds and people.
3 Stare into the light long enough and you'll see the dark.
1 This is no better than what I left behind.
2 All the walls seemed the same. All the world seemed the same.

3 Minute fragments of dirt, and dust and glass bringing tears to the eyes.

1 The midnight city became a blur. A surreal sideshow of the senses.

2 The beat of my heart, the hitch of my breath, the bright halo of colors.

1 I thought I caught sight of a familiar face, but I couldn't be sure.

3 Heavy-lidded eyes, high set ears, pursed lips. Sharp, pointed and severe.

2 Cheeks patchy and pock-marked, with that ever so slightly melted look, as though the invisible touch of once-loving fingertips was pulling them down.

1 Hands in pockets, head held low, the brows of his wandering eyes walk him my way.

2 I've been waiting for you.

3 Toujours. Toujours.

1 It's as thought he is speaking a foreign language.

3 C'est tout. C'est tout qu'il me faut.

1 I smile. I think him to smile.

3 I just don't want him to know.

2 I put on a happy face.

3 I just don't want him to know that I know.

2 Low. Rumbling.

1 He takes me by the arms. Or, rather, but the wrist. Right below the wrist.

3 Such intimacy with a stranger.

1 Tight. So I can't pull away. Not without violence, anyway.

3 Like I've never known it before.

1 In my haste to find shelter, I stumble over the curb.

2 The harsh tones of a curse escape under my breath.

3 Sharp ejaculation of frustration.

1 Teetering from a ground on high, I fall backwards. Bones discarded, crushed by the weight of a dozen layers of sweat-damp clothing. A shock of pain rushes up my spine, bringing a momentary blur in the maelstrom of sight and sound and light.

2 I see my own face.

3 A single bright spot in blackness.

1 A moment of silences as pain blots everything from my mind.

3 You don't want to get emotionally involved.

2 You'd be happier if you didn't feel the pain.

1 Huddled for a moment, hearing attuned only to the catch in my own breath, fleshy, phlegmy pops and gurgles betray the paralysing despair the night has brought.

2 I'm singing again now.

1 My mouth is overfull. Overflowing.

3 The light is changing.

1 The back of my neck is hot.

3 The time is right.

2 Right now.

3 Or never again.

2 I don't care who can see me.

1 Breath. All of me, breath.

2 I don't care who can hear me.

1 Numb. Pain. Moving in parts.

2 I don't care who can understand me. Not now that I'm singing again.

3 It's only a problem if you get emotionally involved.

2 Not now that I'm singing again.

3 No more distractions.

1 I remember.

2 I remember everything and nothing.

1 It's been waiting there behind the buzz, behind the voices, all this time.

   [*Long pause, in which we hear noise, whistling, soft but growing*]

3 Tuesday 16th December 2008, 11:00 p.m.

1 Slowly.

2 Wednesday 17th December 2008, 6:30 p.m.

3 Slowly.

1 Tuesday 18th December 2008, 7:43 p.m.

2 Slowly.

1 I woke to an alien landscape.

   [*The story circles back around to the earlier section, in which Bates found the landscape of the hospital—a maze of glass, and mirrors, wide-set walls and corridors, alien and affronting. Bates' account of being "found" begins again*]

2 Lines and loops and caverns of flesh crowd the false dawn from my mind, their consistency broken by momentary flashes of color branded across the surface.

3 *[Laughs]*

1 A hand lightly tugging my blinking face up from a tangled mess of spit and limbs and sheets.

3 For a moment, I cherish the unfamiliar sensation.

2 Completeness.

3 Connection.

2 With a stranger who'll never know my name.

3 But only for a moment.

1 Words from the wings.

3 Good friend.

2 Dear friend.

3 Best friend.

2 Beloved Friend.

3 Honest friend.

2 I'm pleased to tell you you have been discovered to be a victim.

1 He wants me to believe him. He wants me to believe in him.

3 He's been through the same thing before. Similar, anyway. But he doesn't
   hear what I say.
2 It won't do. You deserve some sort of compensation.
1 Again, the test.
2 It's not too much to ask.
3 Nothing, in fact. Nothing at all.
1 His fingers like little insect, crawling over my flesh.
2 All right, then, let's take a look at what we've got here.
1 Eyes raised, papers ruffled, he can't even meet my eyes.
3 Glasses. Keys. Teacup. Letters. Books. A lot of books.
2 Does that mean anything to you?
3 The limiting mindset of medical orthodoxy leaves him trapped in the
   beam of his own unbroken sight, a shallow catalogue of cut-and-dried
   complaints.
1 A heart attack, cancer, a stroke, cancer combined with a stroke.
2 Things that ought to be private, but aren't.
3 All lit up and decorated by his dull-witted langue to look like the final face
   of truth.
1 A car crash, an accident, a collision at sea.
2 I see.
1 A sea of hands.
2 Slowly turning green.
3 He's blind. He can't see past what he can see.
1 A sea of hands lifting me, and I'm off my feet and flying.
3 He won't breach the bounds of what is palpable, perceptible and
   immediate. He won't push past the mass of shapes and colors and sounds
   he mistakes for progress into the dense heart of things, where he might
   discover the secret spaces hidden inside his tightly wrought catalogue,
   spaces where sight, and memory and imagination meet, betraying the
   hidden depth of things.
2 I need to choose my words wisely.
1 I think they were trying to help me.
2 But the mind is not a perfect mechanism.
1 It hurts me.
3 I waste my breath blaming him for the all-too-human maladjustments to
   which his sight is subject.
2 After all. It has taken an insight—far more exacting than my own infantile
   musings on stolen collections might every have hoped to be—to find my
   way into the heart of things.
1 Saturday 20th December 2008, 8:33 p.m.
2 Again.
3 Saturday.
1 Again, the test.
2 The machine.

1 It's not a merry-go-round but a machine.

2 It doesn't look like much—bolts and globes and bits of glass.

3 But when you see it from within, you understand.

1 Whatever it is, it has taken me on quite a ride.

2 For absolute accuracy, the head of the subject should be held immobile. The only equipment wanted is an ordinary electric globe. And a mirror which moves back and forth so that it can be brought closer to the eye.

  The heat is not enough to interfere with the experiment.

  It is, in fact, essential—the sizzling glare of an artificial sun pulls the images to the surface, to be captured, photographed, measured and catalogued.

  When you understand what the images mean, it not longer bothers you.

  It begins with lines, spots, specks and bubbles, with flashes, and with little squares of light. It's the square lights that are important. Squares passing slowly, erratically, across the darkened surface of the lens, ill-defined at first. But if you wait, if you get beyond the tears, and track what lies beyond those shifting squares of light as the move from left, to right, to centre, you will see.

3 Central fixation.

1 [*Almost simultaneously*] Central fixation.

3 The machine magnifies the image.

2 A snapshot of what the eye has seen.

1 A mirror, a reflection of a memory, fragmented and intensified.

3 Everything the eye has missed.

1 Stare into the light long enough and you'll see the dark.

2 At first such a vision may come only in flashes.

1 Glasses. Keys. Teacup. Letters. Books. A lot of books.

3 Papers flying behind a fast-moving car.

2 An impenetrable fog.

1 A ditch in absolute darkness.

3 Small feet struggling to find purchase.

1 A face looming over me.

2 Misunderstanding.

3 Mistrust.

1 Fear at the fact that he knows me better than I know myself.

3 Fear clouding out thought and confusion.

1 It's not confusion. It's more than that.

1 Saturday 20th December 2008, 8:33 p.m.

3 Things don't always end well of course.

2 The mind is not a perfect mechanism. Mistakes must be expected.

1 Saturday 27th December 2008, 12:36 a.m.

3 You say he overreacts. Overreaches the bounds of his role?

2 I am deaf, and dumb, and blind to their accusations.

1 I wasn't admitted under my own name.

3 Obviously, his methods have never been what we might call orthodox.

1 Unknown male. Another case for the missing person's unit.

2 What you know of me is all lies. What you know of my methods is all lies.

1 You don't to end with a story.

3 You don't want to imagine or guess at the truth.

2 I deny the infectious moralising to which orthodox medicine is subject.

1 Words are not all there is.

2 My judgments are grounded in long exposure to the evidence, long grappling with the given bounds of experience.

3 Or so I used to think.

2 I test. I discover. I demonstrate the facts.

1 Or so I used to think.

2 I don't care what resentments they harbour.
I don't care what allegations they level against me.

1 I used to think I'd agree with whatever they'd say.

2 A moment ago, a lifetime ago, I sat alone, hand working against the clock.

3 But it's not trauma. It's not confusion. It's more than that.

1 I won't lie. I won't deceive. I won't disguise the truth.

2 I hit the pieces in secret places. A bolt here. A bulb there. A bunch of broken tubes and wires.

1 But I know better now.

3 [*Almost simultaneously*] I know better now.

2 A puzzle that can never be put together again.

1 Telling lies is bad for the eyes.

2 I won't blind my patients for the sake of orthodoxy.

1 A knock at the door.

2 Down by the surgery where my façade had first begun to fail.

3 Obviously, then, he overreacts.

2 I knew, then, that I had torn it all apart none too soon.

3 The fact is, except in rare cases, man is not a reasoning being.

1 Slipping into the stairwell, I caught sight of my reflection in the shining class and chrome surfaces.

3 He is dominated by authority.

1 A maze. A maze of sterile white walls, and windows, and glass.

3 And when the facts are not in accord with the view imposed by authority, so much the worse for the facts, I say.

1 The shady, sleep-deprived eyes of a horde of strangers staring back at me.

2 Daring me to turn. Daring me to face my accusers.

1 Another knock, more distant this time.

> A deep voice. Male.
> "Are you there, Bates? Are you there?"
> There.
> Yes.
> But not for long.

2 Midnight. Saturday midnight.

1 I laid out my old leather satchel in a corner of the stairwell, fumbling briefly with the sweat-stained clasp that bound the contents together.

2 I won't be confused by wrong thoughts.

3 Flashes of movement. Faces hidden behind every corner.

1 Bills, and papers, and photos and trinkets, all tied up in plastic bags, beginning to yellow and decay.

3 Pain, fever, discomfort from heat or cold, depression, anxiety.

2 It's getting louder again.

3 TV. CD. DVD.

1 OCD.

2 Louder and more difficult to hear.

1 A hardened, heartless shell my will cannot shift.

3 We always see imperfectly when we hear a loud, unexpected noise.

2 The eye does what the mind desires.

1 Black. A perfectly black period.

3 As a rule, it's the easiest color to remember.

1 It hurts.

3 It helps.

2 Wrong thoughts, whittling away my chances.

1 A single sheet of paper found its way to the floor.

3 Alone, at last, and it isn't so bad.

2 I will concentrate, instead, on the measured cycles of my own breath.

3 It's all that is needed.

1 Past the wide-set walls and doors, past the whirring machines, the broken bodes, the bright lights, the burning ignorance.

2 I know the way the puzzle works now.

3 Windows into the dark.

1 I don't need to hold on to each piece safe in its clear plastic gage.

2 I don't need to turn my head to see.

1 [*Overlaps*] I don't need to be like you.

2 [*Overlaps*] I don't want to be like you.

3 I'm not confused.

1 I will concentrate on the door, the dark black mouth—close now—waiting to draw me into its warm, murmuring anonymity.

2 Let them make what they will of what is left behind.

1 When the unrelenting glare of light and sound and life starts to close in, it is the memory of black that puts your mind at rest.

3 If you can close your eyes, and remember this perfectly realised black, you can clear your mind of the cacophonous assaults. Calmed by a central fixation.

1 You can remember.

3 Sights, sounds, smells and tastes.

1 Distraction

2 The tick of a clock, the turn of a conversation.

1 No longer startles me.

3 You can remember one thing, that one thing, better than all others.

1 You can't ever tell.

3 You can open your mind—to time, to memory, to imagination. You can hold the image firm, and you can see.

1 Sunday 4th January 2009, 12:07 a.m.

2 Like a stranger holding me

3 Firm.

2 Comforting.

3 The horizon of an unwanted future.

1 No confusion here.

3 It's like nothing you've ever known.

2 I breathe.

3 I believe.

1 And I leave behind but an outline of myself.

End of play.

The Plague Plays

Notes from a Pandemic in Progress

BRADLEY CHERNA

The process of collecting and editing this anthology took just shy of two years; six weeks before we handed the manuscript to the publisher, the U.S. began responding to the growing threat of the novel coronavirus. COVID-19 has affected every person in our country and most people around the world. It is one of those disasters in which just speaking about it factually sounds very much like hyperbole or dystopian science fiction.

While there is nothing in the human experience that cannot be further complicated through the lens of disability, disasters and crises tend to be particularly effective at highlighting challenges. As we entered these final weeks of editing while sheltered in our home offices, we knew we could not go to print without addressing this phenomenon. How long, after all, will it be before we can forget that, when the shutdown came, so many of our fellow citizens argued against safety measures, casually claiming that it was "only" the elderly and those with compromised immune systems that were affected?

New York playwright and theatre artist Bradley Cherna was, at that point, already represented in this collection. Their play, *Modern Medicine [for amateurs]*, a phenomenologically rich and poetically rendered meditation on the serpentine linguistics of the medical world, occupied a proud spot among the other selections. When we saw, however, the in-progress play cycle Bradley was posting online, we knew we had to make a change. *The Plague Plays: Notes from a Pandemic in Progress* offers desperate vulnerability juxtaposed against a performatively sparse form. It is the cacophony of anxiety in the stillness of isolation; the labored breathing of a patient in a plain white mask; the messes of disease in the sterile hospital. It is, in short, an artistic expression which we found captured the moment in a way no essay could.

We approached Bradley about the last-minute switch, and they graciously agreed. As we hand this collection off to our publisher, this play cycle is still in progress, since the emergency is still in progress. One day—likely very soon—there will be an abundance of scholarship and art exploring COVID-19 through a lens of Critical Disability Studies and Disability activism. There have been some notable voices claiming we should not create art in this moment—we are too "close" to it, it is too immediate. As this work points out, a play, quilt, or song written in remembrance of a deadly crisis is lovely and important but, by definition, is voiced entirely by survivors. Those saying to wait clearly assume they will still be here when it is over; not all of us who are immunocompromised are quite as confident. For now, the crisis is ongoing, and so is Bradley Cherna's art.

—John Michael Sefel

The Plague Plays: Notes from a Pandemic in Progress

Illness is the night-side of life, a more onerous citizenship. Everyone who is born holds dual citizenship, in the kingdom of the well and in the kingdom of the sick. Although we all prefer to use only the good passport, sooner or later each of us is obliged, at least for a spell, to identify ourselves as citizens of that other place.
—Susan Sontag, *Illness as Metaphor* (1978)

Author's Note: On the following pages are ten collected and connected plays, composed in various locations in Manhattan during the early days of the COVID-19 pandemic's rapid expansion in the United States, amid New York City becoming the American epicenter of the pandemic. They were originally published across various social media platforms, allowing them to be written and shared with the same immediacy as the unfolding crisis. Play #6 is verbatim, built from messages received in response to calls for help on social media. This writing effort continues past these 10 plays, and I invite you to make these plague plays your own. The question of performance is implicit in this undertaking. It is a question this anthology is already engaged in, one which the playwrights represented in this collection might be uniquely ready to answer.

All dialogue takes place from a distance—whether that's six feet or over the phone or over social media or via Zoom.

CAST OF CHARACTERS:
There is a character named "Little Red"; that's me.
Additional characters include "Mother," "Father," and many others.
In Play #6 there are many characters named "You," although each one is distinguished from the other by a number or note of some kind; those are all of you. #6 is a verbatim work, authored by all of you. Your words were enormous hands reaching out from the social distance from one to another. Thank you.

With love and gratitude—B.C.

The Plague Plays: Notes from a Pandemic in Progress © Bradley Cherna, all rights reserved.

* * *

1:

Little Red

Mom, I'm very immunocompromised, have an autoimmune disease, and am therefore especially vulnerable. I share an apartment with three room-mates whose movements I can't control. One of them is an essential worker for the city, and his girlfriend works in the morgue. My immune system will be further suppressed after I get my biologic infusion tomorrow. I want to stay safe. My doctor doesn't want me even going to work or school. I can work and study remotely. I don't know what to do. I want to get ahead of the curve. Can I come stay with you?

Mother

I need to think about what's best for my business!

Little Red

I'm your son.

Mother

You're disrespectful!

Little Red

They just declared a state of emergency.

Mother

I have to get my mail!

Little Red

You should wipe down surfaces your students use after they come to study at your home.

Mother

Don't tell me what to do! You're abusive! It will ruin the leather! How dare you! You can't stay here, because you tell me what to do! I have to think about how my business is going to survive!

{end of play}

2:

Little Red

I've noticed you all seem happy to chat about your MFA applications, grant applications, festival applications, Anne Bogart, and hair dye, but you've gone radio silent ever since I brought up this anxiety I have about my vulnerability in the coming days due to being immunocompromised, morbidly obese, and not having the resources to successfully self-isolate in place if it comes to that.

Other Characters

{end of play}

3:

Little Red
   It's official. It's a pandemic now. It's time to stay home and keep safe. Please let me help in whatever way I can.

Father
   Can't talk now. Watching my fav TV show.

   {end of play}

4:

Little Red (over phone)
   I'm sleeping in my office, but no one knows. I don't know if I can shelter here for a week, let alone the month, let alone months.

Mother
   No one knows what will be.

   {end of play}

5:

Little Red
   I think I'm sick.

Friend
   You think it's a flare-up?

Little Red
   I think it's COVID-19.

Friend
   You think it's a flare-up?

Little Red
   Got exposed.

Friend
   Not close, though?

Little Red
   The sick beds aren't separated from the COVID-positive beds. No more isolation or containment plans in place in any of the city hospitals. The staff use the same single-use personal protective equipment every shift. Nurses take their PPE home and back. They're working triples. It is a place of exposure.

Friend
   Can you change your diet?

   {end of play}

6:

Little Red
   I'm in mandatory self-isolation in a friend's studio on the Upper West Side due to being immunocompromised. There's only a minifridge, so I ordered a freezer—but I'm short on foods I can store long-term (i.e., frozen, non-perishable, et cetera). I have to stop sneaking out in the middle of the night to the pharmacy, waiting for them to open the overnight shipments, loitering in the hope of cleaning products. I can't keep risking my life for Lysol. All of the grocery delivery services I know of are completely booked. I need a thermometer. I need an oximeter. I need my medications. I wish I could go out, but I can't anymore. Can anyone help?

You 1
   Here's a grocery store that delivers.

You 2
   Try Invisible Hands!

You 1
   I'll send you screenshots to walk you through it.

Invisible Hands
   Hi, this is—. I received your request through Invisible Hands and will be getting you your stuff within the next hour or so.

You 3
   I'm so sorry you're dealing with this. People are creating groups on Facebook to help with runs for people in your situation.

You 4
   Where in NYC are you? Will think on if I know anyone.

You 5
   (Tags Friend.) I remember you posting about freelancer friends looking for tasks—if anyone is in NYC

You 6
   I got you bb

You 7
   (Tags Friend) do you know anyone available on the UWS?

You 4
   Just messaged you someone!

You 8
   Emailed you.

You Text
   How are you feeling?

You 9
Lemme know if you need help with groceries. I know people up there.

You 10
Good luck, love.

You on the side
Side-note: keep checking Amazon Prime Whole Foods. Delivery windows open.

You 11
Check out the Nextdoor App. There is a section just for this for neighbors to help neighbors!

You 12
I can go tomorrow and find for you. A lot of the smaller stores seem to have stock. I'm happy to go tomorrow to shop for you

You 13
Hey Little Red! I'm not around the UWS, but I'll be checking on a friend's apartment either tomorrow or Sunday and can pick up whatever you need and bring it by. As long as I'm healthy, I'd be happy to help out.

You 14
How can we get you food? I only know two people in NYC and jus asked them.

You 8
I have a delivery slot Monday morning … Let me know if you'd like me to add stuff to my order for you.

You 15
I saw your post.

You 16
Little Red, just saw your Insta.

You 15
Do you need food?

You 16
We can bring things to you tomorrow.

You 15
I can have food delivered to you.

You 16
Are you ok for tonight?

You 15
Please remember that I am here.

Invisible Hands
I see that you want frozen meals. How many and what type?

You 17
Also try Imperfect Produce.

You 18
We are in the same situation and used Whole Foods and Fresh Direct.

You 17
They deliver to your door and have fresh food.

You 18
Be strong.

You 19
I'm part of a volunteer organization. I'm in Brooklyn, but they're city-wide.

You 20
Oh dear.

You 19
Invisible Hands Deliver dot com.

You 20
If I were there I would.

You 22
Sorry we are so far.

You 21
Uber Eats might be helpful in the meanwhile.

You 25
Where on the UWS?

You 22
I am going to see if any of my people are in your neighborhood.

You 23
I'm also immunocompromised (twins!) or else I'd totally go for you!

You 26
I subscribe to Dinnerly and I should be able to send you a free referral box. Let me know!!

You 20
I wish you all my love.

You 24
Love you wish I were there.

You 22
Stay safe.

You 26
Stay safe.

You 4

Here's the number of my friend who lives nearby and is happy to get stuff for you.

You 27

What do you need at the store?

You 33

Like!

You 27

Send me a list and I'll go shopping for you.

You 28

Just let us know what we can bring.

You 30

954-349-****

You 34

Like!

You 29

If you are hungry let me know.

You 35

Love

You 39

If you need help in the coming weeks, shoot me a DM.

You 31

Download the app Mercado.

You 36

Like!

You 39

Have a car and can drop off food.

You 30

Call that number!

You 37

Love

You 32

Here's a coupon!

You 40

Be safe

You 38

Love

You 41
  Like!

You 42
  Love

You 43
  Like!

You 44
  Calling you

You 45
  Here for you

You 46
  Love

You 24-46
  Love

You 1-23
  Like

You 47
  Love

You 48
  Like

All
  Love.

    {end of play}

7:

Little Red
  I can't cook because there's a gas leak.

Friend 2
  What are you going to do for food?

Little Red
  I've got a microwave and microwaveable soup.

Friend 2
  You can't stay in a place with a gas leak.

Little Red
  I can't self-isolate at home if my roommate's an essential worker.

Friend 2
You need to tell the building.

Little Red
I don't want them to know I'm here.

Friend 2
Why would they care?

Little Red
They're not letting anyone in the building besides tenants. I'm lucky I sheltered here early. But I'm somewhat in-hiding.

Friend 2
You need to tell the super. It's no shelter if you can't eat, and you're in danger because of a gas leak, which could kill you.

Little Red
Fine.
(*To the* SUPERINTENDENT) I think there's a gas leak.

Superintendent
Let me check.

   (*He checks.*)

No gas leak.

   (*Time passes.*)

Little Red
I still smell gas.

Friend 3
You need to get out of there.

Little Red
I just won't use the oven or go near the kitchen.

Friend 3
You need to tell the building.

Little Red
What if they evict me?

Friend 3
Let's cross that bridge when we get to it.

Little Red
Fine.
(*To the* SUPERINTENDENT) I really think there's a gas leak. Can you check again?

Superintendent
  No problem.
    (SUPERINTENDENT *checks.*)
  No gas leak.
    (LITTLE RED *calls 911.*)

Little Red
  I think there's a gas leak.
    (*The* FIRE DEPARTMENT *arrives.*)
  Do you have masks? I'm immunocompromised.

Fire Department
  No. We just need to get in your apartment.

Little Red
  Okay. I'll hide by the window.

Fire Department
  There's a gas leak.

Little Red
  I didn't know what to do.

Fire Department
  You did the right thing by calling.
    (*The* UTILITY WORKER *arrives.*)

Utility Worker
  Excuse me, I have to enter your apartment.

Little Red
  I'm self-isolating.

Utility Worker
  I have to fix your gas leak.

Little Red
  Where do I go?

Superintendent
  It's going to take at least five days for us to break open the wall, pull out the pipes, install new pipes, get them approved, rebuild the wall, paint, and get the approval from the city and then the gas company. We're gonna have to let all these workers into your apartment every day.

Little Red
  Okay. I guess I have to go.

Superintendent
  Yeah. I'll call you to update you when we're done so you know when you can come back.

Little Red
Thanks. (*To self.*) I don't know what to do.

Friend 4
Stay in my place. I left town and went home to Florida after I came back from Europe with coronavirus. It's empty. It's been a few weeks so there's no danger anymore. My ex has the keys.

Little Red
You're amazing. Thank you.

Friend 4
I want you to be safe!

Little Red
The apartment's perfect.

Friend 4
Good. I love you.

Little Red
It should only take five days.

Friend 4
No worries.
  (*Five days pass. The* SUPERINTENDENT *calls.*)

Superintendent
It's gonna take another day.

Little Red
Okay.

Superintendent
I'll call you tomorrow to update you.

Little Red
(*To* FRIEND 4) Can I stay another day?

Friend 4
Sure.
  (*A day passes. The* SUPERINTENDENT *calls.*)

Superintendent
It's gonna take another week.

Little Red
Okay.

Superintendent
I'll call you in a week to update you.

Little Red
(*To* FRIEND 4) Can I stay another week?

Friend 4
   Of course. Do you want to just stay there for the next few months? I'm not
sure when I'm ever going to come back.

Little Red
   I'll think about it.

      (*A week passes. The* SUPERINTENDENT *calls.*)

Superintendent
   It's gonna take another day.

Little Red
   Okay.

Superintendent
   I'll call you tomorrow to update you.

Little Red
   (*To* FRIEND 4) Can I stay another day?

Friend 4
   No.

Little Red
   What happened?

Friend 4
   I just got this from my super.

Superintendent 2
   Hello. It has come to our attention that you are not in the apartment and
that there is someone else staying there. We can't have non-tenants occupying
our building, as per your lease. Please take care of this ASAP. I have many
tenants complaining.

Friend 4
   I'm sorry. I can't lose my lease.

Little Red
   I know. I'm sorry.

Friend 4
   Don't be sorry.

Little Red
   I didn't mean to—

Friend 4
   Can I pay for your Uber?

Little Red
   (*To* SUPERINTENDENT) I have to come back today.

Superintendent
  We're still working on the gas.

Little Red
  There's nothing else I can do.

Superintendent
  We'll try to keep six feet from you.

Little Red
  Sounds like a plan.

Superintendent
  See you—

    (LITTLE RED *coughs.*)

You 1–48
  Stay at home!
    {end of play}

8:

Professor 1
  Don't move.

Professor 2
  Don't speak.

Professor 3
  Don't make a sound.

Visiting Artist
  Wait.

Professor 1
  The last thing the world needs right now is self-expression.

Professor 2
  All you can do is tap on the walls of your cell.

Professor 3
  This is not the time.

Professor 1, 2, and 3
  Wait.
    (*YOU 7 dies.*)

Professor 1, 2, and 3
  Wait.
    (*YOU 48 dies.*)

ALL Except the Dead and Little Red

Wait.

(*YOU 2 dies. YOU ON THE SIDE dies. YOU 11–29 die.*)

{end of play}

9:

(ALL *cheer while banging on pots and pans.*)

{end of play}

10:

(*The* FIELD SCOUT *finds* SOMEONE WHO SURVIVED.)

Field Scout
Okay!

Playwright
We're here to make a play about pandemic.

Director
What do you all have to say?

Assistant Director
Do you want to patch a quilt?

Producer
Collab on a song with your favorite musician?

Director
Talk.

Producer
About what it was like.

Playwright
To survive,
(*SOMEONE 1, 2, and 3 enter.*)

Someone 1
Hi! I'm here to do a pandemic play, too.

Director, Producer, Assistant Director, Playwright, Field Scout, Sound Mixer, and *Director of Photography*
We're not doing a pandemic play.

Someone 3
Okay.
(*SOMEONE 1, 2, and 3 leave. The crew speaks to* SOMEONE WHO SURVIVED.)

Producer
So, back to the pandemic play!

Director
    What was

Assistant Director
    It like

Playwright
    For you?

Sound Mixer
    Can we get a mic check? You know, testing, testing—

You
    Testing, one, two, three.

Sound Mixer
    Okay!

Director
    If you can make sure to answer the questions in the first-person, like—

Producer
    "I lost {blank} in the pandemic."

Assistant Director
    "The pandemic affected me by {blank}"

Playwright
    "I {blank} pandemic."

Director
    That'd be great. All right … Final touches. Camera ready?

Director of Photography
    Camera ready.

Sound Mixer
    Roll sound.

Assistant Director
    Pandemic Play 1, Take 1.

Producer
    Set.

Director
    It's time
    to tell
    the true
    story.

        (SOMEONE WHO SURVIVED *opens their mouth to speak.*)

    {end}

End of play.

Still Standing

Anita Hollander

When Marna Michele, who uses a motorized wheelchair due to arthrogryposis, wheeled before *American Idol* judges Lionel Ritchie, Luke Bryant, and Katy Perry, they promised her they would critique her performance as thoroughly as they would any other auditioning singer's.[1] Their attempt to be egalitarian could also be considered a moment of inspiration porn, as they had never reassured an able-bodied contestant that their critiques would be unbiased by the contestant's perceived helplessness. Their attempts to normalize Michele's presence only revealed how unexpected it was to them. Once she was onstage, however, they realized they couldn't treat Michele like any other contestant. They would have to treat her like any other skilled singer who was an exceptionally dynamic performer. They expected to be inspired by Michele, but they were impressed by her instead.

Michele complicated the performer/audience dynamic, or in this case, the performer/judge dynamic, as soon as she wheeled onstage. Any performer who takes a stage has presumably done so in order to communicate an idea to an audience, even if he/she/they does not address that audience directly. An audience watching a performer with a visible or perceived condition onstage must assume that even a moment that could be perceived as inspiration porn has been intentionally created by the performer, though perhaps in consultation with co-performers, a choreographer, a playwright, or a director. The most important difference between conforming to the performance model of disability in the real world and intentionally performing one's disability onstage, then, is that only the latter allows the performer an opportunity to make deliberate physical and vocal choices that will affect how his/her/their condition will be perceived by an audience that has been specifically invited to witness those choices.

Along with actor Nabil Shaban, the late Richard Tomlinson co-founded the Graeae Theatre Company, England's first disabled theatre company, in 1981. Tomlinson says a performer with a disability who is performing for a (mostly) able-bodied audience is reversing the power dynamic of the able-bodied/disabled binary in the real world.[2] Ablebodiedness is privileged in the real world. Onstage, by contrast, a performer has authority over his/her/their audience, even if the performer has a visible or perceived condition, and the audience members are primarily able-bodied. Of course, a performer cannot entirely control the audience's perception, but the performer can use physicality and vocal choices to frame how the audience evaluates him/her/them. Therefore, a performer who is performing his/her/their disability onstage can affect the audience's evaluation by re-presenting his/her/their disability.

A performer onstage who is embodying a moment that could be perceived as inspiration porn, for example, also uses specific physical and vocal choices to show an audience how to interpret that moment. An audience member will also witness scenes before and after that moment, giving their interpretation more complexity than it would have otherwise. Unlike someone embodying the performance model of disability in the real world, someone who is performing onstage is deliberately creating an interaction with an audience, through which that audience can be encouraged to evaluate the performer on his/her/their own terms.

Moments of inspiration porn in the real world are never experienced from the perspective of a person with a disability. Instead, they are evaluated based on how a person with a disability makes the able-bodied people who observe him/her/them feel. Anita Hollander's *Still Standing* is a celebration, not an inspiration. Through her onstage persona, Hollander is celebrating her own physical and emotional resilience. She invites able-bodied people, both in the play and in the audience, to celebrate with her; when Hollander tells her daughter that her mommy is a mermaid, she is teaching her daughter to celebrate her mother as she is, instead of solely focusing on how she overcomes her physical difference. Hollander invites an audience to experience moments that could be perceived as inspiration porn from her physical and emotional perspective instead of its own. More importantly, she reveals that confining someone to the role of "inspiration" is reductive, as it denies that person the opportunity to admit frailty or failure. In the play, Anita's friend, Michael, considers her his inspiration. Because he does not see her physical and emotional struggles as she strives to be a reliable role model for him, he judges himself too harshly in comparison with her. When moments that could be represented as inspiration porn are re-presented onstage, the audience is offered an opportunity to analyze its own reaction. Inspiration can serve a positive purpose. It can motivate someone to widen their personal perspective based on admiration for a particular person. Inspiration can only serve that purpose if it is an admiration of who someone is, instead of a confirmation of one's own beliefs about who someone could or could not be.

—Jill Summerville

Notes

1. "Wheelchair-Bound Marna Michele Gives Judges a 'Million Reasons' to Love Her," *American Idol*, YouTube.
2. Richard Tomlinson, *Disability, Theatre and Education* (Bloomington: Indiana University Press, 1984), 10.

Still Standing

Still Standing: A Musical Survival Guide for Life's Catastrophes debuted in 1993. Since then, Anita Hollander has performed it almost uncountable times, both Off-Broadway and in venues such as the Alabama Shakespeare Festival, the Cleveland Playhouse, the Corcoran Gallery, the Kennedy Center for the Performing Arts, the White House, Disney World and throughout the country (CD on iTunes). It won the Audience Award at the United Solo Theatre Festival in NYC and has garnered critical praise and awards from the *New York Times*, ASCAP, *Billboard*, and *Back Stage Magazine*, for writing as well as performance. Her other one-woman musical, *Walking to Canada*, appears in the play collection *Estrogenius 2003*. She has also composed new music and songs for the liturgy of The Village Temple (NYC), where Anita has served as musical director.

Still Standing, © 1996 Anita Hollander (ASCAP), all rights reserved

* * *

in dark
ANITA (*singing a cappella from offstage*):
I had a friend, his name was Michael
One day he told me he was ill
He asked me for some information
And I am searching for it still
> *Lights up*
> *Music begins, "Prologue" / "Why I Prefer One"*
Well, they said I had courage and I thought it queer
I didn't feel courageous, not anywhere near
But then someone told me something made it all clear
He said courage is action you make from your darkest fear
And Here I Stand, oh yea!
And not much less afraid than I was before
Here I Stand, oh yea!
But maybe now I know just a little more…
I live in New York City and get mugged on two legs
but I don't get mugged on one
And the guys who mugged me see me on one leg and say
"God Bless You, hon."
I don't stand in line at the bank or post office
if someone sees me there
And I've got two strong metal weapons for anyone
who thinks that's unfair
And the seats on airplanes are getting kinda small

but with 1 leg, ha, well it's nothing at all
And at movies I've got the perfect spot
for my popcorn where it will still stay hot.
Now let's face it sex is spontaneous
And to "get there" is an art
But when you have to remove your limbs, well
the mood sometimes falls apart
And I only have to shave one leg and I only have to find one sock
But perhaps the main issue to discuss is when I'm on one I get a
seat on the bus
Now I know some amputees who don't quite agree with me
They wear theirs each day and they like it that way
And I think that's perfectly great because we're not the same!
(Okay, that's more than you ever wanted to know about having one leg, but
    hey, that's the kind of gal I am.)
Now, I'm not saying I don't love my other one,
it sure does beat a peg.
(no offense)
And the way it looks well it really proves
you can buy a great pair of L'eggs!
And there's one more thing left to say:
I'm more comfortable this way!

> *Music ends*

In 1977 nine out of ten doctors told me I was perfectly healthy. The tenth
    doctor told me I had cancer. From this I learned that if you're stranded on
    a desert island where nine out of ten doctors choose Bayer aspirin, find
    out what the tenth doctor chooses and take that. Along with an off-the-
    wall sense of humor, I've picked up many tools for survival through my life
    and experiences. Tools like Perspective. I gained my perspective in the fall
    of 1977 when I was on chemotherapy. I had no hair and a brace on what
    was still my left leg. I began each morning at the hospital for radiation
    treatments and ended each evening portraying the ancient grandmother in
    a not so cheerful production of *A Month in the Country*.

> *Music begins, "Dressing"*

(*VOICE-OVER*): *God, it's freezing in here. Sure is. Anybody got a scarf? I'm
    gonna catch pneumonia. Well, you wouldn't have to finish this play if you
    did. Anyone got anything to eat? I'm starving. Ever notice how there's no
    place decent to eat around here? Yea, the food at the Beanery makes me
    sick……*
8:00 on Wednesday night and curtain time is nearer
First put on the eyebrows and keep focused on the mirror
Now apply the eyelash glue and now replace the wig
Damn that chemo garbage has me eating like a pig…

(*VOICE-OVER*): *Anyone seen David? The toilet won't flush. Margaret, is that my eyebrow pencil?*

Actors play some roles that in real-life they never are
Others play the roles most like them, then become a star
What on earth—when I feel I've aged 80 years or more
Would I want to play an 80-year-old woman for?

(*VOICE-OVER*): *Oh, why do they always starch this shirt. I could—*

6:00 tomorrow morning, long before the sun is up
Green linen tie-up gown and water from a paper cup
Hope the boy in 320 makes it through the night
Grey curtains, grey carpets, cold table, get me out … NOW!!!!!!!!

(*VOICE-OVER*): *MARGARET!!!!!! Where's my comb? I don't know, use mine. This is mine! Oh. Fifteen Minutes, ladies & gents!*

8:15 on Wednesday night, it's getting closer now
If my shoe stays on my foot I'll do all right somehow
Hard to think of acting when I'm acting to survive
Does anyone here appreciate the fact that they're alive?

(*VOICE-OVER*): *Get off my back! Who, me? Cool out. Back off! Places!*

WAIT FOR ME!!!!!!!!!

Music ends

ANITA: Of course, it helps to have a great family, and a visit from my sister Rachel was always a highly anticipated event.

Prepping the audience for the next scene, Anita points to herself and says:

I'm Rachel, and

indicating stool

this is me in 1977.

Music in, "Lazy Day"

RACHEL: Listen, the bells of Oz are ringing!
Now that I'm here you haven't got a care.
No time for blues if you keep singing
"You're never fully dressed without your hair!"
(spoken): "Awfully hot for April. don't you want to take that off?"
"…ooh, touchy, touchy!"
We're gonna see some movies, oh 7 or 8,
I brought my VCR & the best of the great.
No watches, no schedules, no problems being late,
You're gonna have a lazy day.
(v-o, Anita): Do you want some granola? It's 17 grain.
We're gonna ditch this birdfood and 7-grain toast;
You work too hard to make it and you're pale as a ghost.

Dialing out for pizza takes a finger at most,
You're gonna have a lazy day.
We can act out the Wizard, but first we'll smoke a jay
(v-o): I don't get high!
You don't? Well, goody for you. You can play Glinda,
We both know what I'll play
"I'll get you my pretty! And your little dog, too! Hahahaha!"
(v-o): Getting high depresses me.
(spoken) It does? How odd. Well, what do you do to relax?
(v-o): Well, I like to go swimming.
"Swimming! Hey, what about my swimming? I gotta do my laps"
No fitness talk today, my dear, concentrate on naps
Nothing but regressive bliss from revelie to taps,
You're gonna have a lazy day.
We could open the window and throw fake snow,
Freak out the neighbors strolling through the park.
Remember what I used to do in Ohio?
(v-o): Oh no, oh no, anything but the bark!
(spoken): A little too much? Okay back to square one.
Maybe we'll just sit around and eat instead,
Let the TV movies drill a hole in your head.
Just lay back, unfocus and then drift off to bed,
You're gonna have a lazy day.
(v-o): It sounds so decadent.
Gonna have a lazy day
(v-o): I guess it's possible but—
Let your mind go hazy,
You won't go crazy,
It's gonna be a lazy day
(*big finish*) bee doo wah
Gonna be a lazy day.

   Music ends

ANITA (as herself): After the amputation I never could quite reconcile where
   my leg went.
I mean I literally LOST my leg, because nobody would (or could) actually say
   what was done with it after they removed it.
I asked my doctor about this (and I liked this guy), but all he said was "The
   hospital's policy on this is very respectful." But he didn't tell me where it went!
   This is where a great imagination comes in handy. I imagined that my leg was
   whisked away on a 50-city tour of the world's most famous research hospitals.
   Somewhere a cure for cancer would be found because of "my left foot."
But wherever it went, late one night I went down to the hospital chapel to give
   it my own send-off.

Music in, "Funeral for a Replaceable Part"

Here I stand like a dunce—someone lend a hand
All I know for sure right now is here I stand,
This isn't how I planned, I mean,
It's not like I thought that I would sob or scream
But I get the feeling that this is not a dream
Here I stand in this place like I'm on remote
All I know for sure right now is I must stay afloat
Without you on the boat, okay,
Forget the jokes here. I shouldn't make a sound
Maybe my sense of humor is in the lost and found
Working all those years for me, you taught me, through the pain
How to be efficient and still let the grace remain
Even sick you carried me through Europe's ice and snow
You let me keep dancing, now how can I let you go?
Here I stand on the brink of a brand new day
All I know for sure right now is I can't make you stay,
But people always say
I'm the one whose independent, so they're all watching me
This is the way I'm gonna stand forever
—forever—
Here I stand without you, now you've gone far;
Sorry for the pain—hope it's better where you are.

Music ends

ANITA: Of course, survival is that much easier when you have one very vital element:
BALLS!

Music begins, "Difficult Woman Blues"
(All voices EXCEPT Anita are Voice-Overs)

MOM: She tells the doctor something serious. He says

DOCTOR: My dear, you're just delirious;
Take this prescription and go home and rest.
You're just a difficult woman.

RACHEL: She has alternatives for coping with stress,
since fate has often made her life a mess,
instead of therapy she talks to her limbs:

ANITA: We're just a difficult woman.

MOM: She wants to sing the songs she hears in her ear

RACHEL: She wants to be the songbird of the year

MOM: But, she won't take garbage from anyone

BOTH: And this is what we call a difficult woman?

MOM: She likes to humanize inanimate things;

ANITA: They make more sense at times than human beings.

RACHEL: At least she knows she'll always have a friend

ANITA: Can we talk?

ALL: This is a difficult woman!

RACHEL (spoken): I just left her in physical therapy. She'd like to use the piano in there to practice.

DOCTOR: Oh, I see. And I suppose she thinks that's going to help?

RACHEL: Well, she has to be back at rehearsal next week. As soon as she learns how to walk.

DOCTOR: Oh my God. (*singing:*)
This lady really has a lot of gall.
She won't do just one thing, she'll do it all.
She'll sing and dance and write and run the show.
She's an IMPOSSIBLE woman!

ALL: She won't give up till things are A-Okay;
She's a perfectionist in every way. Just ask her mother—

MOM: She was born like this. Oy, what a difficult woman!

RACHEL: She's got a walk like they got in the South.
And when she talks she sticks her foot in her mouth.
That's why at parties you'll just see her dance.
To walk or talk is taking too big a chance—Whoa!

MOM: I've known this lady since the day she was born,
And if you think she looks a little war-torn,
Who knows? It may be that she will survive BECAUSE she's difficult

ALL: Yes, she's difficult!

ANITA: I'm just a difficult woman.

ALL: She's very difficult—Oh, what a woman!

Music segues into "Walkman!"

ANITA: And as my buddies in physical therapy and I discovered, it never hurts to have a great sense of (*snap the prosthesis*) rhythm!
Each day in therapy trudging through the bars,
I'm doing sit-ups until I'm seeing stars,
My muscles seem to have taken off to Mars,
The hell with this, that's why God invented cars,
Nothing is working out, my head is so full of doubt,
Suddenly I can feel a thrill that I had never felt
Until I got a WALKMAN! It's a snap!
Hit me with the music and I'll walk, walk, walk,

I'll walk walk walk I got no time to talk
I gotta walk, man YEA!

> *Several voices—Anita's physical therapy buddies—begin to emerge from the theatre speakers:*

(V-O): I get the feel of nobility as I improve my mobility.

ANITA: Once you get past mere ability—

(V-O): Then you move on to agility:
You gotta see my wheelies, baby!

(V-O): I can get down and breakdance—maybe.

(V-O): How about Flashdance? Let's all slam!

ANITA: We got our own moves here,
we're jammin' to the WALKMAN!
Boogie down!
We can move, move, move, yea we can move move move, we're
gettin' in the groove of a WALKMAN! What a blast!

(V-O): See ya later, man, I'm goin' to the can, I gotta walk, man!

ANITA: Okay so it's not for everyone, but hey, look at the variations:
Boardwalk, boardwalk, sidewalk,
Catwalk, catwalk, sleepwalk,
Birdwalk, birdwalk, moonwalk,
Cakewalk, cakewalk, take a walk, Ooh-ah!
And suddenly I get this vision of this world of disabled people—with
wheelchairs and crutches all boogyin' down the street with phones on their
heads and grins on their faces … Of course, in the process of this vision I
dropped and smashed the walkman, but hey, it was great while it lasted!
Hit me with the music and I'll walk walk walk
Hit me with the music and I'll walk walk walk
I'll walk walk walk I got no time to talk I gotta walk, man!
(*Rap*): Don't know what I'm doin';
Don't know if I care;
All I know is that I'm gonna get somewhere!
We're gonna rock, rock, rock, be skippin' down the block with a
WALKMAN! Gimme five!
We're gonna rock, rock, rock, be skippin' down the block with a
WALKMAN! WALKMAN baby!
WALKMAN! WALKMAN honey!
Walk walk walk walk walk WALKMAN! WALKMAN! YEA!

> *End music*

But no matter how many tools you may have—or tricks up your sleeve—it
often comes down to you and the pain; in my case, phantom pain. That's
the pain you feel in the limb that's no longer there.

Now, when this happens, I know of two things you can do. One is cry, a very
useful and important thing.
But, the OTHER thing is what I call my "art therapy."

> *Music in, "The Pain"*

First, I put the pencil on the paper and then I wait. … When the pain comes,
it presses the pencil down hard, but as it progresses it moves the pencil in a
herky-jerky sort of fashion—like an EKG for the pain. … Usually there are 6
to 8 seconds of blissful nothing … and then it starts up again.
If you put your hand on top of a stove
When someone is making tea
Your hand will burn and you'll get quite a shock,
But it's over 1-2-3.
If you touch inside of a light socket
When electric current is on
You'll feel a buzz and you'll get quite a shock,
But you'll know what is going on—

(V-O): You can't explain; you can't express it; you can't describe
The Pain.

ANITA: If you're foot falls asleep, as it often may,
And you cannot feel it at all,
You look at it and you get quite a shock,
'cause without it there, you could fall.
Then you slowly feel the pins and needles come to
Put an end to your strife.
You can handle these little friendly pokes,
'cause you know they won't be there for life—

(V-O): You can't explain; you can't express it; you can't describe
The Pain.

ANITA: If you stick a dagger into your ass
And the dagger is attached to a wire,
And the wire has a plug in it,
Plugged into an amplifier,
And the amplifier is plugged to the wall
With the power switch turned on,
And the volume levels are reaching ten,
And that dagger is still in your bum,
Well, it starts with a scream and it ends with a moan

ANITA: And I can't even think of using the phone
'Cause my fingers are frozen into a clutch
And body is twisted up much too much
And my face is distorted
And my throat closes and

God is nowhere around.
But I feel alive
And I feel very strange
And I see myself
And my life change
How do we learn?
Why do we feel it?
What do we earn from pain?
From pain?

(VOICE-OVER):
I'll be as I always was
And I'll be all right soon
You can't describe.
You can't explain.
You can't.
You can't.
You'll never learn.
You'll never heal it.
You may run but never hide—
I'll be by your side.

> *End music*

ANITA: But, late at night, when I would relive the memory of someone slapping my face to keep me from screaming in the recovery room, I would once again be faced with the choice I'd made to live. Though I was convinced of that choice, I wasn't always sure how to live with it.

> *Music in, "The Choice"*

It's now three o'clock in the morning,
You're lying there wondering why
The radio's murmuring love songs
When you worry today you might die
And that feeling starts growing inside you,
You think that it may never end
You reach for the phone by your bedside,
But you don't want to wake up a friend,
And you cry…
For the eyes of the people who stare
For the ears that don't hear how you try
For the handslap that seemed so unfair
For the mouth that may never reply
How to live, to be alive, and you cry,
And you still wonder why.
So you try to reach out to another,

But the words don't know how to express
The hate that is building inside you
As you're able to do less and less
And you want to be more than just living,
Though you're trying as hard as you can
Just to get from one day to another,
Sick of all those who don't understand.
For you live with the fear and the anger
That makes your life harder to bear
And a flame burns away and surrounds you,
You curse yourself for your despair
You feel yourself begging for pity,
So you try to stand up on your own
When you find you are losing the battle,
There's nobody there,
You're alone.
In a way you are just like a baby,
Afraid of the darkness of night
Attacks of that fear still may hit you,
Though you think that you'll soon be all right
But the sunrise is well on its way now,
As you lie there with eyes open wide
And the radio's still playing love songs
As you stifle a scream deep inside,
As you cry…
For the eyes that are still going to stare
For the ears that won't hear how you try
For the slaps that will be so unfair
For the mouth that may never reply
But you'll live,
You'll be alive,
And you'll cry,
And you'll still wonder why.
You will try … and you'll still … wonder why.

Music ends

ANITA: Of course, I've always had a firm grip on reality, and this has made me an expert in the field of Attitude Adjustment.

Music in, "That's the Way It Is"

See that pretty girl in Bloomingdales,
She's a classy chick in every way
Wait until she steps out from the counter.
She is standing on one foot today

(V-O): That's why I say: HEY! That's the way it is

Don't let her fool ya if she looks jappy
That's why I say: Hey, that's the way it is
And cripples ain't supposed to be happy.

ANITA: See that red-head sittin' in the wheelchair,
She's a tragedy in every way
Gosh it's sad to think she could have made it;
She has quite a set of gams, but hey

(V-O): That's why I say: Hey, that's the way it is
'Cause if you're in a chair you feel crappy
That's why I say: Hey, that's the way it is
And cripples ain't supposed to be happy.

(SPOKEN VOICE-OVER:) Ladies & Gentlemen, you've heard of Lenscrafters:
"Get a great pair of glasses in about an hour?" And Nutri-System 2000:
"Lose the weight and keep it off?" Well, now there's Ampucraft 2000: "Lose
twenty pounds, in about an hour, and keep it off!"

ANITA: Then there's that young boy with the angel face
What mother wouldn't want to weep, wail or moan
To behold such a tragic case?
"He's been like that since the day he was born!"
On the bus you see this tall, blonde and handsome;
Long and lean and rugged—sexy, too.
With your eyes you sort of start to undress him.
Wait until he takes his foot off for you!

(V-O): You know it's true: OOH! That's the way it is
No matter if he dresses real snappy
You know it's true. Ooh, that's the way it is
And cripples ain't supposed to be happy.

(SPOKEN VOICE-OVER:) "The sight of Hollander brightly meeting her
challenge may tend to cramp your digestion of this confection. You're
thinking 'Isn't she spunky?' rather than paying attention to the song she's
performing."

ANITA: Then you gotta wonder, "Who's that woman?
Got her legs and arms, she's using them, too."
So it's really hard to understand why the hell
She should be yelling at you!
There's a fellow who is mighty solid:
Hands so strong and eyes that seem to glow
Now you're thinking maybe "What's his problem?"
Which just goes to show you never know

(V-O): But all I know, OH! is the way it is
You better work it out, make it snappy
That's all I know. Oh, that's the way it is

And cripples ain't supposed to be—
Don't believe a thing you see—
Cripples ain't supposed to be happy. YEA.

End of music

ANITA: Another misconception about disabled people is the "myth of the virtuous cripple." But the day I reported to a nameless communications office to record my first dubious phone "communication," I'd say I felt anything BUT virtuous.

Music in, "Talk to Me"

I've had it on trains, I've had it on bars,
I've had it on dressing room floors and in cars,
But nothing else can match the bliss of hearing
How you'll do this to me. Talk to me.
Doing it's out. Family is in.
Fear of doing to death or of family sin,
Makes it more fun and wiser too,
To do my brain out listening to you.
And it's free ('cept for AT&T). Talk to me.
Now this is all of course aside from the fact
That doing it on one leg's the ultimate act
But my imagination is stronger, and
—oh—Lasts so much longer
Open your shell. Come as you are.
Call from the cellular phone in your car.
Watch your foot accelerate. My master plan to bate you
—aurally—
Is the key
To your own
Fantasy.
Talk to me—
Talk to me—
Talk to—(*musical chord*)

End music

ANITA: Once, on a TV talk show, a "TV psychologist" asked me: "After you lost your leg, did you date only one-legged men?" I mean it, this really happened! But, lo and behold, I actually met and married a two-legged man and discovered yet another tool for survival:
Love.

Music begins, "I Want to Be There"

I want to be there when you come home at night
And you're so exhausted you give up the fight
But all my loving helps you to be strong

I want to be there all along
I want to be there in that special year
When you get your Tony and your friends all cheer
Who's watched you struggle? Who's seen you pay?
I want to be there all the way
You don't have to give anything up for me
You don't have to be afraid that you'll die
We all die, don't we?
But just to be there until we do
That's not so unusual when love is true
To ease the painful times, share the joyful too
I want to be there for you
I want to be there WITH you.

    End music

ANITA: Minor miracle: carrying a baby on one leg for nine months.
Major miracle: giving birth to a healthy baby.
But for those nine months we had absolutely no idea what to expect.

    Music begins, "The Phone Call"

Honey, hi, it's me from the doctor's place
where I saw the sonogram
And our baby's growing inside real well—
I can't tell you how glad I am.
What, dear? What does it look like?
Ah well, on that tiny TV screen…
From what I could see, it appears to be
the most beautiful fish I've ever seen!
Honey…
We're giving birth to a tadpole—
A tadpole, I think, lights were dim
We're giving birth to a tadpole—
Well, dear, we'll at least know it can swim!
Darling, please don't faint and please don't hang up
'cause I'll tell you the best part—
The doctor pointed it out to me:
our dear little baby's heart!
What, dear? What does it look like?
Well, it's round and it's tiny and it's sweet,
It's got some kind of a mouth on the side
that opens and closes on beat.
Sweetheart…
We're giving birth to a Pac-Man!
A pac-man, you know, like the game?
I'm growing this cute little pac-man

NO! I don't think my computer job's to blame!
Dearest, one more thing that I ought to tell you
That I still haven't said…
The doctor, she had a problem, see…
Well, she just, couldn't find the head.
What, dear? What am I saying?
There's seven more months, I'm not afraid!
I'm sure that it's gonna grow a head, and if not,
We'll just have one MADE!!!!!!!
WE'RE GIVING BIRTH TO A HEADLESS BABY!
Okay, so it won't be so smart.
I'm sure we'll still love our headless tadpole
And it will learn to love us with its pac-man heart!
Honey? Sweetheart? Hello?

    Music ends

ANITA: This is how I taught our daughter to walk, and how I measured her height.

    Music begins, "Mommy is a Mermaid"

(AS DAUGHTER, HOLLAND): My mommy's different, I've heard it said.
They say "disabled" and shake their heads.
I never understand what they say;
To me all mommies should be this way,
But mommy says that it isn't so,
But should I let it bother me? Oh no, just tell them:
Mommy is a Mermaid,
Mommy is a Mermaid,
Mommy is a Mermaid,
and watch them wonder.
She takes me swimming most every day;
Doesn't seem to hear what people say.
I see some other kids point and stare;
It doesn't matter, I just don't care
'cause when my
Mommy gets in the pool, she makes those other
Swimmers look so foolish because my
Mommy is a Mermaid,
Mommy is a Mermaid,
Mommy is a Mermaid,
and they wonder.
Mommy says that mermaids may not really exist.
Anyway, we may not ever know.
But lately no one's spotted one in New York
And so … who knows?
Since I was born I could hear the sound

Of mommy singing all around
I've heard some stories and now I see
What I believe could really be, 'cause when the
Mermaids would sing so sweet,
They'd knock those sailors right off their feet
So I know that
Mommy is a Mermaid,
Mommy is a Mermaid,
Mommy is a Mermaid
…No wonder.

    Music ends

ANITA: But no matter what struggles we may have, there is still one tool for
  survival that I hope all of us can find within us, and that is the JOY of simply
  being alive.

    Music Begins, "Here I Stand"

Well, I rolled out of bed this morning, fell on the floor
Got myself to stand and then bumped into the door
By the time I stubbed my toe I couldn't take anymore
But then I started to sing and I remembered what I do it for
And Here I Stand—oh yea—
You see that's really quite a "feet" for me
Here I Stand—oh yea—
And there is no way I would rather be
Though I may be weary from the dusk till the dawn,
When the sun comes up my spirit goes on,
And though it may not be the way that I planned—
Here I Stand.
When you're hot you're hot and when you're not you're not
You hear it enough and you forget what you've got
But when it came down to "would I live or not?"
That's when I began to realize I've got alot and
Here I Stand—yes, indeed—
I got a heart, a brain and chutzpah, too
Here I Stand—what I need is
What I've got inside to see me through
My life changed on me and I counted to ten,
Then I got back up to do it again
And though it may not be the way that I planned—
Here I Stand.
You gotta get on with it.
You can't be discouraged by the things that people say
Cause if you believe in it,
You'll keep on doing what you're doing in your own way

So tomorrow I may wake up
And fall over a chair
Hobble seven blocks
And miss the bus by a hair
And just when I think
I haven't got a prayer
Some guy grabs my purse,
It starts to rain
And I don't care
'cause Here I Stand—I'm alive—
it may be hard but not enough to die
Here I Stand—I can drive—
I may be scared but, baby, I can try
Oh I may be weary but it's less of a climb
When I just take life one step at a time
And maybe later I can dance with the band
But Here I Stand, yea, Here I Stand,
And if you need a helping hand,
Here I Stand—
Here I Stand!
Music Ends.

EPILOGUE. *Anita sits at a piano, and begins to softly play*

I had a friend—his name was Michael.
One day he told me he was ill.
He asked me for some information,
And I am searching for it still.
"Just tell me what you did and I'll do it.
Give me a list, I'll try to pursue it.
I want to know if you ever knew it:
How did you get from there to here?"
How did I get from there to here?
That question rings inside my ear about
A couple times a week I suppose, but,
How did I get from there to here?
I told him that I didn't worry—
I was in quite an awful hurry
I thought that I would not see another year.
That's how I got from there to here
Now, don't get me wrong, I think it's important
To find out what's deep inside.
If you have anger, try to explore it.
If you have fears, they can't be denied.
Let it all go…

What does that mean?
To let it all go—
Lay back and just relax and try to be?
And two months later Michael died.
How could I make it understood
I didn't do a thing that was so good?
What could I do to make it clear?
How do you get from there to here?
But, I don't know how to give up on you,
Knowing that you're gone too soon
Was it because I didn't tell you:
How do you get from there to here?
Let it all go…
But did I let you down?
Did you let it all go—
Give up and say goodbye
And hardly try?
Or did you simply have no choice?
There are many gone that I knew,
There are many trying;
I would truly
Like to help them see it through.
Forget the *there* and just be *here*.
Because it hurts—
Oh God, I know it hurts
And no one knows like you do.
It's oh so hard,
But it's inside you,
So don't give in
And don't give up.
Let it all go…
The fear and the doubt.
Did I let it all go?
I didn't, but I won't let my heart find out
Until I take my one last breath…
He died 10 years ago
And his voice is still ringing loudly in my ears.
"Oh tell me how, how did you do it?
How did you get from there to here?"
Let it all go…

    Music ends. Curtain.

End of play.

Afterword

John Michael Sefel

When Julie Goell, the internationally respected physical artist (and commedia dell'arte performer, and singer, and musician, and educator, and—above all—clown) passed away in 2016, it marked the end of her final work of art: a small collection of poems serving as meditations on her experience with disability and dying.

She was well-known in physical performance circles both as a performer and as a teacher—often doing the latter alongside her husband, the notable clown Avner Eisenberg. Though international travel for performances and teaching was a regular feature in their lives, over the years Maine's Celebration Barn Center for Immersive Physical Theatre became a sort of home base for their "Eccentric Principles," a performance pedagogy the two developed during their roughly quarter-century of teaching together. That was where I met her and had the great fortune to briefly call her "teacher."

From commedia performances for Disney's Epcot Center to directing puppet plays to her popular Carmen "Mopera," her impact on audiences and her peers is incalculable. For my part, along with Sherry Jo Ward and *STIFF*, it was Julie and her final work of art that inspired me to create this collection.

The neurodegenerative condition that would eventually take her life first slowly sapped away her muscle control. As she was a performer whose work was thoroughly based in the physical, I have thought often and marveled at the steps she took to continue creating as each stage of the condition appeared. From adapting her performance when she began losing her balance, to turning more heavily toward directing and teaching when she began having great difficulty standing, to, finally, creating short poems once she could no longer speak clearly and had only minimal muscle control.

Those "hai-kools," as they came to be called, were Julie's way of both expressing the experience of her neurodegenerative condition and of continuing to create art out of her life. They came about with help; the form was designed by Nicole D'Entremont. A book would be flipped opened and a single word randomly chosen. That word would then supply the prompt for Julie's poem.

The poem itself would be dictated by Julie's friends and loved ones. With a spelling board before her, Julie would slowly point to individual letters, which her volunteer secretary would then write down. Most of the poems were three lines long, which I think is where the "hai-kool" pet name came from, though I'd argue the supremacy of the natural world, the passing of seasons, the uncontrollable nature of time and mortality, the battle of the ego—these were all qualities of these short poems that tied them just as strongly to haiku as the number of lines.

While this volume is meant to be a collection of plays, I could not bring myself to create this book without including the poems which inspired the work. The following thirty-four poems are the final artistic gift that Julie gave to the world, and I am extremely thankful to her husband, Avner, for allowing me to share them with you.

Thank you for picking up this book—I hope its contents have made you laugh, cry, think, argue, and dream as much as they have for me. I say goodbye with Julie's beautiful work.

* * *

Julie Goell earned a degree in theatre from Emerson College (1974) and completed the School of Music of the University of Southern Maine, in String Bass (2002), minoring in voice with Margaret Yauger. She completed teacher training for Physical Theatre in Rome, Italy, in 1981 at L'Istituto per lo Studio Dello Spettacolo.

Residing in Rome for a decade, she performed in music and theatre, film, and television. She toured as a clown with La Compagnia I Gesti and taught physical comedy skills with Roy Bosier at Teatro Studio. She toured for a year with the Swiss circus Schaubude, and later toured her live jazz show, *Impromptu*, in Switzerland. She toured Italy for three seasons singing with the big band of Testaccio. She appears in Annette Bercut Lust's book, *From the Greek Mimes to Marcel Marceau and Beyond.*

In the United States, Goell acted in *Ghetto* on Broadway, directed several productions in New York, and directed commedia dell'arte for Spoleto Festival and the Epcot Center in Orlando. She taught physical comedy and commedia dell'arte at Boston University, Colby College, UConn, and Dell'Arte International, as well as trained singers and staged commedia scenes for *Ariadne Auf Naxos* at Sarasota Opera.

Goell was a Henson Foundation-supported artist in residence at UConn Puppet Arts Program, where she developed and directed a full-scale graduate puppet production, *By the Willow*, which subsequently received a successful international tour. From 2005 to 2007 she was Irving Suss Guest Artist at Colby College where she taught musical theatre and commedia and directed *Servant of Two Masters* and *The Fantasticks*.

She played bass with the Casco Bay Tummlers klezmer band which performed at festivals in Italy, Germany, Slovenia, and Lithuania. Her solo opera,

Carmen: The Mopera, headlined at festivals in Andorra, New York, Rome, Spain, and Rio. She taught clowning and developed a training pedagogy, "Eccentric Performance," in collaboration with her husband Avner Eisenberg, eventually developing it into the book *Life in a Clown House: A Manual and a Memoir* (2016). She passed away later that year, on December 12, 2016.

*   *   *

Form designed by Nicole D'Entremont
Lines dictated by Julie's friends and loved ones
Shared with the blessing and permission of Julie's husband, Avner Eisenberg

*   *   *

n.d., *White Dog Fell from the Sky* by Eleanor Morse

1. (prompt: stupid)
Watch out, I'm dangerous.
I'm not as stupid as I look,
only as dumb as I feel.

2. (no prompt)
I didn't expect to see the spring.
In a flurry of efficiency
I threw away my summer clothes.

3. (prompt: life)
Life has me flummoxed
but I'm still racing to the finish line
trying to see who comes in first.

4. (prompt: delicate)
How to say this delicately:
I do not have the plague.
I just want as much love as anyone would.

5. (prompt: she)
She flutters by, full of excuses I didn't ask for.
Why does she bother to come at all,
unless it is not me she's visiting?

6. (prompt: one)
One: Get me out of this skin I'm in.
Two: Give me back my body.
Three: I didn't ask to play this game.

7. (prompt: setting)
The sun was setting behind Great Diamond.
I look at you but say nothing.
So many opportunities lost.

8. (prompt: woke)
   I woke to the sound, reassuring, of your breathing,
   clock doing its familiar ghosting thing.
   I wonder, how much longer?

9. (prompt: prove)
   I see the proof in your worried looks,
   In your frequent awakenings to turn me,
   And in frantic calls to the doctor in the middle of the night.

10. (prompt: local)
    Local flowers in bloom.
    The greenest summer you'll see.
    Hope I'll get to see it through.

11. (prompt: sky)
    Dark grey skies of late.
    Mood around me is grim.
    Somewhere inside a dancer rages.

12. (prompt: handles)
    You ask where did these handles come from
    and look at me accusingly.
    Mystery solved. It's all that cake you ate.

6.17.16, *Wise Blood* by Flannery O'Connor

13. (prompt: settled)
    We settled here thirty years.
    Don't know how much more
    Beauty I can stand.

14. (prompt: stinging)
    The stinging in my eyes is proof.
    I'm a big crybaby and
    I don't know how to hide.

15. (prompt: facing)
    I am facing you
    but don't know if you are in profile
    or about to leave your seat.

   beginning 7.6.16 Julie stayed at Norway Rehab for a week while Avner taught the 25th annual Eccentric Performing workshop at the Celebration Barn in South Paris, Maine

16. (prompt: attention)
    So much attention being sick,
    You'd think the world revolved around me,
    Your usual charm just swept away.

17. (prompt: remember)
    I remember your hands and feet so tiny,
    the wind could blow you away.
    Now a married man so solid.

18. (prompt: museum)
    Our basement is our museum,
    Piles of lives lived everywhere
    A testament to love.

7.15.16, *Outside the Law: A Thief's Primer* by Bruce Jackson

19. (prompt: dance)
    You dance me to bed
    When I have to be moved.
    We waltz blind but carefree.

20. (prompt: peeling)
    Peeling like an onion
    Getting to the core of me.
    I want my layers back.

21. (prompt: minute)
    In a minute I'll be gone.
    Seemed to take forever.
    Time flies when you're having fun.

7.22.16, *The Chairs Are Where the People Go* by Misha Glouberman

22. (prompt: end)
    The end, when it comes, will it hurt?
    My mind plays out all possible scenarios.
    The hardest being the one where you're in the next room.

23. (prompt: important)
    The things that once seemed important
    no longer are.
    You will be the last to go.

24. (no prompt)
    I've often thought,
    when can I stop caring?
    If I call, I'll cry
    and I don't want to do that to him.

7.29.16, *Rashi's Daughters, Book Two: Miriam* by Maggie Anton

25. (prompt: erudite)
    I know I look dumb
    I'm actually quite erudite
    What little pleasure that gives me now.

8.3.16, *Circus World* by Barry B. Longyear

26. (prompt: silence)
    The silence is too loud.
    I have to break it up somehow.
    Let's start with you: How the hell are you?

27. (prompt: boy)
    Boy, what do I do now?
    Caught between, worried that you'll have too much fun
    and that you won't have any.

28. (prompt: dropped)
    You dropped in to visit.
    There is much to say
    and too little time.

8.19.16, *Pale Fire* by Vladimir Nabokov

29. (prompt: characters)
    Many characters come to call,
    from subtle to sublime,
    As if I had some kind of answer.

30. (prompt: slight)
    You entertain the troops
    with sleight of hand and magic.
    If only it were a laughing matter.

31. (prompt: gathers)
    Storm clouds gather ahead.
    I needn't tell you this.
    But we have to talk. Soon.

9.23.16, *Geek Love* by Katherine Dunn

32. (prompt: scrap)
    Let's scrap the whole thing:
    This Julie project with
    all its twists and turns and gyrations.

33. (prompt: dance)
    I danced through it all,
    never knowing it would end
    so abruptly or unbidden.

11.13.16

34. (no prompt)
     Bereft of words
     I didn't catch a wink of sleep
     But lay peering dumbly about.
     My problem is I can't see
     Neither what I have done
     Nor what I'm about to do.

About the Contributors

Anonymous, deeply familiar with the hills and valleys of M.S., is a working theatre professional and an educator at a major U.S.–based university.

Calvin **Arium** was born in the south of France, raised next to the sea, and learned early to sail and to draw dragons. After design courses and a comics specialized formation at the EESI of Angoulême, he now lives in Paris' suburbs with other queer disabled individuals. Being a trans autistic mentally ill kid with hEDS, he learned very late that he was a worthy human being and tries his best to talk about it in his comics. His goals are to save the world, to make the best comics he can, and to kiss cute boys, in this order.

Graham **Bryant** is an American playwright and actor. He was born in Houston, Texas. He graduated from Baylor University in 2019 with a BFA in Theatre Performance. Since the age of 13 when he picked up a DVD copy of *Little Shop of Horrors*, he has sought out opportunities to view, study, and work with theatre productions. Today, he strives to promote great works and help make non-profit theatre accessible to all. He could be easily recognized on the street from his beard, his graphic tees, and the various hats he wears so he doesn't have to manage his hair.

Billy **Butler**'s work as a composer and lyricist include the cult-hit rock musical *Gay Bride of Frankenstein* (NYC), *Ziegfeld's Midnight Frolic* (NYC), *Missing: Wynter*, *The Brechtones*, and *Titus Andronicus Musicus*, as well as his trunk show, *A Bitter Pill: The Songs of Billy Butler*. Billy has been featured on many studio recordings, including his own: *The Lot 20 Sessions*, *Neptune*, and *To the Depth of Jazz*. His most recent credits include the world premiere of *Dolly Parton's Smoky Mountain Christmas* at Boston's Emerson Colonial, as well as performing alongside his daughter and bandmates in the darkly anachronistic folk/blues/jazz/vaudeville band Bitter Pill.

Bradley **Cherna** works across pages, stages, and screens. A member of Dramatists Guild, Bradley studied at Eugene Lang College, The New School for Drama, University of Florida (Honors College), NYU Tisch, and Columbia University, and studied playwriting with Lynn Nottage, David Henry Hwang, reg e gaines, Deborah Brevoort, Ann Marie Healy, Dan Fishback, and Alice Eve Cohen. Plays include *The Forest of Without* (Drama League), *Eggshells on my Back and other fairy tales* (University of Florida/Florida Players New Works Festival), *The Scrap Paper Players Present* (Columbia University), and *The Mixed-Up Letters of Jamie & Claude* (Ugly Rhino).

Kate **Devorak** is a Los Angeles–based writer, comedian, podcaster, actress, and director (more or less in that order). She graduated with a degree in theatre from Drew University in 2013. She has acted, directed, and produced stage productions throughout New England, and has delved into stand-up comedy and podcasting since moving to LA in 2018. Kate was officially declared a bit insane in 2005, with a more fitting diagnosis of bipolar II disorder in 2014. Family legacy and all that. Since then, she's been figuring out how to best keep her head above water. She'll be fine.

Amy Bethan **Evans** is a playwright, dramaturg, and disability activist. She studied at UWE and Royal Holloway before doing Year One of Graeae's Write to Play programme. She wrote *Libby's Eyes* (a dystopian PIP parody) at Soho Writers' Lab, which featured at the Bunker Theatre's Breaking out Festival, receiving five four-star reviews and a write-up in the *Times Literary Supplement*. *Tinted* was commissioned by Extant for the Bloomsbury Festival as an extension of the 10-minute play *To Be My Eyes*, originally performed as part of "The Words Are Coming Now," a rapid response to #metoo at Theatre 503.

Mandy **Fox** is an actor, director, author, and narrator who has spent the last 20 years performing, directing, and coaching all over the world, from Broadway to London's West End. Mandy is a graduate of the Yale School of Drama, a member of the Voice and Speech Trainers Association, and the Actors Equity Association. Mandy is an associate professor and the voice specialist for the Department of Theatre at Ohio State University.

Carolyn **Cage** is a playwright, author, and activist. In 1987, she was stricken with ME/CFS (myalgic encephalomyelitis, previously called "chronic fatigue syndrome"). ME/CFS is a complex and debilitating multisystem, chronic disease with a serious impact on one's quality of life. The author of nine collections of lesbian and feminist themed plays and eighty plays, musicals, and one-woman shows, she specializes in non-traditional roles for women, especially those reclaiming famous lesbians whose stories have been distorted or erased from history. Her work has been widely produced and anthologized. A full catalog of her books and plays is at www.carolyngage.com.

Carly Jo **Geer** is originally from New Hampshire and a Columbia College Chicago theatre alum. There, she learned about solo performance and writing which led to becoming a company member with The LIVINGroom, a theatre company dedicated to theatrically heightened story telling. Being a plus-sized actress, Carly took great joy in writing and performing her own work when her cast-ability seemed daunting. She is an ensemble member of Fat Folx, a theatre company dedicated to telling the stories of larger-bodied people in the Chicago-land area. Carly co-hosts the Degrassi podcast *A Social Disease*, found on all major podcast apps.

Bree **Hadley** is an associate professor in drama at Queensland University of Technology in Brisbane, Australia. An internationally recognized authority in disability arts, culture, and media studies, her key books include *The Routledge Handbook of Disability Art, Culture, and Media* (with Donna McDonald),

Theatre, Social Media & Meaning Making, and *Disability, Public Space Performance and Spectatorship: Unconscious Performers*. Her recent practice-led research has included working with artists, curators, and academics to investigate "creative integration" of sign language, captioning, and audio description into, rather than alongside, visual and performing arts aesthetics.

Katrina **Hall** is a Philadelphia, Pennsylvania-based actor, director, and playwright whose decision to study theatre led to the discovery and diagnosis of her disability. In 2013, her intention to eventually earn a master's degree in library science got derailed by two courses—Acting I and Play Reading Analysis. After having switched her major to theatre, she's steadily worked mastering her craft since. *Dyscalculia* is her first full-length play. Additional works include *The Cuckoo, Chow, Visiting Day*, and *…to God's Ear*.

Anita **Hollander** has performed throughout Europe, Asia and America, at Carnegie Hall, Kennedy Center, London's West End, New York Shakespeare Festival, Chicago's Goodman Theatre, and the White House. A Helen Hayes Award nominee, she's won BackStage Bistro Award and United Solo Audience Award for her original solo musical, *Still Standing,* recently presented in South Korea. Her new show, *Spectacular Falls,* premiered Off-Broadway (CDs on iTunes). Theatre: *The Artificial Jungle* (nominee: Best Revival Off-Broadway Theatre Alliance), *Ragtime, Fiddler, CATS* (Grizabella). Television: *FBI: Most Wanted*, BBC's *From The Edge*. Film: *Handsome Harry, Musical Chairs*. SAG-AFTRA National Chair, Performers With Disabilities. www.anitahollander.com.

Amanda Slamcik **Lassetter** serves as production manager and lecturer for Baylor University's Department of Theatre Arts and as a co-editor for *Texas Theatre Journal*. The focus of her scholarly research is in the underlying civic narrative of performative public events. She is a member of the theatre advisory board for McLennan College and is also on the executive board for Therapy Center Stage Productions, a non-profit designed to bring the spotlight to mental health and healing through the creative and dramatic arts. She recently celebrated the ten-year anniversary of her diagnosis with multiple sclerosis.

Connor **Long** is an actor, athlete, disability advocate and speaker. His stage experience includes studies with the Colorado Shakespeare Festival, being a founding member of Tapestry Theatre all-abilities company in Boulder, and projects with Denver's acclaimed Phamaly Theatre Company. His film projects, which include a Sundance premiere, have played at festivals globally and garnered him several international best actor awards. In 2017, he earned a regional Emmy for his groundbreaking broadcast work as a contributing news reporter. When not traveling for his recognized advocacy and keynote speaking, he enjoys cooking, martial arts, cycling and swimming.

Amy **Oestreicher** is a PTSD specialist, multidisciplinary artist, Audie-award nominated author of *My Beautiful Detour*, Huffington Post columnist, RAINN & NSRVC representative, award-winning health and disability advocate, actress and playwright. She's headlined international conferences with her signature keynotes and toured her one-woman musical *Gutless & Grateful* to over 200 venues as a mental health and sexual assault program since 2012. She's given three TEDx Talks on transforming trauma through creativity and founded the #LoveMyDetour campaign. Her writings have appeared in over 70 online and print publications, and her story has appeared on *TODAY*, in *Cosmopolitan*, and on CBS. www.amyoes.com.

seeley **quest** is a trans writer, performer, organizer, and environmentalist, in Montreal since 2017. Working in literary and body-based composition, and curation, sie presented in the San Francisco Bay Area 2001–14, with the Sins Invalid project 2007–15, and has toured to Vancouver, Toronto, Ottawa, and many U.S. cities. Poems are in the book *Disability Culture and Community Performance: Find a Strange and Twisted Shape*, and in *Fiction International*. Hir first game narrative debuted for Canada's 2020 National AccessAbility Week. Sie has facilitated workshops at arts festivals and for undergrads on disability. Not on social media, sie can be found at https://questletters.substack.com.

Monica **Raymond**'s play *The Owl Girl* won the Jewish Play Project 2015 Boston and was second in JPP's 2015 international competition. It also won the Peacewriting Award, Castillo Theatre prize, Clauder Competition Gold Medal, and was nominated for the Susan Smith Blackburn Award (best play in English by a woman). Her short opera, *Paper or Plastic* (music by Charles Turner), premiered at the ART's Outside the Box Festival 2013. A MacDowell Colony Fellow, Massachusetts Cultural Council Fellow in Dramatic Writing, and Playwrights' Center Jerome Fellow, Raymond has taught writing and interdisciplinary arts at Harvard, CUNY, and the Boston Museum School.

Ben **Rosenblatt** is an actor, writer, musician and radio host. Acting credits include: The Public Theatre, Portland Center Stage, Actors Theatre of Louisville, Berkshire Theatre Festival, City Theatre, Round House, Shakespeare Theatre Company, and Cape May Stage, as well as the 2016 Drama Desk nominated Off-Broadway *Death of a Salesman* and the international tour of *ReEntry*. TV: *Unforgettable* (CBS), *Crashing* (HBO), and *Homicide City*. He co-hosts the popular *Love Bites* on Heritage Radio Network and is lead singer/songwriter of the rock band No Denial. Ben is an associate artist of American Records, a theatre company devoted to building bridges between people.

Kurt **Sass** works for a mental health agency and facilitates their Pet Access program, which assists people with psychiatric disabilities in adopting pets from animal shelters. He considers writing as one of the major contributors in his winning battle against his Major Depressive Disorder Anxiety Disorders.

John Michael **Sefel** is an educator, editor, theatre maker, and Melton Center fellow. Past appointments include theatre program director at Cowley College, lecturer at Ohio State, lecturer at Chester College, and graduate lecturer at Baylor University. His research interests involve theatre's intersections with disability, Yiddish, and horror. His editing credits include *Texas Theatre Journal*, *Lovecraftian Proceedings*, and *Seven Deadly Sins*. His writing has been published by McFarland, *New England Theatre Journal*, *Stage Directions*, and others. He was born with renal-cardio abnormalities requiring nearly twenty years' worth of repeated surgeries. He has, at times, been a urostomy bag wearer and cane user.

Jill **Summerville** is a performer, playwright, and scholar. She earned her Ph.D. in theatre history, dramatic literature, and theatre criticism. Her dissertation is a study of the complexities of putting actors with disabilities onstage, such as finding a place in the spotlight for her own sparkly manual wheelchair, Chitara. She's the recipient of a 2020 Ohio Arts Council Individual Artists with Disabilities grant for *If You Can Order a Cup of Coffee at Starbucks, We Can Be Best Friends!* She works as a freelance writer. Contact her at jillellensummerville.com. She'd love to hear your thoughts.

Sherry Jo **Ward** is a professional theatre artist, seen in acclaimed plays including *International Falls* and *August, Osage County* (WaterTower Theatre), *Precious Little* (Echo Theatre), *Mary Stuart* (Walking Shadow Theatre), *Henry V* (Abilene Shakespeare Festival), and *A Christmas Carol* (Ryman Auditorium), as well as premiering *Scripted* and *Ham and Moon on Rye* (Actors Theatre of Louisville, KY). Her screen credits include *Endings*, *In the Middle*, and Hulu's *Monsterland*, in which she plays a mother who, like Sherry, is a wheelchair user. She has a B.A. in theatre from Abilene Christian University and MFA from University of Alabama/Alabama Shakespeare Festival.

Adam Grant **Warren,** originally from Newfoundland, is now based in Vancouver, Canada, where he lives with his wife, Saleshni, and their collection of stuffed sheep. He's an award-winning writer, performer, and arts educator whose recent productions have sought to honor his experience as a wheelchair user without presenting that experience as a central or sole character conflict. When Adam is not writing or performing, folks can usually find him among friends, embracing a late-blooming passion for *Dungeons & Dragons*. For more about Adam and his work, visit adamgrantwarren.com.

Index